THEA
TEXAS HIGHER EDUCATION ASSESSMENT BONUS EDITION:
THEA
PPR EC-12
GENERALIST 4-8 111

By: Sharon Wynne, M.S.

XAMonline, INC.
Boston

Copyright © 2011 XAMonline, Inc.

All rights reserved. No part of the material protected by this copyright notice may be reproduced or utilized in any form or by any means, electronic or mechanical, including photocopying, recording or by any information storage and retrievable system, without written permission from the copyright holder.

To obtain permission(s) to use the material from this work for any purpose including workshops or seminars, please submit a written request to:

XAMonline, Inc.
25 First Street, Suite 106
Cambridge, MA 02141
Toll Free 1-800-509-4128
Email: info@xamonline.com
Web: www.xamonline.com
Fax: 1-617-583-5552

Library of Congress Cataloging-in-Publication Data

Wynne, Sharon A.
 THEA Texas Higher Education Assessment Bonus Edition: THEA, PPR EC-12, Generalist 4-8 111 / Sharon A. Wynne. 1st ed
 ISBN 978-1-60787-314-3
 1. THEA Texas Higher Education Assessment Bonus Edition: THEA, PPR EC-12, Generalist 4-8 111
 2. Study Guides
 3. THEA
 4. Teachers' Certification & Licensure
 5. Careers

Disclaimer:

The opinions expressed in this publication are the sole works of XAMonline and were created independently from the National Education Association, Educational Testing Service, or any State Department of Education, National Evaluation Systems or other testing affiliates.

Between the time of publication and printing, state specific standards as well as testing formats and Web site information may change and therefore would not be included in part or in whole within this product. Sample test questions are developed by XAMonline and reflect content similar to that on real tests; however, they are not former test questions. XAMonline assembles content that aligns with state standards but makes no claims nor guarantees teacher candidates a passing score. Numerical scores are determined by testing companies such as NES or ETS and then are compared with individual state standards. A passing score varies from state to state.

Printed in the United States of America œ-1

THEA Texas Higher Education Assessment Bonus Edition: THEA, PPR EC-12, Generalist 4-8 111
ISBN: 978-1-60787-314-3

Table of Contents

DOMAIN I
READING 1

COMPETENCY 1
DETERMINE THE MEANING OF WORDS AND PHRASES 3
Skill 1.1: Use the context of a passage to determine the meaning of words with multiple meanings, unfamiliar and uncommon words and phrases, and figurative expressions 3
Skill 1.2: Using figurative expressions 7

COMPETENCY 2
UNDERSTAND THE MAIN IDEA AND SUPPORTING DETAILS IN WRITTEN MATERIAL 9
Skill 2.1: Identify explicit and implicit main ideas 9
Skill 2.2: Recognize ideas that support, illustrate, or elaborate the main idea of a passage 10

COMPETENCY 3
IDENTIFY A WRITER'S PURPOSE, POINT OF VIEW, AND INTENDED MEANING 12
Skill 3.1: Recognize a writer's expressed or implied purpose for writing 12
Skill 3.2: Evaluate the appropriateness of written material for a specific purpose or audience 13
Skill 3.3: Recognize the likely effect on an audience of a writer's choice of words 13
Skill 3.4: Use the content, word choice, and phrasing of a passage to determine a writer's opinion or point of view 14

COMPETENCY 4
ANALYZE THE RELATIONSHIP AMONG IDEAS IN WRITTEN MATERIAL 16
Skill 4.1: Identify sequence of events or steps 16
Skill 4.2: Identify cause-effect relationships 17
Skill 4.3: Analyze relationships between ideas in opposition 18
Skill 4.4: Identify solutions to problems 18
Skill 4.5: Draw conclusions inductively and deductively from information stated or implied in a passage 20

COMPETENCY 5
USE CRITICAL REASONING SKILLS TO EVALUATE WRITTEN MATERIAL 22

Skill 5.1: Evaluate the stated or implied assumptions on which the validity of a writer's argument depends 22

Skill 5.2: Judge the relevance or importance of facts, examples, or graphic data to a writer's argument 22

Skill 5.3: Evaluate the logic of a writer's argument 23

Skill 5.4: Evaluate the validity of analogies 25

Skill 5.5: Distinguish between fact and opinion 26

Skill 5.6: Assess the credibility or objectivity of a writer or source of written material 28

COMPETENCY 6
APPLY STUDY SKILLS TO READING ASSIGNMENTS 31

Skill 6.1: Organize and summarize information for study purposes 31

Skill 6.2: Follow written instructions or directions 32

Skill 6.3: Interpret information presented in charts, graphs, or tables 33

DOMAIN II
MATHEMATICS 35
FUNDAMENTAL MATHEMATICS 39

COMPETENCY 7
SOLVE WORD PROBLEMS INVOLVING INTEGERS, FRACTIONS, DECIMALS, AND UNITS OF MEASUREMENT 39

Skill 7.1: Solve word problems involving integers, fractions, decimals *(including percents)*, ratios, and proportions....................... 39

Skill 7.2: Understand units of measurement and conversions *(including scientific notation)* 52

COMPETENCY 8
SOLVE PROBLEMS INVOLVING DATA INTERPRETATION AND ANALYSIS 57

Skill 8.1: Interpret information from line graphs, bar graphs, pictographs, pie charts, and tables 57

Skill 8.2: Recognize appropriate graphic representations of various data 60

Skill 8.3: Analyze and interpret data using measures of central tendency *(mean, median, and mode)* 60

Skill 8.4: Analyze and interpret data using the concept of variability 61

TABLE OF CONTENTS

ALGEBRA ... 63

COMPETENCY 9
GRAPH NUMBERS OR NUMBER RELATIONSHIPS ... 63

Skill 9.1: Identify the graph of a given equation or a given inequality, find the slope and/or intercepts of a given line, and find the equation of a line ... 63

Skill 9.2: Recognize and interpret information from the graph of a function *(including direct and inverse variation)* ... 68

COMPETENCY 10
SOLVE ONE- AND TWO-VARIABLE EQUATIONS ... 70

Skill 10.1: Find the value of the unknown in a given one-variable equation ... 70

Skill 10.2: Express one variable in terms of a second variable in two-variable equations ... 71

Skill 10.3: Solve systems of two equations in two variables *(including graphical solutions)* ... 72

COMPETENCY 11
SOLVE WORD PROBLEMS INVOLVING ONE AND TWO VARIABLES ... 73

Skill 11.1: Identify the algebraic equivalent of a stated relationship and solve word problems involving one and two unknowns ... 73

COMPETENCY 12
UNDERSTAND OPERATIONS WITH ALGEBRAIC EXPRESSIONS AND FUNCTIONAL NOTATION ... 77

Skill 12.1: Factoring quadratics ... 77

Skill 12.2: Performing operations on and simplifying polynomial expressions ... 78

Skill 12.3: Understand rational expressions and radical expressions ... 78

Skill 12.4: Apply principles of functions and functional notation ... 86

COMPETENCY 13
SOLVE PROBLEMS INVOLVING QUADRATIC EQUATIONS ... 88

Skill 13.1: Graph quadratic functions and quadratic inequalities ... 88

Skill 13.2: Solve quadratic equations using factoring, completing the square, or the quadratic formula ... 92

Skill 13.3: Solve problems involving quadratic models ... 94

GEOMETRY ... 98

COMPETENCY 14
SOLVE PROBLEMS INVOLVING GEOMETRIC FIGURES ... 98

Skill 14.1: Solve problems involving two-dimensional geometric figures *(e.g., perimeter and area problems)* ... 98

Skill 14.2: Solve problems involving three-dimensional geometric figures *(e.g., volume and surface area problems)* ... 104

Skill 14.3: Solve problems using the Pythagorean theorem ... 106

COMPETENCY 15
SOLVE PROBLEMS INVOLVING GEOMETRIC CONCEPTS 108

Skill 15.1: Solve problems using principles of similarity, congruence, parallelism, and perpendicularity 108

PROBLEM SOLVING 112

COMPETENCY 16
APPLY REASONING SKILLS 112

Skill 16.1: Draw conclusions using inductive and deductive reasoning 112

COMPETENCY 17
SOLVE APPLIED PROBLEMS INVOLVING A COMBINATION OF MATHEMATICAL SKILLS 118

Skill 17.1: Apply combinations of mathematical skills to solve problems and to solve a series of related problems 118

DOMAIN III
WRITING 119

ELEMENTS OF COMPOSITION 121

COMPETENCY 18
RECOGNIZE PURPOSE AND AUDIENCE 122

Skill 18.1: Recognize writing that is appropriate for a given purpose 122

Skill 18.2: Recognize writing that is appropriate for a given audience and occasion 122

COMPETENCY 19
RECOGNIZE UNITY, FOCUS, AND DEVELOPMENT IN WRITING 122

Skill 19.1: Recognize unnecessary shifts in point of view or distracting details that impair the development of the main idea in a piece of writing 122

Skill 19.2: Recognize revisions that improve the unity and focus of a piece of writing 123

Skill 19.3: Recognize examples of well-developed writing 125

COMPETENCY 20
RECOGNIZE EFFECTIVE ORGANIZATION IN WRITING 127

Skill 20.1: Recognize methods of paragraph organization and the appropriate use of transitional words or phrases to convey text structure 127

Skill 20.2: Reorganize sentences to improve cohesion and the effective sequence of ideas 131

SENTENCE STRUCTURE, USAGE, AND MECHANICS 132

COMPETENCY 21
RECOGNIZE EFFECTIVE SENTENCES 132

Skill 21.1: Recognize ineffective repetition and inefficiency in sentence construction 132

Skill 21.2: Identify sentence fragments and run-on sentences 134

Skill 21.3: Identify standard subject-verb agreement 137

Skill 21.4: Identify standard placement of modifiers, parallel structure, and use of negatives in sentence formation 140

Skill 21.5: Recognize imprecise and inappropriate word choice 143

COMPETENCY 22
RECOGNIZE EDITED AMERICAN ENGLISH USAGE 146

Skill 22.1: Recognize the standard use of verb forms and pronouns 146

Skill 22.2: Recognize the standard formation and use of adverbs, adjectives, comparatives, superlatives, and plural and possessive forms of nouns 152

Skill 22.3: Recognize standard punctuation 156

SAMPLE TEST

THEA READING 165
Answer Key 172
Rigor Table 173
Sample Test with Rationales 174

THEA MATH 187
Answer Key 198
Rigor Table 199
Sample Test with Rationales 200

THEA WRITING 225
Answer Key 235
Rigor Table 236
Sample Test with Rationales 237

PEDAGOGY AND PROFESSIONAL RESPONSIBILITIES EC-12 255
Answer Key 273
Rigor Table 274
Sample Test with Rationales 275

GENERALIST 4-8 LANGUAGE ARTS	313
Answer Key	321
Rigor Table	322
Sample Test with Rationales	323
GENERALIST 4-8 MATH	**336**
Answer Key	342
Rigor Table	343
Sample Test with Rationales	344
GENERALIST 4-8 SOCIAL SCIENCE	**360**
Answer Key	366
Rigor Table	367
Sample Test with Rationales	368
GENERALIST 4-8 SCIENCE	**379**
Answer Key	387
Rigor Table	388
Sample Test with Rationales	389

THEA
TEXAS HIGHER EDUCATION ASSESSMENT BONUS EDITION

THEA

THEA TEXAS HIGHER EDUCATION ASSESSMENT BONUS EDITIO

SECTION 1
ABOUT XAMONLINE

XAMonline—A Specialty Teacher Certification Company
Created in 1996, XAMonline was the first company to publish study guides for state-specific teacher certification examinations. Founder Sharon Wynne found it frustrating that materials were not available for teacher certification preparation and decided to create the first single, state-specific guide. XAMonline has grown into a company of over 1,800 contributors and writers and offers over 300 titles for the entire PRAXIS series and every state examination. No matter what state you plan on teaching in, XAMonline has a unique teacher certification study guide just for you.

XAMonline—Value and Innovation
We are committed to providing value and innovation. Our print-on-demand technology allows us to be the first in the market to reflect changes in test standards and user feedback as they occur. Our guides are written by experienced teachers who are experts in their fields. And our content reflects the highest standards of quality. Comprehensive practice tests with varied levels of rigor means that your study experience will closely match the actual in-test experience.

To date, XAMonline has helped nearly 600,000 teachers pass their certification or licensing exams. Our commitment to preparation exceeds simply providing the proper material for study—it extends to helping teachers **gain mastery** of the subject matter, giving them the **tools** to become the most effective classroom leaders possible, and ushering today's students toward a **successful future**.

SECTION 2
ABOUT THIS STUDY GUIDE

Purpose of This Guide
Is there a little voice inside of you saying, "Am I ready?" Our goal is to replace that little voice and remove all doubt with a new voice that says, "I AM READY. Bring it on!" by offering the highest quality of teacher certification study guides.

Organization of Content

You will see that while every test may start with overlapping general topics, each is very unique in the skills they wish to test. Only XAMonline presents custom content that analyzes deeper than a title, a subarea, or an objective. Only XAMonline presents content and sample test assessments along with **focus statements**, the deepest-level rationale and interpretation of the skills that are unique to the exam.

<u>Title and field number of test</u>
→Each exam has its own name and number. XAMonline's guides are written to give you the content you need to know for the specific exam you are taking. You can be confident when you buy our guide that it contains the information you need to study for the specific test you are taking.

<u>Subareas</u>
→These are the major content categories found on the exam. XAMonline's guides are written to cover all of the subareas found in the test frameworks developed for the exam.

<u>Objectives</u>
→These are standards that are unique to the exam and represent the main subcategories of the subareas/content categories. XAMonline's guides are written to address every specific objective required to pass the exam.

<u>Focus statements</u>
→These are examples and interpretations of the objectives. You find them in parenthesis directly following the objective. They provide detailed examples of the range, type, and level of content that appear on the test questions. **Only XAMonline's guides drill down to this level.**

How Do We Compare with Our Competitors?

XAMonline—drills down to the focus statement level
CliffsNotes and REA—organized at the objective level
Kaplan—provides only links to content
MoMedia—content not specific to the state test

Each subarea is divided into manageable sections that cover the specific skill areas. Explanations are easy to understand and thorough. You'll find that every test answer contains a rejoinder so if you need a refresher or further review after taking the test, you'll know exactly to which section you must return.

How to Use This Book

Our informal polls show that most people begin studying up to eight weeks prior to the test date, so start early. Then ask yourself some questions: How much do you really know? Are you coming to the test straight from your teacher-education program or are you having to review subjects you haven't considered in ten years? Either way, take a **diagnostic or assessment test** first. Also, spend time on sample tests so that you become accustomed to the way the actual test will appear.

This guide comes with an online diagnostic test of 30 questions found online at www.XAMonline.com. It is a little boot camp to get you up for the task and reveal things about your compendium of knowledge in general. Although this guide is structured to follow the order of the test, you are not required to study in that order. By finding a time-management and study plan that fits your life you will be more effective. The results of your diagnostic or self-assessment test can be a guide for how to manage your time and point you toward an area that needs more attention.

After taking the diagnostic exam, fill out the **Personalized Study Plan** page at the beginning of each chapter. Review the competencies and skills covered in that chapter and check the boxes that apply to your study needs. If there are sections you already know you can skip, check the "skip it" box. Taking this step will give you a study plan for each chapter.

Week	Activity
8 weeks prior to test	Take a diagnostic test found at www.XAMonline.com
7 weeks prior to test	Build your Personalized Study Plan for each chapter. Check the "skip it" box for sections you feel you are already strong in. ✗ SKIP IT ☐
6-3 weeks prior to test	For each of these four weeks, choose a content area to study. You don't have to go in the order of the book. It may be that you start with the content that needs the most review. Alternately, you may want to ease yourself into plan by starting with the most familiar material.
2 weeks prior to test	Take the sample test, score it, and create a review plan for the final week before the test.
1 week prior to test	Following your plan (which will likely be aligned with the areas that need the most review) go back and study the sections that align with the questions you may have gotten wrong. Then go back and study the sections related to the questions you answered correctly. If need be, create flashcards and drill yourself on any area that you makes you anxious.

SECTION 3
ABOUT THE THEA EXAM

What Is the THEA (Texas Higher Education Assessment)?

The Texas Higher Education Assessment (THEA) exam is an exam given to first-year college students in order to assess their reading, writing, and mathematics skills upon entering college or an alternative certification program. It is administered by Pearson Education and was created at the direction of the Texas Higher Education Coordinating Board.

Often **your own state's requirements** determine whether or not you should take any particular test. The most reliable source of information regarding this is your state's Department of Education. This resource should have a complete list of testing centers and dates. Test dates vary by subject area and not all test dates necessarily include your particular test, so be sure to check carefully.

If you are in a teacher-education program, check with the Education Department or the Certification Officer for specific information for testing and testing timelines. The Certification Office should have most of the information you need.

If you choose an alternative route to certification you can either rely on our website at *www.XAMonline.com* or on the resources provided by an alternative certification program. Many states now have specific agencies devoted to alternative certification and there are some national organizations as well, for example:

National Association for Alternative Certification
http://www.alt-teachercert.org/index.asp

Interpreting Test Results

Contrary to what you may have heard, the results of the THEA test are not based on time. More accurately, you will be scored on the raw number of points you earn in relation to the raw number of points available. Each question is worth one raw point. It is likely to your benefit to complete as many questions in the time allotted, but it will not necessarily work to your advantage if you hurry through the test.

Follow the guidelines provided by Pearson for interpreting your score. The Web site offers a sample test score sheet and clearly explains how/whether the scores are scaled and what to expect if you have an essay portion on your test.

Scores are available by mail two weeks after the test date and scores will be sent to you and your chosen institution(s).

TEXAS HIGHER EDUCATION ASSESSMENT BONUS EDITION

What's on the Test?

The THEA exam consists of three sections, each with multiple-choice questions. The writing section also contains an essay portion. The use of a four-function, nonprogrammable calculator is permitted. The breakdown of the questions is as follows:

Category	Approximate Number of Questions	Approximate Percentage of the test
I: Reading	40 multiple choice	31%
II: Mathematics	50 multiple choice	38%
III: Writing	40 multiple choice & 1 essay	31%

Question Types

You're probably thinking, enough already, I want to study! Indulge us a little longer while we explain that there is actually more than one type of multiple-choice question. You can thank us later after you realize how well prepared you are for your exam.

1. **Complete the Statement.** The name says it all. In this question type you'll be asked to choose the correct completion of a given statement. For example:

   > The Dolch Basic Sight Words consist of a relatively short list of words that children should be able to:
   >
   > A. Sound out
   >
   > B. Know the meaning of
   >
   > C. Recognize on sight
   >
   > D. Use in a sentence

   The correct answer is C. In order to check your answer, test out the statement by adding the choices to the end of it.

2. **Which of the Following.** One way to test your answer choice for this type of question is to replace the phrase "which of the following" with your selection. Use this example:

> **Which of the following words is one of the twelve most frequently used in children's reading texts:**
> A. There
> B. This
> C. The
> D. An

Don't look! Test your answer. ____ is one of the twelve most frequently used in children's reading texts. Did you guess C? Then you guessed correctly.

3. **Roman Numeral Choices.** This question type is used when there is more than one possible correct answer. For example:

> **Which of the following two arguments accurately supports the use of cooperative learning as an effective method of instruction?**
> I. Cooperative learning groups facilitate healthy competition between individuals in the group.
> II. Cooperative learning groups allow academic achievers to carry or cover for academic underachievers.
> III. Cooperative learning groups make each student in the group accountable for the success of the group.
> IV. Cooperative learning groups make it possible for students to reward other group members for achieving.
>
> A. I and II
> B. II and III
> C. I and III
> D. III and IV

Notice that the question states there are **two** possible answers. It's best to read all the possibilities first before looking at the answer choices. In this case, the correct answer is D.

4. **Negative Questions.** This type of question contains words such as "not," "least," and "except." Each correct answer will be the statement that does **not** fit the situation described in the question. Such as:

> **Multicultural education is not**
>   A. An idea or concept
>   B. A "tack-on" to the school curriculum
>   C. An educational reform movement
>   D. A process

Think to yourself that the statement could be anything but the correct answer. This question form is more open to interpretation than other types, so read carefully and don't forget that you're answering a negative statement.

5. **Questions that Include Graphs, Tables, or Reading Passages.** As always, read the question carefully. It likely asks for a very specific answer and not a broad interpretation of the visual. Here is a simple (though not statistically accurate) example of a graph question:

> In the following graph in how many years did more men take the NYSTCE exam than women?
>
>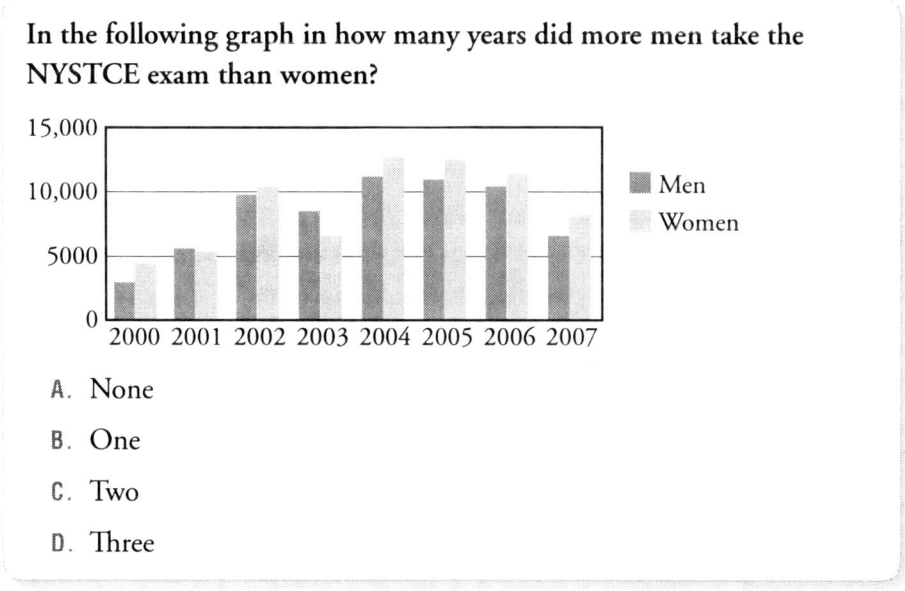
>
>   A. None
>   B. One
>   C. Two
>   D. Three

It may help you to simply circle the two years that answer the question. Make sure you've read the question thoroughly and once you've made your determination, double check your work. The correct answer is C.

SECTION 4
HELPFUL HINTS

Study Tips

1. **You are what you eat.** Certain foods aid the learning process by releasing natural memory enhancers called CCKs (cholecystokinin) composed of tryptophan, choline, and phenylalanine. All of these chemicals enhance the neurotransmitters associated with memory and certain foods release memory enhancing chemicals. A light meal or snacks of one of the following foods fall into this category:

   - Milk
   - Rice
   - Eggs
   - Fish
   - Nuts and seeds
   - Oats
   - Turkey

   The better the connections, the more you comprehend!

2. **See the forest for the trees.** In other words, get the concept before you look at the details. One way to do this is to take notes as you read, paraphrasing or summarizing in your own words. Putting the concept in terms that are comfortable and familiar may increase retention.

3. **Question authority.** Ask why, why, why? Pull apart written material paragraph by paragraph and don't forget the captions under the illustrations. For example, if a heading reads *Stream Erosion* put it in the form of a question (Why do streams erode? What is stream erosion?) then find the answer within the material. If you train your mind to think in this manner you will learn more and prepare yourself for answering test questions.

4. **Play mind games.** Using your brain for reading or puzzles keeps it flexible. Even with a limited amount of time your brain can take in data (much like a computer) and store it for later use. In ten minutes you can: read two paragraphs (at least), quiz yourself with flash cards, or review notes. Even if you don't fully understand something on the first pass, your mind stores it for recall, which is why frequent reading or review increases chances of retention and comprehension.

5. **Get pointed in the right direction.** Use arrows to point to important passages or pieces of information. It's easier to read than a page full of yellow highlights. Highlighting can be used sparingly, but add an arrow to the margin to call attention to it.

6. **The pen is mightier than the sword.** Learn to take great notes. A by-product of our modern culture is that we have grown accustomed to getting our information in short doses. We've subconsciously trained ourselves to assimilate information into neat little packages. Messy notes fragment the flow of information. Your notes can be much clearer with proper formatting. ***The Cornell Method*** is one such format. This method was popularized in *How to Study in College*, Ninth Edition, by Walter Pauk. You can benefit from the method without purchasing an additional book by simply looking up the method online. Below is a sample of how *The Cornell Method* can be adapted for use with this guide.

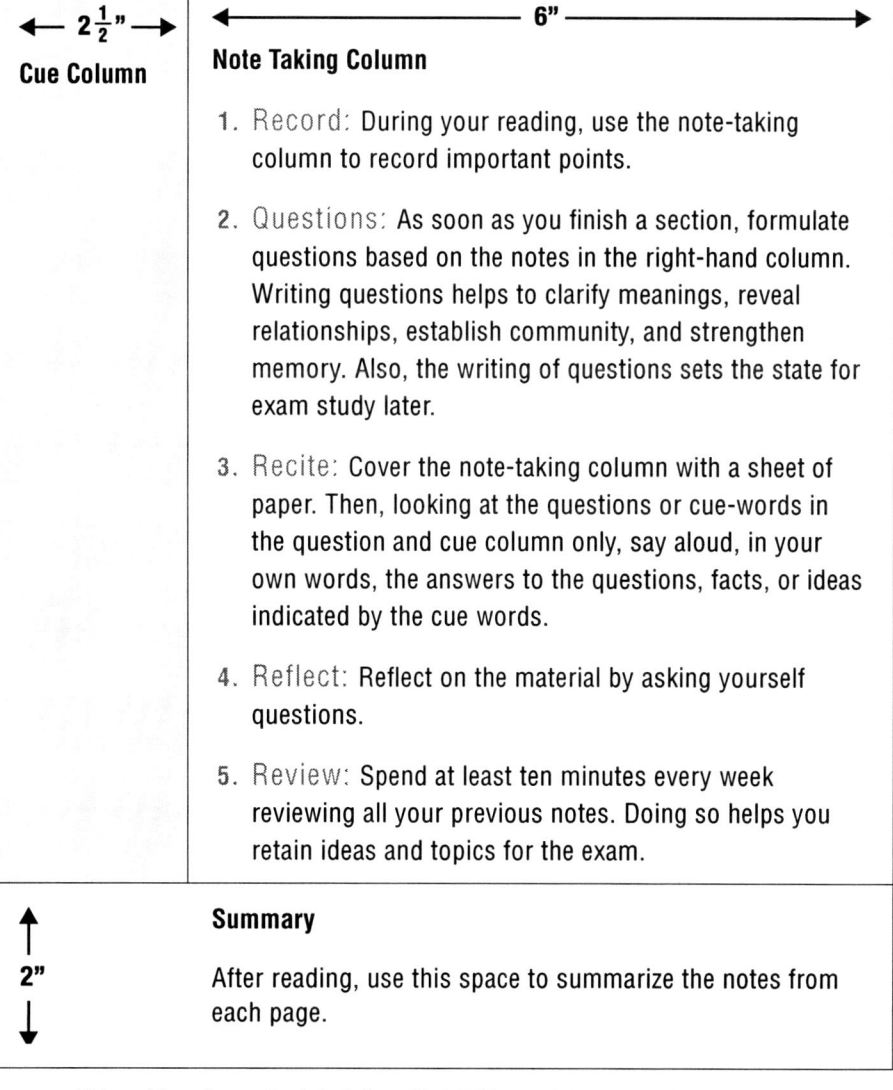

← 2½" → **Cue Column**	← 6" → **Note Taking Column**
	1. Record: During your reading, use the note-taking column to record important points.
	2. Questions: As soon as you finish a section, formulate questions based on the notes in the right-hand column. Writing questions helps to clarify meanings, reveal relationships, establish community, and strengthen memory. Also, the writing of questions sets the state for exam study later.
	3. Recite: Cover the note-taking column with a sheet of paper. Then, looking at the questions or cue-words in the question and cue column only, say aloud, in your own words, the answers to the questions, facts, or ideas indicated by the cue words.
	4. Reflect: Reflect on the material by asking yourself questions.
	5. Review: Spend at least ten minutes every week reviewing all your previous notes. Doing so helps you retain ideas and topics for the exam.
↑ 2" ↓	**Summary** After reading, use this space to summarize the notes from each page.

*Adapted from How to Study in College, Ninth Edition, by Walter Pauk, ©2008 Wadsworth

7. **Place yourself in exile and set the mood.** Set aside a particular place and time to study that best suits your personal needs and biorhythms. If you're a night person, burn the midnight oil. If you're a morning person set yourself up with some coffee and get to it. Make your study time and place as free from distraction as possible and surround yourself with what you need, be it silence or music. Studies have shown that music can aid in concentration, absorption, and retrieval of information. Not all music, though. Classical music is said to work best.

8. **Check your budget.** You should at least review all the content material before your test, but allocate the most amount of time to the areas that need the most refreshing. It sounds obvious, but it's easy to forget. You can use the study rubric above to balance your study budget.

The proctor will write the start time where it can be seen and then, later, provide the time remaining, typically fifteen minutes before the end of the test.

Testing Tips

1. **Get smart, play dumb.** Sometimes a question is just a question. No one is out to trick you, so don't assume that the test writer is looking for something other than what was asked. Stick to the question as written and don't overanalyze.

2. **Do a double take.** Read test questions and answer choices at least twice because it's easy to miss something, to transpose a word or some letters. If you have no idea what the correct answer is, skip it and come back later if there's time. If you're still clueless, it's okay to guess. Remember, you're scored on the number of questions you answer correctly and you're not penalized for wrong answers. The worst case scenario is that you miss a point from a good guess.

3. **Turn it on its ear.** The syntax of a question can often provide a clue, so make things interesting and turn the question into a statement to see if it changes the meaning or relates better (or worse) to the answer choices.

4. **Get out your magnifying glass.** Look for hidden clues in the questions because it's difficult to write a multiple-choice question without giving away part of the answer in the options presented. In most questions you can readily eliminate one or two potential answers, increasing your chances of answering correctly to 50/50, which will help out if you've skipped a question and gone back to it (see tip #2).

5. **Call it intuition.** Often your first instinct is correct. If you've been studying the content you've likely absorbed something and have subconsciously retained the knowledge. On questions you're not sure about trust your instincts because a first impression is usually correct.

6. Graffiti. Sometimes it's a good idea to mark your answers directly on the test booklet and go back to fill in the optical scan sheet later. You don't get extra points for perfectly blackened ovals. If you choose to manage your test this way, be sure not to mismark your answers when you transcribe to the scan sheet.

7. Become a clock-watcher. You have a set amount of time to answer the questions. Don't get bogged down laboring over a question you're not sure about when there are ten others you could answer more readily. If you choose to follow the advice of tip #6, be sure you leave time near the end to go back and fill in the scan sheet.

Do the Drill

No matter how prepared you feel it's sometimes a good idea to apply Murphy's Law. So the following tips might seem silly, mundane, or obvious, but we're including them anyway.

1. Remember, you are what you eat, so bring a snack. Choose from the list of energizing foods that appear earlier in the introduction.

2. You're not too sexy for your test. Wear comfortable clothes. You'll be distracted if your belt is too tight or if you're too cold or too hot.

3. Lie to yourself. Even if you think you're a prompt person, pretend you're not and leave plenty of time to get to the testing center. Map it out ahead of time and do a dry run if you have to. There's no need to add road rage to your list of anxieties.

4. Bring sharp number 2 pencils. It may seem impossible to forget this need from your school days, but you might. And make sure the erasers are intact, too.

5. No ticket, no test. Bring your admission ticket as well as **two** forms of identification, including one with a picture and signature. You will not be admitted to the test without these things.

6. You can't take it with you. Leave any study aids, dictionaries, notebooks, computers, and the like at home. Certain tests **do** allow a scientific or four-function calculator, so check ahead of time to see if your test does.

7. Prepare for the desert. Any time spent on a bathroom break **cannot** be made up later, so use your judgment on the amount you eat or drink.

8. Quiet, Please! Keeping your own time is a good idea, but not with a timepiece that has a loud ticker. If you use a watch, take it off and place it nearby but not so that it distracts you. And **silence your cell phone**.

To the best of our ability, we have compiled the content you need to know in this book and in the accompanying online resources. The rest is up to you. You can use the study and testing tips or you can follow your own methods. Either way, you can be confident that there aren't any missing pieces of information and there shouldn't be any surprises in the content on the test.

If you have questions about test fees, registration, electronic testing, or other content verification issues please visit *www.thea.nesinc.com*.

Good luck!

Sharon Wynne
Founder, XAMonline

DOMAIN I
READING

PERSONALIZED STUDY PLAN

✗ **KNOWN MATERIAL/ SKIP IT**

PAGE	COMPETENCY AND SKILL		KNOWN MATERIAL/ SKIP IT
3	**1:**	**Determine the meaning of words and phrases**	☐
	1.1:	Use context to determine the meaning of words with multiple meanings, unfamiliar and uncommon words and phrases, and figurative expressions	☐
	1.2:	Using figurative expressions	☐
9	**2:**	**Understand the main idea and supporting details in written material**	☐
	2.1:	Identify explicit and implicit main ideas	☐
	2.2:	Recognize ideas that support, illustrate, or elaborate the main idea	☐
12	**3:**	**Identify a writer's purpose, point of view, and intended meaning**	☐
	3.1:	Recognize a writer's expressed or implied purpose	☐
	3.2:	Evaluate the appropriateness of written material for a specific purpose or audience	☐
	3.3:	Recognize the likely effect on an audience of a writer's choice of words	☐
	3.4:	Use the content, word choice, and phrasing of a passage to determine a writer's opinion	☐
16	**4:**	**Analyze the relationship among ideas in written material**	☐
	4.1:	Identify sequence of events or steps	☐
	4.2:	Identify cause-effect relationships	☐
	4.3:	Analyze relationships between ideas in opposition	☐
	4.4:	Identify solutions to problems	☐
	4.5:	Draw conclusions inductively and deductively	☐
22	**5:**	**Use critical reasoning skills to evaluate written material**	☐
	5.1:	Evaluate stated or implied assumptions	☐
	5.2:	Judge the relevance or importance of facts, examples, or graphic data	☐
	5.3:	Evaluate the logic of a writer's argument	☐
	5.4:	Evaluate the validity of analogies	☐
	5.5:	Distinguish between fact and opinion	☐
	5.6:	Assess the credibility or objectivity of a writer or source	☐
31	**6:**	**Apply study skills to reading assignments**	☐
	6.1:	Organize and summarize information for study purposes	☐
	6.2:	Follow written instructions or directions	☐
	6.3:	Interpret information presented in charts, graphs, or tables	☐

COMPETENCY 1
DETERMINE THE MEANING OF WORDS AND PHRASES

> **SKILL 1.1** Use the context of a passage to determine the meaning of words with multiple meanings, unfamiliar and uncommon words and phrases, and figurative expressions

CONTEXT CLUES help readers determine the meanings of words with which they are not familiar. The CONTEXT of a word is the sentence or sentences that surround the word.

Read the following sentences and attempt to determine the meanings of the words in bold print.

> The **luminosity** of the room was so incredible that there was no need for lights.

If there was no need for lights, then one must assume that the word luminosity has something to do with giving off light. The definition of luminosity is "the emission of light."

> Jamie could not understand Joe's feelings. His mood swings made understanding him somewhat of an **enigma**.

The fact that he could not be understood made him somewhat of a puzzle. The definition of enigma is "a mystery or puzzle."

Familiarity with terms, ROOTS (the basic elements of words) and prefixes (affixes that are added to the fronts of words to form derivative words) can help you determine the meanings of unknown words.

Following are some common roots and prefixes.

CONTEXT CLUES: clues that help readers determine the meanings of words with which they are not familiar

CONTEXT: the sentence or sentences that surround a word

ROOTS: the basic elements of words

SOME COMMON ROOTS AND THEIR MEANINGS		
Root	Meaning	Example
aqua	water	aqualung
astro	stars	astrology

Continued on next page

Root	Meaning	Example
bio	life	biology
carn	meat	carnivorous
circum	around	circumnavigate
geo	earth	geology
herb	plant	herbivorous
mal	bad	malicious
neo	new	neonatal
tele	distant	telescope

SOME COMMON PREFIXES AND THEIR MEANINGS

Prefix	Meaning	Example
un-	not	unnamed
re-	again	reenter
il-	not	illegible
pre-	before	preset
mis-	incorrectly	misstate
in-	not	informal
anti-	against	antiwar
de-	opposite	derail
post-	after	postwar
ir-	not	irresponsible

DETERMINE THE MEANING OF WORDS AND PHRASES

Word Forms

Sometimes a very familiar word can appear as a different part of speech, as in the examples below.

> You may have heard that fraud involves a criminal misrepresentation, so when this word appears in the adjective form fraudulent, you can make an educated guess as to its meaning. (Example: He was suspected of fraudulent activities.)

> You probably know that something out-of-date is obsolete; therefore, when you read about "built-in obsolescence," you can detect the meaning of the unfamiliar word.

Practice Exercise: Determining Word Meaning

Choose the option that corrects an error in the underlined portion(s).

1. Farmer John got a two-horse plow and went to work. Straight <u>furrows</u> stretched out behind him.

   The word <u>furrows</u> means

   A. Long cuts made by plow
   B. Vast, open fields
   C. Rows of corn
   D. Pairs of hitched horses

2. The survivors struggled ahead, <u>shambling</u> through the terrible cold, doing their best not to fall.

   The word <u>shambling</u> means

   A. Frozen in place
   B. Running
   C. Shivering uncontrollably
   D. Walking awkwardly

Answer Key: Determining Word Meaning

1. A is the correct answer. The words "straight" and the expression "stretched out behind him" are your clues.

2. D is the correct answer. The words "ahead" and "through" are your clues.

   The context for a word is the written passage that surrounds it. Sometimes the writer offers synonyms—words that have nearly the same meaning. Context clues can appear within the sentence itself, within the preceding and/or following sentence(s), or in the passage as a whole.

Sentence Clues

Often, a writer will actually define a difficult or particularly important word for you the first time it appears in a passage. Phrases such as *that is, such as, which is,* or *is called* might announce the writer's intention to give just the definition you need. Occasionally, a writer will simply use a synonym (a word that means the same thing) or near-synonym joined by the word *or*. Look at the following examples:

> *The credibility, that is to say the believability, of the witness was called into question by evidence of previous perjury.*

> *Nothing would assuage or lessen the child's grief.*

Punctuation at the sentence level is often a clue to the meaning of a word. Commas, parentheses, quotation marks, and dashes tell the reader that the writer is offering a definition.

> *A tendency toward hyperbole, extravagant exaggeration, is a common flaw among persuasive writers.*

> *Political apathy—lack of interest—can lead to the death of the state.*

A writer might simply give an explanation in other words that you can understand in the same sentence:

> *The xenophobic townspeople were suspicious of every foreigner.*

Writers also explain a word in terms of its opposite at the sentence level:

> *His incarceration was ended, and he was elated to be out of jail.*

Adjacent Sentence Clues

The context for a word goes beyond the sentence in which it appears. At times, the writer uses adjacent (adjoining) sentences to present an explanation or definition:

> *The 200 dollars for the car repair would have to come out of the contingency fund. Fortunately, Angela's father had taught her to keep some money set aside for just such emergencies.*

DETERMINE THE MEANING OF WORDS AND PHRASES

Analysis: The second sentence offers a clue to the definition of contingency as used in this sentence: "emergencies." Therefore, a fund for contingencies would be money tucked away for unforeseen and/or urgent events.

Entire Passage Clues

On occasion, you must look at an entire paragraph or passage to figure out the definition of a word or term. In the following paragraph, notice how the word *nostalgia* undergoes a form of extended definition throughout the selection rather than in just one sentence.

> The word nostalgia links the Greek words for "away from home" and "pain." If you are feeling nostalgic, then you are probably in some physical distress or discomfort, suffering from a feeling of alienation and separation from loved ones or loved places. Nostalgia is that awful feeling you remember from the first time you went away to camp or spent the weekend with a friend's family—homesickness, or some condition even more painful than that. However, in common use, nostalgia has come to have associations that are more sentimental. A few years back, for example, a nostalgic craze had to do with the 1950s. We resurrected poodle skirts and saddle shoes, built new restaurants to look like old ones, and tried to make chicken à la king just as Mother probably never made it. In TV situation comedies, we recreated a pleasant world that probably never existed and relished our nostalgia, longing for a homey, comfortable, lost time.

SKILL 1.2 Using figurative expressions

1. **Simile:** Direct comparison between two things. "My love is like a red-red rose."

2. **Metaphor:** Indirect comparison between two things. The use of a word or phrase denoting one kind of object or action in place of another to suggest a comparison between them. While poets use them extensively, they are also integral to everyday speech. For example, chairs are said to have "legs" and "arms" although we know that it's humans and other animals that have these appendages.

3. **Parallelism:** The arrangement of ideas in phrases, sentences, and paragraphs that balance one element with another of equal importance and similar wording. An example from Francis Bacon's *Of Studies*: "Reading maketh a full man, conference a ready man, and writing an exact man."

4. Personification: Human characteristics are attributed to an inanimate object, an abstract quality, or animal. Examples: John Bunyan wrote characters named Death, Knowledge, Giant Despair, Sloth, and Piety in his *Pilgrim's Progress*. The metaphor of an arm of a chair is a form of personification.

5. Euphemism: The substitution of an agreeable or inoffensive term for one that might offend or suggest something unpleasant. Many euphemisms are used to refer to death to avoid using the real word such as "passed away," "crossed over," or nowadays "passed."

6. Hyperbole: Deliberate exaggeration for effect or comic effect. An example from Shakespeare's *The Merchant of Venice*:

> Why, if two gods should play some heavenly match
> And on the wager lay two earthly women,
> And Portia one, there must be something else
> Pawned with the other, for the poor rude world
> Hath not her fellow.

7. Climax: A number of phrases or sentences are arranged in ascending order of rhetorical forcefulness. Example from Melville's *Moby Dick*:

> All that most maddens and torments; all that stirs up the lees of things; all truth with malice in it; all that cracks the sinews and cakes the brain; all the subtle demonisms of life and thought; all evil, to crazy Ahab, were visibly personified and made practically assailable in Moby Dick.

8. Bathos: A ludicrous attempt to portray pathos—that is, to evoke pity, sympathy, or sorrow. It may result from inappropriately dignifying the commonplace, elevated language to describe something trivial, or greatly exaggerated pathos.

9. Oxymoron: A contradiction in terms deliberately employed for effect. It is usually seen in a qualifying adjective whose meaning is contrary to that of the noun it modifies such as wise folly.

10. Irony: Expressing something other than and particularly opposite the literal meaning such as words of praise when blame is intended. In poetry, it is often used as a sophisticated or resigned awareness of contrast between what is and what ought to be and expresses a controlled pathos without sentimentality. It is a form of indirection that avoids overt praise or censure. An early example: the Greek comic character Eiron, a clever underdog who by his wit repeatedly triumphs over the boastful character Alazon.

11. **Alliteration:** The repetition of consonant sounds in two or more neighboring words or syllables. In its simplest form, it reinforces one or two consonant sounds. Example: Shakespeare's Sonnet #12:

> When I do **c**ount the **c**lock that **t**ells the **t**ime.

Some poets have used more complex patterns of alliteration by creating consonants both at the beginning of words and at the beginning of stressed syllables within words. Example: Shelley's "Stanzas Written in Dejection Near Naples:"

> The **C**ity's voice it**s**elf is **s**oft like **S**olitude's

12. **Onomatopoeia:** The naming of a thing or action by a vocal imitation of the sound associated with it, such as "buzz" or "hiss" or the use of words whose sound suggests the sense. A good example from "The Brook" by Tennyson:

> I chatter over stony ways,
> In little sharps and trebles,
> I bubble into eddying bays,
> I babble on the pebbles.

COMPETENCY 2
UNDERSTAND THE MAIN IDEA AND SUPPORTING DETAILS IN WRITTEN MATERIAL

SKILL 2.1 Identify explicit and implicit main ideas

The MAIN IDEA of a passage or paragraph is the basic message, idea, point, concept, or meaning that the author wants to convey to the reader. Understanding the main idea of a passage or paragraph is the key to understanding the more subtle components of the author's message. The main idea is what is being said

MAIN IDEA: the basic message, idea, point, concept, or meaning that the author wants to convey to the reader

READING

about a topic or subject. Once you have identified the basic message, you will have an easier time answering other questions that test critical skills.

Main ideas are either stated or implied. A stated main idea is explicit: it is directly expressed in a sentence or two in the paragraph or passage. An implied main idea is suggested by the overall reading selection. In the first case, you need not pull information from various points in the paragraph or passage in order to form the main idea because the author already states it. If a main idea is implied, however, you must formulate—in your own words—a main idea statement by condensing the overall message contained in the material itself.

> *Sample Passage*
>
> *Sometimes too much of a good thing can become a very bad thing indeed. In an earnest attempt to consume a healthy diet, dietary supplement enthusiasts have been known to overdose. Vitamin C, for example, long thought to help people ward off cold viruses, is currently being studied for its possible role in warding off cancer and other diseases that cause tissue degeneration. Unfortunately, an overdose of vitamin C—more than 10,000 mg—on a daily basis can cause nausea and diarrhea. Calcium supplements, commonly taken by women, are helpful in warding off osteoporosis. More than just a few grams a day, however, can lead to stomach upset and even kidney and bladder stones. Niacin, proven useful in reducing cholesterol levels, can be dangerous in large doses to those who suffer from heart problems, asthma, or ulcers.*

The main idea expressed in this paragraph is:

A. Supplements taken in excess can be a bad thing indeed.

B. Dietary supplement enthusiasts have been known to overdose.

C. Vitamins can cause nausea, diarrhea, and kidney or bladder stones.

D. People who take supplements are preoccupied with their health.

Answer A is a paraphrase of the first sentence and provides a general framework for the rest of the paragraph: excess supplement intake is bad. The rest of the paragraph discusses the consequences of taking too many vitamins. Options B and C refer to major details, and Option D introduces the idea of preoccupation, which is not included in this paragraph.

SKILL 2.2 Recognize ideas that support, illustrate, or elaborate the main idea of a passage

SUPPORTING DETAILS are examples, facts, ideas, illustrations, cases, and anecdotes used by a writer to explain, expand upon, and develop the more general main idea. A writer's choice of supporting details is determined by the nature of the

UNDERSTAND THE MAIN IDEA AND SUPPORTING DETAILS IN WRITTEN MATERIAL

topic being covered. Supporting details are specifics that relate directly to the main idea. Writers select and shape material according to their purposes. An advertisement writer seeking to persuade the reader to buy a particular running shoe, for instance, will emphasize only the positive characteristics of the shoe for advertisement copy. A columnist for a running magazine, on the other hand, might list the good and bad points about the same shoe in an article recommending appropriate shoes for different kind of runners. Both major details (those that directly support the main idea), and minor details (those that provide interesting, but not always essential, information) help create a well-written and fluid passage.

> **SUPPORTING DETAILS:** examples, facts, ideas, illustrations, cases, and anecdotes used by a writer to explain, expand upon, and develop the more general main idea

In the following paragraph, the sentences in **bold print** provide a skeleton of a paragraph on the benefits of recycling. The sentences in bold are generalizations that, by themselves, do not explain the need to recycle. The sentences in *italics* add details to SHOW the general points in bold. Notice how the supporting details help you understand the necessity of recycling.

> **While one day recycling may become mandatory in all states, right now it is voluntary in many communities.** *Those of us who participate in recycling are amazed by how much material is recycled.* **For many communities, the blue-box recycling program has had an immediate effect.** *By just recycling glass, aluminum cans, and plastic bottles, we have reduced the volume of disposable trash by one-third, thus extending the useful life of local landfills by over a decade. Imagine the difference if those dramatic results were achieved nationwide.* **The number of reusable items we thoughtlessly dispose of is staggering.** *For example, Americans dispose of enough steel every day to supply Detroit car manufacturers for three months. Additionally, we dispose of enough aluminum annually to rebuild the nation's air fleet. These statistics, available from the Environmental Protection Agency (EPA), should encourage all of us to watch what we throw away.* **Clearly, recycling in our homes and in our communities directly improves the environment.**

Notice how the author's supporting examples enhance the message of the paragraph and relate to the author's thesis noted above. If you only read the boldface sentences, you have a glimpse of the topic. This paragraph of illustration, however, is developed through numerous details creating specific images: *reduced the volume of disposable trash by one-third; extended the useful life of local landfills by over a decade; enough steel every day to supply Detroit car manufacturers for three months; enough aluminum to rebuild the nation's air fleet.* If the writer had merely written a few general sentences, as those shown in bold, you would not fully understand the vast amount of trash involved in recycling or the positive results of current recycling efforts.

COMPETENCY 3
IDENTIFY A WRITER'S PURPOSE, POINT OF VIEW, AND INTENDED MEANING

SKILL 3.1 Recognize a writer's expressed or implied purpose for writing

> **ESSAY:** an extended discussion of a writer's point of view about a particular topic

An **ESSAY** is an extended discussion of a writer's point of view about a particular topic. This point of view may be supported by using such writing modes as examples, argument and persuasion, analysis, or comparison/contrast. In any case, a good essay is clear, coherent, well organized, and fully developed.

When an author sets out to write a passage, he or she usually has a purpose for doing so. That purpose may be simply to give information that might be interesting or useful to the reader; it may be to persuade the reader to a point of view or to move the reader to act in a particular way; it may be to tell a story; or it may be to describe an experience in such a way that it becomes available to the reader through one of the five senses. Following are the primary devices for expressing a particular purpose in a piece of writing:

- **Basic expository writing** gives information not previously known about a topic or is used to explain or define one. Facts, examples, statistics, cause and effect, direct tone, objective rather than subjective delivery, and non-emotional information are presented in a formal manner.

- **Descriptive writing** centers on a person, place, or object. Descriptive writing uses concrete and sensory words to create a mood or impression, arranging details in a chronological or spatial sequence.

- **Narrative writing** is developed using an incident, an anecdote, or a related series of events. Chronology, the five W's, a topic sentence, and a conclusion are essential ingredients.

- **Persuasive writing** implies the writer's ability to select vocabulary and arrange facts and opinions in such a way as to direct the beliefs or actions of the listener/reader. Persuasive writing may incorporate exposition and narration to illustrate the main idea.

- Journalistic writing is theoretically free of author bias. It is essential, when relaying information about an event, a person, or a thing, that the information be factual and objective. Provide students with an opportunity to examine newspapers and create their own newspaper. Many newspapers have educational programs that are offered free to schools.

SKILL 3.2 Evaluate the appropriateness of written material for a specific purpose or audience

See Skill 3.1

SKILL 3.3 Recognize the likely effect on an audience of a writer's choice of words

Audience

Tailoring language for a particular audience is an important skill. Writing intended to be read by a business associate will surely sound different from writing intended to be read by a young child. Not only are the vocabularies different, but the formality of the discourse needs to be adjusted as well.

Determining the appropriate language for a particular audience hinges on two things: word choice and formality/informality. The most formal language does not use contractions or slang. The most informal language will probably feature a more casual use of common sayings and anecdotes. Formal language will use longer sentences and will not sound like a conversation. The most informal language will use shorter sentences—not necessarily simple sentences, but shorter constructions—and may sound like a conversation.

In both formal and informal writing, there exists a TONE—the writer's attitude toward the material and/or reader. The tone may be playful, formal, intimate, angry, serious, ironic, outraged, baffled, tender, serene, depressed, and so on. Both the subject matter and the audience dictate the overall tone of a piece of writing. Tone is also related to the actual words that make up the document, since we attach affective meanings, called connotations, to words. Gaining conscious control over language makes it possible for the writer to use language appropriately in various situations. By evoking the proper responses from readers/listeners, the writer can prompt them to take action.

TONE: the author's attitude toward the material and/or the reader

READING

The following questions are an excellent way to help the writer choose the appropriate audience and tone for a piece of writing.

1. Who is your audience? (friend, teacher, businessperson, etc.)

2. How much does this person know about you and/or your topic?

3. What is your purpose? (to prove an argument, to persuade, to amuse, to register a complaint, to ask for a raise, etc.)

4. What emotions do you have about the topic? (nervousness, happiness, confidence, anger, sadness, no feelings at all)

5. What emotions do you want to register with your audience? (anger, nervousness, happiness, boredom, interest)

6. What persona do you need to create in order to achieve your purpose?

7. What choice of language is best suited to achieving your purpose with your particular subject? (slang, friendly but respectful, formal)

8. What emotional quality do you want to transmit to achieve your purpose? (matter-of-fact, informative, authoritative, inquisitive, sympathetic, or angry) To what degree do you want to express this tone?

SKILL 3.4 Use the content, word choice, and phrasing of a passage to determine a writer's opinion or point of view

The tone of a written passage is the author's attitude toward the subject matter. The tone (mood, feeling) is revealed through the qualities of the writing itself and is a direct product of such stylistic elements as language and sentence structure. The tone of the written passage is much like a speaker's voice; instead of being spoken, however, it is the product of words on a page.

Often, writers have an emotional stake in their subjects, and their purpose, either explicitly or implicitly, is to convey those feelings to the reader. In such cases, the writing is generally subjective; that is, it stems from opinions, judgments, values, ideas, and feelings. Both sentence structure (syntax) and word choice (diction) are instrumental tools in creating tone.

Tone may be thought of generally as positive, negative, or neutral. Below is a statement about snakes that demonstrates this.

IDENTIFY A WRITER'S PURPOSE, POINT OF VIEW, AND INTENDED MEANING

> *Many species of snakes live here. Some of those species, both poisonous and non-poisonous, have habitats that coincide with those of human residents of the state.*

The voice of the writer in this statement is neutral. The sentences are declarative (not exclamations, fragments, or questions). The adjectives are few and non-descript—*many, some, poisonous* (balanced with *nonpoisonous*). Nothing much in this brief paragraph would alert the reader to the feelings of the writer about snakes. The paragraph has a neutral, objective, detached, impartial tone.

If the writer's attitude toward snakes involved admiration, or even affection, the tone would generally be positive:

> *These snakes are a tenacious bunch. When they find their habitats invaded by humans, they cling to their home territories as long as they can, as if vainly attempting to fight off the onslaught of the human hordes.*

An additional message emerges in this paragraph—the writer quite clearly favors snakes over people. The writer uses adjectives such as tenacious to describe his or her feelings about snakes. The writer also humanizes the reptiles, making them brave, beleaguered creatures. Obviously, the writer is more sympathetic to snakes than to people in this paragraph.

If the writer's attitude toward snakes involved active dislike and fear, then the tone would also reflect that attitude by being negative:

> *Countless species of snakes, some more dangerous than others, still lurk on the urban fringes of towns and cities. They will often invade domestic spaces, terrorizing people and their pets.*

Here, obviously, the snakes are the villains. They *lurk*, they *invade*, and they *terrorize*. The tone of this paragraph might be defined as *distressed*.

In the same manner, a writer can use language to portray characters as good or bad. A writer uses positive and negative adjectives to convey the manner of a character.

COMPETENCY 4
ANALYZE THE RELATIONSHIP AMONG IDEAS IN WRITTEN MATERIAL

SKILL 4.1 Identify sequence of events or steps

The ability to organize events or steps provided in a passage encourages the development of logical thinking and the processes of analysis and evaluation.

The ability to organize events or steps provided in a passage (especially when presented in random order) serves a useful purpose, and it encourages the development of logical thinking and the processes of analysis and evaluation.

Working through and discussing with your students examples like the one below help students to gain valuable practice in sequencing events.

The relationship between sentences is the link that conceptually ties one sentence to another. The relationship may be explicit, in which case a transition or clue word helps identify the connection. The relation may be implicit, in which case you must closely examine the elements found in each sentence and often in the material between the sentences.

Practice Exercise: Identify Sequence of Events

1. **What is the correct order of events listed below?**

   A. Matt had tied a knot in his shoelace.

   B. Matt put on his green socks because they were clean and complimented the brown slacks he was wearing.

   C. Matt took a bath and trimmed his toenails.

   D. Matt put on his brown slacks.

Answer Key: Identify Sequence of Events

1. The proper order of events is:
   C, D, B, and A

ANALYZE THE RELATIONSHIP AMONG IDEAS IN WRITTEN MATERIAL

SKILL 4.2 Identify cause-effect relationships

A CAUSE is the necessary source of a particular outcome. If a writer were addressing the questions, "How will the new tax laws affect small businesses?" or "Why has there been such political unrest in Somalia?" he or she would use cause and effect as an organizational pattern to structure his or her response. In the first case, the writer would emphasize effects of the tax legislation as they apply to owners of small businesses. In the second, they would focus on causes for the current political situation in Somalia.

CAUSE: the necessary source of a particular outcome

Some word clues that identify a cause-effect passage are accordingly, as a result, therefore, because, consequently, hence, in short, thus, then, due to, and so on.

Sample Passage
Simply put, inflation is an increase in price levels. It happens when a government prints more currency than is already in circulation, and there is, consequently, additional money available for the same amount of goods or services. There might be multiple reasons for a government to crank up the printing presses. A war, for instance, could cause an immediate need for steel. A national disaster might create a sudden need for social services. To get the money it needs, a government can raise taxes, borrow, or print more currency. However, raising taxes and borrowing are not always plausible options.

Analysis
The paragraph starts with a definition and proceeds to examine a causal chain. The words consequently, reasons, and cause provide the clues.

Explicit cause and effect

General Hooker failed to anticipate General Lee's bold flanking maneuver. As a result, Hooker's army was nearly routed by a smaller force.

Mindy forgot to bring the lunch her father had packed for her. Consequently, she had to borrow money from her friends at school during lunch period.

Implicit cause and effect

The engine in Lisa's airplane began to sputter. She quickly looked below for a field in which to land.

Luther ate the creamed shrimp that had been sitting in the sun for hours. Later that night, he was so sick he had to be rushed to the hospital.

READING

SKILL 4.3 Analyze relationships between ideas in opposition

See also Skill 4.4

Whenever there are two ideas in opposition there is the ghost of an "either/or" conceptual basis lurking invisibly in the background of the "pro/con" setting.

For example, one person may argue that automobiles are a safer mode of transportation than are motorcycles and support that contention with statistics showing that fatalities are more frequent per accident in motorcycle crashes than in car crashes.

The opposition to this argument may counter that while fatalities are more frequent per accident in motorcycle accidents, it is erroneous to overgeneralize from that statistic that motorcycles are "therefore more dangerous."

Thus, each participant in the argument has assumed a position of "either or," that is to say, the automobile is "either" safer than the motorcycle or it is not (or the motorcycle is "either" safer than the automobile or it is not). With the argument thus formulated, a conclusion acceptable to both sides is not likely to happen.

> Whenever there are two ideas in opposition there is the ghost of an "either/or" conceptual basis lurking invisibly in the background of the "pro/con" setting.

SKILL 4.4 Identify solutions to problems

Within the assessment of reading, working with more than one selection is important in deciding if students can generalize. Utilizing the information read to find the answer to a situation presented is the skill. Sometimes this may involve problems specifically identified within what was read. For example, the characters in the story may be having a specific problem, such as a lack of money. Then, as you continue to read the passage, the characters in the story were hired for a new job, which allowed them to earn more money. Using the information read, identify the problem (a lack of money) and the solution (a new job).

In other cases, generalizations will need to be made across multiple selections. In those cases, selecting problems and solutions may be more evasive. Problems and solutions across texts will require broader thinking. The problems and solutions will not be as clearly spelled out in the text. It will involve your thinking on a different level about how the two passages relate. Connecting texts to other texts

> Connecting texts to other texts and finding common elements within them allows you then to draw out the common problems and solutions. Working through multiple selections requires more complex thinking skills and thinking of problems and solutions sometimes in other terms.

and finding common elements within them allows you then to draw out the common problems and solutions. Working through multiple selections requires more complex thinking skills and thinking of problems and solutions sometimes in other terms. Perhaps thinking of the challenge or issue that was faced and how that issue was overcome would help to broaden the scope and understanding of identifying the common problem and therefore the solution.

Effective writing offers solutions to problems that have been posed during the course of an essay. Take the following example.

> *Which is safer? The car or the motorcycle?*
>
> *Most experienced drivers would agree that while it is more exhilarating to ride a motorcycle than to drive an automobile, it is illogical to conclude that this exhilaration leads to careless driving and, therefore, more accidents, deaths, and injuries to motorcycle readers than car drivers. The critical concept to be understood here is not exhilaration, which is a given, but how the exhilaration comes about and is a cause of serious injury and death of motorcycle riders.*
>
> *There is safe and unsafe thrill seeking. "Exhilaration" is defined as the "state of being stimulated, refreshed, or elated." An example of safe exhilaration is the excitement of sledding downhill, which results in the sled rider feeling stimulated, refreshed, and/or elated.*
>
> *Unsafe exhilaration, which is usually the consequence of reckless thrill seeking, is therefore a state of being overstimulated, frightened, and depressed by terror.*
>
> *Which, then, causes more dangerous exhilarationt—the car or the motorcycle? The answer is that the two forms of exhilaration are the consequence not of the motorcycle or the automobile, per se, but of the operation of the respective vehicles. Without an operator, both vehicles are metal entities, sitting in space, neither threatening nor harmful to anyone.*
>
> *Therefore, neither the motorcycle nor the car is more, or less, dangerous than the other: it is the attitude of their operators that creates the danger, death, and dismemberment resulting from accidents.*

In the concluding paragraph of this essay, the author offers a solution to the problem of safety. The author directly states that it is the attitude of the operator that creates the danger, death, and dismemberment that results from accidents. The reader must therefore infer that the solution to the problem of accidents is for the operator, or driver, to be more cautious.

READING

SKILL 4.5 Draw conclusions inductively and deductively from information stated or implied in a passage

INFERENCE: an educated guess based on given facts and premises

An INFERENCE is sometimes called an "educated guess" because it requires going beyond the strictly obvious to create additional meaning by taking the text one logical step further. Inferences and conclusions are based on the content of the passage—that is, on what the passage says or how the writer says it—and are derived by reasoning.

Inference is an essential and automatic component of most reading. Examples include making educated guesses about the meaning of unknown words, the author's main idea, or the existence of bias. Such is the essence of inference. You use your own ability to reason in order to figure out what the writer is implying.

Consider the following example. Assume you are an employer, and you are reading over the letters of reference submitted by a prospective employee for the position of clerk/typist in your real estate office. The position requires the applicant to be neat, careful, trustworthy, and punctual. You come across this letter of reference submitted by an applicant:

> *To Whom It May Concern:*
>
> *Todd Finley has asked me to write a letter of reference for him. I am well qualified to do so because he worked for me for three months last year. His duties included answering the phone, greeting the public, and producing some simple memos and notices on the computer. Although Todd initially had few computer skills and little knowledge of telephone etiquette, he did acquire some during his stay with us. Todd's manner of speaking, both on the telephone and with the clients who came to my establishment, could be described as casual. He was particularly effective when communicating with peers. Please contact me by telephone if you wish to have further information about my experience with Todd.*

Here the writer implies, rather than openly states, the main idea. This letter calls attention to itself because there is a problem with its tone. A truly positive letter would say something such as, "I have the distinct honor of recommending Todd Finley." Here, however, the letter simply verifies that Todd worked in the office. Second, the praise is obviously lukewarm. For example, the writer says that Todd "was particularly effective when communicating with peers." An educated guess translates that statement into a nice way of saying Todd was not serious about his communication with clients.

In order to draw inferences and make conclusions, a reader must use prior knowledge and apply it to the current situation. A conclusion or inference is never stated. You must rely on your common sense.

ANALYZE THE RELATIONSHIP AMONG IDEAS IN WRITTEN MATERIAL

Practice Exercise: Drawing Conclusions

Read the following passages and select an answer.

1. Tim Sullivan had just turned fifteen. As a birthday present, his parents had given him a guitar and a certificate for ten guitar lessons. He had always shown a love of music and a desire to learn an instrument. Tim began his lessons, and before long, he was making up his own songs. At the music studio, Tim met Josh, who played the piano, and Roger, whose instrument was the saxophone. They all shared the same dream—to start a band—and each was praised by his teacher as having real talent.

   From this passage, one can infer that:

   A. Tim, Roger, and Josh are going to start their own band
   B. Tim is going to give up his guitar lessons
   C. Tim, Josh, and Roger will no longer be friends
   D. Josh and Roger are going to start their own band

2. The Smith family waited patiently around carousel number 7 for their luggage to arrive. They were exhausted after their five-hour trip and were anxious to get to their hotel. After about an hour, they realized that they no longer recognized any of the other passengers' faces. Mrs. Smith asked the person who appeared to be in charge if they were at the right carousel. The man replied, "Yes, this is it, but we finished unloading that baggage almost half an hour ago."

   From the man's response, we can infer that:

   A. The Smiths were ready to go to their hotel
   B. The Smiths' luggage was lost
   C. The man had the Smiths' luggage
   D. The Smiths were at the wrong carousel

Answer Key: Drawing Conclusions

1. A

   Given the facts that Tim wanted to be a musician and start his own band, after he met others who shared the same dreams, we can infer that the friends joined in an attempt to make their dreams become a reality.

2. B

   Because the Smiths were still waiting for their luggage, we know that they were not yet ready to go to their hotel. From the man's response, we know that they were not at the wrong carousel and that he did not have their luggage. Therefore, though not directly stated, it appears that their luggage was lost.

COMPETENCY 5
USE CRITICAL REASONING SKILLS TO EVALUATE WRITTEN MATERIAL

SKILL 5.1 Evaluate the stated or implied assumptions on which the validity of a writer's argument depends

On the certification test, the terms valid and invalid have special meaning. If an argument is valid, it is reasonable. It is objective (not biased) and can be supported by evidence. If an argument is invalid, it is not reasonable and it is not objective. In other words, one can find evidence of bias.

Read the following passage:

> Most dentists agree that Bright Smile Toothpaste is the best for fighting cavities. It tastes good and leaves your mouth minty fresh.

Is this a valid or an invalid argument?

It is invalid. It mentions that most dentists agree. What about those who do not agree? The author is clearly exhibiting bias in leaving those who disagree out.

Read the following passage:

> It is difficult to decide who will make the best presidential candidate, Senator Johnson or Senator Keeley. They have both been involved in scandals and have both gone through messy divorces while in office.

Is this argument valid or invalid?

The argument is valid. The author appears to be listing facts. He does not seem to favor one candidate over the other.

SKILL 5.2 Judge the relevance or importance of facts, examples, or graphic data to a writer's argument

The main idea of a passage may contain a wide variety of supporting information, but it is important that each sentence be related to the main idea. When a sentence contains information that bears little or no connection to the main idea, it is said to be IRRELEVANT. It is important to assess continually whether or not a sentence contributes to the overall task of supporting the main idea. When a sentence is deemed irrelevant, it is best either to omit it from the passage or to make it relevant by one of the following strategies:

1. Adding detail: Sometimes a sentence can seem out of place if it does not contain enough information to link it to the topic. Adding specific information can show how the sentence relates to the main idea.

2. Adding an example: This is especially important in passages in which information is being argued or compared and contrasted. Examples can support the main idea and give the document credibility.

3. Using diction effectively: It is important to understand connotation, avoid ambiguity, and avoid too much repetition when selecting words.

4. Adding transitions: Transitions are extremely helpful for making sentences relevant because they are specifically designed to connect one idea to another. They can also reduce a paragraph's choppiness.

> **IRRELEVANT:** information that bears little or no connection to the main idea

The following passage has several irrelevant sentences that are highlighted in **bold**:

> The New City Planning Committee is proposing a new capitol building to represent the multicultural face of New City. **The current mayor is a Democrat.** The new capitol building will be on 10th Street across from the grocery store and next to the recreational center. It will be within walking distance to the subway and bus depot, as the designers want to emphasize the importance of public transportation. Aesthetically, the building will have a contemporary design, featuring a brushed-steel exterior and large, floor-to-ceiling windows. **It is important for employees to have a connection with the outside world even when they are in their offices.** Inside the building, the walls will be moveable. This will not only facilitate a multitude of creative floor plans, but it will also create a focus on open communication and flow of information. **It sounds a bit gimmicky to me.** Finally, the capitol will feature a large outdoor courtyard full of lush greenery and serene fountains. **Work will now seem like Club Med to those who work at the New City capitol building!**

SKILL 5.3 Evaluate the logic of a writer's argument

An ARGUMENT is a generalization that is proven or supported with facts. If the facts are not accurate, the generalization remains unproven. Using inaccurate "facts" to support an argument is called a FALLACY in reasoning. Some factors to consider in judging whether the facts used to support an argument are accurate are:

> **ARGUMENT:** a generalization that is proven or supported with facts

> **FALLACY:** occurs when inaccurate "facts" are used to support an argument

1. Are the facts current, or are they out-of-date? For example, if the proposition is "birth defects in babies born to drug-using mothers are increasing," then the data must include the latest available.

2. Another important factor to consider in judging the accuracy of a fact is its source. Where were the data obtained, and is that source reliable?

3. The calculations on which the facts are based may be unreliable. It is a good idea to run one's own calculations before using a piece of derived information.

Even facts that are true and have a sharp impact on the argument may not be relevant, as in the following cases:

1. Health statistics drawn from an entire state may have no relevance, or little relevance, to a particular county or zip code. Statistics drawn from an entire country cannot be used to prove very much about a particular state or county.

2. An analogy can be useful in making a point, but the comparison must match up in all characteristics or it will not be relevant. Analogies should be used very carefully. They are often just as likely to destroy an argument as to strengthen one.

The importance or significance of a single fact may not be sufficient to strengthen an argument. For example, using the plight of a particular family as evidence to support a proposed solution to the U.S. immigration problem will not necessarily strengthen the writer's assertion, even though single-example arguments are often used to support one solution or another. If enough cases were cited from a variety of geographical locations, the information might be deemed significant.

How much is enough? Generally speaking, three strong supporting facts are sufficient to establish the thesis of an argument. However, sometimes many more facts are needed, as in the following example:

1. When I was a child, I bit into a green apple from my grandfather's orchard, and it was sour.
2. I once bought green apples from a roadside vendor, and when I bit into one, it was sour.
3. My grocery store had a sale on green Granny Smith apples last week, and I bought several, only to find that they were sour when I bit into one.

Conclusion: All green apples are sour. The fallacy in the above argument is that the sample was insufficient. A more exhaustive search of literature, etc., will probably turn up some green apples that are not sour.

Sometimes more than three arguments are too many. On the other hand, it's not unusual to hear public speakers, particularly politicians, who will cite a long litany of facts to support their positions.

A very good example of the omission of facts in an argument is the résumé of an applicant for a job. The applicant is arguing that he or she should be chosen for a particular job. The application form will ask for information about past employment; the applicant may choose to omit unfavorable dismissals from jobs in the past. Employers are usually suspicious of periods of time when an applicant has not listed any employment.

A writer makes choices about which facts will be used and which will be discarded when developing an argument. Those choices may exclude anything that does not support the point of view that the arguer is taking. It's always a good idea for a reader to do some research to spot omissions and to consider whether they may have an impact on the point of view presented in the argument.

No judgment is either black or white. If an argument seems too neat or too compelling, there may be relevant facts that have not been included.

No judgment is either black or white. If an argument seems too neat or too compelling, there may be relevant facts that have not been included.

SKILL 5.4 Evaluate the validity of analogies

An argument by analogy states that if two things have one thing in common, they probably have other things in common. For example, peaches and plums are both fruits that have nutrients that are good for people to eat. Both peaches and plums are circular in shape; thus, it could be argued by analogy that "because" something is circular in shape, it is fruit and something good for people to eat. However, this analogical deduction is not logical (e.g., a baseball is circular in shape but hardly good to eat).

An ANALOGY is a comparison of the likenesses of two things. The danger of arguing by analogy rests in a failure to correctly perceive the limitations of the likenesses between the two things compared. Because something is like something else does not make it the same as the compared object or, for that matter, put it in the same class as the original object.

ANALOGY: a comparison of the likenesses of two things

For example, a false argument based on analogical thinking could go like this: "Blake and Blunder are both democrats. Both are married. Both have three children, a dog, and a kitten at home. Therefore, because of their similarities, it is likely they will both vote the same way about the school mileage proposal."

READING

This is a false argument by analogy; while the likenesses cited are somewhat striking, these are only likenesses coincidental in nature and not compelling causative roots predictive of behaviors.

However, perceiving the analogical relationship between two things or phenomena is often also the starting point for scientific investigations of reality, and such perceptions are the subjects of a host of scientific theories (e.g., the work of Charles Darwin) and investigations (e.g., "wave/particle" theories in quantum physics). Such analogical relations require austere scrutiny and analysis and, without such, are essentially meaningless or the stuff of poetic comparisons ("*To see the world in a grain of sand*"—William Blake).

Thinking in analogies is the way we all began as children to perceive the world and sort it into categories of "good and bad" (e.g., "water is a liquid that is good for me; hot oil is a liquid that is bad for me"). Mature writers and thinkers discriminate carefully between all elements of an argument by analogy.

> *Perceiving the analogical relationship between two things or phenomena is often also the starting point for scientific investigations of reality, and such perceptions are the subjects of a host of scientific theories.*

SKILL 5.5 Distinguish between fact and opinion

FACTS: verifiable statements that report what has happened or what exists

OPINIONS: statements that must be supported in order to be accepted, such as beliefs, values, judgments, or feelings

JUDGMENTS: opinions, decisions, or declarations based on observation or reasoning that express approval or disapproval

FACTS are verifiable statements. OPINIONS are statements that must be supported in order to be accepted, such as beliefs, values, judgments, or feelings. Facts are objective statements used to support subjective opinions. For example, "Jane is a bad girl" is an opinion. However, "Jane hit her sister with a baseball bat" is a fact upon which the opinion is based. JUDGMENTS are opinions, decisions, or declarations based on observation or reasoning that express approval or disapproval. Facts report what has happened or what exists and come from observation, measurement, or calculation. Facts can be tested and verified, whereas opinions and judgments cannot. They can only be supported with facts.

Most statements cannot be so clearly distinguished. "I believe that Jane is a bad girl" is a fact. The speaker knows what he or she believes. However, it obviously includes a judgment that could be disputed by another person who might believe otherwise. Judgments are not usually so firm. They are, rather, plausible opinions that provoke thought or lead to factual development.

Mickey Mantle replaced Joe DiMaggio, a Yankees centerfielder, in 1952.

USE CRITICAL REASONING SKILLS TO EVALUATE WRITTEN MATERIAL

This is a fact. If necessary, evidence can be produced to support this statement.

First-year players are more ambitious than seasoned players are.

This is an opinion. There is no proof to support that everyone feels this way.

Practice Exercise: Fact and Opinion

1. The Inca were a group of Indians who ruled an empire in South America.
   A. Fact
   B. Opinion

2. The Inca were clever.
   A. Fact
   B. Opinion

3. The Inca built very complex systems of bridges.
   A. Fact
   B. Opinion

Answer Key: Fact and Opinion

1. A

   Research can prove this statement true.

2. B

   It is doubtful that all people who have studied the Inca agree with this statement. Therefore, no proof is available.

3. A

   As with question number one, research can prove this statement true.

READING

SKILL 5.6 Assess the credibility or objectivity of a writer or source of written material

BIAS: an opinion, feeling, or influence that strongly favors one side in an argument

BIAS is defined as an opinion, feeling, or influence that strongly favors one side in an argument. A statement or passage is biased if an author attempts to convince a reader of something.

Is there evidence of bias in the following statement?

> *Using a calculator cannot help a student understand the process of graphing, so its use is a waste of time.*

Since the author makes it perfectly clear that he does not favor the use of the calculator in graphing problems, the answer is yes, there is evidence of bias. He has included his opinion in this statement.

Practice Exercise: Identify Bias and Objectivity

Read the following paragraph and select an answer.

1. There are teachers who feel that computer programs are quite helpful in helping students grasp certain math concepts. There are also those who disagree with this feeling. It is up to each individual math teacher to decide if computer programs benefit her particular group of students.

   Is there evidence of bias in this paragraph?
   A. Yes
   B. No

Answer Key: Identify Bias and Objectivity

1. B is the correct answer. The author seems to state both sides of the argument without favoring a particular side.

"The sky is blue," and "The sky looks like rain"; one is a fact and the other an opinion. This is because one is *readily provable by objective empirical data*, while the other is a *subjective evaluation based upon personal bias*. This means that facts are things that can be proved by the usual means of study and experimentation. We can look and see the color of the sky. Since the shade we are observing is expressed as the color blue and is an accepted norm, the observation that the sky is blue is therefore a fact. (Of course, this depends on other external factors, such as time and weather conditions.)

This brings us to our next idea: that it looks like rain. This is a subjective observation, in that one individual's perception will differ from that of another. What looks like rain to one person will not necessarily look like rain to another person. The question thus remains how to differentiate fact from opinion. The best and only way is to ask oneself if what is being stated can be proved from other sources, by other methods, or by the simple process of reasoning.

Primary and Secondary Sources

The sources used to support a piece of writing can be divided into two major groups: primary sources and secondary sources.

PRIMARY SOURCES are works, records, etc., that were created during the period being studied or immediately after it. SECONDARY SOURCES are works written significantly after the period being studied and based upon primary sources. Primary sources are the basic materials that provide raw data and information. Secondary sources are the works that contain the explications of, and judgments on, this primary material.

Primary sources include the following kinds of materials:

- Documents that reflect the immediate, everyday concerns of people: memoranda, bills, deeds, charters, newspaper reports, pamphlets, graffiti, popular writings, journals or diaries, records of decision-making bodies, letters, receipts, snapshots, etc.

- Theoretical writings that reflect care and consideration in composition and an attempt to convince or persuade. The topic will generally be deeper and have more pervasive values than is the case with "immediate" documents. These may include newspaper or magazine editorials, sermons, political speeches, philosophical writings, etc.

- Narrative accounts of events, ideas, trends, etc., written intentionally by someone contemporary with the events described.

> **PRIMARY SOURCES:** works, records, etc., that were created during the period being studied or immediately after it

> **SECONDARY SOURCES:** works written significantly after the period being studied and based upon primary sources

> *Primary sources are the basic materials that provide raw data and information. Secondary sources are the works that contain the explications of, and judgments on, this primary material.*

- Statistical data, although statistics may be misleading.
- Literature and nonverbal materials such as novels, stories, poetry and essays from the period, as well as coins, archaeological artifacts, and art produced during the period.

Secondary sources include the following kinds of materials:

- Books written on the basis of primary materials about the period of time.
- Books written on the basis of primary materials about people who played a major role in the events under consideration.
- Books and articles written on the basis of primary materials about the culture, the social norms, the language, and the values of the period.
- Quotations from primary sources.
- Statistical data on the period.
- The conclusions and inferences of other historians.
- Multiple interpretations of the ethos of the time.

Guidelines for the use of secondary sources:

1. Do not rely upon a single secondary source only
2. Check facts and interpretations against primary sources whenever possible
3. Do not accept the conclusions of other historians uncritically
4. Place greatest reliance on secondary sources created by the best and most respected scholars
5. Do not use the inferences of other scholars as if they were facts
6. Ensure that you recognize any bias the writer brings to his/her interpretation of history
7. Understand the primary point of the book as a basis for evaluating the material presented in it to answer your questions

COMPETENCY 6
APPLY STUDY SKILLS TO READING ASSIGNMENTS

SKILL 6.1 Organize and summarize information for study purposes

Note Taking Skills and Outlines

Being an effective note taker requires consistent technique, whether the mode of note taking is on 5 × 7 note cards, a lined notebook, or on a computer. Organizing all collected information according to a research outline will allow the user to take notes on each section and begin the writing process. If the computer is used, then the actual format of the report can be word-processed and information can be input to speed up the writing process of the final research report. Creating a title page and the bibliography page will allow each downloaded report to have its resources cited immediately in that section.

Note taking involves identification of specific resources that include the author's or organization's name, year of publication, title, publisher location, and publisher. When taking notes, whether on the computer or using note cards, include the author's last name and page number on cited information. In citing information for major categories and subcategories on the computer, create a file for notes that includes summaries of information and direct quotes. When direct quotes are put into a computer file, the cut and paste process for incorporation into the report is quick and easy.

In outline information, it is crucial to identify the headings and subheadings for the topic being researched. When researching information, it is easier to cut and paste information under the indicated headings to create a visual flow of information for the report. In the actual drafting of the report, the writer is able to lift direct quotations and citations from the posted information to incorporate in the writing.

Mapping

Mapping is a strategy that can be used to reach all learning styles and therefore is an important one to teach. It is exactly what its name implies—a map of the reading. A map helps the reader maneuver through the information in a meaningful manner. Maps can use words with key ideas connected to smaller chunks of

A map helps the reader maneuver through the information in a meaningful manner. Maps can use words with key ideas connected to smaller chunks of information.

information. Teachers can also encourage pictures instead of words to help the more visual learner. Adding color to a map can emphasize certain ideas. Probably the most commonly used types of maps combine words and pictures. This can be particularly helpful for students to begin to understand the process of prioritization in skills. Lines are drawn between connecting concepts to show relationships and because the reader is creating it himself or herself, it is meaningful to them. Maps are individual creations and revolve around reader's learning and prior knowledge.

SKILL 6.2 Follow written instructions or directions

Step by Step

How does one get from here to there, from kindergarten to graduate school or to a trade school? The answer, of course, is by one step at a time, carefully organizing one's courses of action, with each phase building on the previous step and leading to the next.

Similarly, when taking a test, you are asked to follow written instructions or directions because the examiner wants to see how you manage your answer to the exam question. How do you organize your answer logically? How do you support your conclusions? How well connected are your ideas and the support you bring to your argument?

Look at how the writer does these tasks in the following essay:

Parenting Classes

Someone once said that the two most difficult jobs in the world—voting and being a parent — are given to rank amateurs. The consequences of this inequity are voter apathy and inept parenting, leading to, on the one hand, an apparent failure of the democratic process and, on the other hand, misbehaving and misguided children.

The antidote for the first problem is in place in most school systems. Classes in history, civics, government, and student government provide a kind of "hands-on" training in becoming an active member of society so that the step from studenthood to citizenship is clear and expected.

On the other hand, most school systems in the past have avoided or given only lip service to the issue of parenting and parenting skills. The moral issue of illegitimate births aside, the reality of the world is that each year there are large numbers of children born to unwed parents who have had little, or no, training in child rearing.

Continued on next page

> What was done on the farm in the past is irrelevant here: the farm is gone and/or has been replaced by the inner city, and the pressing issue is how to train uneducated new parents in the child-rearing tasks before them. Other issues are secondary to the immediate needs of newborns and their futures. And it is in their futures that the quality of life for all of us is found.
>
> Thus, while we can debate this issue all we wish, we cannot responsibly ignore that uneducated parents need to be educated in the tasks before them, and it is clear that the best way to do this is in the school system, where these new parents are already learning how to be responsible citizens in the civics and other classes currently in place.

Notice how the writer moves sequentially from one idea to the next, maintaining throughout the parallel of citizenship and parenthood, from the opening quotation, paragraph by paragraph to the concluding sentence. Each idea is developed from the preceding idea, and each new idea refers to the preceding ideas, and at no point do related, but irrelevant, issues sidetrack the writer.

SKILL 6.3 Interpret information presented in charts, graphs, or tables

See Skill 8.1

READING

DOMAIN II
MATHEMATICS

MATHEMATICS

PERSONALIZED STUDY PLAN

PAGE	COMPETENCY AND SKILL		KNOWN MATERIAL/ SKIP IT
39	7:	**Solve word problems involving integers, fractions, decimals, and units of measurement**	☐
	7.1:	Solve word problems involving integers, fractions, decimals, ratios, and proportions	☐
	7.2:	Understand units of measurement and conversions	☐
57	8:	**Solve problems involving data interpretation and analysis**	☐
	8.1:	Interpret information from line graphs, bar graphs, pictographs, pie charts, and tables	☐
	8.2:	Recognize appropriate graphic representations of various data	☐
	8.3:	Analyze and interpret data using measures of central tendency	☐
	8.4:	Analyze and interpret data using the concept of variability	☐
63	9:	**Graph numbers or number relationships**	☐
	9.1:	Identify the graph of an equation or inequality, find the slope and/or intercepts and the equation of a line	☐
	9.2:	Recognize and interpret information from the graph of a function	☐
70	10:	**Solve one- and two-variable equations**	☐
	10.1:	Find the value of the unknown in a one-variable equation	☐
	10.2:	Express one variable in terms of a second variable in two-variable equations	☐
	10.3:	Solve systems of two equations in two variables	☐
73	11:	**Solve word problems involving one and two variables**	☐
	11.1:	Identify the algebraic equivalent of a stated relationship and solve word problems	☐
77	12:	**Understand operations with algebraic expressions and functional notation**	☐
	12.1:	Factoring quadratics	☐
	12.2:	Performing operations on and simplifying polynomial expressions	☐
	12.3:	Understand rational expressions and radical expressions	☐
	12.4:	Apply principles of functions and functional notation	☐

MATHEMATICS

PERSONALIZED STUDY PLAN

✗ **KNOWN MATERIAL/ SKIP IT**

PAGE	COMPETENCY AND SKILL	KNOWN MATERIAL/ SKIP IT
88	**13: Solve problems involving quadratic equations**	☐
	13.1: Graph quadratic functions and quadratic inequalities	☐
	13.2: Solve quadratic equations using factoring, completing the square, or the quadratic formula	☐
	13.5: Solve problems involving quadratic models	☐
98	**14: Solve problems involving geometric figures**	☐
	14.1: Solve problems involving two-dimensional geometric figures	☐
	14.2: Solve problems involving three-dimensional geometric figures	☐
	14.3: Solve problems using the Pythagorean Theorem	☐
108	**15: Solve problems involving geometric concepts**	☐
	15.1: Solve problems using principles of similarity, congruence, parallelism, and perpendicularity	☐
112	**16: Apply reasoning skills**	☐
	16.1: Draw conclusions using inductive and deductive reasoning	☐
118	**17: Solve applied problems involving a combination of mathematical skills**	☐
	17.1: Apply combinations of mathematical skills to solve problems	☐

FUNDAMENTAL MATHEMATICS

COMPETENCY 7
SOLVE WORD PROBLEMS INVOLVING INTEGERS, FRACTIONS, DECIMALS, AND UNITS OF MEASUREMENT

SKILL 7.1 Solve word problems involving integers, fractions, decimals (including percents), ratios, and proportions

RATIONAL NUMBERS are numbers that can be expressed as the ratio of two integers, $\frac{a}{b}$, where $b \neq 0$. For example, $\frac{2}{3}$, $-\frac{4}{5}$, and $5 = \frac{5}{1}$ are all rational numbers.

The rational numbers include integers, fractions and mixed numbers, and terminating and repeating decimals. Every rational number can be expressed as a repeating or terminating decimal and can be shown on a number line.

INTEGERS are the positive and negative whole numbers and zero.
...-6, -5, -4, -3, -2, -1, 0, 1, 2, 3, 4, 5, 6,...

WHOLE NUMBERS are the natural numbers and zero.
0, 1, 2, 3, 4, 5, 6...

NATURAL NUMBERS are the counting numbers.
1, 2, 3, 4, 5, 6...

IRRATIONAL NUMBERS are real numbers that cannot be written as the ratio of two integers. They are infinite, nonrepeating decimals.
$\sqrt{5} = 2.2360$, pi $= \pi = 3.1415927...$

A FRACTION is an expression of numbers in the form of $\frac{x}{y}$, where x is the numerator and y is the denominator. The denominator cannot be zero.

$\frac{3}{7}$ 3 is the numerator; 7 is the denominator

If the fraction has common factors in the numerator and denominator, divide both by the common factors to reduce the fraction to its simplest form.
$\frac{13}{39} = \frac{1 \times 13}{3 \times 13} = \frac{1}{3}$ Divide by the common factor 13.

RATIONAL NUMBERS: numbers that can be expressed as the ratio of two integers, $\frac{a}{b}$, where $b \neq 0$

INTEGERS: the positive and negative whole numbers and zero

WHOLE NUMBERS: the natural numbers and zero

NATURAL NUMBERS: the counting numbers

IRRATIONAL NUMBERS: real numbers that cannot be written as the ratio of two integers; they are infinite, nonrepeating decimals

FRACTION: an expression of numbers in the form of $\frac{x}{y}$, where x is the numerator and y is the denominator; the denominator cannot be zero

MATHEMATICS

MIXED NUMBER: one that has an integer part and a fractional part

PERCENT: means "per 100;" ten percent is 10 parts out of 100

DECIMAL: a number written with a whole-number part, a decimal point, and a decimal part

EXPONENT FORM: a shorthand way of writing repeated multiplication; the basic form is b^n, where b is called the *base* and n is the *exponent*

BASE: the number to be multiplied as many times as indicated by the exponent

EXPONET: tells how many times the base is multiplied by itself

A MIXED NUMBER has an integer part and a fractional part.
$2\frac{1}{4}, -5\frac{1}{6}, 7\frac{1}{3}$

PERCENT = per 100 (written with the symbol %). Thus, 10% = $\frac{10}{100} = \frac{1}{10}$.

DECIMALS = deci = part of ten. To find the decimal equivalent of a fraction, use the denominator to divide the numerator, as shown in the following example:
Find the decimal equivalent of $\frac{7}{10}$.
Since 10 cannot divide into 7 evenly,
$\frac{7}{10} = 0.7$

The EXPONENT FORM is a shortcut method to write repeated multiplication. The basic form is b^n, where b is called the BASE and n is the EXPONENT. b and n are both real numbers. b^n implies that the base b is multiplied by itself n times.

Examples:
$3^4 = 3 \times 3 \times 3 \times 3 = 81$
$2^3 = 2 \times 2 \times 2 = 8$
$(-2)^4 = (-2) \times (-2) \times (-2) \times (-2) = 16$
$-2^4 = -(2 \times 2 \times 2 \times 2) = 16$

Caution: The exponent does not affect the sign unless the negative sign is inside the parentheses and the exponent is outside the parentheses.

$(-2)^4$ implies that -2 is multiplied by itself 4 times.

-2^4 implies that 2 is multiplied by itself 4 times, and then the answer becomes. negative.

KEY EXPONENT RULES: FOR 'a' NONZERO AND 'm' AND 'n' REAL NUMBERS	
Product Rule	$a^m \times a^n = a^{(m+n)}$
Quotient Rule	$\frac{a^m}{a^n} = a^{(m-n)}$
Rule of Negative Exponents	$\frac{a^{-m}}{a^{-n}} = \frac{a^n}{a^m}$

When 10 is raised to any power, the exponent tells the numbers of zeros in the product.

Example:
$10^7 = 10,000,000$

SOLVE WORD PROBLEMS INVOLVING INTEGERS, FRACTIONS, DECIMALS, AND UNITS OF MEASUREMENT

Addition of Whole Numbers

Example: At the end of a day of shopping, a shopper had $24 remaining in his wallet. He spent $45 on various goods. How much money did the shopper have at the beginning of the day?

The total amount of money the shopper started with is the sum of the amount spent and the amount remaining at the end of the day.

$$\begin{aligned} \$\ 24 \\ +\ 45 \\ \hline \$\ 69 \end{aligned}$$ The original total was $69.

Example: A race took the winner 1 hr. 58 min. 12 sec. on the first half of the race and 2 hr. 9 min. 57 sec. on the second half of the race. How much time did the entire race take?

1 hr 58 min 12 sec	
+ 2 hr 9 min 57 sec	Add these numbers.
3 hr 67 min 69 sec	
+ 1 min − 60 sec	Change 60 sec to 1 min.
3 hr 68 min 9 sec	
+ 1 hr − 60 min	Change 60 min to 1 hr.
4 hr 8 min 9 sec	Final answer.

Subtraction of Whole Numbers

Example: At the end of his shift, a cashier has $96 in the cash register. At the beginning of his shift, he had $15. How much money did the cashier collect during his shift?

The total collected is the difference between the ending amount and the starting amount.

$$\begin{aligned} \$\ 96 \\ -\ 15 \\ \hline \$\ 81 \end{aligned}$$ The total collected was $81.

Multiplication of Whole Numbers

Multiplication is one of the four basic number operations. In simple terms, multiplication is the addition of a number to itself a certain number of times. For example, 4 multiplied by 3 is equal to 4 + 4 + 4 or 3 + 3 + 3 + 3. Another way of conceptualizing multiplication is to think in terms of groups. For example, if we have 4 groups of 3 students, the total number of students is 4 multiplied by 3. We call the solution to a multiplication problem the PRODUCT.

> Another way of conceptualizing multiplication is to think in terms of groups.

> **PRODUCT:** the solution to a multiplication problem

The basic algorithm for whole number multiplication begins with aligning the numbers by place value, with the number containing more places on top.

$$\begin{array}{r} 172 \\ \times\ 43 \end{array}$$

Note that we placed 172 on top because it has more places than 43 does.

Next, we multiply the ones place of the bottom number by each place value of the top number sequentially.

$$\begin{array}{r} (2) \\ 172 \\ \times\ 43 \\ \hline 516 \end{array}$$

$\{3 \times 2 = 6,\ 3 \times 7 = 21,\ 3 \times 1 = 3\}$

Note that we had to carry a 2 to the hundreds column because $3 \times 7 = 21$. Note also that we add carried numbers to the product.

Next, we multiply the number in the tens place of the bottom number by each place value of the top number sequentially. Because we are multiplying by a number in the tens place, we place a zero at the end of this product.

$$\begin{array}{r} (2) \\ 172 \\ \times\ 43 \\ \hline 516 \\ 6880 \end{array}$$

$\{4 \times 2 = 8,\ 4 \times 7 = 28,\ 4 \times 1 = 4\}$

Finally, to determine the final product, we add the two partial products.

$$\begin{array}{r} 172 \\ \times\ 43 \\ \hline 516 \\ +\ 6880 \\ \hline 7396 \end{array}$$

The product of 172 and 43 is 7396.

Example: A student buys 4 boxes of crayons. Each box contains 16 crayons. How many total crayons does the student have?

The total number of crayons is 16×4.

$$\begin{array}{r} (2) \\ 16 \\ \times\ 4 \\ \hline 64 \end{array}$$

The total number of crayons equals 64.

Division of Whole Numbers

Division, the inverse of multiplication, is another of the four basic number operations. When we divide one number by another, we determine how many times we can multiply the divisor (number divided by) before we exceed the number we are dividing (dividend). For example, 8 divided by 2 equals 4 because we can multiply 2 four times to reach 8 ($2 \times 4 = 8$ or $2 + 2 + 2 + 2 = 8$). Using the grouping conceptualization we used with multiplication, we can divide 8 into 4 groups of 2 or 2 groups of 4. We call the solution to a division problem the QUOTIENT.

If the divisor does not divide evenly into the dividend, we express the leftover amount either as a remainder or as a fraction with the divisor as the denominator. For example, 9 divided by 2 equals 4 with a remainder of 1, or $4\frac{1}{2}$.

> **QUOTIENT:** the solution to a division problem

The basic algorithm for division is long division. We start by representing the quotient as follows.

$14\overline{)293}$ → 14 is the divisor and 293 is the dividend. This represents $293 \div 14$.

Next, we divide the divisor into the dividend, starting from the left.

$14\overline{)293}^{2}$ → 14 divides into 29 two times with a remainder.

Next, we multiply the partial quotient by the divisor, subtract this value from the first digits of the dividend, and bring down the remaining dividend digits to complete the number.

$$\begin{array}{r} 2 \\ 14\overline{)293} \\ -28\downarrow \\ \hline 13 \end{array}$$ → $2 \times 14 = 28$, $29 - 28 = 1$, and bringing down the 3 yields 13.

Finally, we divide again (the divisor into the remaining value) and repeat the preceding process. The number left after the subtraction represents the remainder.

$$\begin{array}{r} 20 \\ 14\overline{)293} \\ -28 \\ \hline 13 \\ -0 \\ \hline 13 \end{array}$$ → The final quotient is 20 with a remainder of 13. We can also represent this quotient as $20\frac{13}{14}$.

Addition and Subtraction of Decimals

When adding and subtracting decimals, we align the numbers by place value as we do with whole numbers. After adding or subtracting each column, we bring the decimal down, placing it in the same location as in the numbers added or subtracted.

> *When adding and subtracting decimals, we align the numbers by place value as we do with whole numbers.*

Example: Find the sum of 152.3 and 36.342.

$$\begin{array}{r} 152.300 \\ +\ 36.342 \\ \hline 188.642 \end{array}$$

Note that we placed two zeros after the final place value in 152.3 to clarify the column addition.

Example: Find the difference of 152.3 and 36.342.

$$\begin{array}{r} 2\ 9\ 10 \qquad\ (4)11(12) \\ 15\cancel{2}.\cancel{3}\cancel{0}0 \qquad 1\cancel{5}\cancel{2}.\cancel{3}\cancel{0}\cancel{0} \\ -\ 36.342 \qquad -\ 36.342 \\ \hline 58 \qquad\qquad 115.958 \end{array}$$

Note how we borrowed to subtract from the zeros in the hundredths and thousandths places of 152.300.

Multiplication of Decimals

When multiplying decimal numbers, we multiply exactly as with whole numbers and place the decimal in from the right the total number of decimal places contained in the two numbers multiplied. For example, when multiplying 1.5 and 2.35, we place the decimal in the product 3 places in from the right (3.525).

Example: Find the product of 3.52 and 4.1.

$$\begin{array}{r} 3.52 \\ \times\ 4.1 \\ \hline 352 \\ +\ 14080 \\ \hline 14.432 \end{array}$$

Note that there are three decimal places in total in the two numbers.

We place the decimal three places in from the right.

Thus, the final product is 14.432.

Example: A shopper has 5 one-dollar bills, 6 quarters, 3 nickels, and 4 pennies in his pocket. How much money does he have?

$$5 \times \$1.00 = \$5.00$$

$$\begin{array}{ccc} 1\ 3 & 1 & \\ \$0.25 & \$0.05 & \$0.01 \\ \times\ 6 & \times\ 3 & \times\ 4 \\ \hline \$1.50 & \$0.15 & \$0.04 \end{array}$$

SOLVE WORD PROBLEMS INVOLVING INTEGERS, FRACTIONS, DECIMALS, AND UNITS OF MEASUREMENT

Note the placement of the decimals in the multiplication products. Thus, the total amount of money in the shopper's pocket is:

$5.00
1.50
0.15
+ 0.04
$6.69

Division of Decimals

When dividing decimal numbers, we first remove the decimal in the divisor by moving the decimal in the dividend the same number of spaces to the right. For example, when dividing 1.45 into 5.3, we convert the numbers to 145 and 530 and perform normal whole-number division.

Example: Find the quotient of 5.3 divided by 1.45.

Convert to 145 and 530.
Divide.

$$145\overline{)530} \quad 3 \qquad 145\overline{)530.00} \quad 3.65$$
$$-435 \qquad\qquad -435$$
$$95 \qquad\qquad 950$$
$$\qquad\qquad -870$$
$$\qquad\qquad 800$$

Note that we insert the decimal to continue division.

Because one of the numbers divided contained one decimal place, we round the quotient to one decimal place. Thus, the final quotient is 3.7.

Operating with Percents

Example: 5 is what percent of 20?

This is the same as converting $\frac{5}{20}$ to % form.

$$\frac{5}{20} \times \frac{100}{1} = \frac{5}{1} \times \frac{5}{1} = 25\%$$

Example: There are 64 dogs in the kennel. 48 are collies. What percent are collies?

Restate the problem.   48 is what percent of 64?
Write an equation. $48 = n \times 64$
Solve. $\frac{48}{64} = n$

$n = \frac{3}{4} = 75\%$

75% of the dogs are collies.

Example: The auditorium was filled to 90% capacity. There were 558 seats occupied. What is the capacity of the auditorium?

Restate the problem.   90% of what number is 558?
Write an equation. $0.9n = 558$
Solve. $n = \frac{558}{.9}$
$n = 620$

The capacity of the auditorium is 620 people.

Example: A pair of shoes costs $42.00. The sales tax is 6%. What is the total cost of the shoes?

Restate the problem.   What is 6% of 42?
Write an equation. $n = 0.06 \times 42$
Solve. $n = 2.52$
Add the sales tax to the cost. $\$42.00 + \$2.52 = \$44.52$

The total cost of the shoes, including sales tax, is $44.52.

Addition and Subtraction of Fractions

Key points

1. You need a common denominator in order to add and subtract reduced and improper fractions.

    Example:
    $$\frac{1}{3} + \frac{7}{3} = \frac{1+7}{3} = \frac{8}{3} = -2\frac{2}{3}$$

    Example:
    $$\frac{4}{12} + \frac{6}{12} - \frac{3}{12} = \frac{4+6-3}{12} = \frac{7}{12}$$

2. Adding an integer and a fraction of the same sign results directly in a mixed fraction.

    Example:
    $$2 + \frac{2}{3} = 2\frac{2}{3}$$

    Example:
    $$-2 - \frac{2}{3} = -2\frac{2}{3}$$

3. Adding an integer and a fraction with different signs involves the following steps.

    - Get a common denominator

SOLVE WORD PROBLEMS INVOLVING INTEGERS, FRACTIONS, DECIMALS, AND UNITS OF MEASUREMENT

- Add or subtract as needed
- Change to a mixed fraction if possible

Example:
$$2 - \frac{1}{3} = \frac{2 \times 3 - 1}{3} = \frac{6 - 1}{3} = \frac{5}{3} = 1\frac{2}{3}$$

Example:
Add $7\frac{3}{8} + 5\frac{2}{7}$

Add the whole numbers, add the fractions, and combine the two results:
$$7\frac{3}{8} + 5\frac{2}{7} = (7 + 5) + \left(\frac{3}{8} + \frac{2}{7}\right)$$
$$= 12 + \frac{(7 \times 3) + (8 \times 2)}{56} \quad \text{(56 is the LCM of 8 and 7)}$$
$$= 12 + \frac{21 + 16}{56} = 12 + \frac{37}{56} = 12\frac{37}{56}$$

Example: Perform the operation.
$$\frac{2}{3} - \frac{5}{6}$$

We first find the LCM of 3 and 6, which is 6.
$$\frac{2 \times 2}{3 \times 2} - \frac{5}{6} \rightarrow \frac{4 - 5}{6} = \frac{-1}{6}$$

Example:
$$-7\frac{1}{4} + 2\frac{7}{8}$$
$$-7\frac{1}{4} + 2\frac{7}{8} = (-7 + 2) + \left(\frac{-1}{4} + \frac{7}{8}\right)$$
$$= (-5) + \frac{-2 + 7}{8} = (-5) + \left(\frac{5}{8}\right)$$
$$= (-5) + \frac{5}{8} = \frac{-5 \times 8}{1 \times 8} + \frac{5}{8} = \frac{-40 + 5}{8}$$
$$= \frac{-35}{8} = -4\frac{3}{8}$$

Divide 35 by 8 to get 4, remainder 3.

Example:

Caution: A common error would be
$$-7\frac{1}{4} + 2\frac{7}{8} = -7\frac{2}{8} + 2\frac{7}{8} = -5\frac{9}{8} \quad \text{Wrong.}$$

It is correct to add -7 and 2 to get -5, but adding $\frac{2}{8} + \frac{7}{8} = \frac{9}{8}$ is wrong. It should have been $\frac{-2}{8} + \frac{7}{8} = \frac{5}{8}$. Then, $-5 + \frac{5}{8} = -4\frac{3}{8}$ as before.

MATHEMATICS

Multiplication of Fractions

Using the following example: $3\frac{1}{4} \times \frac{5}{6}$

1. Convert each number to an improper fraction

   $3\frac{1}{4} = \frac{(12 + 1)}{4} = \frac{13}{4}$ $\frac{5}{6}$ is already in reduced form.

2. Reduce (cancel) common factors of the numerator and denominator if they exist

   $\frac{13}{4} \times \frac{5}{6}$ No common factors exist.

3. Multiply the numerators by each other and the denominators by each other

   $\frac{13}{4} \times \frac{5}{6} = \frac{65}{24}$

4. If possible, reduce the fraction to its lowest term

   $\frac{65}{24}$ Cannot be reduced further.

5. Convert the improper fraction back to a mixed fraction by using long division

   $\frac{65}{24} = 24\overline{)65} \quad = 2\frac{17}{24}$
   $\phantom{\frac{65}{24} = 24\overline{)}}\underline{48}$
   $\phantom{\frac{65}{24} = 24\overline{)6}}17$

Summary of sign changes for multiplication

1. $(+) \times (+) = (+)$
2. $(-) \times (+) = (-)$
3. $(+) \times (-) = (-)$
4. $(-) \times (-) = (+)$

Example: $7\frac{1}{3} \times \frac{5}{11} = \frac{22}{3} \times \frac{5}{11}$
Reduce like terms (22 and 11).
$= \frac{2}{3} \times \frac{5}{1} = \frac{10}{3} = 3\frac{1}{3}$

Example: $-6\frac{1}{4} \times \frac{5}{9} = \frac{-25}{4} \times \frac{5}{9}$
$= \frac{-125}{36} = -3\frac{17}{36}$

Example: $\frac{-1}{4} \times \frac{-3}{7}$
A negative times a negative equals a positive.
$= \frac{1}{4} \times \frac{3}{7} = \frac{3}{28}$

Division of Fractions

1. Change mixed fractions to improper fractions

2. Change the division problem to a multiplication problem by using the reciprocal of the number after the division sign

3. Find the sign of the final product

4. Cancel if common factors exist between the numerator and the denominator

5. Multiply the numerators together and the denominators together

6. Change the improper fraction to a mixed number

Example: $3\frac{1}{5} \div 2\frac{1}{4} = \frac{16}{5} \div \frac{9}{4}$
$= \frac{16}{5} \times \frac{4}{9}$ The reciprocal of $\frac{9}{4}$ is $\frac{4}{9}$.
$= \frac{64}{45} = 1\frac{19}{45}$

Example: $7\frac{3}{4} \div 11\frac{5}{8} = \frac{31}{4} \div \frac{93}{8}$
$= \frac{31}{4} \times \frac{8}{93}$ Reduce like terms.
$= \frac{1}{1} \times \frac{2}{3} = \frac{2}{3}$

Example: $(-2\frac{1}{2}) \div 4\frac{1}{6} = \frac{-5}{2} \div \frac{25}{6}$
$= \frac{-5}{2} \times \frac{6}{25}$ Reduce like terms.
$= \frac{-1}{1} \times \frac{3}{5} = \frac{-3}{5}$

Example: $(-5\frac{3}{8}) \div (\frac{-7}{16}) = \frac{-43}{8} \div \frac{-7}{16}$
$= \frac{-43}{8} \times \frac{-16}{7}$ Reduce like terms.
$= \frac{43}{1} \times \frac{2}{7}$ A negative times a negative equals a positive.
$= \frac{86}{7} = 12\frac{2}{7}$

MATHEMATICS

RATIO: a comparison of two numbers

A RATIO is a comparison of two numbers. If a class had 11 boys and 14 girls, we can write the ratio of boys to girls in three ways:

- 11:14
- 11 to 14
- $\frac{11}{14}$

The ratio of girls to boys is:

- 14:11
- 14 to 11
- $\frac{14}{11}$

We should reduce ratios when possible. A ratio of 12 cats to 18 dogs reduces to 2:3, 2 to 3, or $\frac{2}{3}$.

Note: Read ratio questions carefully. Given a group of 6 adults and 5 children, the ratio of children to the entire group would be 5:11.

PROPORTION: an equation in which one fraction is set equal to another

A PROPORTION is an equation in which one fraction is set equal to another. To solve the proportion, multiply each numerator by the other fraction's denominator. Set these two products equal to each other and solve the resulting equation. This is called cross-multiplying the proportion.

Example: $\frac{4}{5} = \frac{x}{60}$ is a proportion.
To solve, cross multiply.
$(4)(60) = (15)(x)$
$240 = 15x$
$16 = x$

Example: $\frac{x+3}{3x+4} = \frac{2}{5}$ is a proportion.
To solve, cross multiply.
$5(x + 3) = 2(3x + 4)$
$5x + 15 = 6x + 8$
$7 = x$

Example: $\frac{x+2}{8} = \frac{2}{x-4}$ is another proportion.
To solve, cross multiply.
$(x + 2)(x - 4) = 8(2)$
$x^2 - 2x - 8 = 16$
$x^2 - 2x - 24 = 0$
$(x - 6)(x + 4) = 0$
$x = 6$ or $x = -4$

SOLVE WORD PROBLEMS INVOLVING INTEGERS, FRACTIONS, DECIMALS, AND UNITS OF MEASUREMENT

Proportions can be used to solve word problems whenever relationships are compared. Some situations include scale drawings and maps, similar polygons, speed, time and distance, cost, and comparison shopping.

Example: Which is the better buy, 6 items for $1.29 or 8 items for $1.69?
Find the unit price.

$\frac{6}{129} = \frac{1}{x}$ $\quad\quad\quad\quad$ $\frac{8}{169} = \frac{1}{x}$
$6x = 1.29$ $\quad\quad\quad\quad\quad$ $8x = 1.69$
$x = 0.215$ $\quad\quad\quad\quad\quad$ $x = 0.21125$

Thus, 8 items for $1.69 is the better buy.

Example: A car travels 125 miles in 2.5 hours. How far will it go in 6 hours?
Write a proportion comparing the distance and time.
Let x represent distance in miles. Then,

$\frac{125}{2.5} = \frac{x}{6}$ $\quad\quad$ Set up the proportion.
$2.5x = 6 \times 125$ $\quad\quad$ Cross-multiply.
$2.5x = 750$ $\quad\quad$ Simplify.
$\frac{2.5x}{2.5} = \frac{750}{2.5}$ $\quad\quad$ Divide both sides of the equation by 2.5.
$x = 300$ miles $\quad\quad$ Simplify.

Thus, the car can travel 300 miles in 6 hours.

Example: The scale on a map is $\frac{3}{4}$ inch = 6 miles. What is the actual distance between two cities if they are $1\frac{1}{2}$ inches apart on the map?
Write a proportion comparing the scale to the actual distance.

	Scale		Actual
	$\frac{\frac{3}{4}}{1\frac{1}{2}}$	=	$\frac{6}{x}$
	$\frac{3}{4}x$	=	$1\frac{1}{2} \times 6$
	$\frac{3}{4}x$	=	9
	x	=	12

Thus, the actual distance between the cities is 12 miles.

MATHEMATICS

SKILL 7.2 Understand units of measurement and conversions *(including scientific notation)*

SCIENTIFIC NOTATION: a convenient method for writing very large and very small numbers

SCIENTIFIC NOTATION is a convenient method for writing very large and very small numbers. It employs two factors. The first factor is a number between 1 and 10. The second factor is a power of 10. This notation is considered "shorthand" for expressing very large numbers (such as the weight of 100 elephants) or very small numbers (such as the weight of an atom in pounds).

Recall that:

10^n	=	Ten multiplied by itself n times
10^n	=	Any nonzero number raised to the zero power is 1
10^1	=	10
10^2	=	$10 \times 10 = 100$
10^3	=	$10 \times 10 \times 10 = 1000$
10^{-1}	=	$\frac{1}{10}$ (deci)
10^{-2}	=	$\frac{1}{100}$ (centi)
10^{-3}	=	$\frac{1}{1000}$ (milli)
10^{-6}	=	$\frac{1}{1,000,000}$ (micro)

Example: Write 46,368,000 in scientific notation.
1. Introduce a decimal point and decimal places.
   $46,368,000 = 46,368,000.0000$

2. Make a mark between the two digits that give a number between −9.9 and 9.9.
   $4 \wedge 6,368,000.0000$

3. Count the number of digit places between the decimal point and the $\wedge$ mark. This number is the *nth* power of ten.
   So, $46,368,000 = 4.6368 \times 10^7$.

Example: Write 0.00397 in scientific notation.
1. Decimal place is already in place.

SOLVE WORD PROBLEMS INVOLVING INTEGERS, FRACTIONS, DECIMALS, AND UNITS OF MEASUREMENT

2. Make a mark between 3 and 9 to obtain a number between −9.9 and. 9.9.

3. Move decimal place to the mark (three hops).
   0.003 ∧ 97
   Motion is to the right, so n on 10^n is negative.
   Therefore, $0.00397 = 3.97 \times 10^{-3}$.

A *decimal* can be converted to a *percent* by multiplying by 100 or by merely moving the decimal point two places to the right. A percent can be converted to a decimal by dividing by 100 or by moving the decimal point two places to the left.

Examples:

0.375 = 37.5%	84% = 0.84
0.7 = 70%	3% = 0.03
0.04 = 4%	60% = 0.6
3.15 = 315%	110% = 1.1
	$\frac{1}{2}$% = 0.5% = 0.005

A percent can be converted to a *fraction* by placing it over 100 and reducing to simplest terms.

Example: Convert 50% to a fraction.
$50\% = \frac{50}{100} = \frac{1}{2}$

A *decimal* can be converted to a fraction by multiplying by a number that will remove the decimal point and reducing the result to its simplest terms.

Example: Convert 0.056 to a fraction.
Multiply 0.056 by $\frac{1000}{1000}$ to get rid of the decimal point:
$0.056 \times \frac{1000}{1000} = \frac{56}{1000} = \frac{7}{125}$

Example: Convert 6.25% to a decimal and to a fraction.
$6.25\% = 0.0625 = 0.0625 \times \frac{1000}{1000} = \frac{625}{10000} = \frac{1}{16}$

An example of a type of problem involving fractions is the conversion of recipes. For example, if a recipe serves eight people and we want to make enough to serve only four, we must determine how much of each ingredient to use. The conversion factor, or the number we multiply each ingredient by, is:

$$\text{Conversion Factor} = \frac{\text{Number of Servings Needed}}{\text{Number of Servings in Recipe}}$$

Example: Consider the following recipe.

3 cups flour
1/2 tsp. baking powder
2/3 cups butter
2 cups sugar
2 eggs

If this recipe serves eight, how much of each ingredient do we need to serve only four people?

First, determine the conversion factor.

Conversion Factor $= \frac{4}{8} = \frac{1}{2}$

Next, multiply each ingredient by the conversion factor.

$3 \times \frac{1}{2} =$ $1\frac{1}{2}$ cups flour

$\frac{1}{2} \times \frac{1}{2} =$ $\frac{1}{4}$ tsp. baking powder

$\frac{2}{3} \times \frac{1}{2} = \frac{2}{6}$ $\frac{1}{3}$ cup butter

$2 \times \frac{1}{2} =$ 1 cup sugar

$2 \times \frac{1}{2} =$ 1 egg

MEASUREMENTS OF LENGTH (ENGLISH SYSTEM)		
12 inches (in.)	=	1 foot (ft.)
3 ft.	=	1 yd.
1760 yd.	=	1 mi.

MEASUREMENTS OF LENGTH (METRIC SYSTEM)		
kilometer (km)	=	1000 meters (m)
hectometer (hm)	=	100 meters (m)
decameter (dam)	=	10 meters (m)
meter (m)	=	1 meter (m)
decimeter (dm)	=	1/10 meter (m)
centimeter (cm)	=	1/100 meter (m)
millimeter (mm)	=	1/1000 meter (m)

SOLVE WORD PROBLEMS INVOLVING INTEGERS, FRACTIONS, DECIMALS, AND UNITS OF MEASUREMENT

CONVERSION OF LENGTH FROM ENGLISH TO METRIC		
1 inch	=	2.54 centimeters
1 foot	≈	30 centimeters
1 yard	≈	0.9 meters
1 mile	≈	1.6 kilometers

MEASUREMENTS OF WEIGHT (ENGLISH SYSTEM)		
28 grams (g)	=	1 ounce (oz)
16 ounces (oz)	=	1 pound (lb)
2000 pounds (lb)	=	1 ton (t)(short ton)
1.1 ton (t)	=	1 ton (t)

MEASUREMENTS OF WEIGHT (METRIC SYSTEM)		
kilogram (kg)	=	1000 grams (g)
gram (g)	=	1 gram (g)
milligram (mg)	=	1/1000 gram (g)

CONVERSION OF WEIGHT FROM ENGLISH TO METRIC		
1 ounce	≈	28 grams
1 pound	≈	0.45 kilogram
	≈	454 grams

MEASUREMENT OF VOLUME (ENGLISH SYSTEM)		
8 fluid ounces (oz)	=	1 cup (c)
2 cups (c)	=	1 pint (pt)
2 pints (pt)	=	1 quart (qt)
4 quarts (qt)	=	1 gallon (gal)

MATHEMATICS

MEASUREMENT OF VOLUME (METRIC SYSTEM)		
kiloliter (kl)	=	1000 liters (l)
liter (l)	=	1 liter (l)
milliliter (ml)	=	1/1000 liter (ml)

CONVERSION OF VOLUME FROM ENGLISH TO METRIC		
1 teaspoon (tsp)	≈	5 milliliters
1 fluid ounce	≈	15 milliliters
1 cup	≈	0.24 liters
1 pint	≈	0.47 liters
1 quart	≈	0.95 liters
1 gallon	≈	3.8 liters

MEASUREMENT OF TIME		
1 second	=	
1 minute	=	60 seconds
1 hour	=	60 minutes
1 day	=	24 hours
1 week	=	7 days
1 year	=	365 days
1 century	=	100 years

COMPETENCY 8
SOLVE PROBLEMS INVOLVING DATA INTERPRETATION AND ANALYSIS

SKILL 8.1 Interpret information from line graphs, bar graphs, pictographs, pie charts, and tables

To make a bar graph or a pictograph, we determine the scale for the graph. Then we determine the length of each bar on the graph or determine the number of pictures needed to represent each item of information. We need to be sure to include an explanation of the scale in the legend.

Example: A class had the following grades: 4 As, 9 Bs, 8 Cs, 1 D, 3 Fs. Graph these on a pictograph and a bar graph.

Grade	Number of Students
A	☺☺☺☺
B	☺☺☺☺☺☺☺☺☺
C	☺☺☺☺☺☺☺☺
D	☺
F	☺☺☺

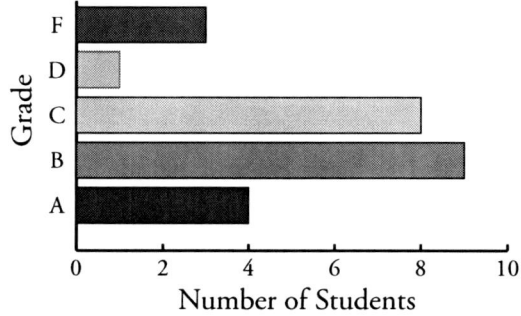

Pictographs can be misleading, especially if drawn to represent 3-dimensional objects. If two or more dimensions are changed in reflecting ratio, the overall visual effect can be misinterpreted. Bar and line graphs can be misleading if the scales are changed. For example, using relatively small scale increments for large numbers will make the comparison differences seem much greater than if larger-scale increments are used. Circle graphs, or pie charts, are excellent for comparing relative amounts; however, they cannot be used to represent absolute amounts, and if interpreted as such, they are misleading.

MATHEMATICS

To make a line graph, we determine appropriate scales for both the vertical and horizontal axes (based on the information we are graphing). Describe what each axis represents and mark the scale periodically on each axis. Graph the individual points of the graph and connect the points on the graph from left to right.

Example: Graph the following information using a line graph.

THE NUMBER OF NATIONAL MERIT FINALISTS PER SCHOOL YEAR						
YEAR	90–91	91–92	92–93	93–94	94–95	95–96
Central	3	5	1	4	6	8
Wilson	4	2	3	2	3	2

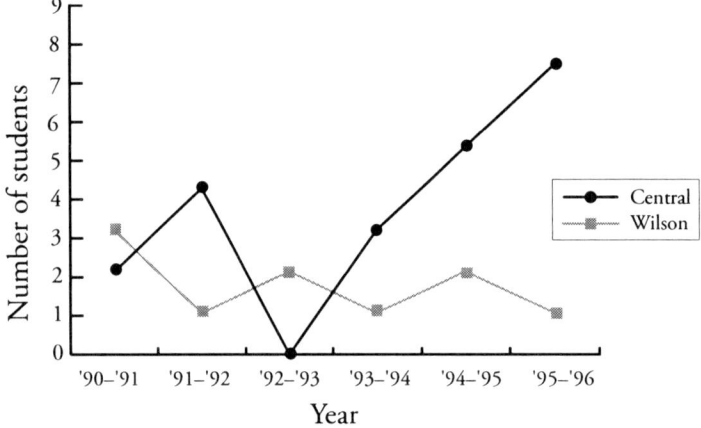

To make a circle graph, we total all the information that is to be included on the graph. We then determine the central angle to be used for each sector of the graph using the following formula:

$$\frac{\text{information}}{\text{total information}} \times 360° = \text{degrees in central } \sphericalangle$$

We lay out the central angles to these sizes, label each section, and include its percent.

Example: Graph the following information on a circle graph

MONTHLY EXPENSES					
Rent	Food	Utilities	Clothes	Church	Misc.
$400	$150	$75	$75	$100	$200

SOLVE PROBLEMS INVOLVING DATA INTERPRETATION AND ANALYSIS

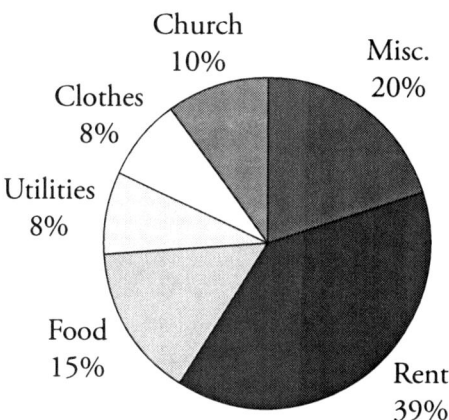

Scatter plots compare two characteristics of the same group of things or people and usually consist of a large body of data. They show how much one variable affects another. The relationship between the two variables is their COR-RELATION. The closer the data points come to forming a straight line when plotted, the closer the correlation.

CORRELATION: the relationship between the two variables in a scatter plot

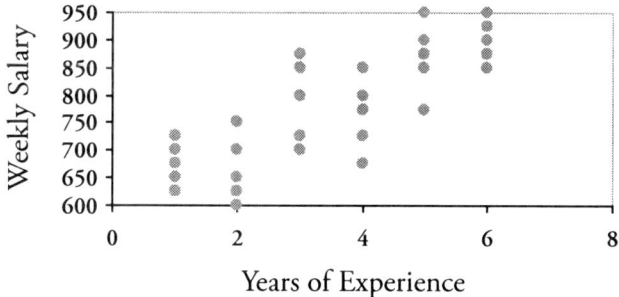

Stem-and-leaf plots are visually similar to line plots. The stems are the digits in the greatest place value of the data values, and the leaves are the digits in the next greatest place value. Stem-and-leaf plots are best suited for small sets of data and are especially useful for comparing two sets of data. The following is an example using test scores:

4	9
5	4 9
6	1 2 3 4 6 7 8 8
7	0 3 4 6 6 6 7 7 7 8 8 8 8
8	3 5 5 7 8
9	0 0 3 4 5
10	0 0

MATHEMATICS

FREQUENCY: the number of times any particular data value occurs

FREQUENCY OF THE INTERVAL: the number of data values in any interval

We use histograms to summarize information from large sets of data that we can naturally group into intervals. The vertical axis indicates FREQUENCY (the number of times any particular data value occurs), and the horizontal axis indicates data values or ranges of data values. The number of data values in any interval is the FREQUENCY OF THE INTERVAL.

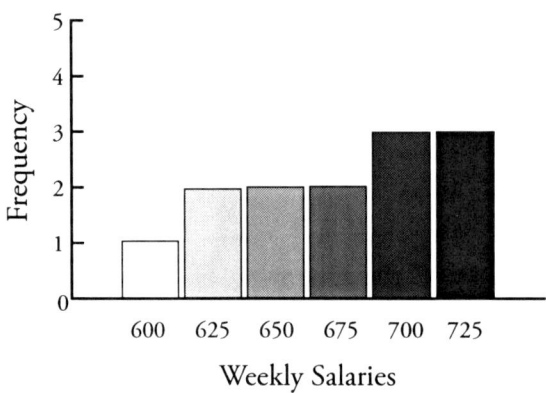

SKILL 8.2 Recognize appropriate graphic representations of various data

See Skill 8.1

SKILL 8.3 Analyze and interpret data using measures of central tendency (mean, median, and mode)

MEAN: the sum of a set of numbers divided by the number of items being averaged; also called the average

The arithmetic MEAN (or average) of a set of numbers is the *sum* of the numbers *divided by* the number of items being averaged.

Example: Find the mean. Round to the nearest tenth.
24.6, 57.3, 44.1, 39.8, 64.5
   The sum is 230.3 ÷ 5 = 46.06, rounded to 46.1

MEDIAN: the middle number when a set of numbers is arranged in order

The MEDIAN of a set of numbers is the middle number when the numbers are arranged in order. To calculate the median, we must arrange the terms in order. If there is an even number of terms, the median is the mean of the two middle terms.

SOLVE PROBLEMS INVOLVING DATA INTERPRETATION AND ANALYSIS

Example: Find the median.

12, 14, 27, 3, 13, 7, 17, 12, 22, 6, 16

Rearrange the terms from least to greatest.

3, 6, 7, 12, 12, 13, 14, 16, 17, 22, 27

Because there are eleven numbers, the middle would be the sixth number, or 13.

The MODE of a set of numbers is the number that occurs with the greatest frequency. A set can have no mode if each term appears exactly one time. Similarly, there can also be more than one mode.

> **MODE:** the number that occurs with the greatest frequency in a set of numbers

Example: Find the mode.

26, 15, 37, **26**, 35, **26**, 15

15 appears twice, but 26 appears three times. Therefore, the mode is 26.

The RANGE of a set of numbers is the difference between the highest and lowest data value.

> **RANGE:** the difference between the highest and lowest data value in a set of numbers

Example: Given the ungrouped data below, calculate the mean, range, standard deviation, and variance.

15	22	28	25	34	38
18	25	30	33	19	23

Mean ($\overline{X}$) = 25.8333333

Range: 38 − 15 = 23

SKILL 8.4 Analyze and interpret data using the concept of variability

The simplest descriptor of data variability or "spread" is the range of a data set described in the previous skill. This, however, depends only on the highest and lowest data points and does not give us any indication of how the other data points deviate from the mean. The variance and standard deviation are more sophisticated measures of the spread (or dispersion) of data around the mean.

The VARIANCE of a data set is the sum of the squares of the differences between each item and the mean divided by the number of items. (The lower case Greek letter sigma squared—σ^2—represents variance.)

$$\sigma^2 = \frac{(X - \overline{X})^2}{N}$$

> **VARIANCE:** the sum of the squares of the differences between each item and the mean divided by the number of items. (the lower case Greek letter sigma squared—σ^2—represents variance)

The larger the value of the variance, the larger the spread.

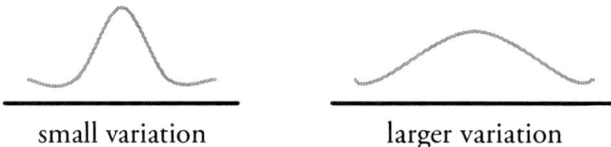

small variation   larger variation

The STANDARD DEVIATION is the square root of the variance. The lower case Greek letter sigma (σ) is used to represent standard deviation.

$$\sigma = \sqrt{\sigma^2}$$

One can think of the standard deviation as a sort of average or typical deviation of a data point from the mean. It may seem like an unnecessary complication to square the deviations in the calculation of the variation and then take the square root while calculating standard deviation. The need for this procedure, however, becomes clear when one considers that a simple average of deviations would cancel out the positive and negative deviations leaving an average deviation of zero. The squaring procedure assures that each deviation, positive or negative, counts as a positive contribution to the measure of variability.

Example: Calculate the range, variance and standard deviation for the following data set: {3, 3, 5, 7, 8, 8, 8, 10, 12, 21}.

The range is simply the largest data value minus the smallest. In this case, the range is $21 - 3 = 18$.

To calculate the variance and standard deviation, first calculate the mean.

$$\mu = \frac{3 + 3 + 5 + 7 + 8 + 8 + 8 + 10 + 12 + 21}{10} = 8.5$$

Use this mean to calculate the variance.

$$\sigma^2 = \frac{1}{10} \Sigma (x_i - 8.5)^2$$
$$\sigma^2 = \frac{1}{10} \{(3 - 8.5)^2 + (3 - 8.5)^2 + (5 - 8.5)^2 + \ldots + (21 - 8.5)^2\}$$
$$\sigma^2 = \frac{246.5}{10} = 24.65$$

The standard deviation is

$$\sigma = \sqrt{\sigma^2} = \sqrt{24.65} \approx 4.96$$

The interquartile range is another measure of dispersion that uses quartiles, which divide the data into four segments. This provides a measure of the spread of the middle 50% of a data set. To find the quartile of a particular datum, first determine the median of the data set (which is labeled Q2), then find the median of the upper half (labeled Q3) and the median of the lower half (labeled Q1) of the data set. To calculate the interquartile range (RIQ), simply subtract Q1 from Q3. Thus,

$$R_{IQ} = Q1 - Q3$$

ALGEBRA

COMPETENCY 9
GRAPH NUMBERS OR NUMBER RELATIONSHIPS

SKILL 9.1 Identify the graph of a given equation or a given inequality, find the slope and/or intercepts of a given line, and find the equation of a line

A relationship between two quantities can be shown using a table, graph, or rule. In this example, the rule $y = 9x$ describes the relationship between the total amount earned, y, and the total amount of $9 sunglasses sold, x.

A table using these data would appear as:

Number of Sunglasses Sold	1	5	10	15
Total Dollars Earned	9	45	90	135

Each (x, y) relationship between a pair of values is called a coordinate pair and can be plotted on a graph. The coordinate pairs $(1, 9)$, $(5, 45)$, $(10, 90)$, and $(15, 135)$ are plotted on the graph below.

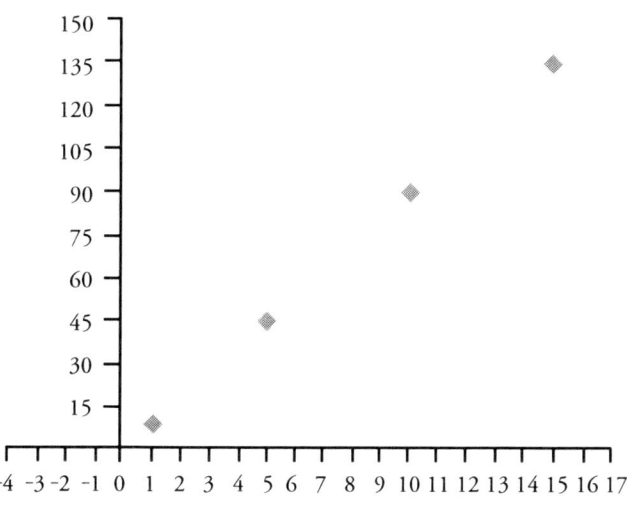

MATHEMATICS

LINEAR RELATIONSHIP: one in which two quantities are proportional to each other

The graph above shows a linear relationship. A LINEAR RELATIONSHIP is one in which two quantities are proportional to each other. Doubling *x* also doubles *y*. On a graph, a straight line depicts a linear relationship.

COORDINATE PLANE: a plane with a point selected as an origin, some length selected as a unit of distance, and two perpendicular lines that intersect at the origin, with positive and negative direction selected on each line

A COORDINATE PLANE is a plane with a point selected as an origin, some length selected as a unit of distance, and two perpendicular lines that intersect at the origin, with positive and negative direction selected on each line. Traditionally, the lines are called *x* (drawn from left to right, with positive direction to the right of the origin) and *y* (drawn from bottom to top, with positive direction upward of the origin). Coordinates of a point are determined by the distance of this point from the lines, and the signs of the coordinates are determined by whether the point is in the positive or in the negative direction from the origin.

The standard coordinate plane consists of a plane divided into four quadrants by the intersection of two axis, the x-axis (horizontal axis), and the y-axis (vertical axis).

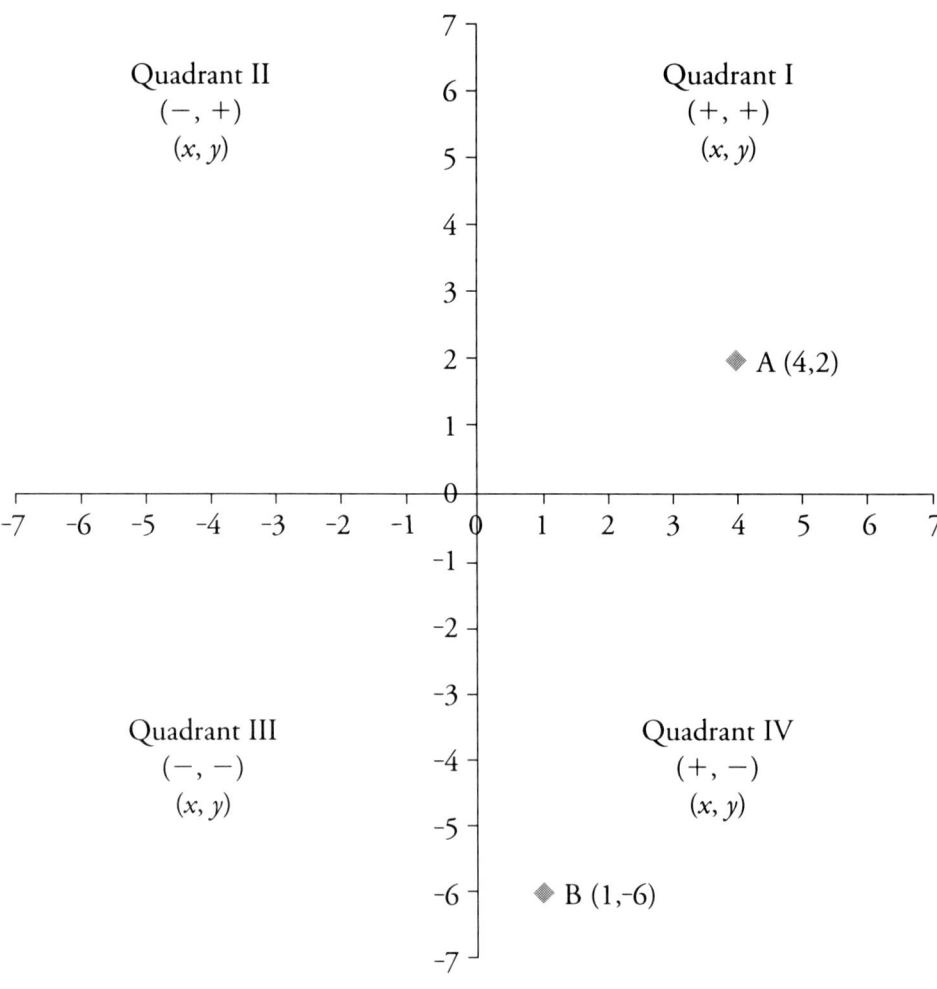

COORDINATES: a unique ordered pair of numbers that identifies a point on the coordinate plane

COORDINATES are a unique *ordered pair* of numbers that identifies a point on the coordinate plane. The first number in the ordered pair identifies the position with regard to the *x*-axis while the second number identifies the position on the *y*-axis (*x*,*y*).

GRAPH NUMBERS OR NUMBER RELATIONSHIPS

In the coordinate plane shown above, point A has the ordered pair (4,2); point B has the ordered pair (1,-6).

The SLOPE of a line is the *slant* of a line. A downward left-to-right slant means a negative slope. An upward slant is a positive slope.

SLOPE: the slant of a line

The formula for calculating the slope of a line with coordinates (x_1, y_1) and (x_2, y_2) is:
$$\text{slope} = \frac{y_2 - y_1}{x_2 - x_1}$$

The top of the fraction represents the change in the *y* coordinates; it is called the RISE.

RISE: the top of the fraction; it represents the change in the *y* coordinates

The bottom of the fraction represents the change in the *x* coordinates, it is called the RUN.

RUN: the bottom of the fraction; it represents the change in the *x* coordinates

Example: Find the slope of a line with points at (2,2) and (7,8).

$\frac{(8) - (2)}{(7) - (2)}$ Plug the values into the formula.

$\frac{6}{5}$ Solve the rise over run.

$= 1.2$ Solve for the slope.

The length of a line segment is the DISTANCE between two different points, A and B.

DISTANCE: the length of a line segment between two different points, A and B

The formula for the length of a line is:
$$\text{length} = \sqrt{(x_1 - x_2)^2 + (y_1 - y_2)^2}$$

Example: Find the length between the points (2,2) and (7,8)

$= \sqrt{(2-7)^2 + (2-8)^2}$ Plug the values into the formula.

$= \sqrt{(-5)^2 + (-6)^2}$ Calculate the *x* and *y* differences.

$= \sqrt{25 + 36}$ Square the values.

$= \sqrt{61}$ Add the two values.

$= 7.81$ Calculate the square root.

A first-degree equation has an equation of the form $ax + by = c$. To find the slope of a line, solve the equation for *y*. This gets the equation into slope-intercept FORM, $y = mx + b$. In this equation, m is the line's slope.

The *y* intercept is the coordinate of the point where a line crosses the *y*-axis. To find the *y* intercept, substitute 0 for *x* and solve for *y*. This is the *y* intercept. In slope-intercept form, $y = mx + b$, b is the *y* intercept.

To find the *x* intercept, substitute 0 for *y* and solve for *x*. This is the *x* intercept. If the equation solves to **x = any number**, then the graph is a vertical line, because it only has an *x* intercept. Its slope is undefined.

If the equation solves to **y = any number**, then the graph is a horizontal line, because it only has a *y* intercept. Its slope is 0 (zero).

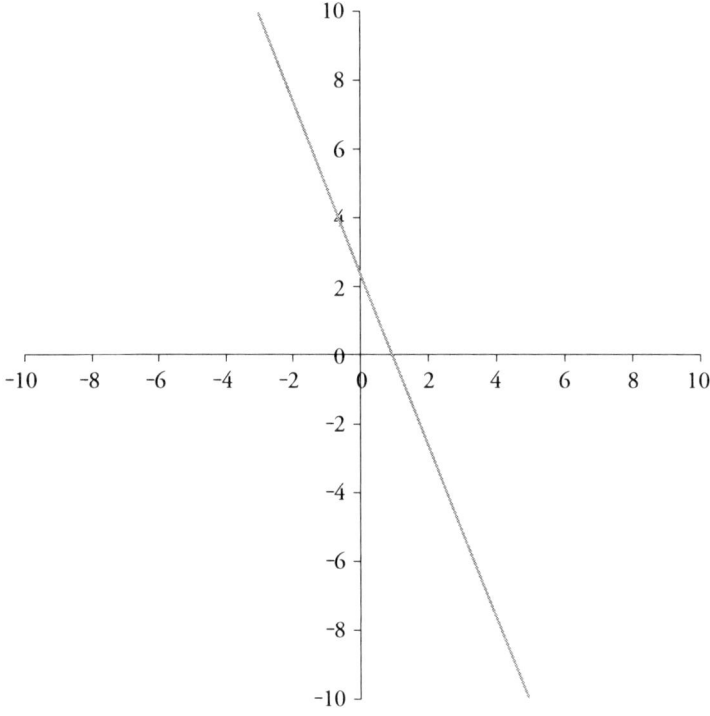

$$5x + 2y = 6$$
$$y = \frac{-5}{2x + 3}$$

The equation of a line can be found from its graph by finding its slope and its intercept. The slope formula looks like this:
$$m = \frac{y_2 - y_1}{x_2 - x_1}$$

The *y* intercept can be found using this equation:
$$Y - y_a = m(X - x_a)$$

(x_a, y_a) can be (x_1, y_1) or (x_2, y_2). If **m**, the value of the slope, is distributed through the parentheses, the equation can be rewritten into other forms of the equation of a line.

Example: Find the equation of a line through (9, -6) and (-1, 2).

$$\text{slope} = \frac{y_2 - y_1}{x_2 - x_1} = \frac{2 - -6}{-1 - 9} = \frac{8}{-10} = \frac{4}{-5}$$

GRAPH NUMBERS OR NUMBER RELATIONSHIPS

$$Y - y_a = m(X - x_a) \rightarrow Y - 2 = \frac{-4}{5(X - -1)} \rightarrow$$
$$Y - 2 = \frac{-4}{5(X + 1)} \rightarrow Y - 2 = \frac{-4}{5}X \frac{-4}{5}$$
$$Y = \frac{-4}{5}X + \frac{6}{5} \qquad \text{This is the slope-intercept form.}$$

Multiplying by 5 to eliminate fractions, it is:
$5Y = -4X + 6 \rightarrow 4X + 5Y = 6$

Example: Find the slope and intercepts of 3x + 2y = 14.
$3x + 2y = 14$
$2y = -3x + 14$
$y = \frac{-3}{2x} + 7$

The slope of the line is $\frac{-3}{2}$. The intercept of the line is 7.

The intercepts can also be found by substituting 0 in place of the other variables in the equation.

To find the y-intercept: To find the x-intercept:
Let $x = 0$; $3(0) + 2y = 14$ Let $y = 0$; $3x + 2(0) = 14$
$0 + 2y = 14$ $3x + 0 = 14$
$2y = 14$ $3x = 14$
$y = 7$ $x = \frac{14}{3}$
$(0,7)$ is the y-intercept. $(\frac{14}{3}, 0)$ is the x-intercept.

Example: Sketch the graph of the line represented by 2x + 3y = 6.
Let $x = 0 \rightarrow 2(0) + 3y = 6$
    $\rightarrow 3y = 6$
    $\rightarrow y = 2$
    $\rightarrow (0,2)$ is the y-intercept

Let $y = 0 \rightarrow 2x + 3(0) = 6$
    $\rightarrow 2x = 6$
    $\rightarrow x = 3$
    $\rightarrow (3,0)$ is the x-intercept

Let $x = 1 \rightarrow 2(1) + 3y = 6$
    $\rightarrow 2 + 3y = 6$
    $\rightarrow 3y = 4$
    $\rightarrow y = \frac{4}{3}$
    $\rightarrow (1, \frac{4}{3})$ is the third point.

Plotting the three points on the coordinate system, we get the following:

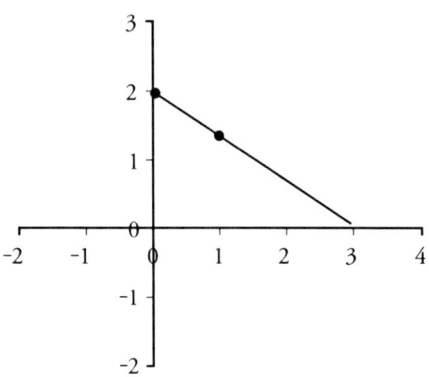

SKILL 9.2 Recognize and interpret information from the graph of a function (including direct and inverse variation)

If two things vary directly, as one gets larger, the other also gets larger. If one gets smaller, then the other gets smaller too. If x and y vary directly, there should be a constant, c, such that $y = cx$. Something can also vary directly with the square of something else: $y = cx^2$.

If two things vary inversely, as one gets larger, the other one gets smaller instead. If x and y vary inversely, there should be a constant, c, such that $xy = c$ or $y = \frac{c}{x}$. Something can also vary inversely with the square of something else: $y = \frac{c}{x^2}$.

Example: If $30 is paid for 5 hours' work, how much would be paid for 19?
This is direct variation and $30 = 5c$, so the constant is 6 ($6/hour). So $y = 6(19)$ or $y = \$114$.

This could also be done as a proportion:
$$\frac{\$30}{5} = \frac{y}{19}$$
$$5y = 570$$
$$y = 114$$

Example: On a 546 mile trip from Miami to Charlotte, one car drove 65 mph while another car drove 70 mph. How does this affect the driving time for the trip?
This is an inverse variation, since increasing your speed should decrease your driving time. Using the equation: rate × time = distance, $rt = d$.

$65t = 546$ and $70t = 546$
$t = 8.4$ and $t = 7.8$
slower speed, more time   faster speed, less time

Example: A 14" pizza from Azzip Pizza costs $8.00. How much would a 20" pizza cost if its price was based on the same price per square inch?

Here the price is directly proportional to the square of the radius. Using a proportion:

$$\frac{\$8.00}{7^2 \pi} = \frac{x}{10^2 \pi}$$

$$\frac{8}{153.86} = \frac{x}{314}$$

$$16.33 = x$$

$16.33 would be the price of the large pizza.

Example: Consider the average monthly temperatures for a hypothetical location.

Month	Jan	March	May	July	Sept	Nov
Avg. Temp. (F)	40	48	65	81	80	60

Note that the graph of the average temperatures resembles the graph of a trigonometric function with a period of one year. We can use the periodic nature of seasonal temperature fluctuation to predict weather patterns.

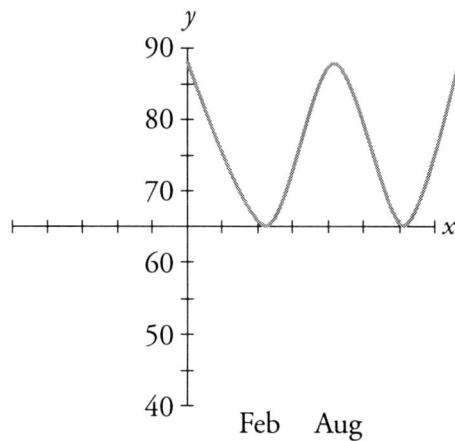

A **LINEAR FUNCTION** is a function whose graph is a line. It has the algebraic form $f(x) = ax + b$. The variables a and b are constants. In order to determine the linear function that best models a set of data, we need to figure out a and b.

LINEAR FUNCTION: a function whose graph is a line

Example: Johnny delivers flyers for ABC Hardware after school. He is paid a weekly salary of $25 plus a 1% commission on any sales resulting from the flyers.

The table of data would look like this:

Sales, *s*	100	200	300	400	500
Earnings, *E(s)*	26	27	28	29	30

The linear function would be $E(s) = (0.01)s + 25$, where $E(s)$ represents total earnings, 0.01 substitutes for a, s represents sales, and 25 substitutes for b.

COMPETENCY 10
SOLVE ONE- AND TWO-VARIABLE EQUATIONS

SKILL 10.1 Find the value of the unknown in a given one-variable equation

The procedure for solving a one-variable equation is explained and demonstrated through the following example.

Example: $3(x + 3) = -2x + 4$. Solve for x.

1. Expand to eliminate all parentheses
   $3x + 9 = -2x + 4$

2. Multiply each term by the LCD to eliminate all denominators

3. Combine like terms on each side when possible

4. Use the properties to put all variables on one side and all constants on the other side

   $\rightarrow 3x + 9 - 9 = -2x + 4 - 9$ Subtract 9 from both sides.
   $\rightarrow 3x = -2x - 5$
   $\rightarrow 3x + 2x = -2x + 2x - 5$ Add $2x$ to both sides.
   $\rightarrow 5x = -5$
   $\rightarrow \frac{5x}{5} = \frac{-5}{5}$ Divide both sides by 5.
   $\rightarrow x = -1$

SOLVE ONE- AND TWO-VARIABLE EQUATIONS

Example: Solve: $3(2x + 5) - 4x = 5(x + 9)$

$6x + 15 - 4x = 5x + 45$

$2x + 15 = 5x + 45$

$-3x + 15 = 45$

$-3x = 30$

$x = -10$

SKILL 10.2 Express one variable in terms of a second variable in two-variable equations

The procedure for expressing one variable in terms of a second variable in a two-variable equation is exactly analogous to the procedure for solving a one-variable equation except that the final answer, instead of being a number, will be an algebraic expression including the other variable. The following example is used to demonstrate and explain the procedure.

Example: Solve for x in terms of y: $\frac{y}{5} + \frac{1}{2}(x - 2) = x$

1. Expand to eliminate all parentheses
   $\frac{y}{5} + \frac{1}{2}x - 1 = x$

2. Multiply each term by the LCD (in this case 10) to eliminate all denominators
   $2y + 5x - 10 = 10x$

3. Combine like terms on each side when possible

4. Use the properties to put all x terms on one side and all constants and y terms on the other side

$2y - 5x - 10 = 10$	Subtract $10x$ from both sides.
$-5x - 10 = -2y$	Subtract $2y$ from both sides.
$-5x = -2y + 10$	Add 10 to both sides.
$5x = 2y - 10$	Multiply both sides by -1.
$x = \frac{2}{5}y - 2$	Divide both sides by 5.

MATHEMATICS

SKILL 10.3 Solve systems of two equations in two variables (including graphical solutions)

The solution set of linear equations is all the ordered pairs of real numbers that satisfy both equations—thus the intersection of the lines. There are two methods for solving linear equations: linear combinations and substitution.

In the SUBSTITUTION method, an equation is solved for either variable. That solution is then substituted in the other equation to find the remaining variable.

SUBSTITUTION: when an equation is solved for either of two variables, then the solution is substituted to find the remaining variable

Example:
1. $2x + 8y = 4$
2. $x - 3y = 5$
2A. $x = 3y + 5$ Solve equation (2) for x.
1A. $2(3y + 5) + 8y = 4$ Substitute for x in equation (1).
     $6y + 10 + 8y = 4$ Solve.
     $14y = -6$
     $y = \frac{-3}{7}$ Solution.
2. $x - 3y = 5$
     $x - 3(\frac{-3}{7}) = 5$ Substitute the value of y.
     $x = \frac{26}{7} = 3\frac{5}{7}$ Solution.

Thus, the solution set of the system of equations is $(3\frac{5}{7}, \frac{-3}{7})$.

In the LINEAR COMBINATIONS method, one or both of the equations are replaced with an equivalent equation so that the two equations can be combined (added or subtracted) to eliminate one variable.

LINEAR COMBINATIONS: when one or both of two equations are replaced with an equivalent equation so that they can be combined and one variable eliminated

Example:
1. $4x + 3y = -2$.
2. $5x - y = 7$
1. $4x + 3y = -2$
2A. $15x - 3y = 2$.   Multiply equation (2) by 3.
     $19x = 19$ Combining (1) and (2a).
     $x = 1$ Solve.

To find y, substitute the value of x in equation 1 (or 2).
     $4x + 3y = -2$
     $4(1) + 3y = -2$
     $4 + 3y = -2$
     $3y = -6$
     $y = -2$

Thus, the solution is $x = 1$ and $y = -2$, or the ordered pair $(1, -2)$.

Example: Solve for x and y.

$4x + 6y = 340$

$3x + 8y = 360$

To solve by linear combinations:

$4(4x + 6y = 340)$ Multiply the first equation by 4

$-3(3x + 8y = 360)$ Multiply the second equation by -3

By doing this, the equations can be added to each other to eliminate one variable and solve for the other variable.

$$16x + 24y = 1360$$
$$-9x - 24y = -1080$$
$$7x = 280$$
$$x = 40$$

Solving for y, $y = 30$

COMPETENCY 11
SOLVE WORD PROBLEMS INVOLVING ONE AND TWO VARIABLES

SKILL 11.1 Identify the algebraic equivalent of a stated relationship and solve word problems involving one and two unknowns

Example: Mark and Mike are twins; 3 times Mark's age, plus 4, equals 4 times Mike's age minus 14. How old are the boys?

Since the boys are twins, their ages are the same. "Translate" the English into algebra. Let $x = $ their age.

$3x + 4 = 4x - 14$

$18 = x$

The boys are each 18 years old.

Example: The YMCA wants to sell raffle tickets to raise at least $32,000. If they must pay $7250 in expenses and prizes out of the money collected from the tickets, how many tickets worth $25 each must they sell?

Since they want to raise at least $32,000, that means they would be happy to get 32,000 or more. This requires an inequality.

Let x = number of tickets sold.
  Then $25x$ = total money collected for x tickets.
  Total money minus expenses must be greater than $32,000.
  $25x - 7250 \geq 3200$
  $25x \geq 39250$
  $x \geq 1570$
  If they sell 1,570 tickets or more, they will raise at least $32,000.

Example: The Simpsons went out for dinner. All 4 of them ordered the aardvark steak dinner. Bert paid for the 4 meals and included a tip of $12 for a total of $84.60. How much was one aardvark steak dinner?

Let x = the price of one aardvark dinner.
So $4x$ = the price of 4 aardvark dinners.
  $4x + 12 = 84.60$
  $4x = 72.60$
  $x = \$18.50$ for each dinner.

Some word problems can be solved using a system (group) of equations or inequalities. Watch for phrases such as *greater than, less than, at least,* and *no more than,* which indicate the need for inequalities.

Example: Farmer Greenjeans bought 4 cows and 6 sheep for $1700. Mr. Ziffel bought 3 cows and 12 sheep for $2400. If all the cows were the same price and all the sheep were another fixed price, find the price charged for a cow and the price charged for a sheep.

Let x = price of a cow
Let y = price of a sheep
  Then Farmer Greenjeans's equation would be: $4x + 6y = 1700$
  Mr. Ziffel's equation would be: $3x + 12y = 2400$

To solve by addition-subtraction:
  Multiply the first equation by -2: $-2(4x + 6y = 1700)$
  Keep the other equation the same: $(3x + 12y = 2400)$

Now the equations can be added to each other to eliminate one variable, and you can solve for the other variable.
  $-8x - 12y = -3400$
  $\underline{3x + 12y = 2400}$ Add these equations.
  $-5x = -1000$
  $x = 200$ ← the price of a cow was $200.
  Solving for y, $y = 150$ ← the price of a sheep was $150.

SOLVE WORD PROBLEMS INVOLVING ONE AND TWO VARIABLES

Solve one of the equations for a variable. (Try to make an equation without fractions if possible.) Substitute this expression into the equation that you have not yet used. Solve the resulting equation for the value of the remaining variable.

$4x + 6y = 1700$
$3x + 12y = 2400$ ← Solve this equation for x.

It becomes $x = 800 - 4y$. Now substitute $800 - 4y$ in place of x in the *other* equation. $4x + 6y = 1700$ now becomes:

$4(800 - 4y) + 6y = 1700$
$3200 - 16y + 6y = 1700$
$3200 - 10y = 1700$
$-10y = -1500$
$y = 150$, or $150 for a sheep.

Substituting 150 back into an equation for y, find x.

$4x + 6(150) = 1700$
$4x + 900 = 1700$
$4x = 800$ so $x = 200$, or $200 for a cow.

Example: Sharon's Bike Shoppe can assemble a three-speed bike in 30 minutes or a ten-speed bike in 60 minutes. The profit on each bike sold is $60 for a three-speed and $75 for a ten-speed bike. How many of each type of bike should the shop assemble during an 8-hour day (480 minutes) to make the maximum profit? Total daily profit must be at least $300.

Let x = number of three-speed bikes.
Let y = number of ten-speed bikes.

Since there are only 480 minutes to use each day, $30x + 60y \leq 480$ is the first inequality.
Since the total daily profit must be at least $300, $60x + 75y \geq 300$ is the second inequality.

$32x + 65y \leq 480$ solves to $y \leq 8 - \frac{1}{2x}$
$60x + 75y \geq 300$ solves to $y \geq 4 - \frac{4}{5x}$

Graph these two inequalities:

$y \leq 8 - \frac{1}{2x}$
$y \geq 4 - \frac{4}{5x}$

MATHEMATICS

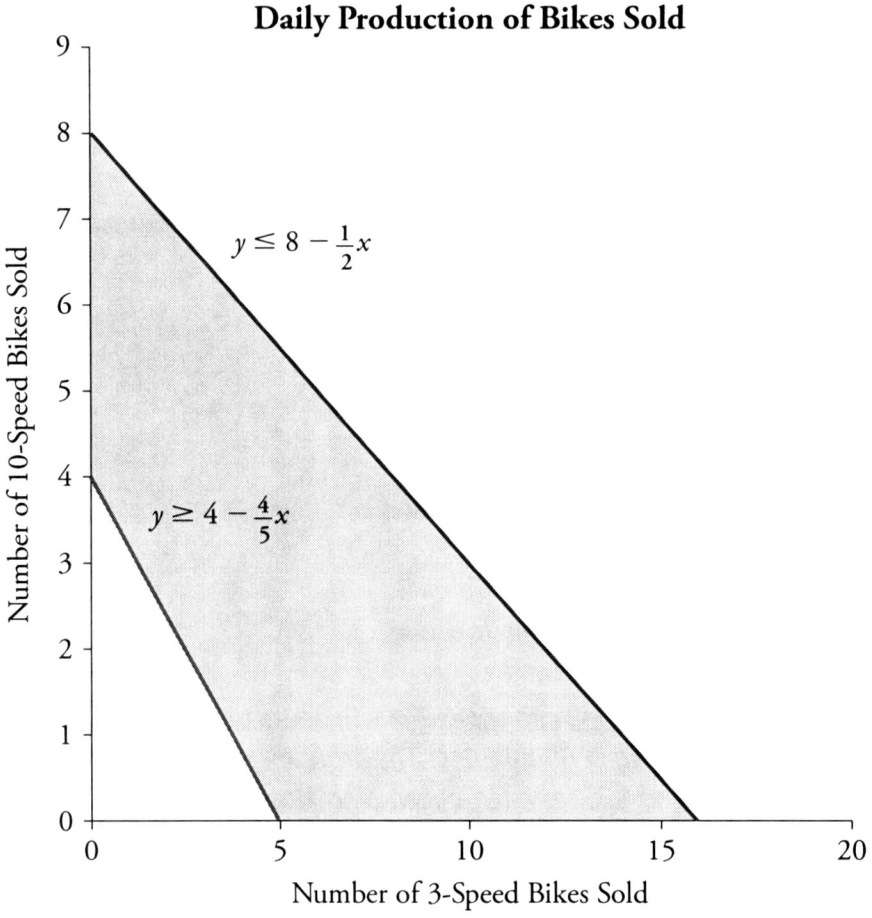

Daily Production of Bikes Sold

Realize that $x \geq 0$ and $y \geq 0$, since the number of bikes assembled cannot be a negative number. Graph these as additional constraints on the problem. The number of bikes assembled must always be an integer value, so points within the shaded area of the graph must have integer values. The maximum profit will occur at or near a corner of the shaded portion of this graph. Those points occur at $(0, 4)$, $(0, 8)$, $(16, 0)$, or $(5, 0)$.

Since profits are $60/three-speed and $75/ten-speed, the profits for these four points would be:

    $(0, 4)$ $60(0) + 75(4) = 300$
    $(0, 8)$ $60(0) + 75(8) = 600$
    $(16, 0)$ $60(16) + 75(0) = 960$ ← Maximum profit
    $(5, 0)$ $60(5) + 75(0) = 300$

The maximum profit will occur if 16 three-speed bikes are made daily.

COMPETENCY 12
UNDERSTAND OPERATIONS WITH ALGEBRAIC EXPRESSIONS AND FUNCTIONAL NOTATION

SKILL 12.1 Factoring quadratics

A quadratic equation is written in the form $ax^2 + bx + c = 0$. To solve a quadratic equation by factoring, at least one of the factors must equal zero.

Example: $3x^2 - 20x - 7$ has two factors:

$(3x + 1)$ and $(x - 7)$

To confirm, we use the FOIL method.

$(3x + 1)$ and $(x - 7)$
  a   b   c   d

1. **F** = multiply the First terms (a and c) → $3x \times x = 3x^2$
2. **O** = multiply the Outside terms (a and d) → $3x \times -7 = -21x$
3. **I** = multiply the Inside terms (b and c) → $1 \times x = x$
   Add the inside and outside answers → $-21x + x = -20x$
4. **L** = multiply the Last terms → $1 \times -7 = -7$
   Corresponding to $3x^2 - 20x - 7$

Example: Solve the equation:

$x^2 + 10x - 24 = 0$	
$(x + 12)(x - 2) = 0$	Factor.
$x + 12 = 0$ or $x - 2 = 0$	Set each factor equal to 0.
$x = -12 \quad\quad x = 2$	Solve.

Check:

$x^2 + 10x - 24 = 0$
$(-12)^2 + 10(-12) - 24 = 0$ $(2)^2 + 10(2) - 24 = 0$
$144 - 120 - 24 = 0$ $4 + 20 - 24 = 0$
$0 = 0$ $0 = 0$

MATHEMATICS

SKILL 12.2 Performing operations on and simplifying polynomial expressions

Whether you are adding, subtracting, or multiplying polynomials, it is always best to write them in standard form; i.e., with the highest degree polynomial first and the others in descending order.

Polynomial expressions are of the form ax^k, where k is the degree of the polynomial and a is the coefficient. Whether you are adding, subtracting, or multiplying polynomials, it is always best to write them in standard form; i.e., with the highest degree polynomial first and the others in descending order.

To add two polynomials, add the coefficients of like terms.

Example: Add $4x^2 + 2x - 10$ and $2x^2 + 2x + 12$:
Solution: $(4x^2 + 2x - 10) + (2x^2 + 2x + 12) =$
$(4x^2 + 2x^2) + (2x + 2x) + (-10 + 12) =$
$6x^2 + 4x + 2$

To subtract a polynomial, you must subtract each of its terms.

Example: Subtract $4x^2 - 2x - 8$ from $6x^2 - 10x + 6$:
Solution: $(6x^2 - 10x + 6) - (4x^2 - 2x - 8) =$
$6x^2 - 10x + 6 - 4x^2 + 2x + 8 =$
$(6x^2 - 4x^2) + (-10x + 2x) + (6 + 8) =$
$2x^2 - 8x + 14$

To multiply two polynomials, each term of one polynomial must be multiplied by each term of the other polynomial.

Example: Multiply: $(2x^2 - 3x - 2)(x - 10)$
Solution: $(2x^2 - 3x - 2)(x - 10) =$
$2x^2(x - 10) - 3x(x - 10) - 2(x - 10) =$
$2x^3 - 20x^2 - 3x^2 + 30x - 2x + 10 =$
$2x^3 - 23x^2 + 28x + 10$

SKILL 12.3 Understand rational expressions and radical expressions

Simplify Rational Expressions

Rational expressions can be changed into other equivalent fractions by either reducing them or by changing them to have a common denominator. When dividing any number of terms by a single term, divide or reduce their coefficients. Then subtract the exponent of a variable on the bottom from the exponent of the same variable from the numerator.

To reduce a rational expression with more than one term in the denominator, the expression must be factored first. Factors that are exactly the same will cancel and each become a 1. Factors that have exactly the opposite signs of each other, such as $(a - b)$ and $(b - a)$, will cancel and one factor becomes a 1 and the other becomes a -1.

To make a fraction have a common denominator, factor the fraction. Determine what factors are missing from that particular denominator, and multiply both the numerator and the denominator by those missing factors. This gives a new fraction which now has the common denominator.

Simplify these fractions:

1. $\dfrac{24x^3y^6z^3}{8x^2y^2z} = 3xy^4z^2$

2. $\dfrac{3x^2 - 14xy - 5y^2}{x^2 - 25y^2} = \dfrac{(3x + y)(x - 5y)}{(x + 5y)(x - 5y)} = \dfrac{3x + y}{x + 5y}$

3. Rewrite this fraction with a denominator of $(x + 3)(x - 5)(x + 4)$

   $\dfrac{x + 2}{x^2 + 7x + 12} = \dfrac{x + 2}{(x + 3)(x + 4)} = \dfrac{(x + 2)(x - 5)}{(x + 3)(x + 4)(x - 5)}$

Add or Subtract Rational Algebraic Fractions

In order to add or subtract rational expressions, they must have a common denominator. If they don't have a common denominator, then factor the denominators to determine what factors are missing from each denominator to make the LCD. Multiply both numerator and denominator by the missing factor(s). Once the fractions have a common denominator, add or subtract their numerators, but keep the common denominator the same. Factor the numerator if possible, and reduce if there are any factors that can be cancelled.

In order to add or subtract rational expressions, they must have a common denominator.

Example: Find the least common denominator for $6a^3b^2$ and $4ab^3$:
These factor into $2 \times 3 \times a^3 \times b^2$ and $2 \times 2 \times a \times b^3$.
The first expression needs to be multiplied by another 2 and b.
The other expression needs to be multiplied by 3 and a^2.
Then both expressions would be $2 \times 2 \times 3 \times a^3 \times b^3 = 12a^3b^3 = $ LCD.

Example: Find the LCD for $x^2 - 4$, $x^2 + 5x + 6$, and $x^2 + x - 6$:

$x^2 - 4$ factors into $(x - 2)(x + 2)$
$x^2 + 5x + 6$ factors into $(x + 3)(x + 2)$
$x^2 + x - 6$ factors into $(x + 3)(x - 2)$

To make these lists of factors the same, they must all be $(x + 3)(x + 2)(x - 2)$. This is the LCD.

Example:
$$\frac{5}{6a^3b^2} + \frac{1}{4ab^3} = \frac{5(2b)}{6a^3b^2(2b)} + \frac{1(3a^2)}{4ab^3(3a^2)} = \frac{10b}{12a^3b^3} + \frac{3a^2}{12a^3b^3} = \frac{10b + 3a^2}{12a^3b^3}$$

This will not reduce as all 3 terms are not divisible by anything.

Example:
$$\frac{2}{x^2 - 4} - \frac{3}{x^2 + 5x + 6} + \frac{7}{x^2 + x - 6} =$$
$$\frac{2}{(x - 2)(x + 2)} - \frac{3}{(x + 3)(x + 2)} + \frac{7}{(x + 3)(x - 2)} =$$
$$\frac{2(x + 3)}{(x - 2)(x + 2)(x + 3)} - \frac{3(x - 2)}{(x + 3)(x + 2)(x - 2)} + \frac{7(x + 2)}{(x + 3)(x - 2)(x + 2)} =$$
$$\frac{2x + 6}{(x - 2)(x + 2)(x + 3)} - \frac{3x - 6}{(x + 3)(x + 2)(x - 2)} + \frac{7x + 14}{(x + 3)(x - 2)(x + 2)} =$$
$$\frac{2x + 6 - (3x - 6) + 7x + 14}{(x + 3)(x - 2)(x + 2)} = \frac{6x + 26}{(x + 3)(x - 2)(x + 2)}$$

This will not reduce.

Solve Rational Algebraic Equations for One Variable

To solve an algebraic formula for some variable, called r, follow these seven steps:

1. Eliminate any parentheses using the distributive property.

2. Multiply every term by the LCD of any fractions to write an equivalent equation without any fractions. This will cancel out all of the denominators and give an equivalent algebraic equation that can be solved.

3. Move all terms containing the variable, r, to one side of the equation. Move all terms without the variable to the opposite side of the equation.

4. If there are 2 or more terms containing the variable r, factor only r out of each of those terms as a common factor.

5. Divide both sides of the equation by the number or expression being multiplied times the variable, r.

6. Reduce fractions if possible.

7. Remember there are restrictions on values allowed for variables because the denominator cannot equal zero.

Examples:

Solve $A = p + prt$ for t.

$$A - p = prt$$
$$\frac{A - p}{pr} = \frac{prt}{pr}$$
$$\frac{A - p}{pr} = t$$

Solve $A = p + prt$ for p.

$$A = p(1 + rt)$$
$$\frac{A}{1 + rt} = \frac{p(1 + rt)}{1 + rt}$$
$$\frac{A}{1 + rt} = p$$

1. Solve $A = \frac{1}{2}h(b_1 + b_2)$ for b_2.

   $A = \frac{1}{2}hb_1 + \frac{1}{2}hb_2$ ← Step a.
   $2A = hb_1 + hb_2$ ← Step b.
   $2A - hb_1 = hb_2$ ← Step c.
   $\frac{2A - hb_1}{h} = \frac{hb_2}{h}$ ← Step d.
   $\frac{2A - hb_1}{h} = hb_2$ ← Will not reduce.

2. Solve $\frac{72}{x + 3} = \frac{32}{x + 3} + 5$ for x LCD $= x + 3$, so multiply by this.

   $(x + 3) \times \frac{72}{x + 3} = (x + 3) \times \frac{32}{x + 3} + 5(x + 3)$
   $72 = 32 + 5(x + 3) \rightarrow 72 = 32 + 5x + 15$
   $72 = 47 + 5x \quad \rightarrow 25 = 5x$
   $5 = x$ (This checks too).

3. Solve $\frac{12}{2x^2 - 4x} + \frac{13}{5} = \frac{9}{x - 2}$ for x: Factor $2x^2 - 4x = 2x(x - 2)$.
                                                   LCD $= 5 \times 2x(x - 2)$ or $10x(x - 2)$

   $10x(x - 2) \times \frac{12}{2x(x - 2)} + 10x(x - 2) \times \frac{13}{5} = \frac{9}{x - 2} \times 10x(x - 2)$
   $60 + 2x(x - 2)(13) = 90x$
   $26x^2 - 142x + 60 = 0$
   $2(13x^2 - 71x + 30) = 0$
   $2(x - 5)(13x - 6)$
   so $x = 5$ or $x = \frac{6}{13}$ ← both check

Solve Word Problems with Rational Algebraic Expressions and Equations

Some problems can be solved using equations with rational expressions. First write the equation. To solve it, multiply each term by the LCD of all fractions. This will cancel out all of the denominators and give an equivalent algebraic equation that can be solved.

Some problems can be solved using equations with rational expressions.

Example: The denominator of a fraction is two less than three times the numerator. If 3 is added to both the numerator and denominator, the new fraction equals $\frac{1}{2}$.

Original fraction: $\frac{x}{3x-2}$

$\frac{x+3}{3x+1} = \frac{1}{2}$

Revised fraction: $\frac{x+3}{3x+1}$

$2x + 6 = 3x + 1$

$x = 5$

So the original fraction is $\frac{5}{13}$.

Example: Elly Mae can feed the animals in 15 minutes. Jethro can feed them in 10 minutes. How long will it take them to feed the animals if they work together?

If Elly Mae can feed the animals in 15 minutes, then she could feed $\frac{1}{15}$ of them in 1 minute, $\frac{2}{15}$ of them in 2 minutes, and $\frac{x}{15}$ of them in x minutes. In the same fashion, Jethro could feed $\frac{x}{10}$ of them in x minutes. Together they complete 1 job. The equation is:

$\frac{x}{15} + \frac{x}{10} = 1$

Multiply each term by the LCD (least common denominator) of 30:

$2x \times 3x = 30$

$x = 6$ minutes

Example: A salesman drove 480 miles from Pittsburgh to Hartford. The next day he returned the same distance to Pittsburgh in half an hour less time than his original trip took, because he increased his average speed by 4 mph. Find his original speed.

Since distance = rate $\times$ time, then time = $\frac{\text{distance}}{\text{rate}}$

original time $-$ 1/2 hour = shorter return time

$\frac{480}{x} - \frac{1}{2} = \frac{480}{x+4}$

Multiplying by the LCD of $2x(x + 4)$, the equation becomes:

$480[2(x + 4)] - 1[x(x + 4)] = 480(2x)$

$960x + 3840 - x^2 - 4x = 960x$

$x^2 + 4x - 3840 = 0$

$(x + 64)(x - 60) = 0$

$x = 60$

60 mph is the original speed, 64 mph is the faster return speed.

Simplifying Radical Expressions

To simplify a radical expression, follow these steps:

1. Factor the number or coefficient completely.

2. For square roots, group like factors in pairs. For cube roots, arrange like factors in groups of three. For nth roots, group like factors in groups of n.

3. For each of these groups, put one of that number outside the radical. Any factors that cannot be combined in groups should be multiplied together and left inside the radical.

4. The index number of a radical is the little number on the front of the radical. For a cube root, the index is 3. If no index appears, then the index is 2 for square roots.

5. For variables inside the radical, divide the index number of the radical into each exponent. The quotient (the answer to the division) is the new exponent to be written on the variable outside the radical. The remainder from the division is the new exponent on the variable remaining inside the radical sign. If the remainder is zero, then the variable no longer appears in the radical sign.

If the index number is an odd number, you can still simplify the radical to get a negative solution.

Note: Remember that the square root of a negative number can be designated by replacing the negative sign inside that square root with an i in front of the radical (to signify an imaginary number). Then simplify the remaining positive radical by the normal method. Include the i outside the radical as part of the answer.

Examples:

$$\sqrt{50a^4b^7} = \sqrt{5 \times 5 \times 2 \times a^4 \times b^7} = 5a^2b^3\sqrt{2b}$$

$$7x\sqrt[3]{16x^5} = 7x\sqrt[3]{2 \times 2 \times 2 \times 2 \times x^5} = 7x \times 2x\sqrt[3]{2x^2} = 14x^2\sqrt[3]{2x^2}$$

Rewrite Expressions Involving Radicals as Expressions with Rational Number Exponents

An expression with a radical sign can be rewritten using a rational exponent. The radicand becomes the base, which will have the rational exponent. The index number on the front of the radical sign becomes the denominator of the rational exponent. The numerator of the rational exponent is the exponent, which was originally inside the radical sign on the original base. *Remember:* if no index number appears on the front of the radical, then it is a 2. If no exponent appears inside the radical, then use a 1 as the numerator of the rational exponent.

$$\sqrt[5]{b^3} = b^{\frac{3}{5}}$$

$$\sqrt[4]{ab^3} = a^{\frac{1}{4}}b^{\frac{3}{4}}$$

When an expression has a rational exponent, it can be rewritten using a radical sign. The denominator of the rational exponent becomes the index number on the front of the radical sign. The base of the original expression goes inside the radical sign. The numerator of the rational exponent is an exponent which can be placed either inside the radical sign on the original base or outside the radical as an exponent on the radical expression.

$$a^{\frac{2}{9}} b^{\frac{4}{9}} c^{\frac{8}{9}} = \sqrt[9]{a^2 b^4 c^8}$$
$$3^{\frac{1}{15}} = \sqrt[15]{3}$$

If an expression contains rational expressions with different denominators, rewrite the exponents with a common denominator and then change the problem into a radical.

$$a^{\frac{2}{3}} b^{\frac{1}{2}} c^{\frac{3}{5}} = a^{\frac{20}{30}} b^{\frac{15}{30}} c^{\frac{18}{30}} = \sqrt[30]{a^{20} b^{15} c^{18}}$$

Add, Subtract, Multiply, Divide, and Simplify Radical Expressions

Before you can add or subtract square roots, the numbers or expressions inside the radicals must be the same. First, simplify the radicals, if possible. If the numbers or expressions inside the radicals are the same, add or subtract the numbers (or like expressions) in front of the radicals. Keep the expression inside the radical the same. Be sure that the radicals are simplified as much as possible.

Note: If the expressions inside the radicals are not the same, and cannot be simplified to become the same, then they cannot be combined by addition or subtraction.

To multiply 2 square roots together, follow these steps:

1. Multiply what is outside the radicals together.

2. Multiply what is inside the radicals together.

3. Simplify the radical if possible. Multiply whatever is in front of the radical times the expression that is coming out of the radical.

To divide one square root by another, follow these steps:

1. Work separately on what is inside or outside the square root sign.

2. Divide or reduce the coefficients outside the radical.

3. Divide any like variables outside the radical.

4. Divide or reduce the coefficients inside the radical.

5. Divide any like variables inside the radical.

6. If there is still a radical in the denominator, multiply both the numerator and denominator by the radical in the denominator. Simplify both resulting radicals and reduce again outside the radical (if possible).

UNDERSTAND OPERATIONS WITH ALGEBRAIC EXPRESSIONS AND FUNCTIONAL NOTATION

Example: Simplify the following expressions

1. $6\sqrt{7} + 2\sqrt{5} + 3\sqrt{7} = 9\sqrt{7} + 2\sqrt{5}$ These cannot be combined further.

2. $5\sqrt{12} + \sqrt{48} - 2\sqrt{75} = 5\sqrt{2 \times 2 \times 3} + \sqrt{2 \times 2 \times 2 \times 2 \times 3} - 2\sqrt{3 \times 5 \times 5} = 5 \times 2\sqrt{3} + 2 \times 2\sqrt{3} - 2 \times 5\sqrt{3} = 10\sqrt{3} + 4\sqrt{3} - 10\sqrt{3} = 4\sqrt{3}$

3. $(6\sqrt{15x})(7\sqrt{10x}) = 42\sqrt{150x^2} = 42\sqrt{2 \times 3 \times 5 \times 5 \times x^2} = 42 \times 5x\sqrt{2 \times 3} = 210x\sqrt{6}$

4. $\dfrac{105x^8 \sqrt{18x^5y^6}}{30x^2 \sqrt{27x^2y^4}} = \dfrac{7x^6(x^2)(y^3) \sqrt{2x}}{2(x)(y^2) \sqrt{3}} = \dfrac{7x^7y \sqrt{2x}}{2\sqrt{3}} = \dfrac{7x^7y \sqrt{2x}}{2\sqrt{3}} \times \dfrac{\sqrt{3}}{\sqrt{3}} = \dfrac{7x^7y \sqrt{6x}}{6}$

Solving Radical Equations

To solve a radical equation, follow these steps:

1. Get a radical alone on one side of the equation.

2. Raise both *sides* of the equation to the power equal to the index number. *Do not raise them to that power term by term, but raise the entire side to that power.* Combine any like terms.

3. If there is another radical still in the equation, repeat steps one and two (i.e., get that radical alone on one side of the equation and raise both sides to a power equal to the index). Repeat as necessary until the radicals are all gone.

4. Solve the resulting equation.

5. Once you have found the answer(s), substitute them back into the original equation to check them. Sometimes there are solutions that do not check in the original equation. These are extraneous solutions, which are not correct and must be eliminated. If a problem has more than one potential solution, each solution must be checked separately.

*Example: Solve and **check** the following expressions*

1. $\sqrt{2x + 1} + 7 = x$
$\sqrt{2x + 1} = x - 7$
$(\sqrt{2x + 1})^2 = (x - 7)^2$ ← BOTH sides are squared.
$2x + 1 = x^2 - 14x + 49$
$0 = x^2 - 16x + 48$
$0 = (x - 12)(x - 4)$
$x = 12, x = 4$

MATHEMATICS

When you check these answers in the original equation, 12 checks; however, *4 does not check in the original equation.* Therefore, the only answer is $x = 12$.

2. $\sqrt{3x + 4} = 2\sqrt{x - 4}$
   $(\sqrt{3x + 4})^2 = (2\sqrt{x - 4})^2$
   $3x + 4 = 4(x - 4)$
   $3x + 4 = 4x - 16$
   $20 = x$ ← This checks in the original equation.

3. $\sqrt[4]{7x - 3} = 3$
   $(\sqrt[4]{7x - 3})^4 = 3^4$
   $7x - 3 = 81$
   $7x = 84$
   $x = 12$ ← This checks out with the original equation.

4. $\sqrt{x} = -3$
   $(\sqrt{x})^2 = (-3)^2$
   $x = 9$ ← This does NOT check in the original equation. Since there is no other answer to check, the correct answer is the empty set or the null set or $\varnothing$.

SKILL 12.4 Apply principles of functions and functional notation

A **RELATION** is any set of ordered pairs. The **DOMAIN** of a relation is the set containing all the first coordinates of the ordered pairs, and the **RANGE** of a relation is the set containing all the second coordinates of the ordered pairs.

A **FUNCTION** is a relation in which each value in the domain corresponds to only one value in the range. It is notable, however, that a value in the range may correspond to any number of values in the domain. Thus, although a function is necessarily a relation, not all relations are functions, since a relation is not bound by this rule.

RELATION: any set of ordered pairs

DOMAIN: the set containing all the first coordinates of the ordered pairs

RANGE: the set containing all the second coordinates of the ordered pairs

UNDERSTAND OPERATIONS WITH ALGEBRAIC EXPRESSIONS AND FUNCTIONAL NOTATION

On a graph, use the **VERTICAL LINE TEST** to check whether a relation is a function. If any vertical line intersects the graph of a relation in more than one point, then the relation is not a function.

A relation is considered **ONE-TO-ONE** if each value in the domain corresponds to only one value in the range, and each value in the range corresponds to only one value in the domain. Thus, a one-to-one relation is also a function, but it adds an additional condition.

In the same way that the graph of a relation can be examined using the vertical line test to determine whether it is a function, the **HORIZONTAL LINE TEST** can be used to determine if a function is a one-to-one relation. If no horizontal lines superimposed on the plot intersect the graph of the relation in more than one place, then the relation is one-to-one (assuming it also passes the vertical line test and, therefore, is a function).

A mapping is essentially the same as a function. Mappings (or maps) can be depicted using diagrams with arrows drawn from each element of the domain to the corresponding element (or elements) of the range. If two arrows originate from any single element in the domain, then the mapping is not a function. Likewise, for a function, if each arrow is drawn to a unique value in the range (that is, there are no cases where more than one arrow is drawn to a given value in the range), then the relation is one-to-one.

Example: Determine the domain and range of this mapping.

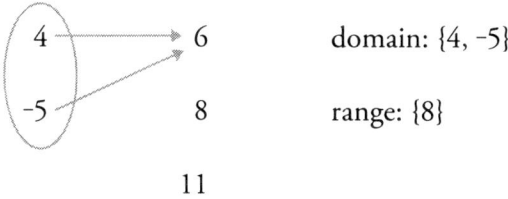

domain: {4, -5}

range: {8}

> **FUNCTION:** a relation in which each value in the domain corresponds to only one value in the range

> **VERTICAL LINE TEST:** states that if any vertical line intersects the graph of a relation in more than one point, then the relation is not a function

> **ONE-TO-ONE RELATIONSHIP:** one in which each value in the domain corresponds to only one value in the range, and each value in the range corresponds to only one value in the domain

> **HORIZONTAL LINE TEST:** states that if no horizontal line intersects the graph of a function in more than one place, then the function is one-to-one

Loosely speaking, an equation like $y = 3x + 5$ describes a relationship between the independent variable x and the dependent variable y. Thus, y is written as $f(x)$ "function of x." But y may not be a "true" function. For a "true" function to exist, there is a relationship between a set of all independent variables (domain) and a set of all outputs or dependent variables (range) such that each element of the domain corresponds to one element of the range. (For any input we get exactly one output).

Example:

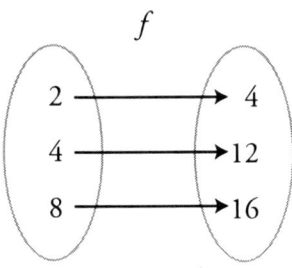 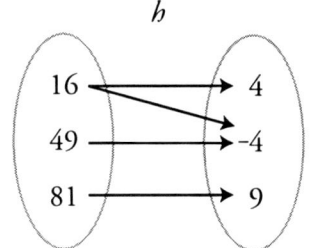

Domain, *X*   Range, *Y*   Domain, *X*   Range, *Y*
This is a "true" function.   This is not a "true" function.

Example: Given a function $f(x) = 3x + 5$, find $f(2); f(0); f(-10)$

$f(2)$ means find the value of the function value at $x = 2$.
$f(2) = 3(2) + 5 = 6 + 5 = 11$
$f(0) = 3(0) + 5 = 0 + 5 = 5$ Substitute for *x*.
$f(-10) = 3(-10) + 5 = -30 + 5 = -25$

Example: Given $h(t) = 3t2 + t - 9$, find $h(-4)$.
$h(-4) = 3(-4)^2 - 4 - 9$
$h(-4) = 3(16) - 13$ Substitute for *t*.
$h(-4) = 48 - 13$
$h(-4) = 35$

COMPETENCY 13
SOLVE PROBLEMS INVOLVING QUADRATIC EQUATIONS

SKILL 13.1 Graph quadratic functions and quadratic inequalities

QUADRATIC FUNCTIONS: functions of the form $f(x) = ax^2 + bx + c$.

QUADRATIC FUNCTIONS are functions of the form $f(x) = ax^2 + bx + c$. A common tool used to solve quadratic equations in scientific problems is the quadratic formula. The quadratic formula produces the solutions of a standard form quadratic equation.

SOLVE PROBLEMS INVOLVING QUADRATIC EQUATIONS

Graphs of Quadratic Functions

The graphs of quadratic functions are parabolas. PARABOLAS are u-shaped curves that may open upward or downward and vary in height and steepness. To graph quadratic functions, it is best to first convert the function to standard form. Standard form for quadratic functions is $f(x) = a(x - h)^2 + k$. Working from standard form, the vertical axis of symmetry is the line $x = h$. The vertex is the point (h, k). Finally, the parabola opens up if a is positive and down if a is negative.

PARABOLAS: graphs of quadratic functions

Quadratic Formula
$$x = \frac{-b \pm \sqrt{b^2 - 4ac}}{2a}$$

Transformations of Quadratic Graphs

Different types of function transformations affect the graph and characteristics of a function in predictable ways. The basic types of transformation are horizontal and vertical shift, horizontal and vertical scaling, and reflection. As an example of the types of transformations, we will consider transformations of the functions $f(x) = x^2$.

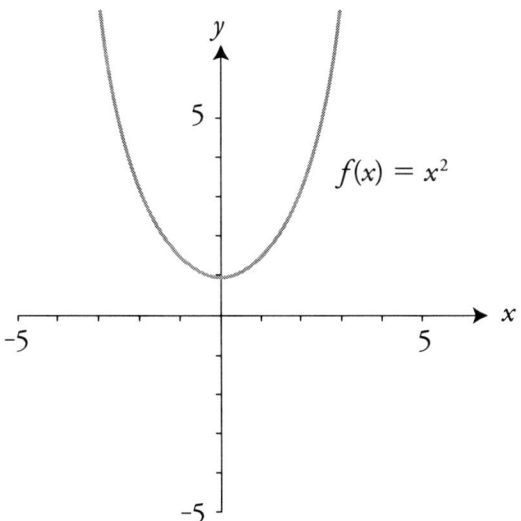

Horizontal shifts take the form $g(x) = f(x \pm c)$. For example, we obtain the graph of the function $g(x) = (x + 2)^2$ by shifting the graph of $f(x) = x^2$ two units to the left. The graph of the function $h(x) = (x - 2)^2$ is the graph of $f(x) = x^2$ shifted two units to the right.

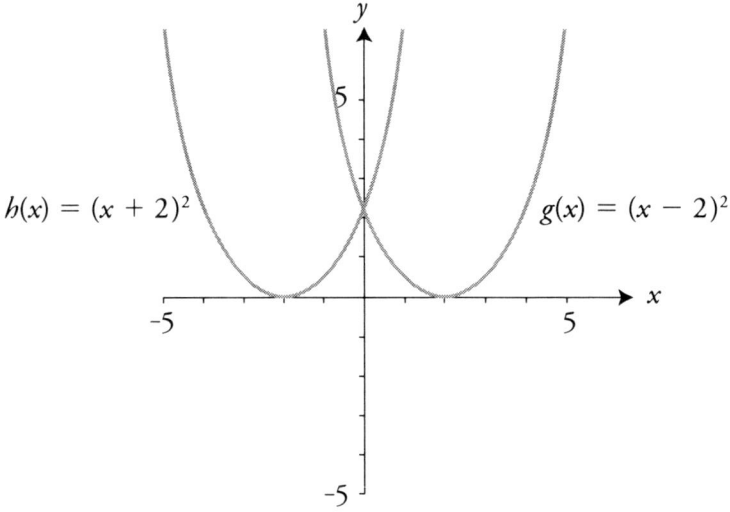

Vertical shifts take the form $g(x) = f(x) \pm c$. For example, we obtain the graph of the function $g(x) = (x^2) - 2$ by shifting the graph of $f(x) = x^2$ two units down. The graph of the function $h(x) = (x^2) + 2$ is the graph of $f(x) = x^2$ shifted two units up.

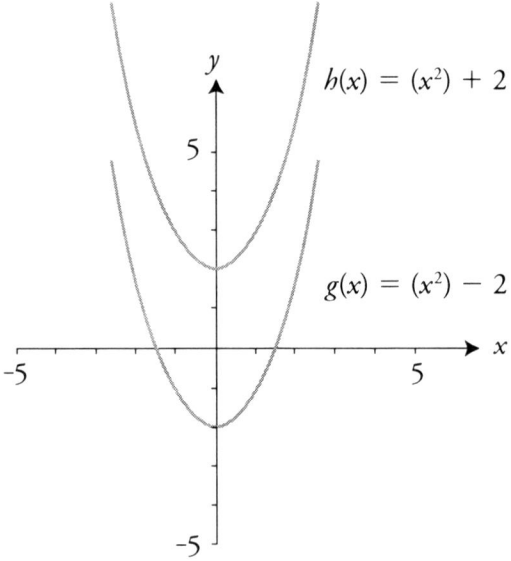

Horizontal scaling takes the form $g(x) = f(cx)$. For example, we obtain the graph of the function $g(x) = (2x)^2$ by compressing the graph of $f(x) = x^2$ in the x-direction by a factor of two. If $c > 1$ the graph is compressed in the x-direction, while if $1 > c > 0$ the graph is stretched in the x-direction.

SOLVE PROBLEMS INVOLVING QUADRATIC EQUATIONS

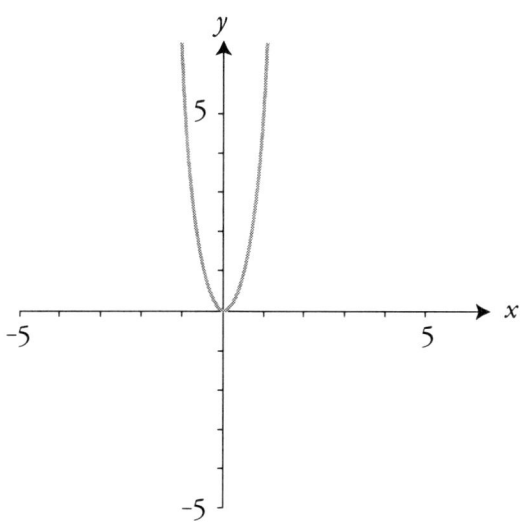

Vertical scaling takes the form $g(x) = cf(x)$. For example, we obtain the graph of $g(x) = \frac{1}{2}(x^2)$ by compressing the graph of $f(x) = x^2$ in the y-direction by a factor of $\frac{1}{2}$. If $c > 1$ the graph is stretched in the y-direction while if $1 > c > 0$ the graph is compressed in the y-direction.

Related to scaling is reflection, in which the graph of a function flips across either the x or y-axis. Reflections take the form of $g(x) = f(-x)$, horizontal reflection, and $g(x) = -f(x)$, vertical reflection. For example, we obtain the graph of $g(x) = -(x^2)$ by reflecting the graph of $f(x) = x^2$ across the x-axis. Note that in the case of $f(x) = x^2$, horizontal reflection produces the same graph because the function is horizontally symmetrical.

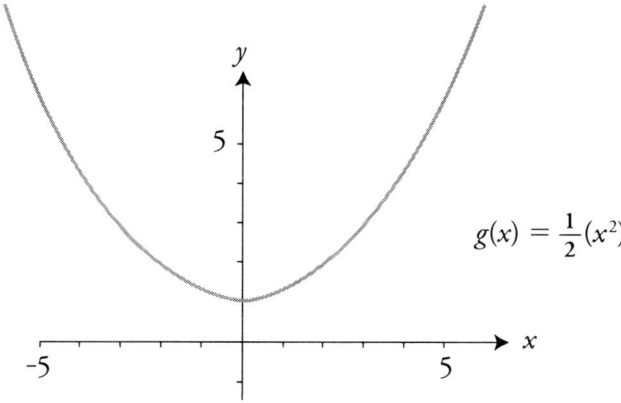

$g(x) = \frac{1}{2}(x^2)$

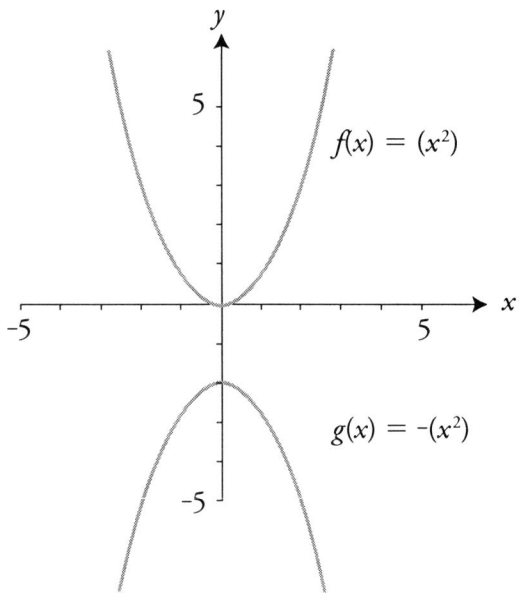

SKILL 13.2 Solve quadratic equations using factoring, completing the square, or the quadratic formula

A quadratic equation that cannot be solved by factoring can be solved by completing the square.

Example: Solve the equation.

$x^2 - 6x + 8 = 0$
$x^2 - 6x = -8$ Move the constant to the right side.
$x^2 - 6x + 9 = -8 + 9$ Add the square of half the coefficient of x to both sides.
$(x - 3)^2 = 1$ Write the left side as a perfect square.
$x - 3 = \pm\sqrt{1}$ Take the square root of both sides.
$x - 3 = 1 \quad x - 3 = -1$ Solve.
$x = 4 \quad\quad x = 2$

Check:
$x^2 - 6x + 8 = 0$
$4^2 - 6(4) + 8 = 0 \quad\quad 2^2 - 6(2) + 8 = 0$
$16 - 24 + 8 = 0 \quad\quad 4 - 12 + 8 = 0$
$0 = 0 \quad\quad\quad\quad\quad 0 = 0$

SOLVE PROBLEMS INVOLVING QUADRATIC EQUATIONS

The general technique for graphing quadratics is the same as for graphing linear equations. Graphing quadratic equations, however, results in a parabola instead of a straight line.

Example: Graph $y = 3x^2 + x - 2$.

x	$y = 3x^2 + x - 2$
-2	8
-1	0
0	-2
1	2
2	12

The general technique for graphing quadratics is the same as for graphing linear equations. Graphing quadratic equations, however, results in a parabola instead of a straight line.

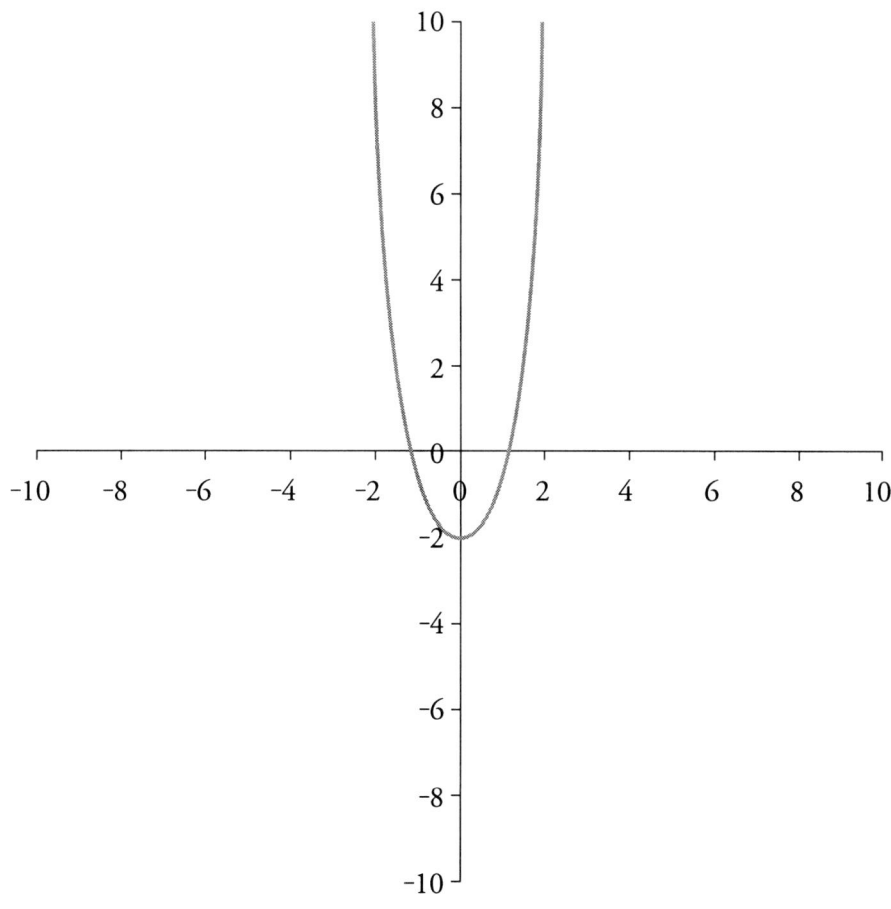

MATHEMATICS

To solve a quadratic equation using the quadratic formula, be sure that your equation is in the form $ax^2 + bx + c = 0$.

To solve a quadratic equation using the quadratic formula, make sure that your equation is in the form $ax^2 + bx + c = 0$. Substitute these values into the formula:

$$x = \frac{-b \pm \sqrt{b^2 - 4ac}}{2a}$$

Example: Solve the equation.

$3x^2 = 7 + 2x \rightarrow 3x^2 - 2x - 7 = 0$

$a = 3 \qquad b = -2 \qquad c = -7$

$$x = \frac{-(-2) \pm \sqrt{(-2)^2 - 4(3)(-7)}}{2(3)}$$

$$x = \frac{2 \pm \sqrt{4 + 84}}{6}$$

$$x = \frac{2 \pm \sqrt{88}}{6}$$

$$x = \frac{2 \pm 2\sqrt{22}}{6}$$

$$x = \frac{1 \pm \sqrt{22}}{3}$$

SKILL 13.3 Solve problems involving quadratic models

Some word problems will give a quadratic equation to be solved. When the quadratic equation is found, set it equal to zero and solve the equation by factoring or the quadratic formula. Examples of this type of problem follow.

Example: Ashland (A) is a certain distance north of Belmont (B). The distance from Belmont east to Carlisle (C) is 5 miles more than the distance from Ashland to Belmont. The distance from Ashland to Carlisle is 10 miles more than the distance from Alberta to Belmont. How far is Ashland from Carlisle?

Solution: Since north and east form a right angle, these distances are the lengths of the legs of a right triangle. If the distance from Ashland to Belmont is x, then from Belmont to Carlisle is $x + 5$, and the distance from Ashland to Carlisle is $x + 10$.

The equation is: $AB^2 + BC^2 = AC^2$

$x^2 + (x + 5)^2 = (x + 10)^2$

$x^2 + x^2 + 10x + 25 = x^2 + 20x + 100$

$2x^2 + 10x + 25 = x^2 + 20x + 100$

SOLVE PROBLEMS INVOLVING QUADRATIC EQUATIONS

$x^2 - 10x - 75 = 0$
$(x - 15)(x + 5) = 0$ Distance cannot be negative.
$x = 15$ Distance from Ashland to Belmont.
$x + 5 = 20$ Distance from Belmont to Carlisle.
$x + 10 = 25$ Distance from Ashland to Carlisle.

Example: The square of a number is equal to 6 more than the original number. Find the original number.

If x = original number, then the equation is:
$x^2 = 6 + x$ Set this equal to zero.
$x^2 - x - 6 = 0$ Now factor.
$(x - 3)(x + 2) = 0$
$x = 3$ or $x = -2$ There are 2 solutions, 3 or -2.

Some word problems can be solved by setting up a quadratic equation or inequality. Examples of this type could be problems that deal with finding a maximum area.

Example: A family wants to enclose 3 sides of a rectangular garden with 200 feet of fence. In order to have a garden with an area of at least 4,800 square feet, find the dimensions of the garden. Assume that a wall or a fence already borders the fourth side of the garden.

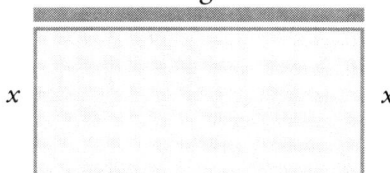

Solution:
Let x = distance from the wall

Then $2x$ feet of fence is used for these 2 sides. The remaining side of the garden would use the rest of the 200 feet of fence, that is, $200 - 2x$ feet of fence. Therefore the width of the garden is x feet and the length is $200 - 2x$ ft.

The area, $200 - 2x$, needs to be greater than or equal to 4,800 sq. ft. So, this problem uses the inequality $4800 \leq 200x - 2x^2$. This becomes $2x^2 - 200x + 4800 \leq 0$. Solving this, we get:

$200x - 2x^2 \geq 4800$
$-2x^2 + 200x - 4800 \geq 0$
$2(-x^2 + 100x - 2400) \geq 0$

$$-x^2 + 100x - 2400 \geq 0$$
$$(-x + 60)(x - 40) \geq 0$$
$$-x + 60 \geq 0$$
$$-x \geq -60$$
$$x \leq 60$$
$$x - 40 \geq 0$$
$$x \geq 40$$

So the area will be at least 4,800 square feet if the width of the garden is from 40 up to 60 feet. (The length of the rectangle would vary from 120 feet to 80 feet depending on the width of the garden.)

Quadratic equations can be used to model different real-life situations. The graphs of these quadratics can be used to determine information about this real life situation.

Example: The height of a projectile fired upward at a velocity of v meters per second from an original height of h meters is $y = h + vx - 4.9x^2$. If a rocket is fired from an original height of 250 meters with an original velocity of 4,800 meters per second, find the approximate time the rocket would drop to sea level (a height of 0).

Solution: The equation for this problem is: $y = 250 + 4800x - 4.9x^2$. If the height at sea level is zero, then $y = 0$ so $0 = 250 + 4800x - 4.9x^2$. Solving this for x could be done by using the quadratic formula. In addition, the approximate time in seconds (x) until the rocket would be at sea level could be estimated by looking at the graph. When the y value of the graph goes from positive to negative then there is a root (also called solution or x intercept) in that interval.

$$x = \frac{-4800 \pm \sqrt{4800^2 - 4(-4.9)(250)}}{2(-4.9)} \approx 980 \text{ or } -0.05 \text{ seconds}$$

Because the time has to be positive, it will be about 980 seconds until the rocket is at sea level.

To graph an inequality, graph the quadratic as if it were an equation; however, if the inequality has just a $>$ or $<$ sign, then make the curve itself dotted. Shade above the curve for $>$ or $\geq$. Shade below the curve for $<$ or $\leq$.

Examples:

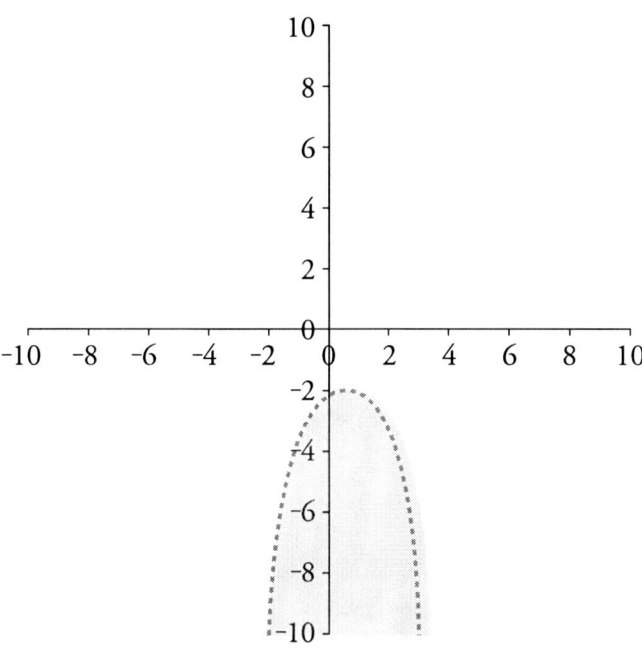

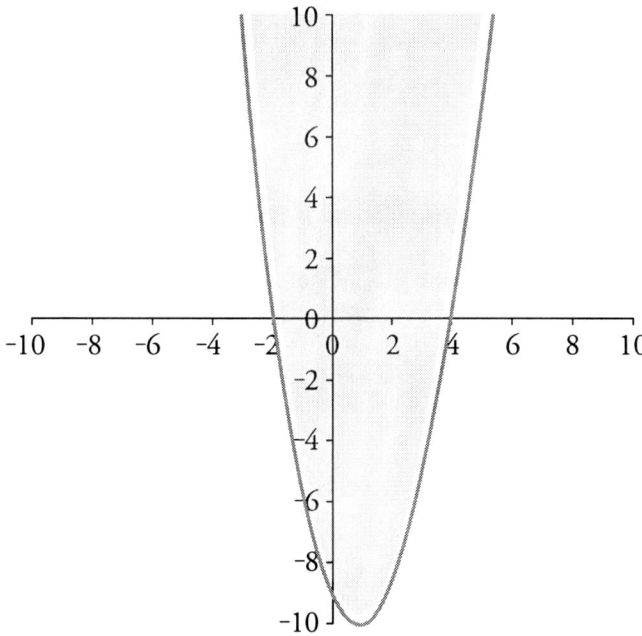

GEOMETRY

COMPETENCY 14
SOLVE PROBLEMS INVOLVING GEOMETRIC FIGURES

> **SKILL 14.1** Solve problems involving two-dimensional geometric figures (e.g., perimeter and area problems)

POLYGON: a simple, closed, two-dimensional figure composed of line segments

We name POLYGONS—simple, closed, two-dimensional figures composed of line segments—according to the number of sides they have.

A QUADRILATERAL is a polygon with four sides.

QUADRILATERAL: a polygon with four sides

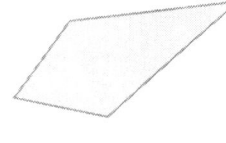
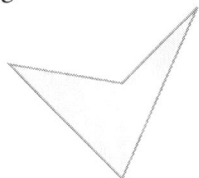

The sum of the measures of the angles of a quadrilateral is 360°.

A TRAPEZOID is a quadrilateral with exactly one pair of parallel sides.

TRAPEZOID: a quadrilateral with exactly *one* pair of parallel sides

In an ISOSCELES TRAPEZOID, the nonparallel sides are congruent.

ISOSCELES TRAPEZOID: a quadrilateral in which the nonparallel sides are congruent

A PARALLELOGRAM is a quadrilateral with two pairs of parallel sides.

PARALLELOGRAM: a quadrilateral with two pairs of parallel sides

SOLVE PROBLEMS INVOLVING GEOMETRIC FIGURES

In a parallelogram:

- The diagonals bisect each other
- Each diagonal divides the parallelogram into two congruent triangles
- Both pairs of opposite sides are congruent
- Both pairs of opposite angles are congruent
- Two adjacent angles are supplementary

A RECTANGLE is a parallelogram with a right angle.

RECTANGLE: a parallelogram with a right angle

A RHOMBUS is a parallelogram with all sides equal in length.

RHOMBUS: a parallelogram with all sides equal in length

A SQUARE is a rectangle with all sides equal in length.

SQUARE: a rectangle with all sides equal in length

Example: True or false?

All squares are rhombuses	True
All parallelograms are rectangles	False—*some* parallelograms are rectangles
All rectangles are parallelograms	True
Some rhombuses are squares	True
Some rectangles are trapezoids	False—trapezoids have only *one* pair of parallel sides
All quadrilaterals are parallelograms	False—some quadrilaterals are parallelograms
Some squares are rectangles	False—all squares are rectangles
Some parallelograms are rhombuses	True

MATHEMATICS

TRIANGLE: a polygon with three sides

ACUTE TRIANGLE: a triangle with exactly three *acute* angles

ACUTE ANGLE: an angle that measures less than 90°

RIGHT TRIANGLE: a triangle with one *right* angle

RIGHT ANGLE: an angle that measures 90°

OBTUSE TRIANGLE: a triangle with one *obtuse* angle

OBTUSE ANGLE: an angle that measures between 90° and 180°

EQUILATERAL TRIANGLE: a triangle in which all sides are the same length

ISOSCELES TRIANGLE: a triangle in which two sides are the same length

SCALENE TRIANGLE: a triangle in which no sides are the same length

PERIMETER: the sum of a polygon the lengths of the sides

A TRIANGLE is a polygon with three sides. We can classify triangles by the types of angles or the lengths of their sides.

An ACUTE TRIANGLE has exactly three *acute* angles. An ACUTE ANGLE is an angle that measures less than 90°.

A RIGHT TRIANGLE has one *right* angle. A RIGHT ANGLE is an angle that measures 90°.

An OBTUSE TRIANGLE has one *obtuse* angle. An OBTUSE ANGLE measures between 90° and 180°.

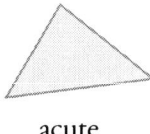 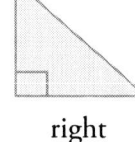 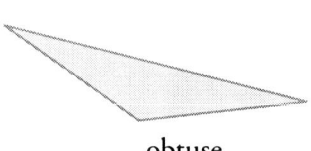

acute   right   obtuse

All three sides of an EQUILATERAL TRIANGLE are the same length.

Two sides of an ISOSCELES TRIANGLE are the same length.

None of the sides of a SCALENE TRIANGLE is the same length.

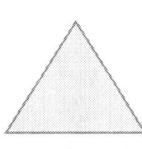 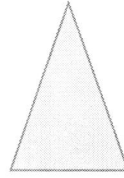 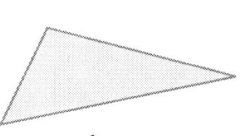

equilateral   isosceles   scalene

Example: Can a triangle have two right angles?
No. A right angle measures 90°; therefore, the sum of two right angles would be 180°, and there could not be a third angle.

Example: Can a triangle have two obtuse angles?
No. Since an obtuse angle measures more than 90°, the sum of two obtuse angles would be greater than 180°.

The PERIMETER of a polygon is the sum of the lengths of the sides.

The AREA of a polygon is the number of square units covered by the figure.

SOLVE PROBLEMS INVOLVING GEOMETRIC FIGURES

FIGURE	AREA FORMULA	PERIMETER FORMULA
Rectangle	LW	2(L + W)
Triangle	$\frac{1}{2}bh$	a + b + c
Parallelogram	bh	sum of lengths of sides
Trapezoid	$\frac{1}{2}h(a + b)$	sum of lengths of sides

AREA: the number of square units covered by a figure; the space a figure occupies

Perimeter of a polygon

Example: A farmer has a piece of land shaped as shown below. He wishes to fence this land at an estimated cost of $25 per linear foot. What is the total cost of fencing this property, to the nearest foot?

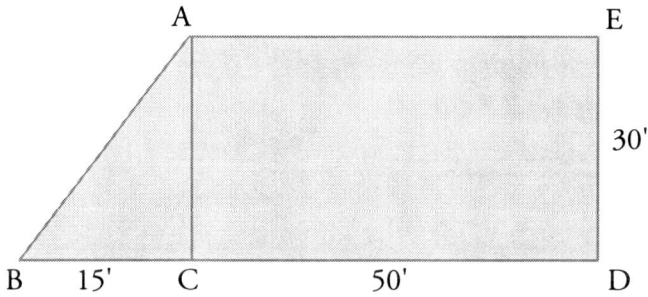

For the right triangle ABC, AC = 30 and BC = 15.
Since $(AB)^2 = (AC)^2 + (BC)^2$
$(AB)^2 = (30)^2 + (15)^2$
So feet $\sqrt{(AB)^2} = AB = \sqrt{1125} = 33.5410$ feet
To the nearest foot, AB = 34 feet.
Perimeter of the piece of land =
34 + 15 + 50 + 30 + 50 = 179 feet
Cost of fencing = $25 × 179 = $4,475

Area of a polygon

Area is the space that a figure occupies.

Example: What will be the cost of carpeting a rectangular office that measures 12 feet by 15 feet if the carpet costs $12.50 per square yard?

The problem is asking you to determine the area of the office. The area of a rectangle is *length × width = A*.

Substitute the given values in the equation $A = lw$.

$A = (12 \text{ ft})(15 \text{ ft})$
$A = 180 \text{ ft}^2$

The problem asks you to determine the cost of the carpet at $12.50 per square yard.

First, you need to convert 180 ft² into yd².

1 yd = 3 ft
(1 yd)(1 yd) = (3 ft)(3 ft)
$1 \text{ yd}^2 = 9 \text{ ft}^2$
Hence, $\frac{180 \text{ ft}^2}{1} = \frac{1 \text{ yd}^2}{9 \text{ ft}^2} = \frac{20}{1} = 20 \text{ yd}^2$

The carpet costs $12.50 per square yard; thus, the cost of carpeting the office is $12.50 × 20 = $250.00.

Example: Find the area of a parallelogram whose base is 6.5 cm and the height of the altitude to that base is 3.7 cm.

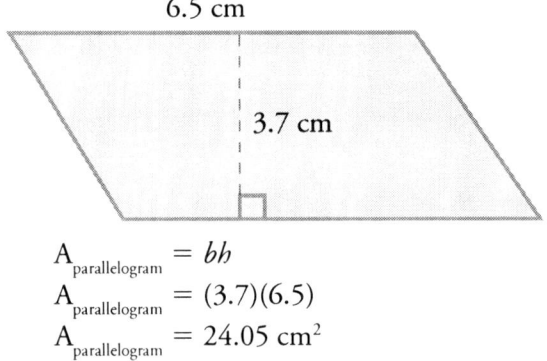

$A_{parallelogram} = bh$
$A_{parallelogram} = (3.7)(6.5)$
$A_{parallelogram} = 24.05 \text{ cm}^2$

Example: Find the area of this triangle.

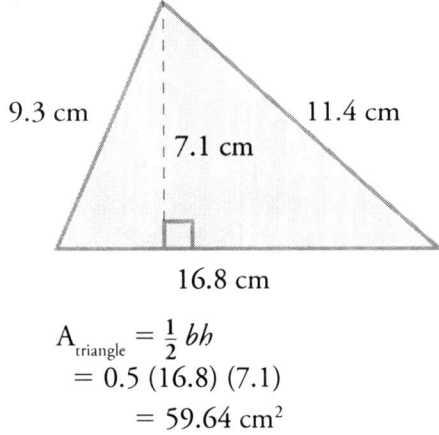

$A_{triangle} = \frac{1}{2}bh$
$= 0.5 (16.8)(7.1)$
$= 59.64 \text{ cm}^2$

SOLVE PROBLEMS INVOLVING GEOMETRIC FIGURES

Example: Find the area of this trapezoid.

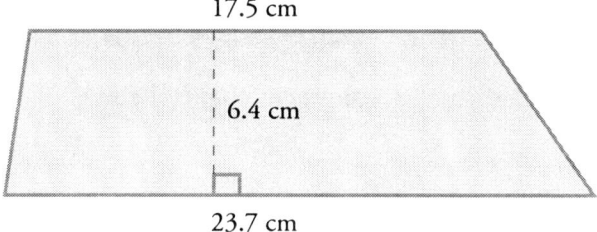

The area of a trapezoid equals one-half the sum of the bases times the altitude.

$A_{trapezoid} = \frac{1}{2} h (b_1 + b_2)$
$= 0.5 (6.4) (17.5 + 23.7)$
$= 131.84 \text{ cm}^2$

Circles

The distance around a circle is called the CIRCUMFERENCE. The Greek letter pi (π) represents the ratio of the circumference to the diameter.

$\pi \approx 3.14 \approx \frac{22}{7}$.

CIRCUMFERENCE: the distance around a circle

The circumference of a circle is found by the formula $C = 2\pi r$ or $C = \pi d$, where r is the radius of the circle and d is the diameter.

The area of a circle is found by the formula $A = \pi r^2$.

Example: Find the circumference and area of a circle whose radius is 7 meters.

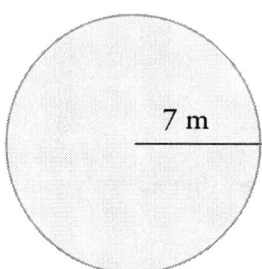

$C = \pi r$
$= 2(3.14)(7)$
$= 43.96 \text{ m}$

$A = \pi r^2$
$= 3.14(7)(7)$
$= 153.86 \text{ m}^2$

MATHEMATICS

> **SKILL 14.2** Solve problems involving three-dimensional geometric figures (e.g., volume and surface area problems)

CYLINDER: a space figure that has two parallel, congruent circular bases

A CYLINDER is a space figure that has two parallel, congruent circular bases.

SPHERE: a space figure having all its points the same distance from the center

A SPHERE is a space figure having all its points the same distance from the center.

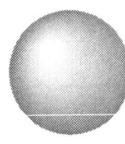

CONE: a space figure having a circular base and a single vertex

A CONE is a space figure having a circular base and a single vertex.

PYRAMID: a space figure with a square base and four triangle-shaped sides

A PYRAMID is a space figure with a square base and four triangle-shaped sides.

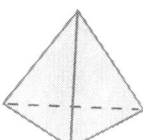

TETRAHEDRON: a four-sided space triangle; each face is a triangle

A TETRAHEDRON is a four-sided space triangle. Each face is a triangle.

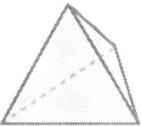

PRISM: a space figure with two congruent, parallel bases that are polygons

A PRISM is a space figure with two congruent, parallel bases that are polygons.

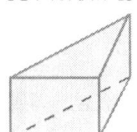

Volume and surface area

We use the following formulas to compute volume and surface area:

FIGURE	LATERAL AREA	TOTAL AREA	VOLUME
Regular Pyramid	$\frac{1}{2}Pl$	$\frac{1}{2}Pl + B$	$\frac{1}{3}Bh$

SOLVE PROBLEMS INVOLVING GEOMETRIC FIGURES

FIGURE	VOLUME	TOTAL SURFACE AREA
Right Cylinder	$\pi r^2 h$	$2\pi rh + 2\pi r^2$
Right Cone	$\dfrac{\pi r^2 h}{3}$	$\pi r \sqrt{r^2 + h^2} + \pi r^2$
Sphere	$\dfrac{4}{3}\pi r^3$	$4\pi r^2$
Rectangular Solid	LWH	$2LW + 2WH + 2LH$

P = Perimeter, h = height, B = Area of Base, l = slant height

Example: What is the volume of a shoe box with a length of 35 cm, a width of 20 cm, and a height of 15 cm?

Volume of a rectangular solid
   = Length × Width × Height
   = 35 × 20 × 15
   = 10,500 cm³

Example: A water company is trying to decide whether to use traditional cylindrical paper cups or to offer conical paper cups, since both cost the same. The traditional cups are 8 cm wide and 14 cm high. The conical cups are 12 cm wide and 19 cm high. The company will use the cup that holds the most water.

Draw and label a sketch of each.

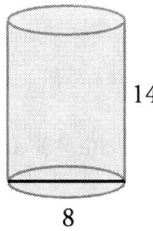
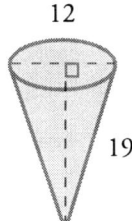

$V = \pi r^2 h$ $V = \dfrac{\pi r^2 h}{3}$ 1. Write a formula.

$V = \pi(4)^2(14)$ $V = \dfrac{1}{3}\pi(6)^2(19)$ 2. Substitute.

$V = 703.717$ cm³ $V = 716.283$ cm³   3. Solve.

The choice should be the conical cup since its volume is more.

MATHEMATICS

Example: How much material is needed to make a basketball that has a diameter of 15 inches? How much air is needed to fill the basketball?

Draw and label a sketch:

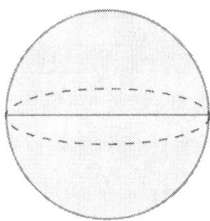

$D = 15$ inches

Total surface area	Volume
$TSA = 4\pi r^2$	$V = \frac{4}{3}\pi r^3$
$= 4\pi(7.5)^2$	$= \frac{4}{3}\pi(7.5)^3$
$= 706.858 \text{ in}^2$	$= 1767.1459 \text{ in}^3$

1. Write a formula.
2. Substitute.
3. Solve.

SKILL 14.3 Solve problems using the Pythagorean theorem

The Pythagorean Theorem

Given any right triangle $\triangle ABC$ the square of the hypotenuse is equal to the sum of the squares of the other two sides.

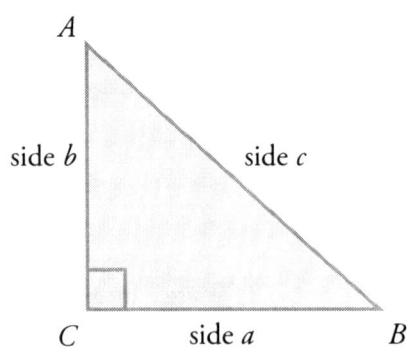

Hypotenuse (side opposite the 90° angle)

This theorem says that $(AB)^2 = (BC)^2 + (AC)^2$
or $c^2 = a^2 + b^2$.

SOLVE PROBLEMS INVOLVING GEOMETRIC FIGURES

Example: Find the area and perimeter of a rectangle if its length is 12 inches and its diagonal is 15 inches.

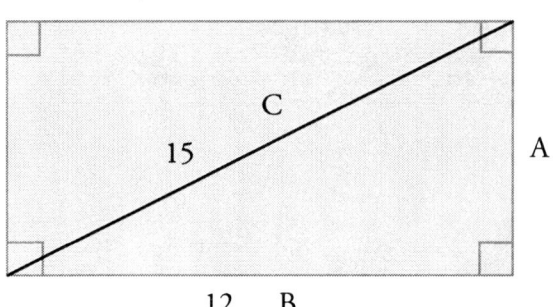

1. Draw and label sketch.
2. Since the height is still needed, use Pythagorean formula to find missing leg of the triangle.

$A^2 + B^2 = C^2$
$A^2 + 12^2 = 15^2$
$A^2 = 15^2 - 12^2$
$A^2 = 81$
$A = 9$

Now use this information to find the area and perimeter.

A = LW	P = 2(L + W)	1. Write formula.
A = (12)(9)	P = 2(12 + 9)	2. Substitute.
A = 108 in²	P = 42 inches	3. Solve.

Example: Two old cars leave a road intersection at the same time. One car traveled due north at 55 mph while the other car traveled due east. After 3 hours, the cars were 180 miles apart. Find the speed of the second car.

Using a right triangle to represent the problem we get the figure:

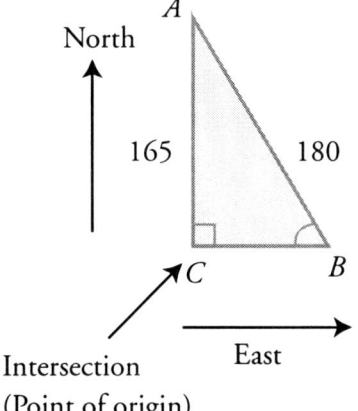

Traveling at 55 mph for 3 hours, the northbound car has driven (55)(3) = 165 miles. This is the side *AC*. The cars are 180 miles apart. This is side *AB*.

Since $\triangle ABC$ is a right triangle, then, by the Pythagorean Theorem, we get:
$(AB)^2 = (BC)^2 + (AC)^2$ or
$(BC)^2 = (AB)^2 + (AC)^2$

$(BC)^2 = 180^2 + 165^2$
$(BC)^2 = 32400 + 27225$
$(BC)^2 = 5175$

Take the square root of both sides to get:
$\sqrt{(BC)^2} = \sqrt{5175} \approx 71.935$ miles

Since the eastbound car has traveled 71.935 miles in 3 hours, then the average speed is:
$\frac{71.935}{3} \approx 23.97$ mph

COMPETENCY 15
SOLVE PROBLEMS INVOLVING GEOMETRIC CONCEPTS

SKILL 15.1 Solve problems using principles of similarity, congruence, parallelism, and perpendicularity

Congruence

CONGRUENT FIGURES have the same size and shape. If one is placed atop the other, it will fit exactly. Congruent lines have the same length. Congruent angles have equal measures.

CONGRUENT FIGURES: figures that have the same size and shape

The symbol for congruent is $\cong$.

Polygons (pentagons) *ABCDE* and *VWXYZ* are congruent. They are exactly the same size and shape.

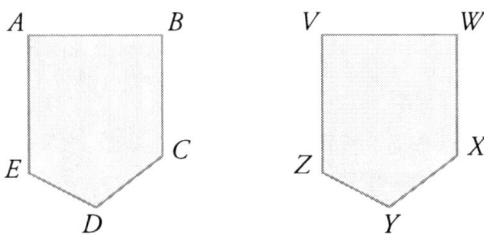

$ABCDE \cong VWXYZ$

SOLVE PROBLEMS INVOLVING GEOMETRIC CONCEPTS

Corresponding parts are the congruent angles and congruent sides. They are:

Corresponding angles	Corresponding sides
$\angle A \leftrightarrow \angle V$	$AB \leftrightarrow VW$
$\angle B \leftrightarrow \angle W$	$BC \leftrightarrow WX$
$\angle C \leftrightarrow \angle X$	$CD \leftrightarrow XY$
$\angle D \leftrightarrow \angle Y$	$DE \leftrightarrow YZ$
$\angle E \leftrightarrow \angle Z$	$AE \leftrightarrow VZ$

Example: Given two similar quadrilaterals, find the lengths of sides x, y, and z.

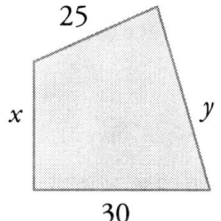
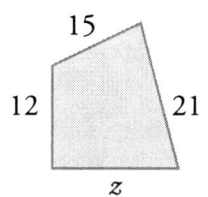

Since corresponding sides are proportional, the scale is:

$\frac{12}{x} = \frac{3}{5}$ $\frac{21}{x} = \frac{3}{5}$ $\frac{z}{30} = \frac{3}{5}$
$3x = 60$ $3y = 105$ $5z = 90$
$x = 20$ $y = 35$ $z = 18$

Similarity

Two figures that have the same shape are SIMILAR. Polygons are similar if and only if corresponding angles are congruent and corresponding sides are in proportion. Corresponding parts of similar polygons are proportional.

SIMILAR: two figures that have the same shape

Example: Given the rectangles below, compare the area and perimeter.

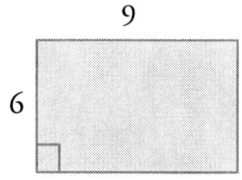
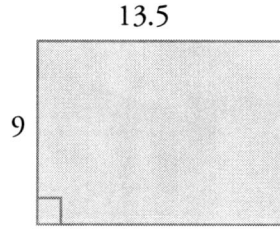

$A = LW$	$A = LW$	1. Write formula.
$A = (6)(9)$	$A = (9)(13.5)$	2. Substitute known values.
$A = 54$ sq. units	$A = 121.5$ sq. units	3. Compute.
$P = 2(L + W)$	$P = 2(L + W)$	1. Write formula.
$P = 2(6 + 9)$	$P = 2(9 + 13.5)$	2. Substitute known values.
$P = 30$ units	$P = 45$ units	3. Compute.

Notice that the areas are related to each other in the following manner:
Ratio of sides $\frac{9}{13.5} = \frac{2}{3}$

Multiply the first area by the square of the reciprocal $(\frac{3}{2})^2$ to get the second area.
$$54 \times (\tfrac{3}{2})^2 = 121.5$$

The perimeters are related to each other in the following manner:
Ratio of sides $\frac{9}{13.5} = \frac{2}{3}$

Multiply the perimeter of the first by the reciprocal of the ratio $(\frac{3}{2})$ to get the perimeter of the second.
$$30 \times \tfrac{3}{2} = 45$$

Example: Given two similar quadrilaterals, find the lengths of sides x, y, and z.

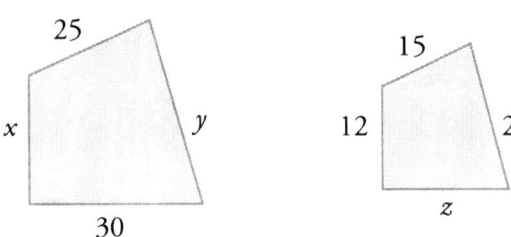

Since corresponding sides are proportional, the scale is:

$\frac{12}{x} = \frac{3}{5}$	$\frac{21}{y} = \frac{3}{5}$	$\frac{z}{30} = \frac{3}{5}$
$3x = 60$	$3y = 105$	$5z = 90$
$x = 20$	$y = 35$	$z = 18$

Example: Tommy draws and cuts out two triangles for a school project. One of them has sides of 3, 6, and 9 inches. The other triangle has sides of 2, 4, and 6 inches. Is there a relationship between the two triangles?

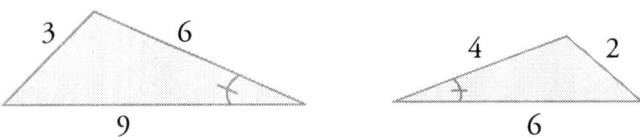

Take the proportion of the corresponding sides.

$$\frac{2}{3} \qquad \frac{4}{6} = \frac{2}{3} \qquad \frac{6}{9} = \frac{2}{3}$$

The smaller triangle is $\frac{2}{3}$ the size of the large triangle.

Parallel and Perpendicular Lines

PARALLEL LINES or planes do not intersect. Two parallel lines have the same slope.

> **PARALLEL LINES:** two or more lines that do not intersect

PERPENDICULAR LINES or planes form a 90° angle to each other. Perpendicular lines have slopes that are negative reciprocals.

> **PERPENDICULAR LINES:** lines that form a 90° angle to each other

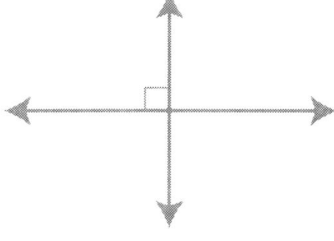

Example: One line passes through the points (-4, -6) and (4, 6); another line passes through the points (-5, -4) and (3, 8). Are these lines parallel, perpendicular, or neither?

Find the slopes.

$$m = \frac{y_2 - y_1}{x_2 - x_1}$$

$$m_1 = \frac{6 - (-6)}{4 - (-4)} = \frac{6 + 6}{4 + 4} = \frac{12}{8} = \frac{3}{2}$$

$$m_2 = \frac{8 - (-4)}{3 - (-5)} = \frac{8 + 4}{3 + 5} = \frac{12}{8} = \frac{3}{2}$$

Since the slopes are the same, the lines are parallel.

Example: One line passes through the points (1, -3) and (0, -6); another line passes through the points (4, 1) and (-2, 3). Are these lines parallel, perpendicular, or neither?

Find the slopes.

$$m = \frac{y_2 - y_1}{x_2 - x_1}$$

$$m_1 = \frac{-6 - (-3)}{0 - 1} = \frac{-6 + 3}{-1} = \frac{-3}{-1} = 3$$

$$m_2 = \frac{3 - 1}{-2 - 4} = \frac{2}{-6} = -\frac{1}{3}$$

The slopes are negative reciprocals, so the lines are perpendicular.

MATHEMATICS

Example: One line passes through the points (-2, 4) and (2, 5); another line passes through the points (-1, 0) and (5, 4). Are these lines parallel, perpendicular, or neither?

Find the slopes.

$$m = \frac{y_2 - y_1}{x_2 - x_1}$$

$$m_1 = \frac{5 - 4}{2 - (-2)} = \frac{1}{2 + 2} = \frac{1}{4}$$

$$m_2 = \frac{4 - 0}{5 - (-1)} = \frac{4}{5 + 1} = \frac{4}{6} = \frac{2}{3}$$

Since the slopes are not the same, the lines are not parallel. Since they are not negative reciprocals, they are not perpendicular either. Therefore, the answer is "neither."

There are four basic transformational symmetries: translation, rotation, reflection, and glide reflection. The transformation of an object is its image. If the original object was labeled with letters, such as *ABCD*, the image may be labeled with the same letters followed by a prime symbol, *A'B'C'D'*.

PROBLEM SOLVING

COMPETENCY 16
APPLY REASONING SKILLS

SKILL 16.1 Draw conclusions using inductive and deductive reasoning

SIMPLE STATEMENT: represents a simple idea that can be described as either true or false, but not both

A SIMPLE STATEMENT represents a simple idea that can be described as either true or false, but not both. A small letter of the alphabet represents a simple statement.

Example: "Today is Monday."

This is a simple statement because we can determine that this statement is either true or false. We can write p = "Today is Monday."

APPLY REASONING SKILLS

Example: "John, please be quiet."
We do not consider this a simple statement in our study of logic because we cannot assign a truth value to it.

Simple statements joined by CONNECTIVES (*and, or, not, if…then*, and *if and only if*) result in COMPOUND STATEMENTS. Note that we can also form compound statements using *but, however,* or *nevertheless*. We can assign a truth value to a compound statement.

> **COMPOUND STATEMENTS:** two simple statements joined by a connective *(and, or, not, if…then, and if and only if, etc.)*

We frequently write conditional statements in *if-then* form. The *if* clause of the conditional is known as the HYPOTHESIS, and the *then* clause is called the CONCLUSION. In a proof, the hypothesis is the information that is assumed to be true, while the conclusion is what is to be proven true. We consider a conditional to be of the form "**if p, then q,**" where p is the hypothesis and q is the conclusion.

$p \rightarrow q$ is read "If p, then q."

~ (statement) is read "It is not true that (statement)."

> **HYPOTHESIS:** the *if* clause of an if-then statement

> **CONCLUSION:** the *then* clause of an if-then statement

QUANTIFIERS are words that describe a quantity under discussion. These include words such as *all, none* (or *no*), and *some*.

NEGATION of a statement: If a statement is true, then its negation must be false (and vice versa).

> **QUANTIFIERS:** words that describe a quantity under discussion

> **NEGATION:** in the case of a statement that is true, its negation must be false (and vice versa)

A SUMMARY OF NEGATION RULES	
STATEMENT	NEGATION
q	not q
not q	q
STATEMENT	NEGATION
π and s	(not π) or (not s)
π or s	(not π) and (not s)
if p, then q	(p) and (not q)

Example: Select the statement that is the negation of "Some winter nights are not cold."

    A. All winter nights are not cold.

    B. Some winter nights are cold.

C. All winter nights are cold.

D. None of the winter nights is cold.

The negation of some are is none is. Therefore, the negation statement is "None of the winter nights is cold." The answer is D.

Example. Select the statement that is the negation of "If it rains, then the beach party will not be held."

A. If it does not rain, then the beach party will be held.

B. If the beach party is held, then it will not rain.

C. It does not rain and the beach party will be held.

D. It rains and the beach party will be held.

The negation of "If p, then q" is "p and (not q)." The negation of the given statement is "It rains and the beach party will be held." Select D.

Example: Select the negation of the statement "If they are elected, then all politicians go back on election promises."

A. If they are elected, then many politicians go back on election promises.

B. They are elected and some politicians go back on election promises.

C. If they are not elected, some politicians do not go back on election promises.

D. None of the above statements is the negation of the given statement.

Identify the key words of "if...then" and "all...go back." The negation of the given statement is "They are elected and none of the politicians goes back on election promises." So select response D, since statements A, B, and C are not the correct negations.

Example: Select the statement that is the negation of "The sun is shining brightly and I feel great."

A. If the sun is not shining brightly, I do not feel great.

B. The sun is not shining brightly and I do not feel great.

C. The sun is not shining brightly or I do not feel great.

D. The sun is shining brightly and I do not feel great.

The negation of "r and s" is "(not r) or (not s)." Therefore, the negation of the given statement is "The sun is not shining brightly or I do not feel great." We select response C.

APPLY REASONING SKILLS

We can diagram conditional statements using a VENN DIAGRAM. We can draw a diagram with one circle inside another circle. The inner circle represents the hypothesis. The outer circle represents the conclusion. If we take the hypothesis to be true, then we are located inside the inner circle. If we are located in the inner circle, then we are also inside the outer circle, so we have proved the conclusion true.

VENN DIAGRAM: a diagram that uses conditional statements

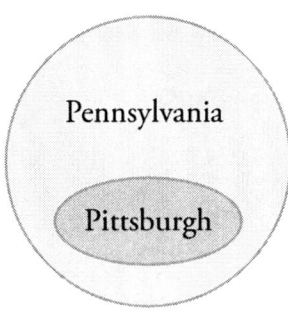

Example: If an angle has a measure of 90°, then it is a right angle.
In this statement, "an angle has a measure of 90°," is the hypothesis. In this statement, "it is a right angle" is the conclusion.

Example: If you are in Pittsburgh, then you are in Pennsylvania.
In this statement, "you are in Pittsburgh" is the hypothesis.
In this statement, "you are in Pennsylvania" is the conclusion.

DEDUCTIVE REASONING is the process of arriving at a conclusion based on other statements that are known to be true.

A symbolic argument consists of a set of premises and a conclusion in the format of of if [premise 1 and premise 2], then [conclusion].

An argument is VALID when the conclusion follows necessarily from the premises. An argument is INVALID or a fallacy when the conclusion does not follow from the premises.

DEDUCTIVE REASONING: the process of arriving at a conclusion based on other statements that are known to be true

VALID: an argument is valid when the conclusion follows necessarily from the premises

INVALID: an argument is invalid when the conclusion does not follow from the premises

FOUR STANDARD FORMS OF VALID ARGUMENTS		
Law of Detachment	If *p*, then *q* *p* Therefore, *q*	(premise 1) (premise 2)
Law of Contraposition	If *p*, then *q* not *q* Therefore, not *p*	

Table continued on next page

Law of Syllogism	If *p*, then *q* If *q*, then *r* Therefore, if *p*, then *r*	
Disjunctive Syllogism	*p* or *q* not *p* Therefore, *q*	

Example: Can we reach a conclusion from these two statements?

A. All swimmers are athletes.
All athletes are scholars.

In "if-then" form, these would be:
If you are a swimmer, then you are an athlete.
If you are an athlete, then you are a scholar.

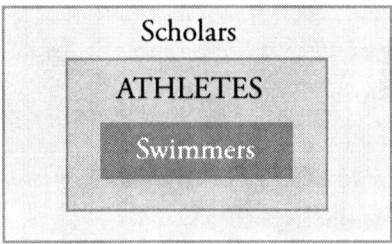

Clearly, if you are a swimmer, then you are also an athlete. This includes you in the group of scholars.

B. All swimmers are athletes.
All wrestlers are athletes.

In "if-then" form, these would be:
If you are a swimmer, then you are an athlete.
If you are a wrestler, then you are an athlete.

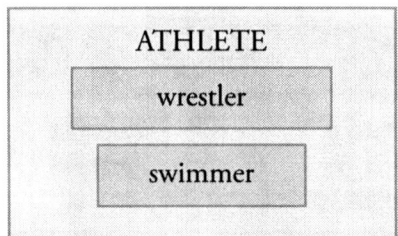

APPLY REASONING SKILLS

Clearly, if you are a swimmer or a wrestler, then you are also an athlete.
This does NOT allow you to come to any other conclusions.
A swimmer may or may NOT also be a wrestler. Therefore, NO CONCLUSION IS POSSIBLE.

Example: Determine whether statement A, B, C, or D can be deduced from the following:

(i) If John drives the big truck, then the shipment will be delivered.
(ii) The shipment will not be delivered.

A. John does not drive the big truck.

B. John drives the big truck.

C. The shipment will not be delivered.

D. None of the above conclusions is valid.

Let p: John drives the big truck.
q: The shipment is delivered.

Statement (i) gives $p \rightarrow q$. Statement (ii) gives $\sim q$ (not q). This is the Law of Contraposition.
Therefore, the logical conclusion is $\sim p$ (not p) or "John does not drive the big truck." The answer is response A.

Example: Determine which conclusion can be logically deduced by the following information:

(i) Peter is a jet pilot or Peter is a navigator.
(ii) Peter is not a jet pilot.

A. Peter is not a navigator.

B. Peter is a navigator.

C. Peter is neither a jet pilot nor a navigator.

D. None of the above is true.

Let p: Peter is a jet pilot.
q: Peter is a navigator.
So we have $p \vee q$ (p or q) from statement (i)
$\sim p$ (not p) from statement (ii)
The answer is response B.

MATHEMATICS

COMPETENCY 17
SOLVE APPLIED PROBLEMS INVOLVING A COMBINATION OF MATHEMATICAL SKILLS

SKILL 17.1 Apply combinations of mathematical skills to solve problems and to solve a series of related problems

See Competencies 7 through 16

DOMAIN III
WRITING

WRITING

PERSONALIZED STUDY PLAN

✘ **KNOWN MATERIAL/ SKIP IT**

PAGE	COMPETENCY AND SKILL	
122	**18: Recognize purpose and audience**	☐
	18.1: Recognize writing that is appropriate for a given purpose	☐
	18.2: Recognize writing that is appropriate for a given audience and occasion	☐
122	**19: Recognize unity, focus, and development in writing**	☐
	19.1: Recognize unnecessary shifts in point of view or distracting details that impair the main idea	☐
	19.2: Recognize revisions that improve unity and focus	☐
	19.3: Recognize examples of well-developed writing	☐
127	**20: Recognize effective organization in writing**	☐
	20.1: Recognize methods of paragraph organization and use of transitional words or phrases	☐
	20.2: Reorganize sentences to improve sequence of ideas	☐
132	**21: Recognize effective sentences**	☐
	21.1: Recognize inefficiency in sentence construction	☐
	21.2: Identify sentence fragments and run-on sentences	☐
	21.3: Identify standard subject-verb agreement	☐
	21.4: Identify standard placement of modifiers, parallel structure, and use of negatives	☐
	21.5: Recognize imprecise and inappropriate word choice	☐
146	**22: Recognize edited American English usage**	☐
	22.1: Recognize the standard use of verb forms and pronouns	☐
	22.2: Recognize the standard formation and use of adverbs, adjectives, comparatives, superlatives, and plural and possessive forms of nouns	☐
	22:3 Recognize standard punctuation	☐

ELEMENTS OF COMPOSITION

The writing subsection of the THEA Test consists of one assignment. Students are asked to prepare a multiple-paragraph writing sample of about 300 to 600 words on an assigned topic. Students' writing samples are scored on the basis of how effectively they communicate a whole message to a specified audience for a stated purpose. Students will be assessed on their ability to express, organize, and support opinions and ideas, rather than on the position they express. The following characteristics may be considered in scoring writing samples:

- **Appropriateness:** The extent to which the student addresses the topic and uses language and style appropriate to the given audience, purpose, and occasion

- **Unity and focus:** The clarity with which the student states and maintains a main idea or point of view

- **Development:** The amount, depth, and specificity of supporting detail the student provides

- **Organization:** The clarity of the student's writing and the logical sequence of the student's ideas

- **Sentence structure:** The effectiveness of the student's sentence structure and the extent to which the student's writing is free of errors in sentence structure

- **Usage:** The extent to which the student's writing is free of errors in usage and shows care and precision in word choice

- **Mechanical conventions:** The student's ability to spell common words and to use the conventions of capitalization and punctuation

Your written response should be your original work, written in your own words, and not copied or paraphrased from some other work.

WRITING

COMPETENCY 18
RECOGNIZE PURPOSE AND AUDIENCE

SKILL 18.1 Recognize writing that is appropriate for a given purpose

See Skill 3.1

SKILL 18.2 Recognize writing that is appropriate for a given audience and occasion

See Skill 3.2

COMPETENCY 19
RECOGNIZE UNITY, FOCUS, AND DEVELOPMENT IN WRITING

SKILL 19.1 Recognize unnecessary shifts in point of view or distracting details that impair the development of the main idea in a piece of writing

Point of view: Defines the focus a writer assumes in relation to a given topic. It is extremely important to maintain a consistent point of view in order to create coherent paragraphs. Point of view is related to matters of person, tense, tone, and number.

Person: A shift in the form that indicates whether a person is speaking (first), is being spoken to (second), or is being spoken about (third) can disrupt continuity of a passage. In your essay, it is recommended that you write in the third person,

RECOGNIZE UNITY, FOCUS, AND DEVELOPMENT IN WRITING

as it is often considered to be the most formal of the modes of person. If you do decide to use the more informal first or second person (I, you, we) in your essay, be careful not to shift between first, second, and third persons from sentence to sentence or paragraph to paragraph.

Tense: Verb tenses indicate the time of an action or state of being—the past, present, or future. It is important to largely stick to a selected tense, though this may not always be the case. For instance, in an essay about the history of environmental protection, it might be necessary to include a paragraph about the future benefits or consequences of protecting the earth.

Tone: The tone of an essay varies greatly with the purpose, subject, and audience. It is best to assume a formal tone for this essay.

Number: Words change when their meanings are singular or plural. Make sure that you do not shift number needlessly; if a meaning is singular in one sentence, do not make it plural in the subsequent sentence.

SKILL 19.2 Recognize revisions that improve the unity and focus of a piece of writing

Techniques for Revising Written Texts to Achieve Clarity and Economy of Expression

Enhancing interest

- Start out with an attention-grabbing introduction. This sets an engaging tone for the entire piece and will be more likely to pull the reader in.

- Use dynamic vocabulary and varied sentence beginnings. Keep the readers on their toes. If they can predict what you are going to say next, switch it up.

- Avoid using clichés (e.g., as cold as ice, the best thing since sliced bread, nip it in the bud). These are easy shortcuts, but they are not interesting, memorable, or convincing.

Ensuring understanding

- Avoid using the words, "clearly," "obviously," and "undoubtedly." Often, things that are clear or obvious to the author are not as apparent to the reader. Instead of using these words, make your point so strongly that it is clear on its own.

WRITING

- Use the word that best fits the meaning you intend for, even if it is longer or a little less common. Try to find a balance, and go with a familiar yet precise word.

- When in doubt, explain further.

Revision of sentences to eliminate wordiness, ambiguity, and redundancy

Sometimes editing is seen by students as simply catching errors in spelling or word use. Students need to reframe their thinking about revising and editing. Some questions that need to be asked include:

- Is the reasoning coherent?
- Is the point established?
- Does the introduction make the reader want to read this discourse?
- What is the thesis? Is it proven?
- What is the purpose? Is it clear? Is it useful, valuable, and interesting?
- Is the style of writing so wordy that it exhausts the reader and interferes with engagement?
- Is the writing so spare that it is boring?
- Are the sentences too uniform in structure?
- Are there too many simple sentences?
- Are too many of the complex sentences the same structure?
- Are the compounds truly compounds or are they unbalanced?
- Are parallel structures truly parallel?
- If there are characters, are they believable?
- If there is dialogue, is it natural or stilted?
- Is the title appropriate?
- Does the writing show creativity or is it boring?
- Is the language appropriate? Is it too formal? Too informal? If jargon is used, is it appropriate?

> *Sometimes editing is seen by students as simply catching errors in spelling or word use. Students need to reframe their thinking about revising and editing.*

Studies have clearly demonstrated that the most fertile area in teaching writing is this one. If students can learn to revise their own work effectively, they are well on their way to becoming effective, mature writers. Word processing is an important tool for teaching this stage in the writing process. Microsoft Word has tracking features that make the revision exchanges between teachers and students more effective than ever before.

Techniques to maintain focus

- **Focus on a main point:** The point should be clear to readers, and all sentences in the paragraph should relate to it.

- **Start the paragraph with a topic sentence:** This should be a general, one-sentence summary of the paragraph's main point, relating both back toward the thesis and toward the content of the paragraph. (A topic sentence is sometimes unnecessary if the paragraph continues a developing idea clearly introduced in a preceding paragraph, or if the paragraph appears in a narrative of events where generalizations might interrupt the flow of the story.)

- **Stick to the point:** Eliminate sentences that do not support the topic sentence.

- **Be flexible:** If there is not enough evidence to support the claim your topic sentence is making, do not fall into the trap of wandering or introducing new ideas within the paragraph. Either find more evidence, or adjust the topic sentence to collaborate with the evidence that is available.

SKILL 19.3 Recognize examples of well-developed writing

Sample of a Well-Written Response

Written on July 15, 1944, three weeks before her family was arrested by the Nazis, Anne Frank's diary entry explains her worldview and future hopes.

> *It's difficult in times like these: ideals, dreams, and cherished hopes rise within us, only to be crushed by grim reality. It's a wonder I haven't abandoned all my ideals; they seem so absurd and impractical. Yet I cling to them because I still believe, in spite of everything, that people are truly good at heart.*
>
> *It's utterly impossible for me to build my life on a foundation of chaos, suffering, and death. I see the world being slowly transformed into a wilderness, I hear the approaching thunder that, one day, will destroy us too. I feel the suffering of millions, and yet, when I look up at the sky, I somehow feel that everything will change for the better, that this cruelty too shall end, that peace and tranquility will return once more. In the meantime, I must hold on to my ideals. Perhaps the day will come when I will be able to realize them!*

WRITING

Using your knowledge of literature, write a response in which you:

1. Compare and contrast Anne's ideals with her awareness of the conditions in which she lives

2. Discuss how the structure of Anne's writing—her sentences and paragraphs—emphasize the above contrast

Sample Response

This excerpt from The Diary of Anne Frank *reveals the inner strength of a young girl who refuses, despite the wartime violence and danger surrounding her, to let her idealism be overcome by hatred and mass killing. This idealism is reflected, in part, by her emphases on universal human hopes, such as peace, tranquility, and goodwill. But Anne Frank is no dreamy Pollyanna. Reflecting on her idealism in the context of the war raging around her, she matter-of-factly writes: "My dreams, they seem so absurd and impractical."*

This indicates Anne Frank's awareness of not only her own predicament, but of human miseries that extend beyond the immediate circumstances of her life. For elsewhere, she writes in a similar vein, "In times like these… I see the world being slowly transformed into a wilderness;" despite her own suffering, she can "feel the suffering of millions."

And yet Anne Frank believes, "in spite of everything, that people are truly good at heart." This statement epitomizes the stark existential contrast of her worldview with the wartime reality that ultimately claimed her life.

The statement also exemplifies how Anne's literary form—her syntax and diction—mirror thematic content and contrasts. "In spite of everything," she still believes in people. She can "hear the approaching thunder…yet, when I look up at the sky, I somehow feel that everything will change for the better." At numerous points in this diary entry, first-hand knowledge of violent tragedy stands side-by-side with belief in humanity and human progress.

"I must hold on to my ideals," Anne concludes. "Perhaps the day will come when I'll be able to realize them!" In her diary, she has done so, and more.

COMPETENCY 20
RECOGNIZE EFFECTIVE ORGANIZATION IN WRITING

SKILL 20.1 Recognize methods of paragraph organization and the appropriate use of transitional words or phrases to convey text structure

The organization of a written work includes two factors: the order in which the writer has chosen to present the different parts of the discussion or argument, and the relationships he or she constructs between these parts.

Written ideas need to be presented in a logical order so that a reader can follow the information easily and quickly. There are many different ways to order a series of ideas, but they all share one goal: to lead the reader along a desired path—while avoiding backtracking and skipping around—in order to give a clear, strong presentation of the writer's main idea. The following are some of the ways in which a paragraph may be organized:

WAYS TO ORGANIZE A WRITTEN WORK	
Sequence of Events	In this type of organization, the details are presented in the order in which they have occurred. Paragraphs that describe a process or procedure, give directions, or outline a given time period (such as a day or a month) are often arranged chronologically.
Statement Support	In this type of organization, the main idea is stated and the rest of the paragraph explains or proves it. This type of organization is also referred to as *relative* or *order of importance*. This type of order is organized in four ways: most to least, least to most, most-least-most, and least-most-least.
Comparison-Contrast	The compare-contrast pattern is used when a paragraph describes the differences or similarities between two or more ideas, actions, events, or things. Usually, the topic sentence describes the basic relationship between the ideas or items, and the rest of the paragraph explains this relationship.
Classification	In this type of organization, the paragraph presents grouped information about a topic. The topic sentence usually states the general category, and the rest of the sentences show how various elements of the category have a common base and how they differ from the common base.

Continued on next page

WRITING

Cause and Effect	This pattern describes how two or more events are connected. The main sentence usually states the primary cause(s) and the primary effect(s) and how they are connected. The rest of the sentences explain the connection—how one event caused the next.
Spatial/Place	In this type of organization, certain descriptions are organized according to the location of items in relation to each other and to a larger context. The orderly arrangement guides the reader's eye as he or she mentally envisions the scene or place being described.
Example, Clarification, and Definition	These types of organization show, explain, or elaborate on the main idea. This can be done by showing specific cases, examining meaning multiple times, or describing one term extensively. Many times, all of these organizations follow the basic P.I.E. sequence: P—the point, or main idea, of the paragraph I—the information (data, details, facts) that supports the main idea E—the explanation or analysis of the information and how it proves, is related to, or connects to the main idea

The relationship between sentences is the link that conceptually ties one sentence to another. The relationship may be explicit, in which case a transition or clue word helps identify the connection. The relation may be implicit, in which case you must closely examine the elements found in each sentence and often in the material between the sentences.

Most sentences cannot meaningfully stand alone. To read a passage without recognizing how each sentence is linked to those around it is to lose the passage's meaning.

Sentences can be connected to one another in many ways.

HOW SENTENCES ARE CONNECTED	
Addition	One sentence is "tacked on" to another without making one sentence depend upon the other. Both are equally important. *Joanna recently purchased a new stereo system, computer, and home alarm system. She **also** put a down payment on a new automobile.*
Clarification	One sentence restates the point of an earlier one but in different terms. *The national debt is growing continually. **In fact**, by next year it may be ten trillion dollars.*
Comparison/Contrast	Connection is one of similarity or difference. *Shelley's strained relationship with his father led the poet to a life of rebellion. **Likewise**, Byron's Bohemian lifestyle may be traced to his ambivalence toward authority.*

Continued on next page

Example	One sentence works to make another more concrete or specific.
	Sarah has always been an optimistic person. She believes that when she graduates from college, she will get the job of her choice. (implicit)
Location/Spatial Order	The relationship between sentences shows the placement of objects or items relative to each other in space.
	The park was darkened by the school building's shadow. However, the sun still splashed the front window with light. (implicit)
Cause/Effect	One event (cause) brings about the second event (effect).
	General Hooker failed to anticipate General Lee's bold maneuver. **As a result**, *Hooker's army was nearly routed by a smaller force.*
Summary	A summary sentence surveys and captures the most important points of the previous sentence(s).
	Every Fourth of July, Ralph brings his whole family to the local parade; every Memorial Day, he displays the flag; and every November 4, he votes. **Overall**, *he is a patriotic American.*
Time	The relationship describes the passage of time or various states of completion of events.
	The car slid down the embankment. **Shortly thereafter**, *curious onlookers had backed up traffic five miles.*

Even if the sentences that make up a given paragraph or passage are arranged in logical order, the document as a whole can still seem choppy, and the various ideas disconnected. TRANSITIONS—words that signal relationships between ideas—can help improve the flow of a document. Transitions can help achieve clear and effective presentation of information by establishing connections between sentences, paragraphs, and sections of a document. With transitions, each sentence builds on the ideas in the last, and each paragraph has clear links to the preceding one. As a result, the reader receives clear directions on how to piece together the writer's ideas in a logically coherent argument. By signaling how to organize, interpret, and react to information, transitions enable writers to explain their ideas effectively and elegantly. Following is a list of common transitional expressions.

> **TRANSITIONS:** words that signal relationships between ideas

COMMON TRANSITIONS	
Similarity	also, in the same way, just as ... so too, likewise, similarly
Exception/Contrast	but, however, in spite of, on the one hand ... on the other hand, nevertheless, nonetheless, notwithstanding, in contrast, on the contrary, still, yet, although

Continued on next page

WRITING

Sequence/Order	first, second, third, ... next, then, finally, until
Time	after, afterward, at last, before, currently, during, earlier, immediately, later, meanwhile, now, presently, recently, simultaneously, since, subsequently, then
Example	for example, for instance, namely, specifically, to illustrate
Emphasis	even, indeed, in fact, of course, truly
Place/Position	above, adjacent, below, beyond, here, in front, in back, nearby, there
Cause and Effect	accordingly, consequently, hence, so, therefore, thus, as a result, because, consequently, hence, if...then, in short
Additional Support or Evidence	additionally, again, also, and, as well, besides, equally important, further, furthermore, in addition, moreover, then
Conclusion/Summary	finally, in a word, in brief, in conclusion, in the end, in the final analysis, on the whole, thus, to conclude, to summarize, in sum, in summary
Statement Support	most important, more significant, primarily, most essential
Addition	again, also, and, besides, equally important, finally, furthermore, in addition, last, likewise, moreover, too
Clarification	actually, clearly, evidently, in fact, in other words, obviously, of course, indeed

The following example shows good logical order and transitions. The transition words are highlighted in bold.

> *No one really knows how Valentine's Day started. There are several legends, **however**, which are often told. The **first** attributes Valentine's Day to a Christian priest who lived in Rome during the third century under the rule of Emperor Claudius. Rome was at war and, **apparently**, Claudius felt that married men did not fight as well as bachelors. **Consequently**, Claudius banned marriage for the duration of the war. **But** Valentinus, the priest, risked his life to marry couples secretly in violation of Claudius's law. The **second** legend is **even more** romantic. In this story, Valentinus is a prisoner, having been condemned to death for refusing to worship pagan deities. **While** in jail, he fell in love with his jailer's daughter, who happened to be blind. Daily, he prayed for her sight to return and miraculously, it did. On February 14, the day that he was condemned to die, he was allowed to write the young woman a note. **In this farewell letter**, he promised eternal love and signed at the bottom of the page the now famous words, "Your Valentine."*

RECOGNIZE EFFECTIVE ORGANIZATION IN WRITING

SKILL 20.2 Reorganize sentences to improve cohesion and the effective sequence of ideas

See also Skill 20.1

Paragraphs should contain concrete, interesting information and supporting details to support the main idea or point of view. Fact statements add weight to opinions, especially when the writer is trying to convince the reader of his or her view. Because every good thesis has an assertion, a well-written passage offers specifics, facts, data, anecdotes, expert opinion, and other details to show or *prove* that assertion. While *the author knows* what he or she wants to convey, the *reader* does not.

Like a whole piece of writing, the paragraphs that make up that piece can take a number of forms or combinations of forms. These forms help create an organized and well-structured document:

- Cause and effect
- Comparison and contrast
- Definition
- Example and illustration
- Sequence and process

Like a whole piece of writing, the paragraphs that make up that piece can take a number of forms or combinations of forms.

A piece of writing should end with a brief straightforward concluding paragraph that ties together the written content and leaves the reader with a sense of its completion. The conclusion should:

- Reinforce the main points and offer some insight into the topic
- Provide a sense of unity for the essay by relating it to the thesis
- Signal clear closure of the essay

A piece of writing should end with a brief straightforward concluding paragraph that ties together the written content and leaves the reader with a sense of its completion.

SENTENCE STRUCTURE, USAGE, AND MECHANICS

COMPETENCY 21
RECOGNIZE EFFECTIVE SENTENCES

SKILL 21.1 Recognize ineffective repetition and inefficiency in sentence construction

Sentence Structure

Recognize simple, compound, complex, and compound-complex sentences. Use dependent (subordinate) and independent clauses correctly to create these sentence structures.

TYPES OF SENTENCES	
Simple	Consists of one independent clause. *Joyce wrote a letter.*
Compound	Consists of two or more independent clauses. The two clauses are usually connected by a coordinating conjunction (and, but, or, nor, for, so, yet). Semicolons sometimes connect compound sentences. *Joyce wrote a letter, and Dot drew a picture.*
Complex	Consists of an independent clause plus one or more dependent clauses. The dependent clause may precede the independent clause or follow it. *While Joyce wrote a letter, Dot drew a picture.*
Compound-Complex	Consists of one or more dependent clauses plus two or more independent clauses. *When Mother asked the girls to demonstrate their newfound skills, Joyce wrote a letter, and Dot drew a picture.*

Note: Do not confuse compound sentence elements with compound sentences.

Simple sentence with compound subject:

> *Joyce* and *Dot* wrote letters.
> The *girl* in row three and the *boy* next to her were passing notes across the aisle.

Simple sentence with compound predicate:

> Joyce *wrote letters* and *drew pictures*.
> The captain of the high school debate team *graduated with honors* and *studied broadcast journalism in college*.

Simple sentence with compound object of preposition:

> Coleen graded the students' essays for *style* and *mechanical accuracy*.

Types of Clauses

CLAUSES are connected word groups that are composed of at least one subject and one verb. (A SUBJECT is the doer of an action or the element that is being joined. A VERB conveys either the action or the link.)

> Students are waiting for the start of the assembly.
> (subject)   (verb)
>
> At the end of the play, students wait for the curtain to come down.
>   (subject) (verb)

Clauses can be independent or dependent.

INDEPENDENT CLAUSES can stand alone or they can be joined to other clauses.

LINKING CLAUSES		
Independent clause	for and nor	Independent clause
Independent clause,	but or yet so	Independent clause

Continued on next page

CLAUSES: connected word groups that are composed of at least one subject and one verb

SUBJECT: the doer of an action or the element that is being joined

VERB: word that conveys either the action or the link

INDEPENDENT CLAUSES: clauses that can stand alone or that can be joined to other clauses

WRITING

Independent clause	;	Independent clause
Dependent clause	,	Independent clause
Independent clause	,	Dependent clause

DEPENDENT CLAUSES: clauses that have a subject and a verb but cannot stand alone as a complete sentence

DEPENDENT CLAUSES, by definition, contain at least one subject and one verb. However, they cannot stand alone as a complete sentence. They are structurally dependent on the main clause.

There are two types of dependent clauses:

1. Those with a subordinating conjunction

2. Those with a relative pronoun

Unless a cure is discovered, many more people will die of the disease.
Dependent clause + Independent clause

The White House has an official Web site, which contains press releases, news updates, and biographies of the President and Vice President.
(independent clause + relative pronoun + relative dependent clause)

SKILL 21.2 Identify sentence fragments and run-on sentences

Fragments

Fragments occur when word groups standing alone are missing either a subject or a verb, or when word groups containing a subject and verb and standing alone are made dependent through the use of subordinating conjunctions or relative pronouns.

Error: *The teacher waiting for the class to complete the assignment.*

Problem: This sentence is not complete because an *-ing* word alone does not function as a verb. When a helping verb is added (for example, *was waiting*), the fragment becomes a sentence.

Correction: *The teacher was waiting for the class to complete the assignment.*

Error: *Until the last toy was removed from the floor.*

Problem: Words such as *until, because, although, when,* and *if* make a clause dependent and thus incapable of standing alone. An independent clause must be added to make the sentence complete.

Correction: *Until the last toy was removed from the floor, the kids could not go outside to play.*

Error: *The city will close the public library. Because of a shortage of funds.*

Problem: The problem is the same as above. The dependent clause must be joined to the independent clause.

Correction: *The city will close the public library because of a shortage of funds.*

Error: *Anyone planning to go on the trip should bring the necessary items. Such as a backpack, boots, a canteen, and bug spray.*

Problem: The second word group is a phrase and cannot stand alone because there is neither a subject nor a verb. The fragment can be corrected by adding the phrase to the sentence.

Correction: *Anyone planning to go on the trip should bring the necessary items, such as a backpack, boots, a canteen, and bug spray.*

Run-on Sentences and Comma Splices

Comma splices appear when a comma joins two sentences. Fused sentences appear when two sentences are run together with no punctuation at all.

Error: *Dr. Sanders is a brilliant scientist, his research on genetic disorders won him a Nobel Prize.*

Problem: A comma alone cannot join two independent clauses (complete sentences). The two clauses can be joined by a semicolon, joined by a conjunction and a comma, or separated into two sentences by a period.

Correction: *Dr. Sanders is a brilliant scientist; his research on genetic disorders won him a Nobel Prize.*
-OR-
Dr. Sanders is a brilliant scientist. His research on genetic disorders won him a Nobel Prize.

-OR-
Dr. Sanders is a brilliant scientist, and his research on genetic disorders won him a Nobel Prize.

Error: *Paradise Island is noted for its beaches they are long, sandy, and beautiful.*

Problem: The first independent clause ends with the word *beaches*, and the second independent clause is fused to the first. The fused sentence error can be corrected in several ways:

1. One clause may be made dependent on another by inserting a subordinating conjunction or a relative pronoun

2. A semicolon may be used to combine two equally important ideas

3. The two independent clauses may be separated by a period

4. The independent clauses may be joined by a conjunction and a comma

Correction: *Paradise Island is noted for its beaches, which are long, sandy, and beautiful.*
-OR-
Paradise Island is noted for its beaches; they are long, sandy, and beautiful.
-OR -
Paradise Island is noted for its beaches. They are long, sandy, and beautiful.
-OR-
Paradise Island is noted for its beaches, for they are long, sandy, and beautiful.

Error: *The number of hotels has increased, however, the number of visitors has grown also.*

Problem: The first sentence ends with the word *increased*, and a comma is not strong enough to connect it to the second sentence. The adverbial transition *however* does not function in the same way as a coordinating conjunction and cannot be used with commas to link two sentences. Several different corrections are available.

Correction: *The number of hotels has increased; however, the number of visitors has grown also.*
[Two separate but closely related sentences are created with the use of the semicolon.]
-OR-

RECOGNIZE EFFECTIVE SENTENCES

The number of hotels has increased. However, the number of visitors has grown also.

[Two separate sentences are created.]

-OR-

Although the number of hotels has increased, the number of visitors has grown also.

[One idea is made subordinate to the other and separated with a comma.]

-OR-

The number of hotels has increased, but the number of visitors has grown also.

[The comma before the coordinating conjunction *but* is appropriate. The adverbial transition *however* does not function in the same way as the coordinating conjunction *but*.]

SKILL 21.3 Identify standard subject-verb agreement

A verb must correspond in the singular or plural form with the simple subject; interfering elements do not affect it.

PRESENT TENSE VERB FORM		
	Singular	Plural
1st person (talking about oneself)	I do	We do
2nd person (talking to another)	You do	You do
3rd person (talking about someone or something)	He does She does It does	They do

Note: A simple subject is never found in a prepositional phrase (that is, a phrase beginning with a word such as *of, by, over, through, until*).

Error: *Sally, as well as her sister, plan to go into nursing.*

Problem: The subject of the sentence is *Sally* and does not include the word *sister*. Therefore, the verb must be singular.

Correction: *Sally, as well as her sister, plans to go into nursing.*

WRITING

Error: *There has been many car accidents lately on that street.*

Problem: The subject *accidents* in this sentence is plural; the verb must be plural also, even though it comes before the subject.

Correction: *There have been many car accidents lately on that street.*

Error: *Every one of us have a reason to attend the school musical.*

Problem: The simple subject is the phrase *every one*, not the *us* in the prepositional phrase. Therefore, the verb must be singular also.

Correction: *Every one of us has a reason to attend the school musical.*

Error: *Either the police captain or his officers is going to the convention.*

Problem: In either/or and neither/nor constructions, the verb agrees with the subject closer to it.

Correction: *Either the police captain or his officers are going to the convention.*

Identify Agreements between Pronoun and Antecedent

A pronoun must correspond to its antecedent in number (singular or plural), person (first, second, or third person), and gender (male, female, or neutral). A pronoun must refer clearly to a single word, not to a complete idea.

A pronoun shift is a grammatical error in which the author starts a sentence, paragraph, or section of a paper using one particular type of pronoun and then suddenly shifts to another. This often confuses the reader.

Error: *A teacher should treat all their students fairly.*

Problem: Since *teacher* is singular, the pronoun referring to it must also be singular. Otherwise, the noun has to be made plural.

Correction: *Teachers should treat all their students fairly.*

Error: *When an actor is rehearsing for a play, it often helps if you can memorize the lines in advance.*

Problem: *Actor* is a third-person word; that is, the writer is talking about the subject. The pronoun *you* is in the second person, which means the writer is talking to the subject.

RECOGNIZE EFFECTIVE SENTENCES

Correction: *When actors are rehearsing for plays, it helps if they can memorize the lines in advance.*

Error: *The workers in the factory were upset when his or her paychecks didn't arrive on time.*

Problem: *Workers* is a plural form, while *his or her* refers to one person.

Correction: *The workers in the factory were upset when their paychecks didn't arrive on time.*

Error: *The charity auction was highly successful, which pleased everyone.*

Problem: In this sentence, the pronoun *which* refers to the idea of the auction's success. In fact, *which* has no antecedent in the sentence; the word *success* is not stated.

Correction: *Everyone was pleased at the success of the auction.*

Error: *Lana told Melanie that she would like aerobics.*

Problem: The person that *she* refers to is unclear; *she* could be either Lana or Melanie.

Correction: *Lana said that Melanie would like aerobics.*

-OR-
Lana told Melanie that she, Melanie, would like aerobics.

Error: *I dislike accounting even though my brother is one.*

Problem: A person's occupation is not the same as a field, and the pronoun *one* is thus incorrect. Note that the word *accountant* is not used in the sentence, so *one* has no antecedent.

Correction: *I dislike accounting even though my brother is an accountant.*

SKILL 21.4 Identify standard placement of modifiers, parallel structure, and use of negatives in sentence formation

Particular phrases that are not placed near the one word they modify often result in misplaced modifiers. Particular phrases that do not relate to the subject being modified result in dangling modifiers.

Error: *Weighing the options carefully, a decision was made regarding the punishment of the convicted murderer.*

Problem: Who is weighing the options? No one capable of weighing is named in the sentence; thus, the participle phrase weighing the options carefully dangles. This problem can be corrected by adding a subject of the sentence capable of doing the action.

Correction: *Weighing the options carefully, the judge made a decision regarding the punishment of the convicted murderer.*

Error: *Returning to my favorite watering hole, brought back many fond memories.*

Problem: The person who returned is never indicated, and the participle phrase dangles. This problem can be corrected by creating a dependent clause from the modifying phrase.

Correction: *When I returned to my favorite watering hole, many fond memories came back to me.*

Error: *One damaged house stood only to remind townspeople of the hurricane.*

Problem: The placement of the misplaced modifier *only* suggests that the sole reason the house remained was to serve as a reminder. The faulty modifier creates ambiguity.

Correction: *Only one damaged house stood, reminding townspeople of the hurricane.*

Faulty Parallelism

Two or more elements stated in a single clause should be expressed with the same (or parallel) structure (e.g., all adjectives, all verb forms, or all nouns).

Error: *She needed to be beautiful, successful, and have fame.*

Problem: The phrase *to be* is followed by two different structures: beautiful and successful are adjectives, and have fame is a verb phrase.

Correction: *She needed to be <u>beautiful</u>, <u>successful</u>, and <u>famous</u>.*
                   (adjective) (adjective) (adjective)
             -OR-
             She needed <u>beauty</u>, <u>success,</u> and <u>fame</u>.
                   (noun) (noun)   (noun)

Error: *I plan either to sell my car during the spring or during the summer.*

Problem: Paired conjunctions (also called *correlative conjunctions*, such as *either-or, both-and, neither-nor,* and *not only-but also*) need to be followed with similar structures. In the sentence above, *either* is followed by *to sell my car during the spring*, while *or* is followed only by the phrase *during the summer*.

Correction: *I plan to sell my car during either the spring or the summer.*

Error: *The President pledged to lower taxes and that he would cut spending to lower the national debt.*

Problem: Since the phrase *to lower taxes* follows the verb *pledged*, a similar structure of *to* is needed with the phrase *cut spending*.

Correction: *The President pledged to lower taxes and to cut spending to lower the national debt.*
             -OR-
             The President pledged that he would lower taxes and cut spending to lower the national debt.

Use of Negatives

Common negative words include: no, not, none, nothing, nowhere, neither, nobody, no one, hardly, scarcely, barely.

POSITIVE	NEGATIVE
TO BE	
<u>I am</u> afraid of the dark.	<u>I am not</u> afraid of the dark. (I'm not)
<u>You are</u> going to the store.	<u>You are not</u> going to the store. (you're not/you aren't)

Continued on next page

WRITING

TO BE	
They were pretty flowers.	They were not pretty flowers. (They weren't)
I was enjoying my day off.	I was not enjoying my day off. (I wasn't)
CONDITIONAL	
Charlotte will arrive at 8.	Charlotte will not arrive at 8.
Robert can run 26 miles.	Robert cannot run 26 miles. (can't run)
I could have been great!	I could not have been great. (couldn't have been)
PRESENT SIMPLE	
I want to go home.	I do not want to go home. (don't want)
Veronica walks too slowly.	Veronica does not walk too slowly. (doesn't walk)
PAST SIMPLE	
I skipped rope daily.	I did not skip rope daily. (didn't skip)
PRESENT PERFECT	
My mom has made my costume.	My mom has not made my costume. (hasn't made)
The Thompsons have just bought a dog.	The Thompsons have not just bought a dog. (haven't just bought)
HAVE VERSUS HAVE GOT	
I have two sisters.	I don't have two sisters.
I have got two sisters.	I haven't got two sisters.
Jeremy has school tomorrow.	Jeremy doesn't have school tomorrow.
Jeremy has got school tomorrow.	Jeremy hasn't got school tomorrow.

RECOGNIZE EFFECTIVE SENTENCES

A **DOUBLE NEGATIVE** occurs when two forms of negation are used in the same sentence. To correct a double negative, remove one of the negative words.

DOUBLE NEGATIVE: when two forms of negation are used in the same sentence

Error: *I haven't got nothing.*

Correction: *I haven't got anything.*
-OR-
I have nothing.

Error: *Don't nobody leave until 7 o'clock.*

Correction: *Do not leave until 7 o'clock.*
-OR-
Nobody leave until 7 o'clock.

It is also incorrect to combine a negative with an adverb such as "barely," "scarcely," or "hardly."

Error: *I can't barely stand it.*

Correction: *I can't stand it.*
-OR-
I can barely stand it.

SKILL 21.5 Recognize imprecise and inappropriate word choice

Practice Exercise: Word Usage

Choose the most effective word or phrase within the context suggested by the sentences.

1. The defendant was accused of _____ money from his employer.
   A. stealing
   B. embezzling
   C. robbing

2. Many tourists are attracted to Paradise Island because of its _____ climate.
   A. friendly
   B. peaceful
   C. balmy

3. The woman was angry because the tomato juice left an _____ stain on her brand new carpet.
   A. unsightly
   B. ugly
   C. unpleasant

WRITING

Practice Exercise: Word Usage

4. After disobeying orders, the army private was _____ by his superior officer.
   A. degraded
   B. attacked
   C. reprimanded

5. Sharon's critical evaluation of the student's book report left him feeling _____, which caused him to want to quit school.
   A. surprised
   B. depressed
   C. discouraged

6. The life-saving medication created by the scientist had a very _____ impact on further developments in the treatment of cancer.
   A. beneficial
   B. fortunate
   C. miraculous

7. *Phantom of The Opera* is one of Andrew Lloyd Webber's most successful musicals, largely because of its _____ themes.
   A. romantic
   B. melodramatic
   C. imaginary

8. The massive Fourth of July fireworks display _____ the partygoers with lots of colored light and sound.
   A. disgusted
   B. captivated
   C. captured

9. Many of the residents of Grand Forks, North Dakota, were forced to _____ their homes because of the flood.
   A. escape
   B. evacuate
   C. exit

10. The six hundred employees of General Electric were _____ by the company due to budgetary cutbacks.
    A. released
    B. terminated
    C. downsized

11. The force of the tornado _____ the many residents of the town of Russell, Kansas.
    A. intimidated
    B. repulsed
    C. frightened

12. Even though his new car was a lot easier to drive, Fred _____ to walk to work every day because he liked the exercise.
    A. needed
    B. preferred
    C. considered

13. June's parents were very upset over the school board's decision to suspend her from Adams High for a week. Before they filed a lawsuit against the board, they _____ with a lawyer to help them make a decision.
    A. consulted
    B. debated
    C. conversed

14. The race car driver's _____ in handling the automobile was a key factor in his victory.
    A. patience
    B. precision
    C. determination

RECOGNIZE EFFECTIVE SENTENCES

Practice Exercise: Word Usage (cont.)

15. After impressing the judges with her talent and charm, the beauty contestant _____ more popularity by singing an aria from *La Boheme.*

    A. captured
    B. scored
    C. gained

16. The stained-glass window was _____ after a large brick flew through it during the riot.

    A. damaged
    B. cracked
    C. shattered

17. The class didn't know what happened to the professor until it was _____ by the principal why he dropped out of school.

    A. informed
    B. discovered
    C. explained

Answer Key: Word Usage

1. A.
2. C.
3. A.
4. C.
5. C.
6. A.
7. A.
8. B.
9. B.
10. C.
11. C.
12. B.
13. A.
14. B.
15. C.
16. C.
17. C.

WRITING

COMPETENCY 22
RECOGNIZE EDITED AMERICAN ENGLISH USAGE

SKILL 22.1 Recognize the standard use of verb forms and pronouns

Past Tense and Past Participles

Both regular and irregular verbs must appear in their standard forms for each tense. Note: The *-ed* or *-d* ending is added to regular verbs in the past tense and to past participles.

REGULAR VERB FORMS		
Infinitive	Past Tense	Past Participle
bake	baked	baked

IRREGULAR VERB FORMS		
Infinitive	Past Tense	Past Participle
be	was/were	been
become	became	become
break	broke	broken
bring	brought	brought
choose	chose	chosen
come	came	come
do	did	done
draw	drew	drawn
eat	ate	eaten

Continued on next page

RECOGNIZE EDITED AMERICAN ENGLISH USAGE

Infinitive	Past Tense	Past Participle
fall	fell	fallen
forget	forgot	forgotten
freeze	froze	frozen
give	gave	given
go	went	gone
frow	grew	grown
have/has	had	had
hide	hid	hidden
know	knew	known
lay	laid	laid
lie	lay	lain
ride	rode	ridden
rise	rose	risen
run	ran	run
see	saw	seen
steal	stole	stolen
take	took	taken
tell	told	told
throw	threw	thrown
wear	wore	worn
write	wrote	written

WRITING

Error: *She should have went to her doctor's appointment at the scheduled time.*

Problem: The past participle of the verb *to go* is *gone*. *Went* expresses the simple past tense.

Correction: *She should have gone to her doctor's appointment at the scheduled time.*

Error: *My train is suppose to arrive before two o'clock.*

Problem: The verb following *train* is a present tense passive construction, which requires the present tense verb *to be* and the past participle.

Correction: *My train is supposed to arrive before two o'clock.*

Error: *Linda should of known that the car wouldn't start after leaving it out in the cold all night.*

Problem: *Should of* is a nonstandard expression. *Of* is not a verb.

Correction: *Linda should have known that the car wouldn't start after leaving it out in the cold all night.*

Verb Tenses

Verb tenses must refer to the same time consistently, unless a change in time is required.

Error: *Despite the increased number of students attending school this year, overall attendance is higher last year at the sporting events.*

Problem: The verb *is* represents an inconsistent shift to the present tense when the action refers to a past occurrence.

Correction: *Despite the increased number of students attending school this year, overall attendance was higher last year at sporting events.*

Error: *My friend Lou, who just competed in the marathon, ran since he was twelve years old.*

Problem: Because Lou continues to run, the present perfect tense is needed.

Correction: *My friend Lou, who just competed in the marathon, has run since he was twelve years old.*

Error: *The mayor congratulated Wallace Mangham, who renovates the city hall last year.*

Problem: Although the speaker is talking in the present, the action of renovating the city hall was in the past.

Correction: *The mayor congratulated Wallace Mangham, who renovated the city hall last year.*

Rules for Clearly Identifying Pronoun Reference

Make sure that the antecedent reference is clear and cannot refer to something else.

A "distant relative" is a relative pronoun or a relative clause that has been placed too far away from the antecedent to which it refers. It is a common error to place a verb between the relative pronoun and its antecedent.

Error: *Return the books to the library that are overdue.*

Problem: The relative clause *that are overdue* refers to the books and should be placed immediately after the antecedent.

Correction: *Return the books that are overdue to the library.*
-OR-
Return the overdue books to the library.

A pronoun should not refer to adjectives or possessive nouns

Adjectives, nouns, or possessive pronouns should not be used as antecedents. This will create ambiguity in sentences.

Error: *In Todd's letter, he told his mom he'd broken the priceless vase.*

Problem: In this sentence, the pronoun *he* seems to refer to the noun phrase *Todd's letter*, though it is probably meant to refer to the possessive noun *Todd's*.

Correction: *In his letter, Todd told his mom that he had broken the priceless vase.*

A pronoun should not refer to an implied idea

A pronoun must refer to a specific antecedent rather than an implied antecedent. When an antecedent is not stated specifically, the reader has to guess or assume

WRITING

> **EXPLETIVE:** a pronoun that does not have an antecedent

the meaning of a sentence. Pronouns that do not have antecedents are called **EXPLETIVES**. "It" and "there" are the most common expletives, though other pronouns can become expletives as well. In informal conversation, expletives allow for casual presentation of ideas without supporting evidence. However, in more formal writing, it is best to be more precise.

Error: *She said that it is important to floss every day.*

Problem: The pronoun *it* refers to an implied idea.

Correction: *She said that flossing every day is important.*

Error: *Milt and Bette returned the books because they had missing pages.*

Problem: The pronoun *they* does not refer to the antecedent.

Correction: *The customers returned the books with missing pages.*

Using Who, That, and Which

Who, whom, and *whose* refer to human beings and can introduce either essential or nonessential clauses. *That* refers to things other than humans and is used to introduce essential clauses. *Which* refers to things other than humans and is used to introduce nonessential clauses.

Error: *The doctor that performed the surgery said the patient would recover fully.*

Problem: Since the relative pronoun is referring to a human, *who* should be used.

Correction: *The doctor who performed the surgery said the patient would recover fully.*

Error: *That ice cream cone that you just ate looked delicious.*

Problem: *That* has already been used, so you must use *which* to introduce the next clause, whether it is essential or nonessential.

Correction: *That ice cream cone, which you just ate, looked delicious.*

Identify Proper Case Forms

Pronouns, unlike nouns, change case forms. Pronouns must be in the subjective, objective, or possessive form, according to their function in the sentence.

PERSONAL PRONOUNS						
	SUBJECTIVE (NOMINATIVE)		POSSESSIVE		OBJECTIVE	
	Singular	Plural	Singular	Plural	Singular	Plural
1st person	I	we	my	our ours	me	us
2nd person	you	you	your yours	your yours	you	you
3rd person	he she it	they	his her/hers its	their theirs	him her it	them

RELATIVE PRONOUNS	
who	Subjective/Nominative
whom	Objective
whose	Possessive

Error: *Tom and me have reserved seats for next week's baseball game.*

Problem: The pronoun *me* is the subject of the verb *have reserved* and should be in the subjective form.

Correction: *Tom and I have reserved seats for next week's baseball game.*

Error: *Mr. Green showed all of we students how to make paper hats.*

Problem: The pronoun *we* is the object of the preposition *of*. It should be in the objective form, us.

Correction: *Mr. Green showed all of us students how to make paper hats.*

WRITING

Error: *Who's coat is this?*

Problem: The interrogative possessive pronoun is *whose*; *who's* is the contraction for *who is*.

Correction: *Whose coat is this?*

Error: *The voters will choose the candidate whom has the best qualifications for the job.*

Problem: The case of the relative pronoun who or whom is determined by the pronoun's function in the clause in which it appears. The word who is in the subjective case, and whom is in the objective. Analyze how the pronoun is being used within the sentence.

Correction: *The voters will choose the candidate who has the best qualifications for the job.*

> **SKILL 22.2** Recognize the standard formation and use of adverbs, adjectives, comparatives, superlatives, and plural and possessive forms of nouns

ADJECTIVES: words that modify or describe nouns or pronouns

ADJECTIVES are words that modify or describe nouns or pronouns. Adjectives usually precede the words they modify but not always; for example, an adjective may occur after a linking verb.

ADVERBS are words that modify verbs, adjectives, or other adverbs. They cannot modify nouns. Adverbs answer such questions as how, why, when, where, how much, or how often. Many adverbs are formed by adding *-ly*.

ADVERBS: words that modify verbs, adjectives, or other adverbs

Error: *The birthday cake tasted sweetly.*

Problem: *Tasted* is a linking verb; the modifier that follows should be an adjective, not an adverb.

Correction: *The birthday cake tasted sweet.*

Error: *You have done good with this project.*

Problem: *Good* is an adjective and cannot be used to modify a verb phrase such as *have done*.

Correction: *You have done well with this project.*

Error: *The coach was positive happy about the team's chance of winning.*

Problem: The adjective positive cannot be used to modify another adjective, *happy*. An adverb is needed instead.

Correction: *The coach was positively happy about the team's chance of winning.*

Error: *The fireman acted quick and brave to save the child from the burning building.*

Problem: *Quick* and *brave* are adjectives and cannot be used to describe a verb. Adverbs are needed instead.

Correction: *The fireman acted quickly and bravely to save the child from the burning building.*

Appropriate Comparative and Superlative Degree Forms

When comparisons are made, the correct form of the adjective or adverb must be used. The comparative form is used for two items. The superlative form is used for more than two items.

	Comparative	Superlative
slow	slower	slowest
young	younger	youngest
tall	taller	tallest

With some words, *more* and *most* are used to make comparisons instead of *-er* and *-est*.

	Comparative	Superlative
energetic	more energetic	most energetic
quickly	more quickly	most quickly

Comparisons must be made between similar structures or items. In the sentence "My house is similar in color to Steve's," one house is being compared to another house, as understood by the use of the possessive *Steve's*.

On the other hand, if the sentence reads "My house is similar in color to Steve," the comparison would be faulty because it would be comparing the house to Steve, not to Steve's house.

Error: *Last year's rides at the carnival were bigger than this year.*

Problem: In the sentence as it is worded, the rides at the carnival are being compared to this year, not to this year's rides.

Correction: *Last year's rides at the carnival were bigger than this year's.*

Plural Nouns

A good dictionary is an invaluable resource that can replace the need to learn complex spelling rules based on phonics or letter doubling, especially when the exceptions to these rules have not been mastered by adulthood. Learning to use a dictionary and thesaurus will be a rewarding use of time.

Most plurals of nouns that end in hard consonants or in hard consonant sounds followed by a silent *e* are made by adding *-s*. Plurals of some words ending in vowels are formed by adding only *-s*.

> fingers, numerals, banks, bugs, riots, homes, gates, radios, bananas

For nouns that end in soft consonant sounds—*s, j, x, z, ch,* and *sh*—the plurals are formed by adding *-es*. Plurals of some nouns ending in *o* are formed by adding *-es*.

> dresses, waxes, churches, brushes, tomatoes

For nouns ending in *y* preceded by a vowel, just add *-s*.

> boys, alleys

For nouns ending in *y* preceded by a consonant, change the *y* to *i* and add *-es*.

> babies, corollaries, frugalities, poppies

Some nouns' plurals are formed irregularly or remain the same.

> sheep, deer, children, leaves, oxen

Some nouns derived from foreign words, especially Latin words, are made plural in two different ways. Sometimes the meanings are the same; other times the two plural forms are used in slightly different contexts. It is always wise to consult the dictionary.

RECOGNIZE EDITED AMERICAN ENGLISH USAGE

appendices, appendixes *criterion, criteria*
indexes, indices *crisis, crises*

Make the plurals of closed (solid) compound words in the usual way.

timelines, hairpins
cupfuls, handfuls

Make the plurals of open or hyphenated compounds by adding the change in inflection to the word that changes in number.

fathers-in-law, courts-martial, masters of art, doctors of medicine

Make the plurals of letters, numbers, and abbreviations by adding *-s*.

fives and tens, IBMs, 1990s, ps *and* qs *(Note that letters are italicized.)*

Possessive Nouns

Make the possessives of singular nouns by adding an apostrophe followed by the letter *s* (*'s*).

baby's bottle, mother's job, elephant's eye, teacher's desk,
sympathizer's protests, week's postponement

Make the possessives of singular nouns ending in *s* by adding either an apostrophe or an apostrophe followed by the letter *s*, depending upon common usage or sound. When the possessive sounds awkward, use a prepositional phrase instead. Even with the sibilant ending, with a few exceptions, it is advisable to use the *'s* construction.

dress's color, species' characteristics (or characteristics of the species),
James' hat (or James's hat), Dolores's shirt

Make the possessives of plural nouns ending in *s* by adding an apostrophe after the *s*.

horses' coats, jockeys' times, four days' time

Make the possessives of plural nouns that do not end in s by adding *'s*, just as with singular nouns.

children's shoes, deer's antlers, cattle's horns

Note: *Because a gerund functions as a noun, any noun preceding it and operating as a possessive adjective must reflect the necessary inflection. However, if the gerundive following the noun is a participle, no inflection is added.*

The general was perturbed by the private's sleeping on duty. *(The word sleeping is a gerund, the object of the preposition* by.*)*
-but-
The general was perturbed to see the private sleeping on duty. *(The word* sleeping *is a participle modifying* private.*)*

WRITING

Make the possessives of compound nouns by adding the inflection at the end of the word or phrase.

> *the mayor of Los Angeles' campaign, the mailman's new truck, the mailmen's new trucks, my father-in-law's first wife, the keepsakes' values, several daughters-in-law's husbands*

SKILL 22.3 Recognize standard punctuation

Commas

COMMA: used to indicate a brief pause

COMMAS are used to indicate a brief pause. They are used to set off dependent clauses and long introductory word groups, to separate words in a series, to set off unimportant material that interrupts the flow of the sentence, and to separate independent clauses joined by conjunctions.

Error: *After I finish my master's thesis I plan to work in Chicago.*

Problem: A comma is needed after an introductory dependent word group containing a subject and verb.

Correction: *After I finish my master's thesis, I plan to work in Chicago.*

Error: *I washed waxed and vacuumed my car today.*

Problem: Commas should separate nouns, phrases, or clauses in a list, as well as two or more coordinate adjectives that modify one word. Although the word *and* is sometimes considered optional, it is often necessary to clarify the meaning.

Correction: *I washed, waxed, and vacuumed my car today.*

Error: *She was a talented dancer but she is mostly remembered for her singing ability.*

Problem: A comma is needed before a conjunction that joins two independent clauses (complete sentences).

Correction: *She was a talented dancer, but she is mostly remembered for her singing ability.*

RECOGNIZE EDITED AMERICAN ENGLISH USAGE

Error: *This incident is I think typical of what can happen when the community remains so divided.*

Problem: Commas are needed between nonessential words or words that interrupt the main clause.

Correction: *This incident is, I think, typical of what can happen when the community remains so divided.*

Semicolons and Colons

SEMICOLONS are needed to separate two or more closely related independent clauses when a transitional adverb introduces the second clause. (These clauses may also be written as separate sentences, preferably by placing the adverb within the second sentence.)

> **SEMICOLONS:** used to separate two or more closely related independent clauses when a transitional adverb introduces the second clause

Error: *I climbed to the top of the mountain, it took me three hours.*

Problem: A comma alone cannot separate two independent clauses. Instead, a semicolon is needed to separate two related sentences.

Correction: *I climbed to the top of the mountain; it took me three hours.*

Error: *In the movie, asteroids destroyed Dallas, Texas, Kansas City, Missouri, and Boston, Massachusetts.*

Problem: Semicolons are needed to separate items in a series that already contain internal punctuation.

Correction: *In the movie, asteroids destroyed Dallas, Texas; Kansas City, Missouri; and Boston, Massachusetts.*

COLONS are used to introduce lists and to emphasize what follows.

> **COLONS:** used to introduce lists and to emphasize the text that follows

Error: *Essays will receive the following grades, A for excellent, B for good, C for average, and D for unsatisfactory.*

Problem: A colon is needed to emphasize the information or list that follows.

Correction: *Essays will receive the following grades: A for excellent, B for good, C for average, and D for unsatisfactory.*

WRITING

Error: *The school carnival included: amusement rides, clowns, food booths, and a variety of games.*

Problem: The material preceding the colon and the list that follows are not complete sentences. Do not separate a verb (or preposition) from the object.

Correction: *The school carnival included amusement rides, clowns, food booths, and a variety of games.*

Apostrophes

APOSTROPHES are used to show contractions or possession.

> **APOSTROPHES:** used to show contractions or possession

Error: *She shouldnt be permitted to smoke cigarettes in the building.*

Problem: An apostrophe is needed in a contraction in place of the missing letter.

Correction: *She shouldn't be permitted to smoke cigarettes in the building.*

Error: *My cousins motorcycle was stolen from his driveway.*

Problem: An apostrophe is needed to show possession.

Correction: *My cousin's motorcycle was stolen from his driveway. (Note: The use of the apostrophe before the letter "s" means that there is just one cousin. The plural form would read as follows: My cousins' motorcycle was stolen from their driveway.)*

Error: *The childrens new kindergarten teacher was also a singer.*

Problem: An apostrophe is needed to show possession.

Correction: *The children's new kindergarten teacher was also a singer.*

Error: *Children screams could be heard for miles.*

Problem: An apostrophe and the letter *s* are needed in the sentence to show who is screaming.

Correction: *Children's screams could be heard for miles. (Note: Because the word children is already plural, the apostrophe and -s must be added afterward to show ownership.)*

Quotation Marks

In a quoted statement that is either declarative or imperative, place the period inside the closing quotation marks.

> "The airplane crashed on the runway during takeoff."

If other words in the sentence follow the quotation, place a comma inside the closing quotations marks and a period at the end of the sentence.

> "The airplane crashed on the runway during takeoff," said the announcer.

Usually, when a quoted title or expression occurs at the end of a sentence, the period is placed before the single or double quotation marks.

> "The middle school readers were unprepared to understand Bryant's poem 'Thanatopsis.'"
>
> Early book-length adventure stories such as Don Quixote and The Three Musketeers were known as "picaresque novels."

The final quotation mark precedes the period if the content of the sentence is about a speech or quote.

> The first thing out of his mouth was "Hi, I'm home."
>
> -BUT-
>
> The first line of his speech began: "I arrived home to an empty house".

In interrogatory or exclamatory sentences, the question mark or exclamation point should be positioned outside the closing quotation marks if the quote itself is a statement, command, or cited title.

> Who decided to lead us in the recitation of the "Pledge of Allegiance"?
>
> Why was Tillie shaking as she began her recitation, "Once upon a midnight dreary . . ."?
>
> I was embarrassed when Mrs. White said, "Your slip is showing"!

In declarative sentences, where the quotation is a question or an exclamation, place the question mark or exclamation point inside the quotation marks.

> The hall monitor yelled, "Fire! Fire!"
>
> "Fire! Fire!" yelled the hall monitor.
>
> Cory shrieked, "Is there a mouse in the room?" (In this instance, the question supersedes the exclamation.)

Quotations—whether words, phrases, or clauses—should be punctuated according to the rules of the grammatical function they serve in the sentence.

> *The works of Shakespeare, "the Bard of Avon," have been contested as originating with other authors.*
>
> *"You'll get my money," the old man warned, "when 'hell freezes over'."*
>
> *Sheila cited the passage that began "Four score and seven years ago . . . ." (Note the ellipsis followed by an enclosed period.)*
>
> *"Old Ironsides" inspired the preservation of the U.S.S. Constitution.*

Use quotation marks to enclose the titles of shorter works: songs, short poems, short stories, essays, and chapters of books. (See "Dashes and Italics" for rules on punctuating longer titles.)

> *"The Tell-Tale Heart" "Casey at the Bat" "America the Beautiful"*

Dashes and Italics

EM DASHES: used to denote sudden breaks in thought or if commas are already used in the sentence for amplification or explanation

Place EM DASHES to denote sudden breaks in thought.

> *Some periods in literature—the Romantic Age, for example—spanned different periods in different countries.*

Use dashes instead of commas if commas are already used elsewhere in the sentence for amplification or explanation.

> *The Fireside Poets included three Brahmans—James Russell Lowell, Henry David Wadsworth, and Oliver Wendell Holmes.*

ITALICS: used to punctuate the titles of long works of literature, names of periodical publications, musical scores, works of art, and motion picture, television, and radio programs

Use ITALICS to punctuate the titles of long works of literature, names of periodical publications, musical scores, works of art, and motion picture, television, and radio programs. (If italic type is unavailable, students should be instructed to use underlining where italics would be appropriate.)

> *The Idylls of the King*   *Hiawatha*   *The Sound and the Fury*
>
> *Mary Poppins*   *Newsweek*   *The Nutcracker Suite*

Capitalize all proper names of persons (including specific organizations or agencies of government); places (countries, states, cities, parks, and specific geographical areas); and things (political parties, structures, historical and cultural terms, and calendar and time designations); and religious terms (any deity, revered person or group, sacred writings).

RECOGNIZE EDITED AMERICAN ENGLISH USAGE

> Percy Bysshe Shelley, Argentina, Mount Rainier National Park, Grand Canyon, League of Nations, the Sears Tower, Birmingham, Lyric Theater, Americans, Midwesterners, Democrats, Renaissance, Boy Scouts of America, Easter, God, Bible, Dead Sea Scrolls, Koran

Capitalize proper adjectives and titles used with proper names.

> California gold rush, President John Adams, French fries, Homeric epic, Romanesque architecture, Senator John Glenn

Note: Some words that represent titles and offices are not capitalized unless used with a proper name.

Capitalized	Not Capitalized
Congressman McKay	the congressman from Florida
Commander Alger	commander of the Pacific Fleet
Queen Elizabeth	the queen of England

Capitalize all main words in titles of works of literature, art, and music.

Error: *Emma went to Dr. Peters for treatment because her own Doctor was on vacation.*

Problem: The use of capital letters with Emma and Dr. Peters is correct since they are specific (proper) names; the title Dr. is also capitalized. However, the word doctor is not a specific name and should not be capitalized.

Correction: *Emma went to Dr. Peters for treatment because her own doctor was on vacation.*

Error: *Our Winter break does not start until next wednesday.*

Problem: Days of the week are capitalized, but seasons are not capitalized.

Correction: *Our winter break does not start until next Wednesday.*

Error: *The exchange student from israel, who came to study Biochemistry, spoke spanish very well.*

Problem: Languages and the names of countries are always capitalized. Courses are also capitalized when they refer to a specific course; they are not capitalized when they refer to courses in general.

Correction: *The exchange student from Israel, who came to study Biochemistry, spoke Spanish very well.*

WRITING

THEA TEXAS HIGHER EDUCATION ASSESSMENT

READING SAMPLE TEST

Read the following paragraph, and answer the questions that follow.

This writer has often been asked to tutor hospitalized children with cystic fibrosis. While undergoing all the precautionary measures to see these children (i.e., scrubbing thoroughly and donning sterilized protective gear—for the children's protection), she has often wondered why their parents subject these children to the pressures of schooling and trying to catch up on what they have missed because of hospitalization, a normal part of cystic fibrosis patients' lives. These children undergo so many tortuous treatments a day that it seems cruel to expect them to learn as normal children do, especially with their life expectancies as short as they are.

1. **What is meant by the word "precautionary" in the second sentence?**
   (Easy) (Skill 1.1)

   A. Careful
   B. Protective
   C. Medical
   D. Sterilizing

2. **What is the main idea of this passage?**
   (Average) (Skill 2.1)

   A. There is a lot of preparation involved in visiting a patient of cystic fibrosis.
   B. Children with cystic fibrosis are incapable of living normal lives.
   C. Certain concessions should be made for children with cystic fibrosis.
   D. Children with cystic fibrosis die young.

3. **What is the author's purpose?**
   (Average) (Skill 3.1)

   A. To inform
   B. To entertain
   C. To describe
   D. To narrate

4. **What is the author's tone?**
   (Rigorous) (Skill 3.3)

   A. Sympathetic
   B. Cruel
   C. Disbelieving
   D. Cheerful

5. **What type of organizational pattern is the author using?**
   (Rigorous) (Skill 4.3)

   A. Classification
   B. Explanation
   C. Compare and contrast
   D. Cause and effect

6. **How is the author so familiar with the procedures used when visiting a child with cystic fibrosis?**
   (Easy) (Skill 4.5)

   A. She has read about it.
   B. She works in a hospital.
   C. She is the parent of one.
   D. She often tutors them.

7. **What kind of relationship is found within the last sentence that starts with "These children undergo..." and ends with "...as short as they are"?**
   (Rigorous) (Skill 4.5)

   A. Addition
   B. Explanation
   C. Generalization
   D. Classification

8. **Does the author present an argument that is valid or invalid concerning the schooling of children with cystic fibrosis?**
   (Easy) (Skill 5.4)

   A. Valid
   B. Invalid

9. **The author states that it is "cruel" to expect children with cystic fibrosis to learn as "normal" children do. Is this a fact or an opinion?**
   (Easy) (Skill 5.5)

   A. Fact
   B. Opinion

10. **Is there evidence of bias in this paragraph?**
    (Rigorous) (Skill 5.6)

    A. Yes
    B. No

Read the following passage, and answer the questions that follow.
Disciplinary practices have been found to affect diverse areas of child development such as moral values, obedience to authority, and performance at school. Even though the dictionary has a specific definition for the word "discipline," it is still open to interpretation by people of different cultures.

There are four types of disciplinary styles: assertion of power, withdrawal of love, reasoning, and permissiveness. Assertion of power involves the use of force to discourage unwanted behavior. Withdrawal of love involves making the love of a parent conditional on children's good behavior. Reasoning involves persuading children to behave one way rather than another. Permissiveness involves allowing children to do as they please and face the consequences of their actions.

11. **What is the meaning of the word "diverse" in the first sentence?**
(Average) (Skill 1.1)

   A. Many
   B. Related to children
   C. Disciplinary
   D. More

12. **What is the main idea of this passage?**
(Easy) (Skill 2.1)

   A. Different people have different ideas of what discipline is.
   B. Permissiveness is the most widely used disciplinary style.
   C. Most people agree on their definition of discipline.
   D. There are four disciplinary styles.

13. **Name the four types of disciplinary styles.**
(Easy) (Skill 2.2)

   A. Reasoning, power assertion, morality, and permissiveness
   B. Morality, reasoning, permissiveness, and withdrawal of love
   C. Withdrawal of love, permissiveness, assertion of power, and reasoning
   D. Permissiveness, morality, reasoning, and power assertion

14. **What does the technique of reasoning involve?**
(Average) (Skill 2.2)

   A. Persuading children to behave in a certain way
   B. Allowing a child to do as he or she pleases
   C. Using force to discourage unwanted behavior
   D. Making love conditional on good behavior

15. **What organizational structure is used in the first sentence of the second paragraph?**
    (Rigorous) (Skill 3.1)

    A. Addition
    B. Explanation
    C. Definition
    D. Simple listing

16. **What is the author's purpose in writing this?**
    (Average) (Skill 3.1)

    A. To describe
    B. To narrate
    C. To entertain
    D. To inform

17. **What is the author's tone?**
    (Rigorous) (Skill 3.3)

    A. Disbelieving
    B. Angry
    C. Informative
    D. Optimistic

18. **What is the overall organizational pattern of this passage?**
    (Rigorous) (Skill 4.3)

    A. Generalization
    B. Cause and effect
    C. Addition
    D. Summary

19. **From reading this passage we can conclude that**
    (Average) (Skill 5.1)

    A. The author is a teacher.
    B. The author has many children.
    C. The author has written a book about discipline.
    D. The author has done a lot of research on discipline.

20. **The author states that "assertion of power involves the use of force to discourage unwanted behavior." Is this a fact or an opinion?**
    (Average) (Skill 5.5)

    A. Fact
    B. Opinion

21. **Is this passage biased?**
    (Rigorous) (Skill 5.6)

    A. Yes
    B. No

Read the following passage, and answer the questions that follow.
One of the most difficult problems plaguing American education is the assessment of teachers. No one denies that teachers ought to be answerable for what they do, but what exactly does that mean? *The Oxford American Dictionary* defines accountability as the obligation to give a reckoning or explanation for one's actions.

Do students have to learn, for teaching to have taken place? Historically, teaching has not been defined in this restrictive manner; teachers were thought to be responsible for the quantity and quality of material covered and for the way in which it was presented. However, some definitions of teaching now imply that students must learn in order for teaching to have taken place.

As a teacher who tries my best to keep current on all the latest teaching strategies, I believe that those teachers who do not bother to read an educational journal every once in a while should be kept under close watch. There are many teachers out there who have been teaching for decades and refuse to change their ways, although research has proven that their methods are outdated and ineffective. There is no place in the profession of teaching for these types of individuals. It is time that the American educational system clean house, for the sake of our children.

22. **What is the meaning of the word "reckoning" in the third sentence?**
(Easy) (Skill 1.1)

A. Thought
B. Answer
C. Obligation
D. Explanation

23. **What is meant by the word "plaguing" in the first sentence?**
(Average) (Skill 1.1)

A. Causing problems
B. Causing illness
C. Causing anger
D. Causing failure

24. **Where does the author get her definition of "accountability?"**
(Average) (Skill 1.1)

A. *Webster's Dictionary*
B. *Encyclopedia Britannica*
C. *Oxford Dictionary*
D. *World Book Encyclopedia*

25. **What is the main idea of the passage?**
(Average) (Skill 2.1)

A. Teachers should not be answerable for what they do.
B. Teachers who do not do their job should be fired.
C. The author is a good teacher.
D. Assessment of teachers is a serious problem in society today.

26. **The author states that teacher assessment is a problem for**
    (Average) (Skill 2.2)

    A. Elementary schools
    B. Secondary schools
    C. American education
    D. Families

27. **What is the author's purpose in writing this?**
    (Average) (Skill 3.1)

    A. To entertain
    B. To narrate
    C. To describe
    D. To persuade

28. **The author's tone is one of**
    (Rigorous) (Skill 3.3)

    A. Disbelief
    B. Excitement
    C. Support
    D. Concern

29. **Is there evidence of bias in this passage?**
    (Rigorous) (Skill 3.4)

    A. Yes
    B. No

30. **What is the organizational pattern of the second paragraph?**
    (Rigorous) (Skill 4.3)

    A. Cause and effect
    B. Classification
    C. Addition
    D. Explanation

31. **From the passage, one can infer that**
    (Average) (Skill 4.5)

    A. The author considers himself or herself to be a good teacher.
    B. Poor teachers should be fired.
    C. Students have to learn for teaching to take place.
    D. The author will be fired.

32. **Is this a valid argument?**
    (Easy) (Skill 5.3)

    A. Yes
    B. No

33. **Teachers who do not keep current on educational trends should be fired. Is this a fact or an opinion?**
    (Easy) (Skill 5.5)

    A. Fact
    B. Opinion

34. **What is the best summary for the passage?**
    (Average) (Skill 6.1)

    A. Teachers need to be more accountable.
    B. Today's teachers must be responsible for student learning.
    C. Older teachers have no place in the classroom.
    D. Teachers are responsible for the quantity they teach, not the quality.

Read the following paragraph, and answer the questions that follow.
Mr. Smith gave instructions for the painting to be hung on the wall. And then it leaped forth before his eyes: the little cottages on the river, the white clouds floating over the valley, and the green of the towering mountain ranges which were seen in the distance. The painting was so vivid that it seemed almost real. Mr. Smith was now absolutely certain that the painting had been worth the money.

35. **What is the meaning of the word "vivid" in the third sentence?**
    (Easy) (Skill 1.1)

    A. Lifelike
    B. Dark
    C. Expensive
    D. Big

36. **What does the author mean by the expression "it leaped forth before his eyes"?**
    (Average) (Skill 1.2)

    A. The painting fell off the wall.
    B. The painting appeared so real it was almost three-dimensional.
    C. The painting struck Mr. Smith in the face.
    D. Mr. Smith was hallucinating.

37. **What is the main idea of this passage?**
    (Average) (Skill 2.1)

    A. The painting that Mr. Smith purchased is expensive.
    B. Mr. Smith purchased a painting.
    C. Mr. Smith was pleased with the quality of the painting he had purchased.
    D. The painting depicted cottages and valleys.

38. **The author's purpose is to**
    (Average) (Skill 3.1)

    A. Inform
    B. Entertain
    C. Persuade
    D. Narrate

39. **From the last sentence, one can infer that**
    (Rigorous) (Skill 4.5)

    A. The painting was expensive.
    B. The painting was cheap.
    C. Mr. Smith was considering purchasing the painting.
    D. Mr. Smith thought the painting was too expensive and decided not to purchase it.

40. **Is this passage biased?**
    (Rigorous) (Skill 5.6)

    A. Yes
    B. No

THEA Sample Test

Answer Key

1.	B		21.	B
2.	C		22.	D
3.	C		23.	A
4.	A		24.	C
5.	B		25.	D
6.	D		26.	C
7.	B		27.	D
8.	B		28.	D
9.	B		29.	A
10.	A		30.	D
11.	A		31.	A
12.	A		32.	B
13.	C		33.	B
14.	A		34.	B
15.	D		35.	A
16.	D		36.	B
17.	C		37.	C
18.	C		38.	D
19.	D		39.	A
20.	A		40.	B

Rigor Table

Easy
1, 6, 8, 9, 12, 13, 22, 32, 33, 35

Average
2, 3, 11, 14, 16, 19, 20, 23, 24, 25, 26, 27, 31, 34, 36, 37, 38

Rigorous
4, 5, 7, 10, 15, 17, 18, 21, 28, 29, 30, 39, 40

READING SAMPLE TEST WITH RATIONALES

Read the following paragraph, and answer the questions that follow.
This writer has often been asked to tutor hospitalized children with cystic fibrosis. While undergoing all the precautionary measures to see these children (i.e., scrubbing thoroughly and donning sterilized protective gear—for the children's protection), she has often wondered why their parents subject these children to the pressures of schooling and trying to catch up on what they have missed because of hospitalization, a normal part of cystic fibrosis patients' lives. These children undergo so many tortuous treatments a day that it seems cruel to expect them to learn as normal children do, especially with their life expectancies as short as they are.

1. **What is meant by the word "precautionary" in the second sentence?**
   (Easy) (Skill 1.1)

   A. Careful
   B. Protective
   C. Medical
   D. Sterilizing

Answer: B. Protective
The writer uses expressions such as "protective gear" and "child's protection" to emphasize this.

2. **What is the main idea of this passage?**
   (Average) (Skill 2.1)

   A. There is a lot of preparation involved in visiting a patient of cystic fibrosis.
   B. Children with cystic fibrosis are incapable of living normal lives.
   C. Certain concessions should be made for children with cystic fibrosis.
   D. Children with cystic fibrosis die young.

Answer: C. Certain concessions should be made for children with cystic fibrosis
The author states that she wonders "why parents subject these children to the pressures of schooling," and that "it seems cruel to expect them to learn as normal children do." In making these statements, she appears to be expressing the belief that these children should not have to do what "normal" children do. They have enough to deal with—their illness itself.

3. **What is the author's purpose?**
   (Average) (Skill 3.1)

   A. To inform
   B. To entertain
   C. To describe
   D. To narrate

Answer: C. To describe
The author is simply describing her experience in working with children with cystic fibrosis.

4. **What is the author's tone?**
   (Rigorous) (Skill 3.3)

   A. Sympathetic
   B. Cruel
   C. Disbelieving
   D. Cheerful

Answer: A. Sympathetic
The author states that "it seems cruel to expect them to learn as normal children do," thereby indicating that she feels sorry for them.

5. **What type of organizational pattern is the author using?**
   (Rigorous) (Skill 4.3)

   A. Classification
   B. Explanation
   C. Compare and contrast
   D. Cause and effect

Answer: B. Explanation
The author mentions tutoring children with cystic fibrosis in her opening sentence and goes on to "explain" some of these issues that are involved with her job.

6. **How is the author so familiar with the procedures used when visiting a child with cystic fibrosis?**
    (Easy) (Skill 4.5)

    A. She has read about it.
    B. She works in a hospital.
    C. She is the parent of one.
    D. She often tutors them.

Answer: D. She often tutors them.
The writer states this fact in the opening sentence.

7. **What kind of relationship is found within the last sentence that starts with "These children undergo..." and ends with "...as short as they are"?**
    (Rigorous) (Skill 4.5)

    A. Addition
    B. Explanation
    C. Generalization
    D. Classification

Answer: B. Explanation
In mentioning that their life expectancies are short, she is explaining by giving one reason why it is cruel to expect them to learn as normal children do.

8. **Does the author present an argument that is valid or invalid concerning the schooling of children with cystic fibrosis?**
    (Easy) (Skill 5.4)

    A. Valid
    B. Invalid

Answer: B. Invalid
Even though to most readers, the writer's argument makes good sense, it is biased and lacks real evidence.

9. The author states that it is "cruel" to expect children with cystic fibrosis to learn as "normal" children do. Is this a fact or an opinion?
 (Easy) (Skill 5.5)

   A. Fact
   B. Opinion

Answer: B. Opinion
The fact that she states that it "seems" cruel indicates that there is no evidence to support this belief.

10. Is there evidence of bias in this paragraph?
 (Rigorous) (Skill 5.6)

   A. Yes
   B. No

Answer: A. Yes
The writer clearly feels sorry for these children and gears her writing in that direction.

Read the following passage, and answer the questions that follow.
Disciplinary practices have been found to affect diverse areas of child development such as moral values, obedience to authority, and performance at school. Even though the dictionary has a specific definition for the word "discipline," it is still open to interpretation by people of different cultures.

There are four types of disciplinary styles: assertion of power, withdrawal of love, reasoning, and permissiveness. Assertion of power involves the use of force to discourage unwanted behavior. Withdrawal of love involves making the love of a parent conditional on children's good behavior. Reasoning involves persuading children to behave one way rather than another. Permissiveness involves allowing children to do as they please and face the consequences of their actions.

11. **What is the meaning of the word "diverse" in the first sentence?**
    (Average) (Skill 1.1)

    A. Many
    B. Related to children
    C. Disciplinary
    D. More

Answer: A. Many
Any of the other choices would be redundant in this sentence.

12. **What is the main idea of this passage?**
    (Easy) (Skill 2.1)

    A. Different people have different ideas of what discipline is.
    B. Permissiveness is the most widely used disciplinary style.
    C. Most people agree on their definition of discipline.
    D. There are four disciplinary styles.

Answer: A. Different people have different ideas of what discipline is.
Choice C is not true; the opposite is stated in the passage. Choice B could be true, but we have no evidence of this. Choice D is just one of the many facts listed in the passage.

13. **Name the four types of disciplinary styles.**
    (Easy) (Skill 2.2)

    A. Reasoning, power assertion, morality, and permissiveness
    B. Morality, reasoning, permissiveness, and withdrawal of love
    C. Withdrawal of love, permissiveness, assertion of power, and reasoning
    D. Permissiveness, morality, reasoning, and power assertion

Answer: C. Withdrawal of love, permissiveness, assertion of power, and reasoning
This is directly stated in the second paragraph.

14. **What does the technique of reasoning involve?**
    (Average) (Skill 2.2)

    A. Persuading children to behave in a certain way
    B. Allowing a child to do as he or she pleases
    C. Using force to discourage unwanted behavior
    D. Making love conditional on good behavior

Answer: A. Persuading children to behave in a certain way
This fact is directly stated in the second paragraph.

15. **What organizational structure is used in the first sentence of the second paragraph?**
    (Rigorous) (Skill 3.1)

    A. Addition
    B. Explanation
    C. Definition
    D. Simple listing

Answer: D. Simple listing
The author simply states the types of disciplinary styles.

16. **What is the author's purpose in writing this?**
    (Average) (Skill 3.1)

    A. To describe
    B. To narrate
    C. To entertain
    D. To inform

Answer: D. To inform
The author is providing the reader with information about disciplinary practices.

17. **What is the author's tone?**
    (Rigorous) (Skill 3.3)

    A. Disbelieving
    B. Angry
    C. Informative
    D. Optimistic

Answer: C. Informative
The author appears to simply be stating the facts.

18. **What is the overall organizational pattern of this passage?**
    (Rigorous) (Skill 4.3)

    A. Generalization
    B. Cause and effect
    C. Addition
    D. Summary

Answer: C. Addition
The author has taken a subject, in this case discipline, and developed it point by point.

19. **From reading this passage we can conclude that**
    (Average) (Skill 5.1)

    A. The author is a teacher.
    B. The author has many children.
    C. The author has written a book about discipline.
    D. The author has done a lot of research on discipline.

Answer: D. The author has done a lot of research on discipline.
Given all the facts mentioned in the passage, this is the only inference one can make.

20. **The author states that "assertion of power involves the use of force to discourage unwanted behavior." Is this a fact or an opinion?**
    (Average) (Skill 5.5)

    A. Fact
    B. Opinion

Answer: A. Fact
The author appears to have done extensive research on this subject.

21. **Is this passage biased?**
    (Rigorous) (Skill 5.6)

    A. Yes
    B. No

Answer: B. No
If the reader were so inclined, he could research discipline and find this information.

Read the following passage, and answer the questions that follow.
One of the most difficult problems plaguing American education is the assessment of teachers. No one denies that teachers ought to be answerable for what they do, but what exactly does that mean? *The Oxford American Dictionary* defines accountability as the obligation to give a reckoning or explanation for one's actions.

Do students have to learn, for teaching to have taken place? Historically, teaching has not been defined in this restrictive manner; teachers were thought to be responsible for the quantity and quality of material covered and for the way in which it was presented. However, some definitions of teaching now imply that students must learn in order for teaching to have taken place.

As a teacher who tries my best to keep current on all the latest teaching strategies, I believe that those teachers who do not bother to read an educational journal every once in a while should be kept under close watch. There are many teachers out there who have been teaching for decades and refuse to change their ways, although research has proven that their methods are outdated and ineffective. There is no place in the profession of teaching for these types of individuals. It is time that the American educational system clean house, for the sake of our children.

22. **What is the meaning of the word "reckoning" in the third sentence?**
    (Easy) (Skill 1.1)

    A. Thought
    B. Answer
    C. Obligation
    D. Explanation

Answer: D. Explanation
The meaning of this word is directly stated in the same sentence.

23. **What is meant by the word "plaguing" in the first sentence?**
    (Average) (Skill 1.1)

    A. Causing problems
    B. Causing illness
    C. Causing anger
    D. Causing failure

Answer: A. Causing problems
The first paragraph makes this definition clear.

24. **Where does the author get her definition of "accountability?"**
    (Average) (Skill 1.1)

    A. *Webster's Dictionary*
    B. *Encyclopedia Britannica*
    C. *Oxford Dictionary*
    D. *World Book Encyclopedia*

Answer: C. *Oxford Dictionary*
This is directly stated in the third sentence of the first paragraph.

25. **What is the main idea of the passage?**
    (Average) (Skill 2.1)

    A. Teachers should not be answerable for what they do.
    B. Teachers who do not do their job should be fired.
    C. The author is a good teacher.
    D. Assessment of teachers is a serious problem in society today.

Answer: D. Assessment of teachers is a serious problem in society today.
Most of the passage is dedicated to elaborating on why teacher assessment is such a problem.

26. **The author states that teacher assessment is a problem for**
    (Average) (Skill 2.2)

    A. Elementary schools
    B. Secondary schools
    C. American education
    D. Families

Answer: C. American education
This fact is directly stated in the first paragraph.

27. What is the author's purpose in writing this?
(Average) (Skill 3.1)

- A. To entertain
- B. To narrate
- C. To describe
- D. To persuade

Answer: D. To persuade
The author does some describing, but the majority of her statements seemed geared towards convincing the reader that teachers who are lazy or who do not keep current should be fired.

28. The author's tone is one of
(Rigorous) (Skill 3.3)

- A. Disbelief
- B. Excitement
- C. Support
- D. Concern

Answer: D. Concern
The author appears concerned with the future of education.

29. Is there evidence of bias in this passage?
(Rigorous) (Skill 3.4)

- A. Yes
- B. No

Answer: A. Yes
The entire third paragraph is the author's opinion on the matter.

30. What is the organizational pattern of the second paragraph?
(Rigorous) (Skill 4.3)

- A. Cause and effect
- B. Classification
- C. Addition
- D. Explanation

Answer: D. Explanation
The author further explains what she meant by "...what exactly does that mean?" in the first paragraph.

31. **From the passage, one can infer that**
    (Average) (Skill 4.5)

    A. The author considers himself or herself to be a good teacher.
    B. Poor teachers should be fired.
    C. Students have to learn for teaching to take place.
    D. The author will be fired.

Answer: A. The author considers himself or herself to be a good teacher.
The first sentence of the third paragraph alludes to this.

32. **Is this a valid argument?**
    (Easy) (Skill 5.3)

    A. Yes
    B. No

Answer: B. No
In the third paragraph, the author appears to be resentful of lazy teachers.

33. **Teachers who do not keep current on educational trends should be fired. Is this a fact or an opinion?**
    (Easy) (Skill 5.5)

    A. Fact
    B. Opinion

Answer: B. Opinion
There may be those who feel they can be good teachers by using old methods.

34. **What is the best summary for the passage?**
    (Average) (Skill 6.1)

    A. Teachers need to be more accountable.
    B. Today's teachers must be responsible for student learning.
    C. Older teachers have no place in the classroom.
    D. Teachers are responsible for the quantity they teach, not the quality.

Answer: B. Today's teachers must be responsible for student learning.
The one idea that applies to the whole passage is Choice B.

Read the following paragraph, and answer the questions that follow.
Mr. Smith gave instructions for the painting to be hung on the wall. And then it leaped forth before his eyes: the little cottages on the river, the white clouds floating over the valley, and the green of the towering mountain ranges which were seen in the distance. The painting was so vivid that it seemed almost real. Mr. Smith was now absolutely certain that the painting had been worth the money.

35. What is the meaning of the word "vivid" in the third sentence?
    (Easy) (Skill 1.1)

    A. Lifelike
    B. Dark
    C. Expensive
    D. Big

Answer: A. Lifelike
This is reinforced by the second half of the same sentence.

36. What does the author mean by the expression "it leaped forth before his eyes"?
    (Average) (Skill 1.2)

    A. The painting fell off the wall.
    B. The painting appeared so real it was almost three-dimensional.
    C. The painting struck Mr. Smith in the face.
    D. Mr. Smith was hallucinating.

Answer: B. The painting appeared so real it was almost three-dimensional
This is almost directly stated in the third sentence.

37. What is the main idea of this passage?
    (Average) (Skill 2.1)

    A. The painting that Mr. Smith purchased is expensive.
    B. Mr. Smith purchased a painting.
    C. Mr. Smith was pleased with the quality of the painting he had purchased.
    D. The painting depicted cottages and valleys.

Answer: C. Mr. Smith was pleased with the quality of the painting he had purchased.
Every sentence in the paragraph alludes to this fact.

38. **The author's purpose is to**
    (Average) (Skill 3.1)

    A. Inform
    B. Entertain
    C. Persuade
    D. Narrate

Answer: D. Narrate
The author is simply narrating or telling the story of Mr. Smith and his painting.

39. **From the last sentence, one can infer that**
    (Rigorous) (Skill 4.5)

    A. The painting was expensive.
    B. The painting was cheap.
    C. Mr. Smith was considering purchasing the painting.
    D. Mr. Smith thought the painting was too expensive and decided not to purchase it.

Answer: A. The painting was expensive.
Choice B is incorrect because, had the painting been cheap, chances are that Mr. Smith would not have considered his purchase. Choices C and D are ruled out by the fact that the painting had already been purchased. The author makes this clear when she says, "...the painting had been worth the money."

40. **Is this passage biased?**
    (Rigorous) (Skill 5.6)

    A. Yes
    B. No

Answer: B. No
The author appears merely to be telling what happened when Mr. Smith had his new painting hung on the wall.

MATHEMATICS SAMPLE TEST

1. $\left(\dfrac{-4}{9}\right) + \left(\dfrac{-7}{10}\right) =$

   (Rigorous) (Skill 7.1)

   A. $\dfrac{23}{90}$

   B. $\dfrac{-23}{90}$

   C. $\dfrac{103}{90}$

   D. $\dfrac{-103}{90}$

2. $0.74 =$
   (Easy) (Skill 7.1)

   A. $\dfrac{74}{100}$

   B. 7.4%

   C. $\dfrac{33}{50}$

   D. $\dfrac{74}{10}$

3. $-9\dfrac{1}{4}$ ☐ $-8\dfrac{2}{3}$

   (Average) (Skill 7.1)

   A. =
   B. <
   C. >
   D. ≤

4. 303 is what percent of 600?
   (Average) (Skill 7.1)

   A. 0.505%
   B. 5.05%
   C. 505%
   D. 50.5%

5. An item that sells for $375 is put on sale at $120. What is the percent of decrease?
   (Average) (Skill 7.1)

   A. 25%
   B. 28%
   C. 68%
   D. 34%

6. Two mathematics classes have a total of 410 students. The 8:00 am class has 40 more than the 10:00 am class. How many students are in the 10:00 am class?
   (Average) (Skill 7.1)

   A. 123.3
   B. 370
   C. 185
   D. 330

7. A restaurant employs 465 people. There are 280 waiters and 185 cooks. If 168 waiters and 85 cooks receive pay raises, what percent of the waiters will receive a pay raise?
   (Average) (Skill 7.1)

   A. 36.13%
   B. 60%
   C. 60.22%
   D. 40%

8. $\frac{7}{9} + \frac{1}{3} \div \frac{2}{3} =$
   (Average) (Skill 7.1)

   A. $\frac{5}{3}$

   B. $\frac{3}{2}$

   C. 2

   D. $\frac{23}{18}$

9. Choose the statement that is true for all real numbers.
   (Rigorous) (Skill 7.1)

   A. $a = 0, b \neq 0$, then $\frac{b}{a} =$ undefined.

   B. $^-(a + (^-a)) = 2a$

   C. $2(ab) =^- (2a)b$

   D. $^-a(b+1) = ab - a$

10. The price of gas was $3.27 per gallon. Your tank holds 15 gallons of fuel. You are using two tanks a week. How much will you save weekly if the price of gas goes down to $2.30 per gallon.
    (Average) (Skill 7.1)

    A. $26.00
    B. $29.00
    C. $15.00
    D. $17.00

11. In a sample of 40 full-time employees at a particular company, 35 were also holding down a part-time job requiring at least 10 hours/week. If this proportion holds for the entire company of 25,000 employees, how many full-time employees at this company are actually holding down a part-time job of at least 10 hours per week.
    (Rigorous) (Skill 7.1)

    A. 714
    B. 625
    C. 21,875
    D. 28,571

12. A sofa sells for $520. If the retailer makes a 30% profit, what was the wholesale price?
    (Average) (Skill 7.1)

    A. $400
    B. $676
    C. $490
    D. $364

13. A car gets 25.36 miles per gallon. The car has been driven 83,310 miles. What is a reasonable estimate for the number of gallons of gas used?
    (Average) (Skill 7.2)

    A. 2,087 gallons
    B. 3,000 gallons
    C. 1,800 gallons
    D. 164 gallons

14. **What unit of measurement could we use to report the distance traveled walking around a track?**
(Easy) (Skill 7.2)

   A. degrees
   B. square meters
   C. kilometers
   D. cubic feet

15. **What unit of measurement would describe the spread of a forest fire in a unit time?**
(Average) (Skill 7.2)

   A. 10 square yards per second
   B. 10 yards per minute
   C. 10 feet per hour
   D. 10 cubic feet per hour

16. **Express .0000456 in scientific notation.**
(Easy) (Skill 7.2)

   A. 4.56×10^{-4}
   B. 45.6×10^{-6}
   C. 4.56×10^{-6}
   D. 4.56×10^{-5}

17. **A student organization is interested in determining how strong the support is among registered voters in the United States for the president's education plan. Which of the following procedures would be most appropriate for selecting a statistically unbiased sample?**
(Average) (Skill 8.1)

   A. Having viewers call in to a nationally broad-cast talk show and give their opinions.
   B. Survey registered voters selected by blind drawing in the three largest states.
   C. Select regions of the country by blind drawing and then select people from the voter's registration list by blind drawing.
   D. Pass out survey forms at the front entrance of schools selected by blind drawing and ask people entering and exiting to fill them in.

18. The following chart shows the yearly average number of international tourists visiting Palm Beach for 1990-1994. How many more international tourists visited Palm Beach in 1994 than in 1991?
(Easy) (Skill 8.1)

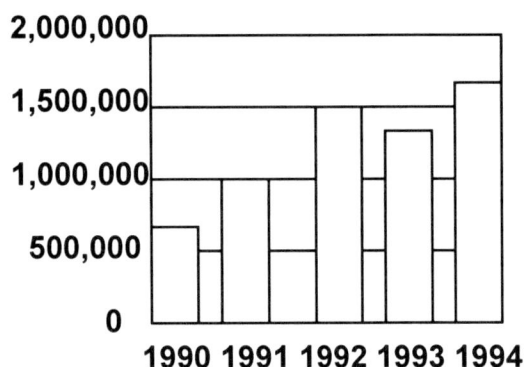

A. 100,000
B. 600,000
C. 1,600,000
D. 8,000,000

19. Consider the graph of the distribution of the length of time it took individuals to complete an employment form.
(Average) (Skill 8.1)

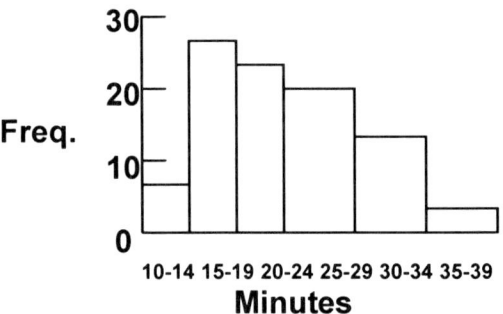

Approximately how many individuals took less than 15 minutes to complete the employment form?

A. 35
B. 28
C. 7
D. 4

20. Which statement is true about George's budget? *(Easy) (Skill 8.1)*

   A. George spends the greatest portion of his income on food.
   B. George spends twice as much on utilities as he does on his mortgage.
   C. George spends twice as much on utilities as he does on food.
   D. George spends the same amount on food and utilities as he does on mortgage.

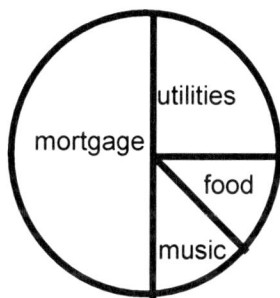

21. Corporate salaries are listed for several employees. Which is the best measure of central tendency? *(Average) (Skill 8.3)*

   $24,000 $24,000 $26,000
   $28,000 $30,000 $120,000

   A. Mean
   B. Median
   C. Mode
   D. No difference

22. Compute the median for the following data set: *(Easy) (Skill 8.3)*

   {12, 19, 13, 16, 17, 14}

   A. 14.5
   B. 15.17
   C. 15
   D. 16

23. State the domain of the function $f(x) = \dfrac{3x-6}{x^2 - 25}$ *(Rigorous) (Skill 12.4)*

   A. $x \neq 2$
   B. $x \neq 5, -5$
   C. $x \neq 2, -2$
   D. $x \neq 5$

24. Which graph represents the equation of $y = x^2 + 3x$? *(Rigorous) (Skill 9.1)*

   A.   B.

   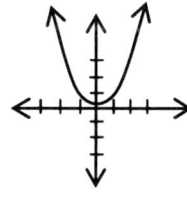   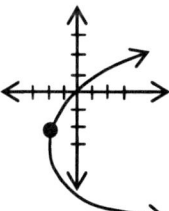

   C.   D.

   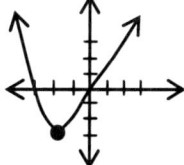   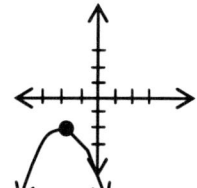

25. Choose the equation that is equivalent to the following:
    (Rigorous) (Skill 10.1)

    $$\frac{3x}{5} - 5 = 5x$$

    A. $3x - 25 = 25x$

    B. $x - \frac{25}{3} = 25x$

    C. $6x - 50 = 75x$

    D. $x + 25 = 25x$

26. If $4x - (3 - x) = 7(x - 3) + 10$, then
    (Rigorous) (Skill 10.1)

    A. $x = 8$
    B. $x = -8$
    C. $x = 4$
    D. $x = -4$

27. Solve for x.

    $$3x - \frac{2}{3} = \frac{5x}{2} + 2$$

    (Rigorous) (Skill 10.1)

    A. $5\frac{1}{3}$

    B. $\frac{17}{3}$

    C. 2

    D. $\frac{16}{2}$

28. Given the formula $d = rt$, (where d = distance, r = rate, and t = time), calculate the time required for a vehicle to travel 585 miles at a rate of 65 miles per hour.
    (Average) (Skill 10.2)

    A. 8.5 hours
    B. 6.5 hours
    C. 9.5 hours
    D. 9 hours

29. Solve the system of equations for x, y and z.
    (Rigorous) (Skill 10.3)

    $3x + 2y - z = 0$
    $2x + 5y = 8z$
    $x + 3y + 2z = 7$

    A. $(-1, 2, 1)$
    B. $(1, 2, -1)$
    C. $(-3, 4, -1)$
    D. $(0, 1, 2)$

30. What is the equation that expresses the relationship between x and y in the table below?
    (Average) (Skill 11.1)

x	y
-2	4
-1	1
0	-2
1	-5
2	-8

    A. $y = -x - 2$
    B. $y = -3x - 2$
    C. $y = 3x - 2$
    D. $y = \frac{1}{3}x - 1$

31. Choose the expression that is not equivalent to 5x + 3y + 15z:
    (Average) (Skill 12.2)

    A. 5(x + 3z) + 3y
    B. 3(x + y + 5z)
    C. 3y + 5(x + 3z)
    D. 5x + 3(y + 5z)

32. Simplify: $\sqrt{27} + \sqrt{75}$
    (Average) (Skill 12.3)

    A. $8\sqrt{3}$
    B. 34
    C. $34\sqrt{3}$
    D. $15\sqrt{3}$

33. What is the equation of the graph below?
    (Rigorous) (Skill 9.1)

    A. 2x + y − 2
    B. 2x - y = -2
    C. 2x - y = 2
    D. 2x + y = -2

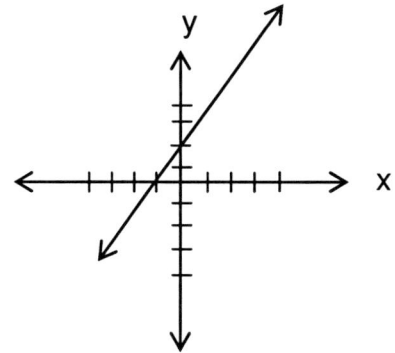

34. $f(x) = 3x - 2; f^{-1}(x) =$
    (Rigorous) (Skill 12.4)

    A. $3x + 2$
    B. $x/6$
    C. $2x - 3$
    D. $(x+2)/3$

35. What is the area of a square whose side is 13 feet?
    (Easy) (Skill 14.1)

    A. 169 feet
    B. 169 square feet
    C. 52 feet
    D. 52 square feet

36. The trunk of a tree has a 2.1 meter radius. What is its circumference?
    (Easy) (Skill 14.1)

    A. 2.1π square meters
    B. 4.2π meters
    C. 2.1π meters
    D. 4.2π square meters

37. The figure below shows a running track and the shape of an inscribed rectangle with semicircles at each end.
(Rigorous) (Skill 14.1)

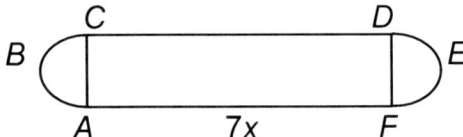

Calculate the distance around the track. (r = 1.5y)

A. $6\pi y + 14x$
B. $3\pi y + 7x$
C. $6\pi y + 7x$
D. $3\pi y + 14x$

38. What type of triangle is triangle ABC?
(Easy) (Skill 14.1)

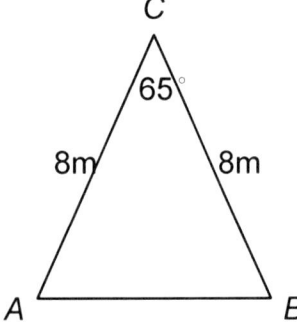

A. right
B. equilateral
C. scalene
D. isosceles

39. What is the area of this triangle?
(Easy) (Skill 14.1)

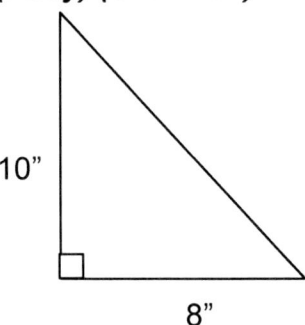

A. 80 square inches
B. 20 square inches
C. 40 square inches
D. 30 square inches

40. For the following statements
(Average) (Skill 14.1)

I. All parallelograms are rectangles
II. Some rhombi are squares

A. Both statements are correct
B. Both statements are incorrect
C. Only II is correct
D. Only I is correct

41. Find the surface area of a box which is 3 feet wide, 5 feet tall, and 4 feet deep.
(Average) (Skill 14.2)

A. 47 sq. ft.
B. 60 sq. ft.
C. 94 sq. ft
D. 188 sq. ft.

42. The owner of a rectangular piece of land 40 yards in length and 30 yards in width wants to divide it into two parts. She plans to join two opposite corners with a fence as shown in the diagram below. The cost of the fence will be approximately $25 per linear foot. What is the estimated cost for the fence needed by the owner?
(Rigorous) (Skill 14.3)

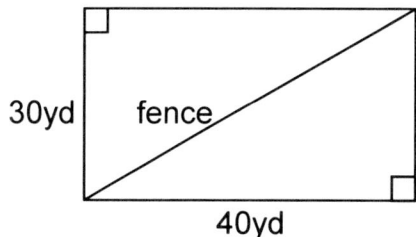

A. $1,250
B. $62,500
C. $5,250
D. $3,750

43. Which term most accurately describes two coplanar lines without any common points?
(Average) (Skill 15.1)

A. perpendicular
B. parallel
C. intersecting
D. skew

44. Set A, B, C, and U are related as shown in the diagram.
(Rigorous) (Skill 16.1)

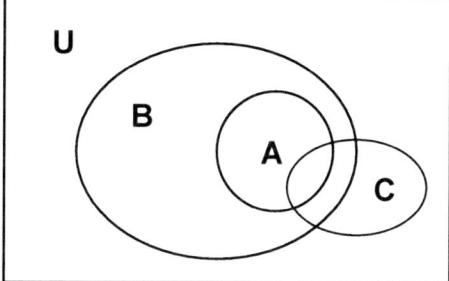

Which of the following is true, assuming not one of the six regions is empty?

A. Any element that is a member of set B is also a member of set A.
B. No element is a member of all three sets A, B, and C.
C. Any element that is a member of set U is also a member of set B.
D. None of the above statements is true.

THEA Sample Test

45. **Select the statement that is the negation of the statement, "If the weather is cold, then the soccer game will be played."**
(Rigorous) (Skill 16.1)

   A. If the weather is not cold, then the soccer game will be played.
   B. The weather is cold and the soccer game was not played.
   C. If the soccer game is played, then the weather is not cold.
   D. The weather is cold and the soccer game will be played.

46. **Select the statement below that is logically equivalent to "If Mary works late, then Bill will prepare lunch."**
(Rigorous) (Skill 16.1)

   A. Bill prepares lunch or Mary does not work late.
   B. If Bill does not prepare lunch, then Mary did not work late.
   C. If Bill prepares lunch, then Mary works late.
   D. Mary does not work late or Bill prepares lunch.

47. **Select the rule of logical equivalence that directly (in one step) transforms the statement (i) into statement (ii),**
(Average) (Skill 16.1)

   i. Not all the students have books.
   ii. Some students do not have books.

   A. "If p, then q" is equivalent to "if not q, then b."
   B. "Not all are p" is equivalent to "some are not p."
   C. "Not q" is equivalent to "p."
   D. "All are not p" is equivalent to "none are p"

48. **Given that:**
   i. No athletes are weak.
   ii. All football players are athletes.

   Determine which conclusion can be logically deduced.
   (Average) (Skill 16.1)

   A. Some football players are weak.
   B. All football players are weak.
   C. No football player is weak.
   D. None of the above is true.

THEA Sample Test

49. Study the information given below. If a logical conclusion is given, select that conclusion.
(Rigorous) (Skill 16.1)

    Bob eats donuts or he eats yogurt. If Bob eats yogurt, then he is healthy. If Bob is healthy, then he can run the marathon. Bob does not eat yogurt.

    A. Bob does not eat donuts.
    B. Bob is healthy.
    C. If Bob runs the marathon then he eats yogurt.
    D. None of the above is warranted.

50. Given $K(-4, y)$ and $M(2, -3)$ with midpoint $L(x, 1)$, determine the values of x and y.
    (Rigorous) (Skill 17.1)

    A. $x = -1, y = 5$
    B. $x = 3, y = 2$
    C. $x = 5, y = -1$
    D. $x = -1, y = -1$

Answer Key

1.	D		26.	C
2.	A		27.	A
3.	B		28.	D
4.	D		29.	A
5.	C		30.	B
6.	C		31.	B
7.	B		32.	A
8.	D		33.	B
9.	A		34.	D
10.	B		35.	B
11.	C		36.	B
12.	A		37.	D
13.	B		38.	D
14.	C		39.	C
15.	A		40.	C
16.	D		41.	C
17.	C		42.	D
18.	B		43.	B
19.	C		44.	D
20.	C		45.	B
21.	B		46.	B
22.	C		47.	B
23.	B		48.	C
24.	C		49.	D
25.	A		50.	A

Rigor Table

Easy
2, 14, 16, 18, 20, 22, 35, 36, 38, 39

Average
3, 4, 5, 6, 7, 8, 10, 12, 13, 15, 17, 19, 21, 28, 30, 31, 32, 40, 41, 43, 47, 48

Rigorous
1, 9, 11, 23, 24, 25, 26, 27, 29, 33, 34, 37, 42, 44, 45, 46, 49, 50

MATHEMATICS SAMPLE TEST WITH RATIONALES

1. $\left(\dfrac{-4}{9}\right) + \left(\dfrac{-7}{10}\right) =$

   (Rigorous) (Skill 7.1)

   A. $\dfrac{23}{90}$

   B. $\dfrac{-23}{90}$

   C. $\dfrac{103}{90}$

   D. $\dfrac{-103}{90}$

   Answer: D. $\dfrac{-103}{90}$

   Find the LCD of $\dfrac{-4}{9}$ and $\dfrac{-7}{10}$. The LCD is 90, so you get $\dfrac{-40}{90} + \dfrac{-63}{90} = \dfrac{-103}{90}$

2. $0.74 =$

   (Easy) (Skill 7.1)

   A. $\dfrac{74}{100}$

   B. 7.4%

   C. $\dfrac{33}{50}$

   D. $\dfrac{74}{10}$

   Answer: A. $\dfrac{74}{100}$

   0.74 ⊛ the 4 is in the hundredths place, so the answer is $\dfrac{74}{100}$

3. $-9\dfrac{1}{4}$ ☐ $-8\dfrac{2}{3}$
   (Average) (Skill 7.1)

   A. =
   B. <
   C. >
   D. ≤

Answer: B. <
The larger the absolute value of a negative number, the smaller the negative number is. The absolute value of $-9\dfrac{1}{4}$ is $9\dfrac{1}{4}$ which is larger than the absolute value of $-8\dfrac{2}{3}$, which is $8\dfrac{2}{3}$. Therefore, the relationship should be $-9\dfrac{1}{4} < -8\dfrac{2}{3}$

4. **303 is what percent of 600?**
   (Average) (Skill 7.1)

   A. 0.505%
   B. 5.05%
   C. 505%
   D. 50.5%

Answer: D. 50.5%
Use x for the percent. $600x = 303$. $\dfrac{600x}{600} = \dfrac{303}{600} \rightarrow x = 0.505 = 50.5\%$

5. **An item that sells for $375 is put on sale at $120. What is the percent of decrease?**
   (Average) (Skill 7.1)

   A. 25%
   B. 28%
   C. 68%
   D. 34%

Answer: C. 68%
Use $(1 - x)$ as the discount. $375x = 120$.
$375(1 - x) = 120 \rightarrow 375 - 375x = 120 \rightarrow 375x = 255 \rightarrow x = 0.68 = 68\%$

6. Two mathematics classes have a total of 410 students. The 8:00 am class has 40 more than the 10:00 am class. How many students are in the 10:00 am class?
   (Average) (Skill 7.1)

   A. 123.3
   B. 370
   C. 185
   D. 330

Answer: C. 185
Let x = # of students in the 8 am class and $x - 40$ = # of students in the 10 am class. $x + (x - 40) = 410 \rightarrow 2x - 40 = 410 \rightarrow 2x = 450 \rightarrow x = 225$. So there are 225 students in the 8 am class, and 225 − 40 = 185 in the 10 am class.

7. A restaurant employs 465 people. There are 280 waiters and 185 cooks. If 168 waiters and 85 cooks receive pay raises, what percent of the waiters will receive a pay raise?
   (Average) (Skill 7.1)

   A. 36.13%
   B. 60%
   C. 60.22%
   D. 40%

Answer: B. 60%
The total number of waiters is 280 and only 168 of them get a pay raise. Divide the number getting a raise by the total number of waiters to get the percent. $\frac{168}{280} = 0.6 = 60\%$

8. $\dfrac{7}{9}+\dfrac{1}{3}\div\dfrac{2}{3}=$

   (Average) (Skill 7.1)

   A. $\dfrac{5}{3}$

   B. $\dfrac{3}{2}$

   C. 2

   D. $\dfrac{23}{18}$

Answer: D. $\dfrac{23}{18}$

First, do the division.
$\dfrac{1}{3}\div\dfrac{2}{3}=\dfrac{1}{3}\times\dfrac{3}{2}=\dfrac{1}{2}$
Add.
$\dfrac{7}{9}+\dfrac{1}{2}=\dfrac{14}{18}+\dfrac{9}{18}=\dfrac{23}{18}$

9. **Choose the statement that is true for all real numbers.**
   (Rigorous) (Skill 7.1)

   A. $a=0, b\neq 0,$ then $\dfrac{b}{a}=$ undefined.

   B. $^-(a+(^-a))=2a$

   C. $2(ab)=^-(2a)b$

   D. $^-a(b+1)=ab-a$

Answer: A. $a=0, b\neq 0,$ then $\dfrac{b}{a}=$ undefined.
A is the correct answer because any number divided by 0 is undefined.

10. The price of gas was $3.27 per gallon. Your tank holds 15 gallons of fuel. You are using two tanks a week. How much will you save weekly if the price of gas goes down to $2.30 per gallon.
    (Average) (Skill 7.1)

    A. $26.00
    B. $29.00
    C. $15.00
    D. $17.00

Answer: B. $29.00
15 gallons x 2 tanks = 30 gallons a week
= 30 gallons x $3.27 = $98.10
30 gallons x $2.30 = $69.00
$98.10 - $69.00 = $29.10 is approximately $29.00.

11. In a sample of 40 full-time employees at a particular company, 35 were also holding down a part-time job requiring at least 10 hours/week. If this proportion holds for the entire company of 25000 employees, how many full-time employees at this company are actually holding down a part-time job of at least 10 hours per week.
    (Rigorous) (Skill 7.1)

    A. 714
    B. 625
    C. 21,875
    D. 28,571

Answer: C. 21, 875
$\frac{35}{40}$ full time employees have a part time job also. Out of 25,000 full time employees, the number that also have a part time job is
$\frac{35}{40} = \frac{x}{25000} \rightarrow 40x = 875000 \rightarrow x = 21875$, so 21875 full time employees also have a part time job.

12. **A sofa sells for $520. If the retailer makes a 30% profit, what was the wholesale price?**
    (Average) (Skill 7.1)

    A. $400
    B. $676
    C. $490
    D. $364

Answer: A. $400
$400; Let x be the wholesale price, then x + .30x = 520, 1.30x = 520. divide both sides by 1.30.

13. **A car gets 25.36 miles per gallon. The car has been driven 83,310 miles. What is a reasonable estimate for the number of gallons of gas used?**
    (Average) (Skill 7.2)

    A. 2,087 gallons
    B. 3,000 gallons
    C. 1,800 gallons
    D. 164 gallons

Answer: B. 3,000 gallons
Divide the number of miles by the miles per gallon to determine the approximate number of gallons of gas used. $\frac{83310 \text{ miles}}{25.36 \text{ miles per gallon}} = 3285$ gallons. This is approximately 3000 gallons.

14. **What unit of measurement could we use to report the distance traveled walking around a track?**
    (Easy) (Skill 7.2)

    A. degrees
    B. square meters
    C. kilometers
    D. cubic feet

Answer: C. kilometers
Degrees measures angles, square meters measures area, cubic feet measure volume, and kilometers measures length. Kilometers is the only reasonable answer.

15. **What unit of measurement would describe the spread of a forest fire in a unit time?**
    (Average) (Skill 7.2)

    A. 10 square yards per second
    B. 10 yards per minute
    C. 10 feet per hour
    D. 10 cubic feet per hour

Answer: A. 10 square yards per second
The only appropriate answer is one that describes "an area" of forest consumed per unit time. All answers are not units of area measurement except answer A.

16. **Express .0000456 in scientific notation.**
    (Easy) (Skill 7.2)

    A. 4.56×10^{-4}
    B. 45.6×10^{-6}
    C. 4.56×10^{-6}
    D. 4.56×10^{-5}

Answer: D. 4.56×10^{-5}
In scientific notation, the decimal point belongs to the right of the 4, the first significant digit. To get from 4.56×10^{-5} back to 0.0000456, we would move the decimal point 5 places to the left.

17. **A student organization is interested in determining how strong the support is among registered voters in the United States for the president's education plan. Which of the following procedures would be most appropriate for selecting a statistically unbiased sample?**
    (Average) (Skill 8.1)

    A. Having viewers call in to a nationally broad-cast talk show and give their opinions.
    B. Survey registered voters selected by blind drawing in the three largest states.
    C. Select regions of the country by blind drawing and then select people from the voter's registration list by blind drawing.
    D. Pass out survey forms at the front entrance of schools selected by blind drawing and ask people entering and exiting to fill them in.

Answer: C. Select regions of the country by blind drawing and then select people from the voter's registration list by blind drawing.
C is the best answer because it is random and it surveys a larger population.

18. The following chart shows the yearly average number of international tourists visiting Palm Beach for 1990-1994. How many more international tourists visited Palm Beach in 1994 than in 1991? *(Easy) (Skill 8.1)*

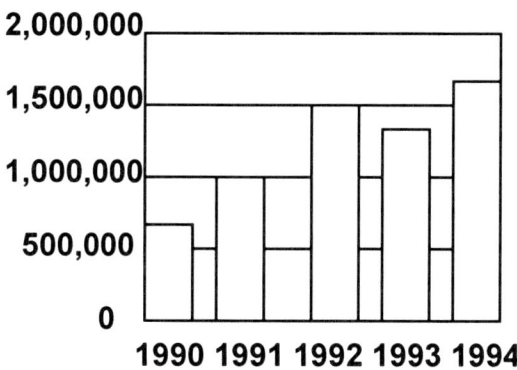

A. 100,000
B. 600,000
C. 1,600,000
D. 8,000,000

Answer: B. 600,000
The number of tourists in 1991 was 1,000,000 and the number in 1994 was 1,600,000. Subtract to get a difference of 600,000.

19. Consider the graph of the distribution of the length of time it took individuals to complete an employment form.
   (Average) (Skill 8.1)

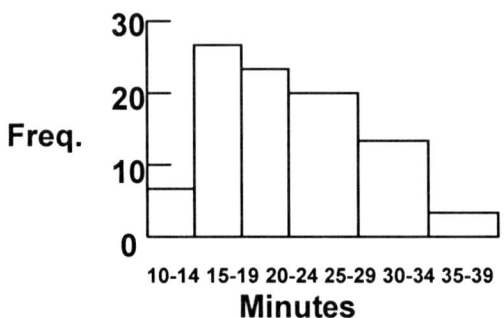

Approximately how many individuals took less than 15 minutes to complete the employment form?

   A. 35
   B. 28
   C. 7
   D. 4

Answer: C. 7
According to the chart, the number of people who took under 15 minutes is 7.

20. Which statement is true about George's budget?
   (Easy) (Skill 8.1)

   A. George spends the greatest portion of his income on food.
   B. George spends twice as much on utilities as he does on his mortgage.
   C. George spends twice as much on utilities as he does on food.
   D. George spends the same amount on food and utilities as he does on mortgage.

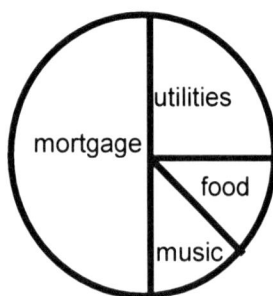

Answer: C. George spends twice as much on utilities as he does on food.
The wedge representing utilities is twice as large as the wedge representing food.

21. **Corporate salaries are listed for several employees. Which is the best measure of central tendency?**
    (Average) (Skill 8.3)

    $24,000 $24,000 $26,000 $28,000 $30,000 $120,000

    A. Mean
    B. Median
    C. Mode
    D. No difference

Answer: B. Median
The median provides the best measure of central tendency in this case where the mode is the lowest number and the mean is disproportionately skewed by the outlier $120,000.

22. **Compute the median for the following data set:**
    (Easy) (Skill 8.3)

    {12, 19, 13, 16, 17, 14}

    A. 14.5
    B. 15.17
    C. 15
    D. 16

Answer: C. 15
Arrange the data in ascending order: 12,13,14,16,17,19. The median is the middle value in a list with an odd number of entries. When there is an even number of entries, the median is the mean of the two center entries. Here the average of 14 and 16 is 15.

23. **State the domain of the function** $f(x) = \dfrac{3x-6}{x^2-25}$

    (Rigorous) (Skill 12.4)

    A. $x \neq 2$
    B. $x \neq 5, -5$
    C. $x \neq 2, -2$
    D. $x \neq 5$

Answer: B. $x \neq 5, -5$
The values of 5 and –5 must be omitted from the domain of all real numbers because if x took on either of those values, the denominator of the fraction would have a value of 0, and therefore the fraction would be undefined.

24. Which graph represents the equation of $y = x^2 + 3x$?
    (Rigorous) (Skill 9.1)

    A.   B.

    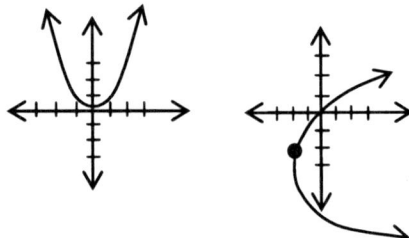

    C.   D.

    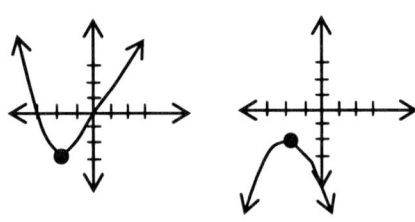

Answer: C.
B is not the graph of a function. D is the graph of a parabola where the coefficient of x^2 is negative. A appears to be the graph of $y = x^2$. To find the x-intercepts of $y = x^2 + 3x$, set y = 0 and solve for x: $0 = x^2 + 3x = x(x + 3)$ to get x = 0 or x = -3. Therefore, the graph of the function intersects the x-axis at x=0 and x=-3.

25. **Choose the equation that is equivalent to the following:**
    (Rigorous) (Skill 10.1)

    $$\frac{3x}{5} - 5 = 5x$$

    A. $3x - 25 = 25x$

    B. $x - \frac{25}{3} = 25x$

    C. $6x - 50 = 75x$

    D. $x + 25 = 25x$

Answer: A. $3x - 25 = 25x$
A is the correct answer because it is the original equation multiplied by 5. The other choices alter the answer to the original equation.

26. **If $4x - (3 - x) = 7(x - 3) + 10$, then**
    (Rigorous) (Skill 10.1)

    A. $x = 8$
    B. $x = -8$
    C. $x = 4$
    D. $x = -4$

Answer: C. $x = 4$
Solve for x.
$$4x - (3 - x) = 7(x - 3) + 10$$
$$4x - 3 + x = 7x - 21 + 10$$
$$5x - 3 = 7x - 11$$
$$5x = 7x - 11 + 3$$
$$5x - 7x = {}^-8$$
$${}^-2x = {}^-8$$
$$x = 4$$

27. Solve for x.
$$3x - \frac{2}{3} = \frac{5x}{2} + 2$$
(Rigorous) (Skill 10.1)

  A. $5\frac{1}{3}$

  B. $\frac{17}{3}$

  C. 2

  D. $\frac{16}{2}$

Answer: A. $5\frac{1}{3}$

$$3x(6) - \frac{2}{3}(6) = \frac{5x}{2}(6) + 2(6) \quad\quad \text{6 is the LCD of 2 and 3}$$
$$18x - 4 = 15x + 12$$
$$18x = 15x + 16$$
$$3x = 16$$
$$x = \frac{16}{3} = 5\frac{1}{3}$$

28. **Given the formula *d* = *rt*, (where *d* = distance, *r* = rate, and *t* = time), calculate the time required for a vehicle to travel 585 miles at a rate of 65 miles per hour.**
    (Average) (Skill 10.2)

    A. 8.5 hours
    B. 6.5 hours
    C. 9.5 hours
    D. 9 hours

Answer: D. 9 hours
We are given $d = 585$ miles and $r = 65$ miles per hour and $d = rt$. Solve for t.
$585 = 65t \rightarrow t = 9$ hours.

29. **Solve the system of equations** for x, y and z.
(Rigorous) (Skill 10.3)

$3x + 2y - z = 0$

$2x + 5y = 8z$

$x + 3y + 2z = 7$

A. $(-1, 2, 1)$
B. $(1, 2, -1)$
C. $(-3, 4, -1)$
D. $(0, 1, 2)$

Answer: A. $(-1, 2, 1)$
Multiplying equation 1 by 2, and equation 2 by –3, and then adding together the two resulting equations gives -11y + 22z = 0. Solving for y gives y = 2z. In the meantime, multiplying equation 3 by –2 and adding it to equation 2 gives –y – 12z = -14. Then substituting 2z for y, yields the result z = 1. Subsequently, one can easily find that y = 2, and x = -1.

30. What is the equation that expresses the relationship between x and y in the table below?
(Average) (Skill 11.1)

x	y
-2	4
-1	1
0	-2
1	-5
2	-8

A. y = -x – 2
B. y = -3x – 2
C. y = 3x – 2
D. y = $\frac{1}{3}$x – 1

Answer: B. y = -3x - 2
Solve by plugging the values of x and y into the equations to see if they work. The answer is B because it is the only equation for which the values of x and y are correct.

31. Choose the expression that is not equivalent to
5x + 3y + 15z:
(Average) (Skill 12.2)

    A. 5(x + 3z) + 3y
    B. 3(x + y + 5z)
    C. 3y + 5(x + 3z)
    D. 5x + 3(y + 5z)

Answer: B. 3(x + y +5z)
5x + 3y + 15z = (5x + 15z) + 3y = 5(x + 3z) + 3y   A. is true
               = 5x + (3y + 15z) = 5x + 3(y + 5z)   D. is true
               = 3y + (5x + 15z) = 3y + 5(x + 3z)   C. is true

We can solve all of these using the associative property and then factoring. However, in B 3(x + y + 5z) by distributive property = 3x + 3y + 15z, which does not equal 5x + 3y + 15z.

32. Simplify: $\sqrt{27} + \sqrt{75}$
(Average) (Skill 12.3)

    A. $8\sqrt{3}$
    B. 34
    C. $34\sqrt{3}$
    D. $15\sqrt{3}$

Answer: A. $8\sqrt{3}$
Simplifying radicals gives $\sqrt{27} + \sqrt{75} = 3\sqrt{3} + 5\sqrt{3} = 8\sqrt{3}$.

33. What is the equation of the graph below?
    (Rigorous) (Skill 9.1)

    A. $2x + y = 2$
    B. $2x - y = -2$
    C. $2x - y = 2$
    D. $2x + y = -2$

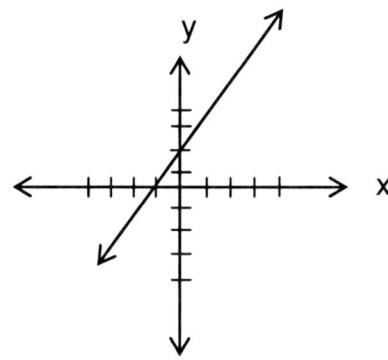

Answer: B. $2x - y = -2$

By observation, we see that the graph has a y-intercept of 2 and a slope of 2/1 = 2. Therefore its equation is y = mx + b = 2x + 2. Rearranging the terms gives 2x – y = -2.

34. $f(x) = 3x - 2;\ f^{-1}(x) =$
    (Rigorous) (Skill 12.4)

    A. $3x + 2$
    B. $x/6$
    C. $2x - 3$
    D. $(x + 2)/3$

Answer: D. $(x+2)/3$

To find the inverse, f⁻¹(x), of the given function, reverse the variables in the given equation, y = 3x – 2, to get x = 3y – 2. Then solve for y as follows:
x+2 = 3y, and y = $\dfrac{x+2}{3}$.

35. **What is the area of a square whose side is 13 feet?**
    (Easy) (Skill 14.1)

    A. 169 feet
    B. 169 square feet
    C. 52 feet
    D. 52 square feet

Answer: B. 169 square feet
Area = length times width (*lw*).
Length = 13 feet
Width = 13 feet (square, so length and width are the same).
Area = $13 \times 13 = 169$ square feet.
Area is measured in square feet.

36. **The trunk of a tree has a 2.1 meter radius. What is its circumference?**
    (Easy) (Skill 14.1)

    A. 2.1π square meters
    B. 4.2π meters
    C. 2.1π meters
    D. 4.2π square meters

Answer: B. 4.2π meters
Circumference is $2\pi r$, where r is the radius. The circumference is $2\pi 2.1 = 4.2\pi$ meters (not square meters because we are not measuring area).

37. The figure below shows a running track and the shape of an inscribed rectangle with semicircles at each end.
(Rigorous) (Skill 14.1)

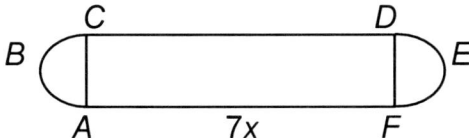

Calculate the distance around the track (r = 1.5y).

A. $6\pi y + 14x$
B. $3\pi y + 7x$
C. $6\pi y + 7x$
D. $3\pi y + 14x$

Answer: D. $3\pi y + 14x$
The two semicircles of the track create one circle with a diameter 3y. The circumference of a circle is $C = \pi d$ so $C = 3\pi y$. The length of both sides of the track is 7x each side, so the total circumference around the track is
$3\pi y + 7x + 7x = 3\pi y + 14x$

38. What type of triangle is triangle ABC?
(Easy) (Skill 14.1)

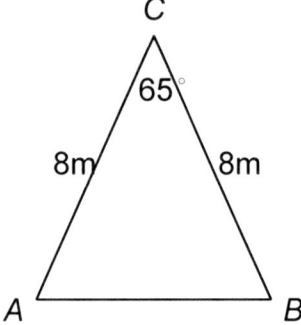

A. right
B. equilateral
C. scalene
D. isosceles

Answer: D. isosceles
Two of the sides are the same length, so we know the triangle is either equilateral or isosceles. ∡CAB and ∡CBA are equal, because their sides are. Therefore, $180° = 65° - 2x = \frac{115°}{2} = 57.5°$. Because all three angles are not equal, the triangle is isosceles.

39. What is the area of this triangle?
(Easy) (Skill 14.1)

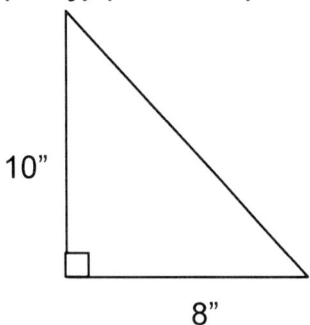

A. 80 square inches
B. 20 square inches
C. 40 square inches
D. 30 square inches

Answer: C. 40 square inches
The area of a triangle is $\frac{1}{2}bh$.
$\frac{1}{2} \times 8 \times 10 = 40$ square inches.

40. **For the following statements**
    (Average) (Skill 14.1)

    I. All parallelograms are rectangles
    II. Some rhombi are squares

    A. Both statements are correct
    B. Both statements are incorrect
    C. Only II is correct
    D. Only I is correct

Answer: C. Only II is correct
I is false because only some parallelograms are rectangles. II is true. So only II is correct.

41. **Find the surface area of a box which is 3 feet wide, 5 feet tall, and 4 feet deep.**
    (Average) (Skill 14.2)

    A. 47 sq. ft.
    B. 60 sq. ft.
    C. 94 sq. ft
    D. 188 sq. ft.

Answer: C. 94 sq. ft.
Let's assume the base of the rectangular solid (box) is 3 by 4, and the height is 5. Then the surface area of the top and bottom together is 2(12) = 24. The sum of the areas of the front and back are 2(15) = 30, while the sum of the areas of the sides are 2(20)=40. The total surface area is therefore 94 square feet.

42. The owner of a rectangular piece of land 40 yards in length and 30 yards in width wants to divide it into two parts. She plans to join two opposite corners with a fence as shown in the diagram below. The cost of the fence will be approximately $25 per linear foot. What is the estimated cost for the fence needed by the owner?
(Rigorous) (Skill 14.3)

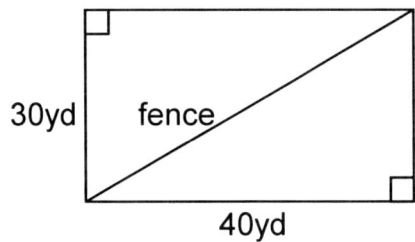

A. $1,250
B. $62,500
C. $5,250
D. $3,750

Answer: D. $3,750
Find the length of the diagonal by using the Pythagorean theorem. Let x be the length of the diagonal.

$$30^2 + 40^2 = x^2 \rightarrow 900 + 1600 = x^2$$
$$2500 = x^2 \rightarrow \sqrt{2500} = \sqrt{x^2}$$
$$x = 50 \text{ yards}$$

Convert to feet.

50 yards x 3 feet per yard = 150 feet

It cost $25.00 per linear foot, so the cost is (150 ft)($25) = $3750.

43. Which term most accurately describes two coplanar lines without any common points?
(Average) (Skill 15.1)

A. perpendicular
B. parallel
C. intersecting
D. skew

Answer: B. parallel
By definition, parallel lines are coplanar lines without any common points.

44. Set A, B, C, and U are related as shown in the diagram.
    (Rigorous) (Skill 16.1)

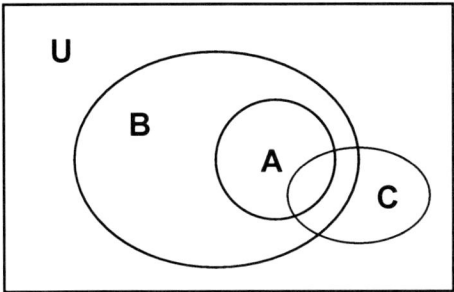

Which of the following is true, assuming not one of the six regions is empty?

    A. Any element that is a member of set B is also a member of set A.
    B. No element is a member of all three sets A, B, and C.
    C. Any element that is a member of set U is also a member of set B.
    D. None of the above statements is true.

Answer: D. None of the above statements is true.
Answer A is incorrect because not all members of set B are also in set A. Answer B is incorrect because there are elements that are members of all three sets A, B, and C. Answer C is incorrect because not all members of set U are members of set B. This leaves answer D, which states that none of the above choices are true.

THEA Sample Test

45. **Select the statement that is the negation of the statement, "If the weather is cold, then the soccer game will be played."**
    (Rigorous) (Skill 16.1)

    A. If the weather is not cold, then the soccer game will be played.
    B. The weather is cold and the soccer game was not played.
    C. If the soccer game is played, then the weather is not cold.
    D. The weather is cold and the soccer game will be played.

Answer: B. The weather is cold and the soccer game was not played.
Negation of "if p, then q" is "p and (not q)". So the negation of the given statement is "The weather is cold and the soccer game was not played ".

46. **Select the statement below that is logically equivalent to "If Mary works late, then Bill will prepare lunch."**
    (Rigorous) (Skill 16.1)

    A. Bill prepares lunch or Mary does not work late.
    B. If Bill does not prepare lunch, then Mary did not work late.
    C. If Bill prepares lunch, then Mary works late.
    D. Mary does not work late or Bill prepares lunch.

Answer: B. If Bill does not prepare lunch, then Mary did not work late.
The contrapositive of a statement is always logically equivalent to the statement. The contrapositive of "if p then q" is "if not q then not p". Since statement B is the contrapositive of the given statement, it is logically equivalent.

The other answer choices assume that if Mary does not work late then Bill does not prepare lunch. This is not a valid deduction from the original statement which merely states that Bill prepares lunch when Mary works late. It does not eliminate the possibility that Bill prepares lunch when Mary does not work late. Hence these statements are not logically equivalent to the given statement.

47. **Select the rule of logical equivalence that directly (in one step) transforms the statement (i) into statement (ii),**
    (Average) (Skill 16.1)

    i. Not all the students have books.
    ii. Some students do not have books.

    A. "If p, then q" is equivalent to "if not q, then b."
    B. "Not all are p" is equivalent to "some are not p."
    C. "Not q" is equivalent to "p."
    D. "All are not p" is equivalent to "none are p"

Answer: B. "Not all are p" is equivalent to "some are not p."
If we assume that the statement p is "students have books", then "not p" is "students do not have books". It is clear that statements (i) and (ii) are equivalent to the choice B.

48. **Given that:**
    i. No athletes are weak.
    ii. All football players are athletes.

    Determine which conclusion can be logically deduced.
    (Average) (Skill 16.1)

    A. Some football players are weak.
    B. All football players are weak.
    C. No football player is weak.
    D. None of the above is true.

Answer: C. No football player is weak.
According to the law of syllogism, "if p then q and if q then r" implies "if p then r". We can rephrase the statements above to read:

   i. If a person is a football player, he or she is an athlete.
   ii. If a person is an athlete, he or she is not weak.

Then, using the law of syllogism, we can conclude:
If a person is a football player, he or she is not weak.
This statement is equivalent to the one in choice C.

49. Study the information given below. If a logical conclusion is given, select that conclusion.
    (Rigorous) (Skill 16.1)

    Bob eats donuts or he eats yogurt. If Bob eats yogurt, then he is healthy. If Bob is healthy, then he can run the marathon. Bob does not eat yogurt.

    A. Bob does not eat donuts.
    B. Bob is healthy.
    C. If Bob runs the marathon then he eats yogurt.
    D. None of the above is warranted.

Answer: D. None of the above is warranted.
Statement A is not warranted since "Bob eats donuts or he eats yogurt" and "Bob does not eat yogurt" implies that "Bob eats donuts".

Statement B is not warranted since according to the given statements, Bob does not eat yogurt and Bob is healthy if he eats yogurt. The statements do not say anything about Bob's health if he does not eat yogurt.

Statement C is not warranted since Bob may run the marathon even if he does not eat yogurt. The given statements do not say anything about Bob's ability to run the marathon if he does not eat yogurt. It merely implies that he can run the marathon if he does eat yogurt.

50. Given $K(-4, y)$ and $M(2, -3)$ with midpoint $L(x, 1)$, determine the values of x and y.
    (Rigorous) (Skill 17.1)

    A. $x = -1, y = 5$
    B. $x = 3, y = 2$
    C. $x = 5, y = -1$
    D. $x = -1, y = -1$

Answer: A. $x = -1, y = 5$
The formula for finding the midpoint (a,b) of a segment passing through the points (x_1, y_1) and (x_2, y_2) is $(a,b) = (\frac{x_1 + x_2}{2}, \frac{y_1 + y_2}{2})$. Setting up the corresponding equations from this information gives us $x = \frac{-4 + 2}{2}$, and $1 = \frac{y - 3}{2}$. Solving for x and y gives x = -1 and y = 5.

ELEMENTS OF COMPOSITION SAMPLE TEST

Directions: The passage below contains many errors. Read the passage. Then, answer each test item by choosing the option that corrects an error in the underlined portion(s). No more than one underlined error will appear in each item. If no error exists, choose "No change is necessary."

Climbing to the top of Mount Everest is an adventure. One which everyone--whether physically fit or not--seems eager to try. The trail stretches for miles, the cold temperatures are usually frigid and brutal.

Climbers must endure severel barriers on the way, including other hikers, steep jagged rocks, and lots of snow. Plus, climbers often find the most grueling part of the trip is their climb back down, just when they are feeling greatly exhausted. Climbers who take precautions are likely to find the ascent less arduous than the unprepared. By donning heavy flannel shirts, gloves, and hats, climbers prevented hypothermia, as well as simple frostbite. A pair of rugged boots is also one of the necesities. If climbers are to avoid becoming dehydrated, there is beverages available for them to transport as well.

Once climbers are completely ready to begin their lengthy journey, they can comfortable enjoy the wonderful scenery. Wide rock formations dazzle the observers eyes with shades of gray and white, while the peak forms a triangle that seems to touch the sky. Each of the climbers are reminded of the splendor and magnificence of God's great Earth.

1. If climbers are to avoid **becoming** dehydrated, there **is** beverages available for **them** to transport as well.
   (Rigorous) (Skill 21.3)

   A. becoming
   B. are
   C. him
   D. No change is necessary.

2. Each of the climbers **are** reminded of the splendor and **magnificence** of **God's** great Earth.
   (Rigorous) (Skill 21.3)

   A. is
   B. magnifisence
   C. Gods
   D. No change is necessary.

3. Climbing to the top of Mount Everest is an **adventure. One** which everyone **—whether** physically fit or not—**seems** eager to try.
   (Average) (Skill 21.5)

   A. adventure, one
   B. everyone, whether
   C. seem
   D. No change is necessary.

THEA Sample Test   225

4. **A pair of rugged boots is also one of the necesities.**
   (Average) (Skill 21.5)

   A. are
   B. also, one
   C. necessities
   D. No change is necessary.

5. **Plus, climbers often find the most grueling part of the trip is their climb back down, just when they are feeling greatly exhausted.**
   (Rigorous) (Skill 22.1)

   A. his
   B. down; just
   C. were
   D. No change is necessary.

6. **By donning heavy flannel shirts, boots, and hats, climbers prevented hypothermia, as well as simple frostbite.**
   (Average) (Skill 22.1)

   A. hats climbers
   B. can prevent
   C. hypothermia;
   D. No change is necessary.

7. **Climbers must endure severel barriers on the way, including other hikers, steep jagged rocks, and lots of snow.**
   (Average) (Skill 22.2)

   A. several
   B. on the way: including
   C. hikers'
   D. No change is necessary.

8. **Climbers who take precautions are likely to find the ascent less difficult than the unprepared.**
   (Easy) (Skill 22.2)

   A. Climbers, who
   B. least difficult
   C. then
   D. No change is necessary.

9. **Once climbers are completely prepared for their lengthy journey, they can comfortable enjoy the wonderful scenery.**
   (Easy) (Skill 22.2)

   A. they're
   B. journey; they
   C. comfortably
   D. No change is necessary.

10. **Wide rock formations dazzle the observers eyes with shades of gray and white, while the peak forms a triangle that seems to touch the sky.**
    (Average) (Skill 22.2)

    A. observers' eyes
    B. white; while
    C. formed
    D. No change is necessary.

11. **The trail stretches for miles, the cold temperatures are usually frigid and brutal.**
    (Rigorous) (Skill 22.3)

    A. trails
    B. miles;
    C. usual
    D. No change is necessary.

THEA Sample Test

Directions: The passage below contains several errors. Read the passage. Then, answer each test item by choosing the option that corrects an error in the underlined portion(s). No more than one underlined error will appear in each item. If no error exists, choose "No change is necessary."

Every job places different kinds of demands on their employees. For example, whereas such jobs as accounting and bookkeeping require mathematical ability; graphic design requires creative/artistic ability.

Doing good at one job does not usually guarantee success at another. However, one of the elements crucial to all jobs are especially notable: the chance to accomplish a goal.

The accomplishment of the employees varies according to the job. In many jobs, the employees become accustom to the accomplishment provided by the work they do every day.

In medicine, for example, every doctor tests him self by treating badly injured or critically ill people. In the operating room, a team of Surgeons, is responsible for operating on many of these patients. In addition to the feeling of accomplishment that the workers achieve, some jobs also give a sense of identity to the employees'. Profesions like law, education, and sales offer huge financial and emotional rewards. Politicians are public servants: who work for the federal and state governments. President obama is basically employed by the American people to make laws and run the country.

Finally; the contributions that employees make to their companies and to the world cannot be taken for granted. Through their work, employees are performing a service for their employers and are contributing something to the world.

12. **Every job places different kinds of demands on their employees.**
    (Average) (Skill 21.3)

    A. place
    B. its
    C. employes
    D. No change is necessary.

13. **However, one of the elements crucial to all jobs are especially notable: the accomplishment of a goal.**
    (Average) (Skill 21.3)

    A. However
    B. is
    C. notable;
    D. No change is necessary.

14. **The accomplishment of the employees varies according to the job.**
    (Average) (Skill 21.3)

    A. accomplishment,
    B. employee's
    C. vary
    D. No change is necessary.

15. Profesions like law, education, and sales offer huge financial and emotional rewards.
    (Easy) (Skill 21.4)

    A. Professions
    B. education;
    C. offered
    D. No change is necessary.

16. Doing good at one job does not usually guarantee success at another.
    (Average) (Skill 21.5)

    A. well
    B. usualy
    C. succeeding
    D. No change is necessary.

17. In many jobs, the employees become accustom to the accomplishment provided by the work they do every day.
    (Rigorous) (Skill 21.5)

    A. became
    B. accustomed
    C. provides
    D. No change is necessary.

18. In medicine, for example, every doctor tests him self by treating badly-injured and critically ill people.
    (Easy) (Skill 21.5)

    A. test
    B. himself
    C. critical
    D. No change is necessary.

19. In addition to the feeling of accomplishment that the workers achieve, some jobs also give a sense of self-identity to the employees'.
    (Average) (Skill 22.1)

    A. acheve
    B. gave
    C. employees
    D. No change is necessary.

20. For example, whereas such jobs as accounting and bookkeeping require mathematical ability; graphic design requires creative/artistic ability.
    (Rigorous) (Skill 22.3)

    A. For example
    B. whereas,
    C. ability,
    D. No change is necessary.

21. In the operating room, a team of Surgeons, is responsible for operating on many of these patients.
    (Easy) (Skill 22.3)

    A. operating room:
    B. surgeons is
    C. those
    D. No change is necessary.

22. Politicians are public servants: who work for the federal and state governments.
    (Average) (Skill 22.3)

    A. were
    B. servants who
    C. worked
    D. No change is necessary.

23. **President obama is basically employed <u>by</u> the American people to <u>make</u> laws and run the country.**
    (Easy) (Skill 22.3)

    A. Obama
    B. to
    C. made
    D. No change is necessary.

24. <u>**Finally;**</u> **the contributions that employees make to <u>their</u> companies and to the world cannot be <u>taken</u> for granted.**
    (Average) (Skill 22.3)

    A. Finally,
    B. thier
    C. took
    D. No change is necessary.

Directions: For the underlined sentence(s), choose the option that expresses the meaning with the most fluency and the clearest logic within the context. If the underlined sentence should not be changed, choose Option A, which shows no change.

25. **Which of the following sentences logically and correctly expresses the comparison?**
    (Rigorous) (Skill 19.2)

    A. The Empire State Building in New York is taller than buildings in the city.
    B. The Empire State Building in New York is taller than any other building in the city.
    C. The Empire State Building in New York is tallest than other buildings in the city.

26. **Treating patients for drug and/or alcohol abuse is a sometimes difficult process. Even though there are a number of different methods for helping the patient overcome a dependency, there is no way of knowing which is best in the long run.**
(Rigorous) (Skill 20.1)

   A. Even though there are a number of different methods for helping the patient overcome a dependency, there is no way of knowing which is best in the long run.
   B. Even though different methods can help a patient overcome a dependency, there is no way to know which is best in the long run.
   C. Even though there is no way to know which way is best in the long run, patients can overcome their dependencies when they are helped.
   D. There is no way to know which method will help the patient overcome a dependency in the long run, even though there are many different ones.

27. **Selecting members of a President's cabinet can often be an aggravating process. Either there are too many or too few qualified candidates for a certain position, and then they have to be confirmed by the Senate, where there is the possibility of rejection.**
(Rigorous) (Skill 20.2)

   A. Either there are too many or too few qualified candidates for a certain position, and then they have to be confirmed by the Senate, where there is the possibility of rejection.
   B. Qualified candidates for certain positions face the possibility of rejection, when they have to be confirmed by the Senate.
   C. The Senate has to confirm qualified candidates, who face the possibility of rejection.
   D. Because the Senate has to confirm qualified candidates; they face the possibility of rejection.

28. Many factors account for the decline in the quality of public education. <u>**Overcrowding, budget cutbacks, and societal deterioration which have greatly affected student learning.**</u>
(Rigorous) (Skill 20.2)

   A. Overcrowding, budget cutbacks, and societal deterioration which have greatly affected student learning.
   B. Student learning has been greatly affected by overcrowding, budget cutbacks, and societal deterioration.
   C. Due to overcrowding, budget cutbacks, and societal deterioration, student learning has been greatly affected.
   D. Overcrowding, budget cutbacks, and societal deterioration have affected students learning greatly.

Directions: Choose the most effective word within the context of the sentence.

29. Many of the clubs in Boca Raton are noted for their _____ elegance.
(Average) (Skill 19.2)

   A. vulgar
   B. tasteful
   C. ordinary

30. When a student is expelled from school, the parents are usually _____ in advance.
(Easy) (Skill 19.2)

   A. rewarded
   B. congratulated
   C. notified

31. Before appearing in court, the witness was _____ the papers requiring her to show up.
(Easy) (Skill 19.2)

   A. condemned
   B. served
   C. criticized

Directions: Choose the underlined word or phrase that is unnecessary within the context of the passage.

32. <u>**Considered by many to be**</u> one of the worst <u>**terrorist**</u> incidents <u>**on American soil**</u> was the bombing of the Oklahoma City Federal Building, which will be remembered <u>**for years to come**</u>.
(Rigorous) (Skill 19.1)

   A. considered by many to be
   B. terrorist
   C. on American soil
   D. for years to come

33. The flu epidemic struck most of the respected faculty and students of The Woolbright School, forcing the Boynton Beach School Superintendent to close it down for two weeks.
    (Rigorous) (Skill 19.1)

    A. flu
    B. most of
    C. respected
    D. for two weeks

34. The expanding number of television channels has prompted cable operators to raise their prices, even though many consumers do not want to pay a higher increased amount for their service.
    (Average) (Skill 21.1)

    A. expanding
    B. prompted
    C. even though
    D. increased

Directions: The passage below contains several errors. Read the passage. Then, answer each test item by choosing the option that corrects an error in the underlined portion(s). No more than one underlined error will appear in each item. If no error exists, choose "No change is necessary."

The discovery of a body at Paris Point marina in Boca Raton shocked the residents of Palmetto Pines, a luxury condominium complex located next door to the marina.

The victim is a thirty-five year old woman who had been apparently bludgeoned to death and dumped in the ocean late last night. Many neighbors reported terrible screams, gunshots: as well as the sound of a car backfiring loudly to Boca Raton Police shortly after midnight. The woman had been spotted in the lobby of Palmetto Pines around ten thirty, along with an older man, estimated to be in his fifties, and a younger man, in his late twenties.

"Apparently, the victim had been driven to the complex by the older man and was seen arguing with him when the younger man intervened," said Sheriff Fred Adams, "all three of them left the building together and walked to the marina, where gunshots rang out an hour later." Deputies found five bullets on the sidewalk and some blood, along with a steel pipe that is assumed to be the murder weapon. Two men were seen fleeing the scene in a red Mercedes shortly after, rushing toward the Interstate. The Palm Beach County Coroner, Melvin Watts, said he concluded the victim's skull had been crushed by a blunt tool, which resulted in a brain hemorrhage. As of now, there is no clear motive for the murder.

35. **The victim is a thirty-five-year-old who had been apparently bludgeoned to death and dumped in the ocean late last night.**
    (Rigorous) (Skill 21.3)

    A. was
    B. bludgoned
    C. ocean: late
    D. No change is necessary.

36. **The discovery of a body at Paris Point marina in Boca Raton shocked the residents of Palmetto Pines, a luxury condominium complex located next door to the marina.**
    (Rigorous) (Skill 21.5)

    A. Marina
    B. residence
    C. condominnium
    D. No change is necessary.

37. **Deputies found five bullets on the sidewalk and some blood, along with a steel pipe that is assumed to be the murder weapon.**
    (Rigorous) (Skill 22.1)

    A. blood;
    B. assuming
    C. to have been
    D. No change is necessary.

38. Many <u>neighbors</u> reported terrible screams, <u>gunshots: as</u> well as the sound of a car, backfiring <u>loudly</u> to Boca Raton Police shortly after midnight.
(Average) (Skill 22.3)

   A. nieghbors
   B. gunshots, as
   C. loud
   D. No change is necessary.

39. The woman <u>had</u> been spotted in the lobby of Palmetto Pines around ten <u>thirty,</u> along with an older <u>man, estimated</u> to be in his fifties, and a younger man in his late twenties.
(Average) (Skill 22.3)

   A. has
   B. thirty;
   C. man estimated
   D. No change is necessary.

40. "Apparently, the victim had been driven to the complex by the older man and was seen arguing with him when the younger man intervened," said <u>Sheriff Fred Adams, "all</u> three of them left the building together and walked to the marina, where gunshots rang out an hour later."
(Rigorous) (Skill 22.3)

   A. sheriff Fred Adams, "all
   B. sheriff Fred Adams, "All
   C. Sheriff Fred Adams. "All
   D. No change is necessary.

Answer Key

1.	B	21.	B
2.	A	22.	B
3.	A	23.	A
4.	C	24.	A
5.	D	25.	B
6.	B	26.	B
7.	A	27.	C
8.	D	28.	B
9.	C	29.	B
10.	A	30.	C
11.	B	31.	B
12.	B	32.	A
13.	B	33.	C
14.	C	34.	D
15.	A	35.	A
16.	A	36.	A
17.	B	37.	C
18.	B	38.	B
19.	C	39.	C
20.	C	40.	C

Rigor Table

Easy
8, 9, 15, 18, 21, 23, 30, 31

Average
3, 4, 6, 7, 10, 12, 13, 14, 16, 19, 22, 24, 29, 34, 38, 39

Rigorous
1, 2, 5, 11, 17, 20, 25, 26, 27, 28, 32, 33, 35, 36, 37, 40

ELEMENTS OF COMPOSITION SAMPLE TEST WITH RATIONALES

Directions: The passage below contains many errors. Read the passage. Then, answer each test item by choosing the option that corrects an error in the underlined portion(s). No more than one underlined error will appear in each item. If no error exists, choose "No change is necessary."

Climbing to the top of Mount Everest is an adventure. One which everyone--whether physically fit or not--seems eager to try. The trail stretches for miles, the cold temperatures are usually frigid and brutal.

Climbers must endure severel barriers on the way, including other hikers, steep jagged rocks, and lots of snow. Plus, climbers often find the most grueling part of the trip is their climb back down, just when they are feeling greatly exhausted. Climbers who take precautions are likely to find the ascent less arduous than the unprepared. By donning heavy flannel shirts, gloves, and hats, climbers prevented hypothermia, as well as simple frostbite. A pair of rugged boots is also one of the necesities. If climbers are to avoid becoming dehydrated, there is beverages available for them to transport as well.

Once climbers are completely ready to begin their lengthy journey, they can comfortable enjoy the wonderful scenery. Wide rock formations dazzle the observers eyes with shades of gray and white, while the peak forms a triangle that seems to touch the sky. Each of the climbers are reminded of the splendor and magnificence of God's great Earth.

1. If climbers are to avoid <u>becoming</u> dehydrated, there <u>is</u> beverages available for <u>them</u> to transport as well.
   (Rigorous) (Skill 21.3)

   A. becommming
   B. are
   C. him
   D. No change is necessary.

Answer: B. are
The plural verb *are* must be used with the plural subject *beverages*. Option A is incorrect because *becoming* has only one *m*. Option C is incorrect because the plural pronoun *them* is needed to agree with the referent *climbers*.

2. Each of the climbers <u>are</u> reminded of the splendor and <u>magnificence</u> of <u>God's</u> great Earth.
   (Rigorous) (Skill 21.3)

   A. is
   B. magnifisence
   C. Gods
   D. No change is necessary.

Answer: A. is
The singular verb *is* agrees with the singular subject *each*. Option B is incorrect because *magnificence* is misspelled. Option C is incorrect because an apostrophe is needed to show possession.

3. Climbing to the top of Mount Everest is an <u>adventure. One</u> which everyone <u>—whether</u> physically fit or not—<u>seems</u> eager to try.
   (Average) (Skill 21.5)

   A. adventure, one
   B. everyone, whether
   C. seem
   D. No change is necessary.

Answer: A. adventure, one
A comma is needed between *adventure* and *one* to avoid creating a fragment of the second part. In Option B, a comma after *everyone* would not be appropriate when the dash is used on the other side of *not*. In Option C, the singular verb *seems* is needed to agree with the singular subject *everyone*.

4. A pair of rugged boots <u>is</u> <u>also one</u> of the <u>necesities</u>.
   (Average) (Skill 21.5)

   A. are
   B. also, one
   C. necessities
   D. No change is necessary.

Answer: C. necessities
The word *necessities* is misspelled in the text. Option A is incorrect because the singular verb *is* must agree with the singular noun *pair* (a collective singular). Option B is incorrect because *is also* is set off with commas (potential correction); it should be set off on both sides.

5. **Plus, climbers often find the most grueling part of the trip is <u>their</u> climb back <u>down, just</u> when they <u>are</u> feeling greatly exhausted.**
    (Rigorous) (Skill 22.1)

    A. his
    B. down; just
    C. were
    D. No change is necessary.

Answer: D. No change is necessary.
The present tense must be used consistently throughout; therefore, Option C is incorrect. Option A is incorrect because the singular pronoun *his* does not agree with the plural antecedent *climbers*. Option B is incorrect because a comma, not a semicolon, is needed to separate the dependent clause from the main clause.

6. **By donning heavy flannel shirts, boots, and <u>hats, climbers</u> <u>prevented</u> hypothermia, as well as simple frostbite.**
    (Average) (Skill 22.1)

    A. hats climbers
    B. can prevent
    C. hypothermia;
    D. No change is necessary.

Answer: B. can prevent
The verb *prevented* is in the past tense and must be changed to the present *can prevent* to be consistent. Option A is incorrect because a comma is needed after a long introductory phrase. Option C is incorrect because the semicolon creates a fragment of the phrase *as well as simple frostbite*.

7. **Climbers must endure <u>severel</u> barriers <u>on the way, including</u> other <u>hikers</u>, steep jagged rocks, and lots of snow.**
    (Average) (Skill 22.2)

    A. several
    B. on the way: including
    C. hikers'
    D. No change is necessary.

Answer: A. several
The word *several* is misspelled in the text. Option B is incorrect because a comma, not a colon, is needed to set off the modifying phrase. Option C is incorrect because no apostrophe is needed after *hikers* since possession is not involved.

8. **Climbers who** take precautions are likely to find the ascent **less difficult than** the unprepared.
   (Easy) (Skill 22.2)

   A. Climbers, who
   B. least difficult
   C. then
   D. No change is necessary.

Answer: D. No change is necessary.
No change is needed. Option A is incorrect because a comma would make the phrase *who take precautions* seem less restrictive or less essential to the sentence. Option B is incorrect because *less* is appropriate when two items—the prepared and the unprepared—are compared. Option C is incorrect because the comparative adverb *than*, not *then*, is needed.

9. Once climbers are completely prepared for **their** lengthy **journey, they** can **comfortable** enjoy the wonderful scenery.
   (Easy) (Skill 22.2)

   A. they're
   B. journey; they
   C. comfortably
   D. No change is necessary.

Answer: C. comfortably
The adverb form *comfortably* is needed to modify the verb phrase *can enjoy*. Option A is incorrect because the possessive plural pronoun is spelled *their*. Option B is incorrect because a semicolon would make the first half of the item seem like an independent clause when the subordinating conjunction *once* makes that clause dependent.

10. Wide rock formations dazzle the <u>observers eyes</u> with shades of gray and <u>white, while</u> the peak <u>forms</u> a triangle that seems to touch the sky.
    (Average) (Skill 22.2)

    A. observers' eyes
    B. white; while
    C. formed
    D. No change is necessary.

Answer: A. observers' eyes
An apostrophe is needed to show the plural possessive form *observers' eyes*. Option B is incorrect because the semicolon would make the second half of the item seem like an independent clause when the subordinating conjunction *while* makes that clause dependent. Option C is incorrect because *formed* is in the wrong tense.

11. The <u>trail</u> stretches for <u>miles</u>, the cold temperatures are <u>usually</u> frigid and brutal.
    (Rigorous) (Skill 22.3)

    A. trails
    B. miles;
    C. usual
    D. No change is necessary.

Answer: B. miles;
A semicolon, not a comma, is needed to separate the first independent clause from the second independent clause. Option A is incorrect because the plural subject *trails* needs the singular verb *stretch*. Option C is incorrect because the adverb form *usually* is needed to modify the adjective *frigid*.

Directions: The passage below contains several errors. Read the passage. Then, answer each test item by choosing the option that corrects an error in the underlined portion(s). No more than one underlined error will appear in each item. If no error exists, choose "No change is necessary."

Every job places different kinds of demands on their employees. For example, whereas such jobs as accounting and bookkeeping require mathematical ability; graphic design requires creative/artistic ability.

Doing good at one job does not usually guarantee success at another. However, one of the elements crucial to all jobs are especially notable: the chance to accomplish a goal.

The accomplishment of the employees varies according to the job. In many jobs, the employees become accustom to the accomplishment provided by the work they do every day.

In medicine, for example, every doctor tests him self by treating badly injured or critically ill people. In the operating room, a team of Surgeons, is responsible for operating on many of these patients. In addition to the feeling of accomplishment that the workers achieve, some jobs also give a sense of identity to the employees'. Profesions like law, education, and sales offer huge financial and emotional rewards. Politicians are public servants: who work for the federal and state governments. President obama is basically employed by the American people to make laws and run the country.

Finally; the contributions that employees make to their companies and to the world cannot be taken for granted. Through their work, employees are performing a service for their employers and are contributing something to the world.

12. **Every job <u>places</u> different kinds of demands on <u>their</u> <u>employees</u>.** *(Average) (Skill 21.3)*

   A. place
   B. its
   C. employes
   D. No change is necessary.

Answer: B. its
The singular possessive pronoun *its* must agree with its antecedent *job*, which is singular also. Option A is incorrect because *place* is a plural form, and the subject, *job*, is singular. Option C is incorrect because the correct spelling of employees is given in the sentence.

13. **However, one of the elements crucial to all jobs are especially notable: the accomplishment of a goal.**
    (Average) (Skill 21.3)

    A. However
    B. is
    C. notable;
    D. No change is necessary.

Answer: B. is
The singular verb *is* is needed to agree with the singular subject *one*. Option A is incorrect because a comma is needed to set off the transitional word *however*. Option C is incorrect because a colon, not a semicolon, is needed to set off an item.

14. **The accomplishment of the employees varies according to the job.**
    (Average) (Skill 21.3)

    A. accomplishment,
    B. employee's
    C. vary
    D. No change is necessary.

Answer: C. vary
The singular verb *vary* is needed to agree with the singular subject *accomplishment*. Option A is incorrect because a comma after *accomplishment* would suggest that the modifying phrase *of the employees* is additional instead of essential. Option B is incorrect because *employees* is not possessive.

15. **Profesions like law, education, and sales offer huge financial and emotional rewards.**
    (Easy) (Skill 21.4)

    A. Professions
    B. education;
    C. offered
    D. No change is necessary.

Answer: A. Professions
Option A is correct because *professions* is misspelled in the sentence. Option B is incorrect because a comma, not a semi-colon, is needed after *education*. In Option C, *offered* is in the wrong tense.

16. Doing <u>good</u> at one job does not <u>usually</u> guarantee <u>success</u> at another.
(Average) (Skill 21.5)

   A. well
   B. usualy
   C. succeeding
   D. No change is necessary.

Answer: A. well
The adverb *well* modifies the word *doing*. Option B is incorrect because *usually* is spelled correctly in the sentence. Option C is incorrect because *succeeding* is in the wrong tense.

17. In many jobs, the employees <u>become</u> <u>accustom</u> to the accomplishment <u>provided</u> by the work they do every day.
(Rigorous) (Skill 21.5)

   A. became
   B. accustomed
   C. provides
   D. No change is necessary.

Answer: B. accustomed
The past participle *accustomed* is needed with the verb *become*. Option A is incorrect because the verb tense does not need to change to the past *became*. Option C is incorrect because *provides* is the wrong tense.

18. In medicine, for example, every doctor <u>tests</u> <u>him self</u> by treating badly-injured and critically ill people.
(Easy) (Skill 21.5)

   A. test
   B. himself
   C. critical
   D. No change is necessary.

Answer: B. himself
The reflexive pronoun *himself* is needed. (Him self is nonstandard and never correct.) Option A is incorrect because the singular verb *test* is needed to agree with the singular subject *doctor*. Option C is incorrect because the adverb *critically* is needed to modify the verb *ill*.

19. In addition to the feeling of accomplishment that the workers <u>achieve</u>, some jobs also <u>give</u> a sense of self-identity to the <u>employees'</u>.
    (Average) (Skill 22.1)

    A. acheve
    B. gave
    C. employees
    D. No change is necessary.

Answer: C. employees
Option C is correct because *employees* is not possessive. Option A is incorrect because *achieve* is spelled correctly in the sentence. Option B is incorrect because *gave* is the wrong tense.

20. <u>For example, whereas</u> such jobs as accounting and bookkeeping require mathematical <u>ability;</u> graphic design requires creative/artistic ability.
    (Rigorous) (Skill 22.3)

    A. For example
    B. whereas,
    C. ability,
    D. No change is necessary.

Answer: C. ability,
An introductory dependent clause is set off with a comma, not a semicolon. Option A is incorrect because the transitional phrase *for example* should be set off with a comma. Option B is incorrect because the adverb *whereas* functions like *while* and does not take a comma after it.

21. In the <u>operating room,</u> a team of <u>Surgeons, is</u> responsible for operating on many of <u>these</u> patients.
    (Easy) (Skill 22.3)

    A. operating room:
    B. surgeons is
    C. those
    D. No change is necessary.

Answer: B. surgeons is
Surgeons is not a proper name, so it does not need to be capitalized. A comma is not needed to break up *a team of surgeons* from the rest of the sentence. Option A is incorrect because a comma, not a colon, is needed to set off an item. Option C is incorrect because *those* is an incorrect pronoun.

22. **Politicians <u>are</u> public <u>servants: who</u> <u>work</u> for the federal and state governments.**
    (Average) (Skill 22.3)

    A. were
    B. servants who
    C. worked
    D. No change is necessary.

Answer: B. servants who
A colon is not needed to set off the introduction of the sentence. In Option A, *were* is the incorrect tense of the verb. In Option C, *worked* is in the wrong tense.

23. **President obama is basically employed <u>by</u> the American people to <u>make</u> laws and run the country.**
    (Easy) (Skill 22.3)

    A. Obama
    B. to
    C. made
    D. No change is necessary.

Answer: A. Obama
Obama is a proper name and should be capitalized. In Option B, *to* does not fit with the verb *employed*. Option C uses the wrong form of the verb *make*.

24. **<u>Finally;</u> the contributions that employees make to <u>their</u> companies and to the world cannot be <u>taken</u> for granted.**
    (Average) (Skill 22.3)

    A. Finally,
    B. thier
    C. took
    D. No change is necessary.

Answer: A. Finally,
A comma is needed to separate *Finally* from the rest of the sentence. *Finally* is a preposition which usually heads a dependent sentence, hence a comma is needed. Option B is incorrect because *their* is misspelled. Option C is incorrect because *took* is the wrong form of the verb.

Directions: For the underlined sentence(s), choose the option that expresses the meaning with the most fluency and the clearest logic within the context. If the underlined sentence should not be changed, choose Option A, which shows no change.

25. Which of the following sentences logically and correctly expresses the comparison?
    (Rigorous) (Skill 19.2)

    A. The Empire State Building in New York is taller than buildings in the city.
    B. The Empire State Building in New York is taller than any other building in the city.
    C. The Empire State Building in New York is tallest than other buildings in the city.

Answer: B. The Empire State Building in New York is taller than any other building in the city.
Because the Empire State Building is a building in New York City, the phrase *any other* must be included. Option A is incorrect because the Empire State Building is implicitly compared to itself since it is one of the buildings. Option C is incorrect because *tallest* is the incorrect form of the adjective.

26. Treating patients for drug and/or alcohol abuse is a sometimes difficult process. <u>Even though there are a number of different methods for helping the patient overcome a dependency, there is no way of knowing which is best in the long run.</u>
    (Rigorous) (Skill 20.1)

    A. Even though there are a number of different methods for helping the patient overcome a dependency, there is no way of knowing which is best in the long run.
    B. Even though different methods can help a patient overcome a dependency, there is no way to know which is best in the long run.
    C. Even though there is no way to know which way is best in the long run, patients can overcome their dependencies when they are helped.
    D. There is no way to know which method will help the patient overcome a dependency in the long run, even though there are many different ones.

Answer: B. Even though different methods can help a patient overcome a dependency, there is no way to know which is best in the long run.
Option B is concise and logical. Option A tends to ramble with the use of *there are* and the verbs *helping* and *knowing*. Option C is awkwardly worded and repetitive in the first part of the sentence, and vague in the second because it never indicates how the patients can be helped. Option D contains the unnecessary phrase *even though there are many different ones*.

27. **Selecting members of a President's cabinet can often be an aggravating process.** <u>Either there are too many or too few qualified candidates for a certain position, and then they have to be confirmed by the Senate, where there is the possibility of rejection.</u>
(Rigorous) (Skill 20.2)

   A. Either there are too many or too few qualified candidates for a certain position, and then they have to be confirmed by the Senate, where there is the possibility of rejection.
   B. Qualified candidates for certain positions face the possibility of rejection, when they have to be confirmed by the Senate.
   C. The Senate has to confirm qualified candidates, who face the possibility of rejection.
   D. Because the Senate has to confirm qualified candidates; they face the possibility of rejection.

Answer: C. The Senate has to confirm qualified candidates, who face the possibility of rejection.
Option C is the most straightforward and concise sentence. Option A is too unwieldy with the wordy *Either...or* phrase at the beginning. Option B doesn't make clear the fact that candidates face rejection by the Senate. Option D illogically implies that candidates face rejection because they have to be confirmed by the Senate.

28. **Many factors account for the decline in the quality of public education.** <u>Overcrowding, budget cutbacks, and societal deterioration which have greatly affected student learning</u>.
(Rigorous) (Skill 20.2)

   A. Overcrowding, budget cutbacks, and societal deterioration which have greatly affected student learning.
   B. Student learning has been greatly affected by overcrowding, budget cutbacks, and societal deterioration.
   C. Due to overcrowding, budget cutbacks, and societal deterioration, student learning has been greatly affected.
   D. Overcrowding, budget cutbacks, and societal deterioration have affected students learning greatly.

Answer: B. Student learning has been greatly affected by overcrowding, budget cutbacks, and societal deterioration.
Option B is concise and best explains the causes of the decline in student education. The unnecessary use of *which* in Option A makes the sentence feel incomplete. Option C has weak coordination between the reasons for the decline in public education and the fact that student learning has been affected. Option D incorrectly places the adverb *greatly* after learning, instead of before *affected*.

Directions: Choose the most effective word within the context of the sentence.

29. Many of the clubs in Boca Raton are noted for their _____ elegance.
    (Average) (Skill 19.2)

    A. vulgar
    B. tasteful
    C. ordinary

Answer: B. tasteful
Tasteful means beautiful or charming, which would correspond to an elegant club. The words *vulgar* and *ordinary* have negative connotations.

30. When a student is expelled from school, the parents are usually _____ in advance.
    (Easy) (Skill 19.2)

    A. rewarded
    B. congratulated
    C. notified

Answer: C. notified
Notified means informed or told, which fits into the logic of the sentence. The words *rewarded* and *congratulated* are positive actions, which don't make sense regarding someone being expelled from school.

31. Before appearing in court, the witness was _____ the papers requiring her to show up.
    (Easy) (Skill 19.2)

    A. condemned
    B. served
    C. criticized

Answer: B. served
Served means given, which makes sense in the context of the sentence. *Condemned* and *criticized* do not make sense within the context of the sentence.

Directions: Choose the underlined word or phrase that is unnecessary within the context of the passage.

32. **Considered by many to be** one of the worst **terrorist** incidents **on American soil** was the bombing of the Oklahoma City Federal Building, which will be remembered **for years to come**.
(Rigorous) (Skill 19.1)

   A. considered by many to be
   B. terrorist
   C. on American soil
   D. for years to come

Answer: A. considered by many to be
Considered by many to be is a wordy phrase and unnecessary in the context of the sentence. All other words are necessary within the context of the sentence.

33. The **flu** epidemic struck **most of** the **respected** faculty and students of The Woolbright School, forcing the Boynton Beach School Superintendent to close it down **for two weeks.**
(Rigorous) (Skill 19.1)

   A. flu
   B. most of
   C. respected
   D. for two weeks

Answer: C. respected
The fact that the faculty might have been *respected* is not really necessary to mention in the sentence. The other words and phrases are all necessary to complete the meaning of the sentence. The correct answer is C.

34. The **expanding** number of television channels has **prompted** cable operators to raise their prices, **even though** many consumers do not want to pay a higher **increased** amount for their service.
(Average) (Skill 21.1)

   A. expanding
   B. prompted
   C. even though
   D. increased

Answer: D. increased
The word *increased* is redundant with *higher* and should be removed. All the other words are necessary within the context of the sentence.

Directions: The passage below contains several errors. Read the passage. Then, answer each test item by choosing the option that corrects an error in the underlined portion(s). No more than one underlined error will appear in each item. If no error exists, choose "No change is necessary."

The discovery of a body at Paris Point marina in Boca Raton shocked the residents of Palmetto Pines, a luxury condominium complex located next door to the marina.

The victim is a thirty-five year old woman who had been apparently bludgeoned to death and dumped in the ocean late last night. Many neighbors reported terrible screams, gunshots: as well as the sound of a car backfiring loudly to Boca Raton Police shortly after midnight. The woman had been spotted in the lobby of Palmetto Pines around ten thirty, along with an older man, estimated to be in his fifties, and a younger man, in his late twenties.

"Apparently, the victim had been driven to the complex by the older man and was seen arguing with him when the younger man intervened," said Sheriff Fred Adams, "all three of them left the building together and walked to the marina, where gunshots rang out an hour later." Deputies found five bullets on the sidewalk and some blood, along with a steel pipe that is assumed to be the murder weapon. Two men were seen fleeing the scene in a red Mercedes shortly after, rushing toward the Interstate. The Palm Beach County Coroner, Melvin Watts, said he concluded the victim's skull had been crushed by a blunt tool, which resulted in a brain hemorrhage. As of now, there is no clear motive for the murder.

35. The victim <u>is</u> a thirty-five-year-old who had been apparently <u>bludgeoned</u> to death and dumped in the <u>ocean late</u> last night.
    (Rigorous) (Skill 21.3)

    A. was
    B. bludgoned
    C. ocean: late
    D. No change is necessary.

Answer: A. was
The past tense *was* is needed to maintain consistency. Option B creates a misspelling. Option C incorrectly uses a colon when none is needed.

36. **The discovery of a body at Paris Point <u>marina</u> in Boca Raton shocked the <u>residents</u> of Palmetto Pines, a luxury <u>condominium</u> complex located next door to the marina.**
 (Rigorous) (Skill 21.5)

   A. Marina
   B. residence
   C. condominnium
   D. No change is necessary.

Answer: A. Marina
Marina is a name that needs to be capitalized. Options B and C create misspellings.

37. **Deputies found five bullets on the sidewalk and some <u>blood,</u> along with a steel pipe that is <u>assumed</u> <u>to be</u> the murder weapon.**
 (Rigorous) (Skill 22.1)

   A. blood;
   B. assuming
   C. to have been
   D. No change is necessary.

Answer: C. to have been
The past tense *to have been* is needed to maintain consistency. Option A incorrectly uses a semicolon, instead of a comma. Option B uses the wrong form of the verb *assumed*.

38. **Many <u>neighbors</u> reported terrible screams, <u>gunshots: as</u> well as the sound of a car, backfiring <u>loudly</u> to Boca Raton Police shortly after midnight.**
 (Average) (Skill 22.3)

   A. nieghbors
   B. gunshots, as
   C. loud
   D. No change is necessary.

Answer: B. gunshots, as
Option B correctly uses a comma, not a colon to separate the items. Option A creates a misspelling. Option C incorrectly changes the adverb into an adjective.

39. The woman <u>had</u> been spotted in the lobby of Palmetto Pines around ten <u>thirty,</u> along with an older <u>man, estimated</u> to be in his fifties, and a younger man in his late twenties.
    (Average) (Skill 22.3)

    A. has
    B. thirty;
    C. man estimated
    D. No change is necessary.

Answer: C. man estimated
A comma is not needed to separate the item because *an older man estimated to be in his fifties* is one complete fragment. Option A incorrectly uses the present tense *has* instead of the past tense *had*. Option B incorrectly uses a colon when a comma is needed.

40. "Apparently, the victim had been driven to the complex by the older man and was seen arguing with him when the younger man intervened," said <u>Sheriff Fred Adams, "all</u> three of them left the building together and walked to the marina, where gunshots rang out an hour later."
    (Rigorous) (Skill 22.3)

    A. sheriff Fred Adams, "all
    B. sheriff Fred Adams, "All
    C. Sheriff Fred Adams. "All
    D. No change is necessary.

Answer: C. Sheriff Fred Adams. "All
The quote's source comes in the middle of two independent clauses, so a period should follow *Adams*. Option A is incorrect because titles, when they come before a name, must be capitalized. Punctuation is also faulty. Option B is incorrect because the word *Adams* ends a sentence; a comma is not strong enough to support two sentences.

TExES PEDAGOGY AND PROFESSIONAL RESPONSIBILITIES EC-12

SAMPLE TEST

Directions: Read each item and select the best response.

1. **What developmental patterns should a professional teacher assess to meet the needs of the student?**
   (Average)

   A. Academic, regional, and family background
   B. Social, physical, and cognitive
   C. Academic, physical, and family background
   D. Physical, family, and ethnic background

2. **According to Piaget, what stage is characterized by the ability to think abstractly and to use logic?**
   (Easy)

   A. Concrete operations
   B. Pre-operational
   C. Formal operations
   D. Conservative operational

3. **At approximately what age is the average child able to define abstract terms such as honesty and justice?**
   (Rigorous)

   A. 10–12 years old
   B. 4–6 years old
   C. 14–16 years old
   D. 6–8 years old

4. **What would improve planning for instruction?**
   (Average)

   A. Describe the role of the teacher and student
   B. Evaluate the outcomes of instruction
   C. Rearrange the order of activities
   D. Give outside assignments

5. **What is the most significant development emerging in children at age two?**
   (Easy)

   A. Immune system develops
   B. Socialization occurs
   C. Language develops
   D. Perception develops

6. **You are leading a substance abuse discussion for health class. The students present their belief that marijuana is not harmful to their health. What set of data would refute their claim?**
(Rigorous)

   A. It is more carcinogenic than nicotine, lowers resistance to infection, worsens acne, and damages brain cells
   B. It damages brain cells, causes behavior changes in prenatally exposed infants, leads to other drug abuse, and causes short-term memory loss
   C. It lowers tolerance for frustration, causes eye damage, increases paranoia, and lowers resistance to infection
   D. It leads to abusing alcohol, lowers white blood cell count, reduces fertility, and causes gout

7. **Bobby, a nine-year-old, has been caught stealing frequently in the classroom. What might be a factor contributing to this behavior?**
(Average)

   A. Need for the items stolen
   B. Serious emotional disturbance
   C. Desire to experiment
   D. A normal stage of development

8. **What strategy can teachers incorporate in their classrooms that will allow students to acquire the same academic skills even though the students are at various learning levels?**
(Rigorous)

   A. Create learning modules
   B. Apply concrete rules to abstract theories
   C. Incorporate social learning skills
   D. Follow cognitive development progression

9. **The process approach is a three-phase model approach that aims directly at the enhancement of self concept among students. Which of the following are components of this process approach?**
(Rigorous)

   A. Sensing function, transforming function, acting function
   B. Diversity model, ethnicity model, economic model
   C. Problem approach, acting function, diversity model
   D. Ethnicity approach, sensing model, problem approach

10. **Andy shows up to class abusive and irritable. He is often late, sleeps in class, sometimes slurs his speech, and has an odor of drinking. What is the first intervention to take?**
    (Rigorous)

    A. Confront him, relying on a trusting relationship you think you have
    B. Do a lesson on alcohol abuse, making an example of him
    C. Do nothing, it is better to err on the side of failing to identify substance abuse
    D. Call administration, avoid conflict, and supervise others carefully

11. **What is a good strategy for teaching ethnically diverse students?**
    (Average)

    A. Do not focus on the students' culture
    B. Expect them to assimilate easily into your classroom
    C. Imitate their speech patterns
    D. Include ethnic studies in the curriculum

12. **Which of the following is an accurate description of an English Language Learner student?**
    (Average)

    A. Remedial students
    B. Exceptional education students
    C. Are not a homogeneous group
    D. Feel confident in communicating in English when with their peers

13. **What is an effective way to help an English Language Learner student succeed in class?**
    (Average)

    A. Refer the child to a specialist
    B. Maintain an encouraging, success-oriented atmosphere
    C. Help them assimilate by making them use English exclusively
    D. Help them cope with the content materials you presently use

14. **Johnny, a middle-schooler, comes to class uncharacteristically tired, distracted, withdrawn, and sullen and cries easily. What should be the teacher's first response?**
    (Average)

    A. Send him to the office to sit
    B. Call his parents
    C. Ask him what is wrong
    D. Ignore his behavior

15. **What should be considered when evaluating textbooks for content?**
    (Easy)

    A. Type of print used
    B. Number of photographs used
    C. Free of cultural stereotyping
    D. Outlines at the beginning of each chapter

16. **What steps are important in the review of subject matter in the classroom?**
    (Rigorous)

    A. A lesson-initiating review, topic, and a lesson-end review
    B. A preview of the subject matter, an in-depth discussion, and a lesson-end review
    C. A rehearsal of the subject matter and a topic summary within the lesson
    D. A short paragraph synopsis of the previous day's lesson and a written review at the end of the lesson

17. **What are critical elements of the instructional process?**
    (Rigorous)

    A. Content, goals, teacher needs
    B. Means of getting money to regulate instruction
    C. Content, materials, activities, goals, learner needs
    D. Materials, definitions, assignments

18. **The teacher states that the lesson the students will be engaged in will consist of a review of the material from the previous day, a demonstration of the scientific principles of an electronic circuit, and small group work on setting up an electronic circuit. What has the teacher demonstrated?**
    (Rigorous)

    A. The importance of reviewing
    B. Giving the general framework for the lesson to facilitate learning
    C. Giving students the opportunity to leave if they are not interested in the lesson
    D. Providing momentum for the lesson

19. **What is one component of the instructional planning model that must be given careful evaluation?**
    (Rigorous)

    A. Students' prior knowledge and skills
    B. The script the teacher will use in instruction
    C. Future lesson plans
    D. Parent participation

20. **How many stages of intellectual development does Piaget define?**
    (Average)

    A. Two
    B. Four
    C. Six
    D. Eight

21. Who developed the theory of multiple intelligences?
 (Average)

 A. Bruner
 B. Gardner
 C. Kagan
 D. Cooper

22. What is an example of a low order question?
 (Easy)

 A. "Why is it important to recycle items in your home?"
 B. "Compare how glass and plastics are recycled"
 C. "What items do we recycle in our county?"
 D. "Explain the importance of recycling in our county"

23. Bloom's taxonomy references six skill levels within the cognitive domain. The top three skills are known as higher-order thinking skills (HOTS). Which of the following are the three highest order skills?
 (Rigorous)

 A. Comprehension, application, analysis
 B. Knowledge, comprehension, evaluation
 C. Application, synthesis, comprehension
 D. Analysis, synthesis, and evaluation

24. Teachers have a responsibility to help students learn how to organize their classroom environments. Which of the following is NOT an effective method of teaching responsibility to students?
 (Rigorous)

 A. Dividing responsibilities among students
 B. Doing "spot-checks" of notebooks
 C. Cleaning up after students leave the classroom
 D. Expecting students to keep weekly calendars

25. How can students use a computer desktop publishing center?
 (Easy)

 A. To set up a classroom budget
 B. To create student made books,reports, essays, and more
 C. To design a research project
 D. To create a classroom behavior management system

26. Which of the following is considered a study skill?
 (Average)

 A. Using graphs, tables, and maps
 B. Using a desktop publishing program
 C. Explaining important vocabulary words
 D. Asking for clarification

27. According to research, what can be a result of specific teacher actions on behavior?
    (Rigorous)

    A. Increase in student misconduct
    B. Increase in the number of referrals
    C. Decrease in student participation
    D. Decrease in student retentions

28. When using a kinesthetic approach, what would be an appropriate activity?
    (Average)

    A. List
    B. Match
    C. Define
    D. Debate

29. How can the teacher establish a positive climate in the classroom?
    (Average)

    A. Help students see the unique contributions of individual differences
    B. Use whole group instruction for all content areas
    C. Help students divide into cooperative groups based on ability
    D. Eliminate teaching strategies that allow students to make choices

30. How can the teacher help students become more work-oriented and less disruptive?
    (Rigorous)

    A. Seek their input for content instruction
    B. Challenge the students with a task and show genuine enthusiasm for it
    C. Use behavior modification techniques with all students
    D. Make sure lesson plans are complete for the week

31. What has been established to increase student originality, intrinsic motivation, and higher-order thinking skills?
    (Rigorous)

    A. Classroom climate
    B. High expectations
    C. Student choice
    D. Use of authentic learning opportunities

32. Which of the following is NOT a component of the invitational learning theory?
    (Rigorous)

    A. Proper arrangement of classroom furniture
    B. Adequate ventilation and classroom lighting
    C. The regular use of substitute teachers
    D. Neutral hues for coloration of walls

33. **How can student misconduct be redirected at times?**
    (Easy)

    A. The teacher threatens the students
    B. The teacher assigns detention to the whole class
    C. The teacher stops the activity and stares at the students
    D. The teacher effectively handles changing from one activity to another

34. **The concept of efficient use of time includes which of the following?**
    (Rigorous)

    A. Daily review, seatwork, and recitation of concepts
    B. Lesson initiation, transition, and comprehension check
    C. Review, test, and review
    D. Punctuality, management transition, and wait time avoidance

35. **Reducing off-task time and maximizing the amount of time students spend attending to academic tasks is closely related to which of the following?**
    (Rigorous)

    A. Using whole class instruction only
    B. Business-like behaviors of the teacher
    C. Dealing only with major teaching functions
    D. Giving students a maximum of two minutes to come to order

36. **What do cooperative learning methods all have in common?**
    (Rigorous)

    A. Philosophy
    B. Cooperative task/cooperative reward structures
    C. Student roles and communication
    D. Teacher roles

37. **The use of volunteers and paraprofessionals within a classroom enriches the setting by:**
    (Easy)

    A. Providing more opportunity for individual student attention
    B. Offering a perceived sense of increased security for students
    C. Modifying the behavior of students
    D. All of the above

38. **What is the definition of proactive classroom management?**
    (Rigorous)

    A. Management that is constantly changing
    B. Management that is downplayed
    C. Management that gives clear and explicit instructions and rewards compliance
    D. Management that is designed by the students

39. **Which of the following significantly increases appropriate behavior in the classroom?**
    (Average)

    A. Monitoring the halls
    B. Having class rules
    C. Having class rules, giving feedback, and having individual consequences
    D. Having class rules, and giving feedback

40. **What have recent studies regarding effective teachers concluded?**
    (Average)

    A. Effective teachers let students establish rules
    B. Effective teachers establish routines by the sixth week of school
    C. Effective teachers state their own policies and establish consistent class rules and procedures on the first day of class
    D. Effective teachers establish flexible routines

41. **What is one way of effectively managing student conduct?**
    (Average)

    A. State expectations about behavior
    B. Let students discipline their peers
    C. Let minor infractions of the rules go unnoticed
    D. Increase disapproving remarks

42. **When is utilization of instructional materials most effective?**
    (Average)

    A. When the activities are organized and sequenced
    B. When the materials are prepared weeks in advance
    C. When the students choose the pages to work on
    D. When the students create the instructional materials

43. **Why is it important for a teacher to pose a question before calling on students to answer?**
    (Rigorous)

    A. It helps manage student conduct
    B. It keeps the students as a group focused on the class work
    C. It allows students time to collaborate
    D. It gives the teacher time to walk among the students

44. **Wait-time has what effect?**
    (Average)

    A. Gives structure to the class discourse
    B. Fewer chain and low-level questions are asked with more high-level questions included
    C. Gives the students time to evaluate the response
    D. Gives the opportunity for in-depth discussion about the topic

45. What is one benefit of amplifying a student's response?
    (Rigorous)

    A. It helps the student develop a positive self-image
    B. It is helpful to other students who are in the process of learning the reasoning or steps in answering the question
    C. It allows the teacher to cover more content
    D. It helps to keep the information organized

46. What is not a way that teachers show acceptance and give value to a student response?
    (Rigorous)

    A. Acknowledging
    B. Correcting
    C. Discussing
    D. Amplifying

47. What is an effective amount of wait-time?
    (Easy)

    A. 1 second
    B. 5 seconds
    C. 15 seconds
    D. 10 seconds

48. Ms. Smith says, "Yes, exactly what do you mean by 'It was the author's intention to mislead you'" What does this illustrate?
    (Rigorous)

    A. Digression
    B. Restates response
    C. Probes a response
    D. Amplifies a response

49. The teacher responds, "Yes, that is correct" to a student's answer. What is this an example of?
    (Average)

    A. Academic feedback
    B. Academic praise
    C. Simple positive response
    D. Simple negative response

50. When are students more likely to understand complex ideas?
    (Rigorous)

    A. If they do outside research before coming to class
    B. Later when they write out the definitions of complex words
    C. When they attend a lecture on the subject
    D. When they are clearly defined by the teacher and are given examples and non-examples of the concept

51. What are the two ways concepts can be taught?
    (Easy)

    A. Factually and interpretively
    B. Inductively and deductively
    C. Conceptually and inductively
    D. Analytically and facilitatively

52. **According to Piaget, when does the development of symbolic functioning and language take place?**
    (Average)

    A. Concrete operations stage
    B. Formal operations stage
    C. Sensorimotor stage
    D. Preoperational stage

53. **What should a teacher do when students have not responded well to an instructional activity?**
    (Average)

    A. Reevaluate learner needs
    B. Request administrative help
    C. Continue with the activity another day
    D. Assign homework on the concept

54. **How could a KWL chart be used in instruction?**
    (Average)

    A. To motivate students to do a research paper
    B. To assess prior knowledge of the students
    C. To assist in teaching skills
    D. To put events in sequential order

55. **Which of the following is an example of a synthesis question according to Bloom's taxonomy?**
    (Rigorous)

    A. "What is the definition of_____?"
    B. "Compare ____ to ____."
    C. "Match column A to column B."
    D. "Propose an alternative to_____."

56. **Which statement is an example of specific praise?**
    (Average)

    A. "John, you are the only person in class not paying attention"
    B. "William, I thought we agreed that you would turn in all of your homework"
    C. "Robert, you did a good job staying in line. See how it helped us get to music class on time?"
    D. "Class, you did a great job cleaning up the art room"

57. Mrs. Grant is providing her students with many extrinsic motivators in order to increase their intrinsic motivation. Which of the following best explains this relationship?
(Rigorous)

    A. This is a good relationship and will increase intrinsic motivation
    B. The relationship builds animosity between the teacher and the students
    C. Extrinsic motivation does not in itself help to build intrinsic motivation
    D. There is no place for extrinsic motivation in the classroom

58. Which of the following is NOT a factor in student self-motivation?
(Rigorous)

    A. Breaking larger tasks into more manageable steps
    B. Permitting students to turn in assignments late
    C. Offering students control over the assignment
    D. Allowing students to create dream boards

59. Which of the following is NOT a part of the hardware of a computer system?
(Easy)

    A. Storage device
    B. Input devices
    C. Software
    D. Central Processing Unit

60. When pulling educational information from shared drives what is the MOST important factor to consider?
(Rigorous)

    A. What is the intended use of the information
    B. What age group is the information best suited for
    C. Where the information came from
    D. Who the author of the information is

61. Which of the following are the three primary categories of instructional technology tools?
(Rigorous)

    A. Creation/design/implementation
    B. Research/implementation/assessment
    C. Assessment/creation/research
    D. Design/research/usage

62. When a teacher is evaluating a student's technologically produced product, which of the following is considered the MOST important factor to consider?
(Rigorous)

    A. Content
    B. Design
    C. Audience
    D. Relevance

63. You are a classroom teacher in a building that does not have a computer lab for your class to use. However, knowing that you enjoy incorporating technology into the classroom, your principal has worked to find computers for your room. They are set up in the back of your classroom and have software loaded, but have no access to the intranet or internet within your building. Which of the following is NOT an acceptable method for using these computers within your classroom instruction? *(Rigorous)*

    A. Rotating the students in small groups through the computers as centers
    B. Putting students at the computers individually for skill-based review or practice
    C. Dividing your classroom into three groups and putting each group at one computer and completing a whole class lesson
    D. Using the computers for students to complete their writing assignments with an assigned sign-up sheet, so the students know the order in which they will type their stories

64. What are three steps, in the correct order, for evaluating software before purchasing it for use within the classroom? *(Rigorous)*

    A. Read the instructions to ensure it will work with the computer you have, try it out as if you were a student, and examine how the program handles errors or mistakes the student may make
    B. Try the computer program as if you were a student, read any online information about the program, have a student use the program and provide feedback
    C. Read the instructions and load it onto your computer, try out the program yourself as if you were a student, have a student use the program and provide feedback
    D. Read the instructions, have a student use the program, try it out yourself

65. When a teacher wants to utilize an assessment that is subjective in nature, which of the following is the most effective method for scoring? *(Easy)*

    A. Rubric
    B. Checklist
    C. Alternative assessment
    D. Subjective measures should not be utilized

66. **What is an example of formative feedback?**
    (Average)

    A. The results of an intelligence test
    B. Correcting the tests in small groups
    C. Verbal behavior that expresses approval of a student response to a test item
    D. Scheduling a discussion prior to the test

67. **Norm-referenced tests:**
    (Rigorous)

    A. Give information only about the local samples results
    B. Provide information about how the local test takers did compared to a representative sampling of national test takers
    C. Make no comparisons to national test takers
    D. None of the above

68. **What is the best definition for an achievement test?**
    (Average)

    A. It measures mechanical and practical abilities
    B. It measures broad areas of knowledge that are the result of cumulative learning experiences
    C. It measures the ability to learn to perform a task
    D. It measures performance related to specific, recently acquired information

69. **How are standardized tests useful in assessment?**
    (Average)

    A. For teacher evaluation
    B. For evaluation of the administration
    C. For comparison from school to school
    D. For comparison to the population on which the test was normed

70. **Mr. Brown wishes to improve his parent communication skills. Which of the following is a strategy he can utilize to accomplish this goal?**
    (Easy)

    A. Hold parent-teacher conferences
    B. Send home positive notes
    C. Have parent nights where the parents are invited into his classroom
    D. All of the above

71. **When communicating with parents for whom English is not the primary language, you should:**
    (Easy)

    A. Provide materials whenever possible in their native language
    B. Use an interpreter
    C. Provide the same communication as you would to native English speaking parents
    D. All of the above

TX THEA BONUS EDITION

72. **Which statement best reflects why family involvement is important to a student's educational success?**
    (Easy)

    A. Reading the class newsletter constitutes strong family involvement
    B. Family involvement means to attend graduation
    C. There are limited ways a parent can be active in their child's education
    D. The more family members are involved, the more success a student is likely to experience

73. **Which of the following is NOT an appropriate method for teachers to interact with families of diverse backgrounds?**
    (Easy)

    A. Show respect to parents
    B. Share personal stories concerning the student
    C. Display patience with parents
    D. Disregard culture of student

74. **A parent has left an angry message on the teacher's voicemail. The message relates to a concern about a student and is directed at the teacher. The teacher should:**
    (Average)

    A. Call back immediately and confront the parent
    B. Cool off, plan what to discuss with the parent, then call back
    C. Question the child to find out what set off the parent
    D. Ignore the message, since feelings of anger usually subside after a while

75. **Which is NOT considered a good practice when conducting parent-teacher conferences?**
    (Average)

    A. Ending the conference with an agreed plan of action
    B. Figure out questions for parents during the conference
    C. Prepare work samples, records of behavior, and assessment information
    D. Prepare a welcoming environment, set a good mood, and be an active listener

76. **Which of the following should NOT be a purpose of a parent-teacher conference?**
    (Average)

    A. To involve the parent in their child's education
    B. To establish a friendship with the child's parents
    C. To resolve a concern about the child's performance
    D. To inform parents of positive behaviors by the child

77. **Which of the following is a technological strategy that keeps students and teachers interactively communicating about issues in the classroom and beyond?**
    (Rigorous)

    A. Distance learning
    B. Mentoring support system
    C. Conceptual learning modalities
    D. Community resources

78. **In the past, teaching has been viewed as _____ while in more current society it has been viewed as _____.**
    (Rigorous)

    A. isolating…collaborative
    B. collaborative…isolating
    C. supportive…isolating
    D. isolating…supportive

79. **Which of the following is a good reason to collaborate with a pee?**
    (Easy)

    A. To increase your knowledge in areas where you feel you are weak, but the peer is strong
    B. To increase your planning time and that of your peer by combining the classes and taking more breaks
    C. To have fewer lesson plans to write
    D. To teach fewer subjects

80. **Which of the following is responsible for working with the school in matters concerning the business of running a school?**
    (Rigorous)

    A. Curriculum coordinators
    B. Administrators
    C. Board of Education
    D. Parent-Teacher organizations

81. **What would happen if a school utilized an integrated approach to professional development?**
    (Average)

    A. All stakeholders needs are addressed
    B. Teachers and administrators are on the same page
    C. High-quality programs for students are developed
    D. Parents drive the curriculum and instruction

82. **Which is true of child protective services?**
    (Rigorous)

    A. They have been forced to become more punitive in their attempts to treat and prevent child abuse and neglect
    B. They have become more a means for identifying cases of abuse and less an agent for rehabilitation due to the large volume of cases
    C. They have become advocates for structured discipline within the school
    D. They have become a strong advocate in the court system

83. **What is a benefit of frequent self-assessment?**
    (Average)

    A. Opens new venues for professional development
    B. Saves teachers the pressure of being observed by others
    C. Reduces time spent on areas not needing attention
    D. Offers a model for students to adopt in self-improvement

84. **Mrs. Graham has taken the time to reflect, completed observations, and asked for feedback about the interactions between her and her students from her principal. It is obvious by seeking this information out that Mrs. Graham understands which of the following?**
    (Rigorous)

    A. The importance of clear communication with the principal
    B. She needs to analyze her effectiveness of classroom interactions
    C. She is clearly communicating with the principal
    D. She cares about her students

85. **Which of the following are ways a professional can assess his/her teaching strengths and weaknesses?**
    (Rigorous)

    A. Examining how many students were unable to understand a concept
    B. Asking peers for suggestions or ideas
    C. Self-evaluation/reflection of lessons taught
    D. All of the above

86. **In successful inclusion of students with disabilities:** *(Average)*

    A. A variety of instructional arrangements are available
    B. School personnel shift the responsibility for learning outcomes to the student
    C. The physical facilities are used as they are
    D. Regular classroom teachers have sole responsibility for evaluating student progress

87. **Teachers may duplicate copies of informational materials provided that they meet the following requirement/s:** *(Rigorous)*

    A. Brevity
    B. Spontaneity
    C. Cumulative effect
    D. All of the above

88. **Which of the following is one of the greatest obstacles that new teachers face when first entering the profession?** *(Rigorous)*

    A. Dealing with behavioral issues in the classroom
    B. Monitoring daily student success
    C. Developing rapport with parents and caretakers
    D. Creating weekly lesson plans

89. **How can a teacher use a student's permanent record?** *(Average)*

    A. To develop a better understanding of the needs of the student
    B. To record all instances of student disruptive behavior
    C. To brainstorm ideas for discussing with parents at parent-teacher conferences
    D. To develop realistic expectations of the student's performance early in the year

90. **To what does the validity of a test refer?** *(Rigorous)*

    A. Its consistency
    B. Its usefulness
    C. Its accuracy
    D. The degree of true scores it provide

Answer Key

1.	B	31.	C	61.	C
2.	C	32.	C	62.	D
3.	A	33.	D	63.	C
4.	B	34.	D	64.	A
5.	C	35.	B	65.	A
6.	B	36.	B	66.	C
7.	B	37.	D	67.	B
8.	A	38.	C	68.	B
9.	A	39.	C	69.	D
10.	D	40.	C	70.	D
11.	D	41.	A	71.	D
12.	C	42.	A	72.	D
13.	B	43.	B	73.	D
14.	C	44.	B	74.	B
15.	C	45.	B	75.	B
16.	A	46.	B	76.	B
17.	C	47.	B	77.	A
18.	B	48.	C	78.	A
19.	A	49.	C	79.	A
20.	B	50.	D	80.	C
21.	B	51.	B	81.	C
22.	C	52.	D	82.	B
23.	D	53.	A	83.	A
24.	C	54.	B	84.	B
25.	B	55.	D	85.	D
26.	A	56.	C	86.	A
27.	A	57.	C	87.	D
28.	B	58.	B	88.	A
29.	A	59.	C	89.	A
30.	B	60.	A	90.	B

Rigor Table

Easy
2, 5, 15, 22, 25, 33, 37, 47, 51, 59, 65, 70, 71, 72, 73, 79

Average
1, 4, 7, 11, 12, 13, 14, 20, 21, 26, 28, 29, 39, 40, 41, 42, 44, 49, 52, 53, 54, 56, 66, 68, 69, 74, 75, 76, 81, 83, 86, 89

Rigorous
3, 6, 8, 9, 10, 16, 17, 18, 19, 23, 24, 27, 30, 31, 32, 34, 35, 36, 38, 43, 45, 46, 48, 50, 55, 57, 58, 60, 61, 62, 63, 64, 67, 77, 78, 80, 82, 84, 85, 87, 88, 90

SAMPLE TEST WITH RATIONALES

Directions: Read each item and select the best response.

1. **What developmental patterns should a professional teacher assess to meet the needs of the student?**
   (Average)

   A. Academic, regional, and family background
   B. Social, physical, and cognitive
   C. Academic, physical, and family background
   D. Physical, family, and ethnic background

Answer: B. Social, physical, and cognitive
The effective teacher applies knowledge of physical, social, and cognitive developmental patterns and of individual differences to meet the instructional needs of all students in the classroom. The most important premise of child development is that all domains of development (physical, social, and academic) are integrated. The teacher has a broad knowledge and thorough understanding of the development that typically occurs during the students' current period of life. More importantly, the teacher understands how children learn best during each period of development. An examination of the student's file coupled with ongoing evaluation assures a successful educational experience for both teacher and students.

2. **According to Piaget, what stage is characterized by the ability to think abstractly and to use logic?**
   (Easy)

   A. Concrete operations
   B. Pre-operational
   C. Formal operations
   D. Conservative operational

Answer: C. Formal operations
The four development stages are described in Piaget's theory as follows:

1. Sensorimotor stage: from birth to age 2 years (children experience the world through movement and senses)
2. Preoperational stage: from ages 2 to 7 (acquisition of motor skills)
3. Concrete operational stage: from ages 7 to 11 (children begin to think logically about concrete events)
4. Formal operational stage: after age 11 (development of abstract reasoning)

These chronological periods are approximate and, in light of the fact that studies have demonstrated great variation between children, cannot be seem as rigid norms. Furthermore, these stages occur at different ages, depending upon the domain of knowledge under consideration. The ages normally given for the stages reflect when each stage tends to predominate even though one might elicit examples of two, three, or even all four stages of thinking at the same time from one individual, depending upon the domain of knowledge and the means used to elicit it.

3. **At approximately what age is the average child able to define abstract terms such as honesty and justice?**
   (Rigorous)

   A. 10–12 years old
   B. 4–6 years old
   C. 14–16 years old
   D. 6–8 years old

Answer: A. 10–12 years old
The usual age for the fourth stage (the formal operational stage) as described by Piaget is from 10 to 12 years old. It is in this stage that children begin to be able to define abstract terms.

4. **What would improve planning for instruction?**
   (Average)

   A. Describe the role of the teacher and student
   B. Evaluate the outcomes of instruction
   C. Rearrange the order of activities
   D. Give outside assignments

Answer: B. Evaluate the outcomes of instruction
Important as it is to plan content, materials, activities, and goals taking into account learner needs and to base what goes on in the classroom on the results of that planning, it makes no difference if students are not able to demonstrate improvement in the skills being taught. An important part of the planning process is for the teacher to constantly adapt all aspects of the curriculum to what is actually happening in the classroom. Planning frequently misses the mark or fails to allow for unexpected factors. Evaluating the outcomes of instruction regularly and making adjustments accordingly will have a positive impact on the overall success of a teaching methodology.

5. **What is the most significant development emerging in children at age two?**
   (Easy)

   A. Immune system develops
   B. Socialization occurs
   C. Language develops
   D. Perception develops

Answer: C. Language develops
Language begins to develop in an infant not long after birth. Chomsky claims that children teach themselves to speak using the people around them for resources. Several studies of the sounds infants make in their cribs seem to support this. The first stage of meaningful sounds is the uttering of a word that obviously has meaning for the child, for example "bird," when the child sees one flying through the air. Does the development of real language begin when the noun is linked with a verb ("bird fly")? When language begins and how it develops has been debated for a long time. It is useful for a teacher to investigate those theories and studies.

6. **You are leading a substance abuse discussion for health class. The students present their belief that marijuana is not harmful to their health. What set of data would refute their claim?**
   (Rigorous)

   A. It is more carcinogenic than nicotine, lowers resistance to infection, worsens acne, and damages brain cells
   B. It damages brain cells, causes behavior changes in prenatally exposed infants, leads to other drug abuse, and causes short-term memory loss
   C. It lowers tolerance for frustration, causes eye damage, increases paranoia, and lowers resistance to infection
   D. It leads to abusing alcohol, lowers white blood cell count, reduces fertility, and causes gout

Answer: B. It damages brain cells, causes behavior changes in prenatally exposed infants, leads to other drug abuse, and causes short-term memory loss
The student tending toward the use of drugs and/or alcohol will exhibit losses in social and academic functional levels that were previously attained. He may begin to experiment with substances. The adage "Pot makes a smart kid average and an average kid dumb" is right on the mark. There exist not a few families where pot smoking is a known habit of the parents. The children start their habit by stealing from the parents, making it almost impossible to convince the child that drugs and alcohol are not good for them. Parental use is hampering national efforts to clean up America. The school may be the only source for the real information that children need in order to make intelligent choices about drug use. It's important to remember that if children start using drugs early, it will interfere with their accomplishing developmental tasks and will likely lead to a lifetime of addiction.

7. **Bobby, a nine-year-old, has been caught stealing frequently in the classroom. What might be a factor contributing to this behavior?**
   (Average)

   A. Need for the items stolen
   B. Serious emotional disturbance
   C. Desire to experiment
   D. A normal stage of development

   Answer: B. Serious emotional disturbance
   Lying, stealing, and fighting are atypical behaviors that most children may exhibit occasionally, but if a child lies, steals, or fights regularly or blatantly, these behaviors may be indicative of emotional distress. Emotional disturbances in childhood are not uncommon and take a variety of forms. Usually these problems show up in the form of uncharacteristic behaviors. Most of the time, children respond favorably to brief treatment programs of psychotherapy. At other times, disturbances may need more intensive therapy and are harder to resolve. All stressful behaviors need to be addressed, and any type of chronic antisocial behavior needs to be examined as a possible symptom of deep-seated emotional upset.

8. **What strategy can teachers incorporate in their classrooms that will allow students to acquire the same academic skills even though the students are at various learning levels?**
   (Rigorous)

   A. Create learning modules
   B. Apply concrete rules to abstract theories
   C. Incorporate social learning skills
   D. Follow cognitive development progression

   Answer: A. Create learning modules
   Teachers should be aware of the fact that each student develops cognitively, mentally, emotionally, and physically at different levels. Each student is a unique person and may require individualized instruction. This may require teachers to adapt their lesson plans according to a student's developmental progress.

9. The process approach is a three-phase model approach that aims directly at the enhancement of self concept among students. Which of the following are components of this process approach?
(Rigorous)

   A. Sensing function, transforming function, acting function
   B. Diversity model, ethnicity model, economic model
   C. Problem approach, acting function, diversity model
   D. Ethnicity approach, sensing model, problem approach

Answer: A. Sensing function, transforming function, acting function
This three-phase approach can be simplified into the words by which the model is usually known: reach, touch, and teach. The sensing function integrates information. The transforming function conceptualizes and provides meaning and value to perceived information. The acting function chooses actions from several different alternatives to be acted upon. This three-phase approach can be applied to any situation.

10. Andy shows up to class abusive and irritable. He is often late, sleeps in class, sometimes slurs his speech, and has an odor of drinking. What is the first intervention to take?
(Rigorous)

   A. Confront him, relying on a trusting relationship you think you have
   B. Do a lesson on alcohol abuse, making an example of him
   C. Do nothing, it is better to err on the side of failing to identify substance abuse
   D. Call administration, avoid conflict, and supervise others carefully

Answer: D. Call administration, avoid conflict, and supervise others carefully
Educators are not only likely to, but often do, face students who are high on something. Of course, they are not only a hazard to their own safety and those of others, but their ability to be productive learners is greatly diminished, if not non-existent. They show up instead of skip, because it is not always easy or practical for them to spend the day away from home but not in school. Unless they can stay inside they are at risk of being picked up for truancy. Some enjoy being high in school, getting a sense of satisfaction by putting something over on the system. Some just do not take drug use seriously enough to think usage at school might be inappropriate. The first responsibility of the teacher is to assure the safety of all of the children. Avoiding conflict with the student who is high and obtaining help from administration is the best course of action.

11. **What is a good strategy for teaching ethnically diverse students?**
    (Average)

    A. Do not focus on the students' culture
    B. Expect them to assimilate easily into your classroom
    C. Imitate their speech patterns
    D. Include ethnic studies in the curriculum

Answer: D. Include ethnic studies in the curriculum
Exploring a student's own culture increases their confidence levels in the group. It is also a very useful tool when students are struggling to develop identities that they can feel comfortable with. The bonus is that this is good training for living in the world.

12. **Which of the following is an accurate description of an English Language Learner student?**
    (Average)

    A. Remedial students
    B. Exceptional education students
    C. Are not a homogeneous group
    D. Feel confident in communicating in English when with their peers

Answer: C. Are not a homogenous group
Because ELL students are often grouped in classes that take a different approach to teaching English than those for native speakers, it is easy to assume that they are all present with the same needs and characteristics. Nothing could be further from the truth, even in what they need when it comes to learning English. It is important that their backgrounds and personalities be observed just as with native speakers. It was very surprising several years ago when Vietnamese children began arriving in American schools with little training in English and went on to excel in their classes, often even beyond their American counterparts. In many schools, there were Vietnamese merit scholars in the graduating classes.

13. **What is an effective way to help an English Language Learner student succeed in class?**
    (Average)

    A. Refer the child to a specialist
    B. Maintain an encouraging, success-oriented atmosphere
    C. Help them assimilate by making them use English exclusively
    D. Help them cope with the content materials you presently use

Answer: B. Maintain an encouraging, success-oriented atmosphere
Anyone who is in an environment where his language is not the standard one feels embarrassed and inferior. The student who is in that situation expects to fail.

Encouragement is even more important for these students. They need many opportunities to succeed.

14. **Johnny, a middle-schooler, comes to class uncharacteristically tired, distracted, withdrawn, and sullen and cries easily. What should be the teacher's first response?**
    (Average)

    A. Send him to the office to sit
    B. Call his parents
    C. Ask him what is wrong
    D. Ignore his behavior

Answer: C. Ask him what is wrong
If a teacher has developed a trusting relationship with a child, the reasons for the child's behavior may come out. It might be that the child needs to tell someone what is going on and is seeking a confidant, and a trusted teacher can intervene. If the child is unwilling to talk to the teacher about what is going on, the next step is to contact the parents, who may or may not be willing to explain why the child is the way he/she is. If they simply do not know, then it is time to add a professional physician or counselor to the mix.

15. **What should be considered when evaluating textbooks for content?**
    (Easy)

    A. Type of print used
    B. Number of photographs used
    C. Free of cultural stereotyping
    D. Outlines at the beginning of each chapter

Answer: C. Free of cultural stereotyping
While textbook writers and publishers have responded to the need to be culturally diverse in recent years, a few texts are still being offered that do not meet these standards. When teachers have an opportunity to be involved in choosing textbooks, they can be watchdogs for the community in keeping the curriculum free of matter that reinforces bigotry and discrimination.

16. **What steps are important in the review of subject matter in the classroom?**
    (Rigorous)

    A. A lesson-initiating review, topic, and a lesson-end review
    B. A preview of the subject matter, an in-depth discussion, and a lesson-end review
    C. A rehearsal of the subject matter and a topic summary within the lesson
    D. A short paragraph synopsis of the previous day's lesson and a written review at the end of the lesson

Answer: A. A lesson-initiating review, topic, and a lesson-end review
The effective teacher utilizes all three of these together with comprehension checks to make sure the students are processing the information. Lesson-end reviews are restatements (by the teacher or teacher and students) of the content of discussion at the end of a lesson. Subject matter retention increases when lessons include an outline at the beginning of the lesson and a summary at the end of the lesson. This type of structure is utilized in successful classrooms. Moreover, when students know what is coming next and what is expected of them, they feel more a part of their learning environment, and deviant behavior is lessened.

17. **What are critical elements of the instructional process?**
    (Rigorous)

    A. Content, goals, teacher needs
    B. Means of getting money to regulate instruction
    C. Content, materials, activities, goals, learner needs
    D. Materials, definitions, assignments

Answer: C. Content, materials, activities, goals, learner needs
Goal-setting is a vital component of the instructional process. The teacher will, of course, have overall goals for her class, both short-term and long-term. However, perhaps even more important than that is the setting of goals that take into account the individual learner's needs, background, and stage of development. Making an educational program child-centered involves building on the natural curiosity children bring to school and asking children what they want to learn. Student-centered classrooms contain not only textbooks, workbooks, and literature but also rely heavily on a variety of audiovisual equipment and computers. There are tape recorders, language masters, filmstrip projectors, and laser disc players to help meet the learning styles of the students. Planning for instructional activities entails identification or selection of the activities the teacher and students will engage in during a period of instruction.

18. **The teacher states that the lesson the students will be engaged in will consist of a review of the material from the previous day, a demonstration of the scientific principles of an electronic circuit, and small group work on setting up an electronic circuit. What has the teacher demonstrated?**
    (Rigorous)

    A. The importance of reviewing
    B. Giving the general framework for the lesson to facilitate learning
    C. Giving students the opportunity to leave if they are not interested in the lesson
    D. Providing momentum for the lesson

    Answer: B. Giving the general framework for the lesson to facilitate learning
    If children know where they're going, they're more likely to be engaged in getting there. It's important to give them a road map whenever possible for what is coming in their classes.

19. **What is one component of the instructional planning model that must be given careful evaluation?**
    (Rigorous)

    A. Students' prior knowledge and skills
    B. The script the teacher will use in instruction
    C. Future lesson plans
    D. Parent participation

    Answer: A. Students' prior knowledge and skills
    The teacher will, of course, have certain expectations regarding where the students will be physically and intellectually when he/she plans for a new class. However, there will be wide variations in the actual classroom. If he/she does not make the extra effort to understand where there are deficiencies and where there are strengths in the individual students, the planning will probably miss the mark, at least for some members of the class. This can be obtained through a review of student records, by observation, and by testing.

20. **How many stages of intellectual development does Piaget define?**
    (Average)

    A. Two
    B. Four
    C. Six
    D. Eight

    Answer: B. Four
    The stages are:
    1. Sensorimotor stage: from birth to age 2 years (children experience the world through movement and senses)

2. Preoperational stage: from ages 2 to 7 (acquisition of motor skills)
3. Concrete operational stage: from ages 7 to 11 (children begin to think logically about concrete events)
4. Formal operational stage: after age 11 (development of abstract reasoning)

21. Who developed the theory of multiple intelligences?
(Average)

A. Bruner
B. Gardner
C. Kagan
D. Cooper

Answer: B. Gardner
Howard Gardner's most famous work is probably *Frames of Mind*, which details seven dimensions of intelligence (visual/spatial intelligence, musical intelligence, verbal intelligence, logical/mathematical intelligence, interpersonal intelligence, intrapersonal intelligence, and bodily/kinesthetic intelligence). Gardner's claim that pencil and paper IQ tests do not capture the full range of human intelligences has garnered much praise within the field of education but has also met criticism, largely from psychometricians. Since the publication of *Frames of Mind*, Gardner has additionally identified the 8th dimension of intelligence: naturalist intelligence, and is still considering a possible ninth—existentialist intelligence.

22. What is an example of a low order question?
(Easy)

A. "Why is it important to recycle items in your home?"
B. "Compare how glass and plastics are recycled"
C. "What items do we recycle in our county?"
D. "Explain the importance of recycling in our county"

Answer: C. "What items do we recycle in our county?"
Remember that the difference between specificity and abstractness is a continuum. The most specific is something that is concrete and can be seen, heard, smelled, tasted, or felt, like cans, bottles, and newspapers. At the other end of the spectrum is an abstraction like importance. Lower-order questions are on the concrete end of the continuum; higher-order questions are on the abstract end.

23. **Bloom's taxonomy references six skill levels within the cognitive domain. The top three skills are known as higher-order thinking skills (HOTS). Which of the following are the three highest order skills?**
    (Rigorous)

    A. Comprehension, application, analysis
    B. Knowledge, comprehension, evaluation
    C. Application, synthesis, comprehension
    D. Analysis, synthesis, and evaluation

Answer: D. Analysis, synthesis, and evaluation
The six skill levels of Bloom's taxonomy are: knowledge, comprehension, application, analysis, synthesis, and evaluation. Key instructional approaches that utilize HOTS are inquiry-based learning, problem solving, and open-ended questioning. It is crucial for students to use and refine these skills in order to apply them to everyday life and situations outside of school.

24. **Teachers have a responsibility to help students learn how to organize their classroom environments. Which of the following is NOT an effective method of teaching responsibility to students?**
    (Rigorous)

    A. Dividing responsibilities among students
    B. Doing "spot-checks" of notebooks
    C. Cleaning up after students leave the classroom
    D. Expecting students to keep weekly calendars

Answer: C. Cleaning up after students leave the classroom
Teachers of young children can help students learn how to behave appropriately and take care of their surroundings by providing them with opportunities to practice ownership, chores, and leadership. Allowing students to leave a messy and disorganized class at the end of the day does not teach them responsibility.

25. **How can students use a computer desktop publishing center?**
    (Easy)

    A. To set up a classroom budget
    B. To create student made books, reports, essays, and more
    C. To design a research project
    D. To create a classroom behavior management system

Answer: B. To create student made books, reports, essays, and more
By creating a book, students gain new insights into how communication works. Suddenly, the concept of audience for what they write and create becomes real. They also have an opportunity to be introduced to graphic arts, an exploding field. In addition,

just as computers are a vital part of the world they will be entering as adults, so is desktop publishing. It is universally used by businesses of all kinds.

26. **Which of the following is considered a study skill?**
    (Average)

    A. Using graphs, tables, and maps
    B. Using a desktop publishing program
    C. Explaining important vocabulary words
    D. Asking for clarification

Answer: A. Using graphs, tables, and maps
In studying, it is certainly true that "a picture is worth a thousand words." Not only are these devices useful in making a point clear, they are excellent mnemonic devices for remembering facts.

27. **According to research, what can be a result of specific teacher actions on behavior?**
    (Rigorous)

    A. Increase in student misconduct
    B. Increase in the number of referrals
    C. Decrease in student participation
    D. Decrease in student retentions

Answer: A. Increase in student misconduct
Unfortunately, at times, misbehavior is the result of specific teacher actions. There is considerable research that indicates that some teacher behavior is upsetting to students and increases the occurrence of student misbehavior. Such teacher behavior may include any action that a child perceives as being unfair; punitive remarks about the child, his behavior, or his work; or harsh responses to the child.

28. **When using a kinesthetic approach, what would be an appropriate activity?**
    (Average)

    A. List
    B. Match
    C. Define
    D. Debate

Answer: B. Match
Brain lateralization theory emerged in the 1970s and demonstrated that the left hemisphere appeared to be associated with verbal and sequential abilities whereas the right hemisphere appeared to be associated with emotions and with spatial, holistic processing. Although those particular conclusions continue to be challenged, it is clear that people concentrate, process, and remember new and difficult information under

very different conditions. For example, auditory and visual perceptual strengths, passivity, and self-oriented or authority-oriented motivation often correlate with high academic achievement, whereas tactual and kinesthetic strengths, a need for mobility, nonconformity, and peer motivation often correlate with school underachievement (Dunn & Dunn, 1992, 1993). Understanding how students perceive the task of learning new information differently is often helpful in tailoring the classroom experience for optimal success.

29. **How can the teacher establish a positive climate in the classroom?**
    (Average)

    A. Help students see the unique contributions of individual differences
    B. Use whole group instruction for all content areas
    C. Help students divide into cooperative groups based on ability
    D. Eliminate teaching strategies that allow students to make choices

Answer: A. Help students see the unique contributions of individual differences
In the first place, an important purpose of education is to prepare students to live successfully in the real world, and this is an important insight and understanding for them to take into that world. In the second place, the most fertile learning environment is one in which all viewpoints and backgrounds are respected and where everyone has equal respect.

30. **How can the teacher help students become more work-oriented and less disruptive?**
    (Rigorous)

    A. Seek their input for content instruction
    B. Challenge the students with a task and show genuine enthusiasm for it
    C. Use behavior modification techniques with all students
    D. Make sure lesson plans are complete for the week

Answer: B. Challenge the students with a task and show genuine enthusiasm for it
Many studies have demonstrated that the enthusiasm of the teacher is infectious. If students feel that the teacher is ambivalent about a task, they will also catch that attitude.

31. **What has been established to increase student originality, intrinsic motivation, and higher-order thinking skills?**
    (Rigorous)

    A. Classroom climate
    B. High expectations
    C. Student choice
    D. Use of authentic learning opportunities

Answer: C. Student choice
While all of the descriptors are good attributes for students to demonstrate, it has been shown through research that providing student choice can increase all of the described factors.

32. **Which of the following is NOT a component of the invitational learning theory?**
    (Rigorous)

    A. Proper arrangement of classroom furniture
    B. Adequate ventilation and classroom lighting
    C. The regular use of substitute teachers
    D. Neutral hues for coloration of walls

Answer: C. The regular use of substitute teachers
The physical environment is one of the main principles of the invitational learning theory. The teacher can create and design their classroom to cultivate a warm and caring environment for their students. This thoughtful atmosphere can create positive learning experiences for their students.

33. **How can student misconduct be redirected at times?**
    (Easy)

    A. The teacher threatens the students
    B. The teacher assigns detention to the whole class
    C. The teacher stops the activity and stares at the students
    D. The teacher effectively handles changing from one activity to another

Answer: D. The teacher effectively handles changing from one activity to another
Appropriate verbal techniques include a soft non-threatening voice void of undue roughness, anger, or impatience regardless of whether the teacher is instructing, providing student alerts, or giving a behavior reprimand. Verbal techniques that may be effective in modifying student behavior include simply stating the student's name, explaining briefly and succinctly what the student is doing that is inappropriate and what the student should be doing. Verbal techniques for reinforcing behavior include both encouragement and praise delivered by the teacher. In addition, for verbal techniques to

positively affect student behavior and learning, the teacher must give clear, concise directives while implying her warmth toward the students.

34. **The concept of efficient use of time includes which of the following?**
    (Rigorous)

    A. Daily review, seatwork, and recitation of concepts
    B. Lesson initiation, transition, and comprehension check
    C. Review, test, and review
    D. Punctuality, management transition, and wait time avoidance

Answer: D. Punctuality, management transition, and wait time avoidance
The "benevolent boss" concept applies here. One who succeeds in managing a business follows these rules; so does the successful teacher.

35. **Reducing off-task time and maximizing the amount of time students spend attending to academic tasks is closely related to which of the following?**
    (Rigorous)

    A. Using whole class instruction only
    B. Business-like behaviors of the teacher
    C. Dealing only with major teaching functions
    D. Giving students a maximum of two minutes to come to order

Answer: B. Business-like behaviors of the teacher
The effective teacher continually evaluates his/her own physical/mental/social/emotional well-being with regard to the students in his/her classroom. There is always the tendency to satisfy social and emotional needs through relationships with the students. A good teacher genuinely likes his/her students, and that is a positive thing. However, if students are not convinced that the teacher's purpose for being there is to get a job done, the atmosphere in the classroom becomes difficult to control. This is the job of the teacher. Maintaining a business-like approach in the classroom yields many positive results. It is a little like a benevolent boss.

36. **What do cooperative learning methods all have in common?**
    (Rigorous)

    A. Philosophy
    B. Cooperative task/cooperative reward structures
    C. Student roles and communication
    D. Teacher roles

Answer: B. Cooperative task/cooperative reward structures
Cooperative learning situations, as practiced in today's classrooms, grew out of searches conducted by several groups in the early 1970s. Cooperative learning situations can range from very formal applications such as STAD (Student Teams-

Achievement Divisions) and CIRC (Cooperative Integrated Reading and Composition) to less formal groupings known variously as "group investigation," "learning together," and "discovery groups." Cooperative learning as a general term is now firmly recognized and established as a teaching and learning technique in American schools. Since cooperative learning techniques are so widely diffused in the schools, it is necessary to orient students in the skills by which cooperative learning groups can operate smoothly, and thereby enhance learning. Students who cannot interact constructively with other students will not be able to take advantage of the learning opportunities provided by the cooperative learning situations and will furthermore deprive their fellow students of the opportunity for cooperative learning.

37. **The use of volunteers and paraprofessionals within a classroom enriches the setting by:**
    (Easy)

    A. Providing more opportunity for individual student attention
    B. Offering a perceived sense of increased security for students
    C. Modifying the behavior of students
    D. All of the above

Answer: D. All of the above
Research has shown that volunteers and paraprofessionals involvement in the educational process positively impacts the attitude and conduct of children in the classroom. Always be cautious in choosing classroom helpers that you trust and are competent.

38. **What is the definition of proactive classroom management?**
    (Rigorous)

    A. Management that is constantly changing
    B. Management that is downplayed
    C. Management that gives clear and explicit instructions and rewards compliance
    D. Management that is designed by the students

Answer: C. Management that gives clear and explicit instructions and rewards compliance
Classroom management plans should be in place when the school year begins. Developing a management plan takes a proactive approach—that is, decide what behaviors will be expected of the class as a whole, anticipate possible problems, and teach the behaviors early in the school year. Involving the students in the development of the classroom rules lets the students know the rationale for the rules and allows them to assume responsibility in the rules because they had a part in developing them.

39. **Which of the following significantly increases appropriate behavior in the classroom?**
    (Average)

    A. Monitoring the halls
    B. Having class rules
    C. Having class rules, giving feedback, and having individual consequences
    D. Having class rules, and giving feedback

Answer: C. Having class rules, giving feedback, and having individual consequences
Clear, consistent class rules go a long way to preventing inappropriate behavior. Effective teachers give immediate feedback to students regarding their behavior or misbehavior. If there are consequences, they should be as close as possible to the outside world, especially for adolescents. Consistency, especially with adolescents, reduces the occurrence of power struggles and teaches them that predictable consequences follow for their choice of actions.

40. **What have recent studies regarding effective teachers concluded?**
    (Average)

    A. Effective teachers let students establish rules
    B. Effective teachers establish routines by the sixth week of school
    C. Effective teachers state their own policies and establish consistent class rules and procedures on the first day of class
    D. Effective teachers establish flexible routines

Answer: C. Effective teachers state their own policies and establish consistent class rules and procedures on the first day of class
The teacher can get ahead of the game by stating clearly on the first day of school in her introductory information for the students exactly what the rules are. These should be stated firmly but unemotionally. When one of those rules is broken, he/she can then refer to the rules, rendering enforcement much easier to achieve. It is extremely difficult to achieve goals with students who are out of control. Establishing limits early and consistently enforcing them enhances learning. It is also helpful for the teacher to display prominently the classroom rules. This will serve as a visual reminder of the students' expected behaviors. In a study of classroom management procedures, it was established that the combination of conspicuously displayed rules, frequent verbal references to the rules, and appropriate consequences for appropriate behaviors led to increased levels of on-task behavior.

41. What is one way of effectively managing student conduct?
(Average)

A. State expectations about behavior
B. Let students discipline their peers
C. Let minor infractions of the rules go unnoticed
D. Increase disapproving remarks

Answer: A. State expectations about behavior
The effective teacher demonstrates awareness of what the entire class is doing and is in control of the behavior of all students even when the teacher is working with only a small group of the children. In an attempt to prevent student misbehaviors the teacher makes clear, concise statements about what is happening in the classroom directing attention to content and the students' accountability for their work rather than focusing the class on the misbehavior. It is also effective for the teacher to make a positive statement about the appropriate behavior that is observed. If deviant behavior does occur, the effective teacher will specify who the deviant is, what he or she is doing wrong, and why this is unacceptable conduct or what the proper conduct would be. This can be a difficult task to accomplish as the teacher must maintain academic focus and flow while addressing and desisting misbehavior. The teacher must make clear, brief statements about the expectations without raising his/her voice and without disrupting instruction.

42. When is utilization of instructional materials most effective?
(Average)

A. When the activities are organized and sequenced
B. When the materials are prepared weeks in advance
C. When the students choose the pages to work on
D. When the students create the instructional materials

Answer: A. When the activities are organized and sequenced
Most assignments will require more than one educational principle. It is helpful to explain to students the proper order in which these principles must be applied to complete the assignment successfully. Subsequently, students should also be informed of the nature of the assignment (i.e., cooperative learning, group project, individual assignment, etc). This is often done at the start of the assignment.

43. **Why is it important for a teacher to pose a question before calling on students to answer?**
    (Rigorous)

    A. It helps manage student conduct
    B. It keeps the students as a group focused on the class work
    C. It allows students time to collaborate
    D. It gives the teacher time to walk among the students

Answer: B. It keeps the students as a group focused on the class work
It does not take much distraction for a class's attention to become diffused. Once this happens, effectively teaching a principle or a skill is very difficult. The teacher should plan presentations that will keep students focused on the lesson. A very useful tool is effective, well thought-out, pointed questions.

44. **Wait-time has what effect?**
    (Average)

    A. Gives structure to the class discourse
    B. Fewer chain and low-level questions are asked with more high-level questions included
    C. Gives the students time to evaluate the response
    D. Gives the opportunity for in-depth discussion about the topic

Answer: B. Fewer chain and low-level questions are asked with more high-level questions included
One part of the questioning process for the successful teacher is *wait-time*: the time between the question and either the student response or a follow-up. Many teachers vaguely recommend some general amount of wait-time (until the student starts to get uncomfortable or is clearly perplexed), but here the focus is on wait-time as a specific and powerful communicative tool that speaks through its structured silences. Embedded in wait-time are subtle clues about judgments of a student's abilities and expectations of individuals and groups. For example, the more time a student is allowed to mull through a question, the more the teacher trusts his or her ability to answer that question without getting flustered. As a rule, the practice of prompting is not a problem. Giving support and helping students reason through difficult conundrums is part of being an effective teacher.

45. **What is one benefit of amplifying a student's response?**
    (Rigorous)

    A. It helps the student develop a positive self-image
    B. It is helpful to other students who are in the process of learning the reasoning or steps in answering the question
    C. It allows the teacher to cover more content
    D. It helps to keep the information organized

Answer: B. It is helpful to other students who are in the process of learning the reasoning or steps in answering the question
Not only does the teacher show acceptance and give value to student responses by acknowledging, amplifying, discussing, or restating the comment or question, she also helps the rest of the class learn to reason. If a student response is allowed, even if it is blurted out, it must be acknowledged and the student made aware of the quality of the response. A teacher acknowledges a student response by commenting on it. For example, the teacher states the definition of a noun, and then asks for examples of nouns in the classroom. A student responds, "My pencil is a noun." The teacher answers, "Okay, let us list that on the board." By this response and the action of writing "pencil" on the board, the teacher has just incorporated the student's response into the lesson.

46. **What is not a way that teachers show acceptance and give value to a student response?**
    (Rigorous)

    A. Acknowledging
    B. Correcting
    C. Discussing
    D. Amplifying

Answer: B. Correcting
There are ways to treat every answer as worthwhile even if it happens to be wrong. The objective is to keep students involved in the dialogue. If their efforts to participate are "rewarded" with what seems to them to be a rebuke or that leads to embarrassment, they will be less willing to respond the next time.

47. **What is an effective amount of wait-time?**
 (Easy)

   A. 1 second
   B. 5 seconds
   C. 15 seconds
   D. 10 seconds

Answer: B. 5 seconds
See rationale for question 44.

48. **Ms. Smith says, "Yes, exactly what do you mean by 'It was the author's intention to mislead you'" What does this illustrate?**
 (Rigorous)

   A. Digression
   B. Restates response
   C. Probes a response
   D. Amplifies a response

Answer: C. Probes a response
From ancient times, notable teachers such as Socrates have employed oral-questioning to enhance their discourse, to stimulate thinking, and/or to stir emotion among their audiences. Educational researchers and practitioners virtually all agree that teachers' effective use of questioning promotes student learning. Effective teachers continually develop their questioning skills.

49. **The teacher responds, "Yes, that is correct" to a student's answer. What is this an example of?**
 (Average)

   A. Academic feedback
   B. Academic praise
   C. Simple positive response
   D. Simple negative response

Answer: C. Simple positive response
The reason for praise in the classroom is to increase the desirable in order to eliminate the undesirable. This refers to both conduct and academic focus. It further states that effective praise should be authentic, it should be used in a variety of ways, and it should be low-keyed. Academic praise is a group of specific statements that give information about the value of the response or its implications. For example, a teacher using academic praise would respond, "That is an excellent analysis of Twain's use of the river in Huckleberry Finn." Whereas a simple positive response to the same question would be, "That's correct."

50. **When are students more likely to understand complex ideas?**
(Rigorous)

A. If they do outside research before coming to class
B. Later when they write out the definitions of complex words
C. When they attend a lecture on the subject
D. When they are clearly defined by the teacher and are given examples and non-examples of the concept

Answer: D. When they are clearly defined by the teacher and are given examples and non-examples of the concept
Several studies have been carried out to determine the effectiveness of giving examples as well as the difference in effectiveness of various types of examples. It was found conclusively that the most effective method of concept presentation included giving a definition along with examples and non-examples and also providing an explanation of them. These same studies indicate that boring examples were just as effective as interesting examples in promoting learning. Additional studies have been conducted to determine the most effective number of examples that will result in maximum student learning. These studies concluded that a few thoughtfully selected examples are just as effective as many examples. It was determined that the actual number of examples necessary to promote student learning was relative to the learning characteristics of the learners. It was again ascertained that learning is facilitated when examples are provided along with the definition.

51. **What are the two ways concepts can be taught?**
(Easy)

A. Factually and interpretively
B. Inductively and deductively
C. Conceptually and inductively
D. Analytically and facilitatively

Answer: B. Inductively and deductively
Induction is reasoning from the particular to the general—that is, looking at a feature that exists in several examples and drawing a conclusion about that feature. Deduction is the reverse; it is the statement of the generality and then supporting it with specific examples.

52. **According to Piaget, when does the development of symbolic functioning and language take place?**
   (Average)

   A. Concrete operations stage
   B. Formal operations stage
   C. Sensorimotor stage
   D. Preoperational stage

Answer: D. Preoperational stage
Although there is no general theory of cognitive development, the most historically influential theory was developed by Jean Piaget, a Swiss psychologist (1896-1980). His theory provided many central concepts in the field of developmental psychology. His theory concerned the growth of intelligence, which for Piaget meant the ability to more accurately represent the world and perform logical operations on representations of concepts grounded in the world. His theory concerns the emergence and acquisition of schemata - schemes of how one perceives the world - in "developmental stages," times when children are acquiring new ways of mentally representing information.

His theory is considered "constructivist," meaning that, unlike nativist theories (which describe cognitive development as the unfolding of innate knowledge and abilities) or empiricist theories (which describe cognitive development as the gradual acquisition of knowledge through experience), asserts that we construct our cognitive abilities through self-motivated action in the world. For his development of the theory, Piaget was awarded the Erasmus Prize.

53. **What should a teacher do when students have not responded well to an instructional activity?**
   (Average)

   A. Reevaluate learner needs
   B. Request administrative help
   C. Continue with the activity another day
   D. Assign homework on the concept

Answer: A. Reevaluate learner needs
The value of teacher observations cannot be underestimated. It is through the use of observations that the teacher is able to informally assess the needs of the students during instruction. These observations will drive the lesson and determine the direction that the lesson will take based on student activity and behavior. After a lesson is carefully planned, teacher observation is the single most important component of an instructional presentation. If the teacher observes that a particular student is not on task, she will change the method of instruction accordingly. She may change from a teacher-directed approach to a more interactive approach. Questioning will increase in order to increase the participation of the students. If appropriate, the teacher will introduce manipulative materials to the lesson. In addition, teachers may switch to a

cooperative group activity, thereby removing the responsibility of instruction from the teacher and putting it on the students.

54. **How could a KWL chart be used in instruction?**
    (Average)

    A. To motivate students to do a research paper
    B. To assess prior knowledge of the students
    C. To assist in teaching skills
    D. To put events in sequential order

    Answer: B. To assess prior knowledge of the students
    To understand information, not simply repeat it, students must connect it to their previous understanding. Textbooks cannot do that. Instead, teachers—the people who know students best—have to find out what they know and how to build on that knowledge. In science, having students make predictions before conducting experiments is an obvious way of finding out what they know and having them compare their observations to those predictions helps connect new knowledge and old. In history, teachers can also ask students what they know about a topic before they begin studying it or ask them to make predictions about what they will learn. KWL charts, in which students discuss what they know, what they want to know, and (later), what they have learned, are one way to activate this prior knowledge.

55. **Which of the following is an example of a synthesis question according to Bloom's taxonomy?**
    (Rigorous)

    A. "What is the definition of _____?"
    B. "Compare _____ to _____."
    C. "Match column A to column   B."
    D. "Propose an alternative to_____."

    Answer: D. "Propose an alternative to_____"
    There are six levels to the taxonomy: knowledge, comprehension, application, analysis, synthesis, and evaluation. Synthesis is compiling information together in a different way by combining elements in a new pattern or proposing alternative solutions to produce a unique communication, plan, or proposed set of operations or to derive a set of abstract relations.

56. **Which statement is an example of specific praise?**
    (Average)

    A. "John, you are the only person in class not paying attention"
    B. "William, I thought we agreed that you would turn in all of your homework"
    C. "Robert, you did a good job staying in line. See how it helped us get to music class on time?"
    D. "Class, you did a great job cleaning up the art room"

Answer: C. "Robert, you did a good job staying in line. See how it helped us get to music class on time?"
Praise is a powerful tool in obtaining and maintaining order in a classroom. In addition, it is an effective motivator. It is even more effective if the positive results of good behavior are included.

57. **Mrs. Grant is providing her students with many extrinsic motivators in order to increase their intrinsic motivation. Which of the following best explains this relationship?**
    (Rigorous)

    A. This is a good relationship and will increase intrinsic motivation
    B. The relationship builds animosity between the teacher and the students
    C. Extrinsic motivation does not in itself help to build intrinsic motivation
    D. There is no place for extrinsic motivation in the classroom

Answer: C. Extrinsic motivation does not in itself help to build intrinsic motivation
There are some cases where it is necessary to utilize extrinsic motivation; however, the use of extrinsic motivation is not alone a strategy to use to build intrinsic motivation. Intrinsic motivation comes from within the student themselves, while extrinsic motivation comes from outside parties.

58. **Which of the following is NOT a factor in student self-motivation?**
    (Rigorous)

    A. Breaking larger tasks into more manageable steps
    B. Permitting students to turn in assignments late
    C. Offering students control over the assignment
    D. Allowing students to create dream boards

Answer: B. Permitting students to turn in assignments late
Student motivation in the classroom is an essential component of teaching. Highly motivated students actively engage more in the learning process than less motivated students. Teachers should have a firm understanding of the diverse aspects that influence student motivation and then incorporate strategies for encouraging motivation in the classroom.

59. **Which of the following is NOT a part of the hardware of a computer system?**
    (Easy)

    A. Storage device
    B. Input devices
    C. Software
    D. Central Processing Unit

    Answer: C. Software
    Software is not a part of the hardware of a computer but instead consists of all of the programs which allow the computer to run. Software is either an operating system or an application program.

60. **When pulling educational information from shared drives what is the MOST important factor to consider?**
    (Rigorous)

    A. What is the intended use of the information
    B. What age group is the information best suited for
    C. Where the information came from
    D. Who the author of the information is

    Answer: A. What is the intended use of the information
    The concept of using shared drives is well established and as with most educational network operating systems, retrieving information is relatively straightforward. However, it is fundamentally important to know that not all information is the best suited for classroom instruction. Each lesson will need to be tailored and adjusted to students' needs.

61. **Which of the following are the three primary categories of instructional technology tools?**
    (Rigorous)

    A. Creation/design/implementation
    B. Research/implementation/assessment
    C. Assessment/creation/research
    D. Design/research/usage

    Answer: C. Assessment/creation/research
    Assessment programs may not necessarily teach students about technology but are very clear-cut and simple programs to use. Creation is the category where students can practice their technology skills. Teachers can permit students to utilize their researching skills by allowing classroom time to research the topics they are studying. This also allows them to keep them abreast of technological advances.

62. When a teacher is evaluating a student's technologically produced product, which of the following is considered the MOST important factor to consider?
(Rigorous)

   A. Content
   B. Design
   C. Audience
   D. Relevance

Answer: D. Relevance
All of the above are important; however, relevance is of utmost importance. It is imperative that students are aware of how to design a technologically based assignment and also to incorporate effective content. However, if the content is not relevant and pertinent to the topic studied, it is not considered an effective learning strategy.

63. You are a classroom teacher in a building that does not have a computer lab for your class to use. However, knowing that you enjoy incorporating technology into the classroom, your principal has worked to find computers for your room. They are set up in the back of your classroom and have software loaded, but have no access to the intranet or internet within your building. Which of the following is NOT an acceptable method for using these computers within your classroom instruction?
(Rigorous)

   A. Rotating the students in small groups through the computers as centers
   B. Putting students at the computers individually for skill-based review or practice
   C. Dividing your classroom into three groups and putting each group at one computer and completing a whole class lesson
   D. Using the computers for students to complete their writing assignments with an assigned sign-up sheet, so the students know the order in which they will type their stories

Answer: C. Dividing your classroom into three groups and putting each group at one computer and completing a whole class lesson
Three computers are not enough for a typical class size across the country. This would involve too many students at one computer and could result in behavioral issues. Additionally, it would be difficult for the students to all have the ability to interact in a meaningful way with the software. If you would like to complete a whole class lesson using the technology, it would be best to find a projector that connects to the computer so all students have equal opportunity to participate and see.

64. **What are three steps, in the correct order, for evaluating software before purchasing it for use within the classroom?**
    (Rigorous)

    A. Read the instructions to ensure it will work with the computer you have, try it out as if you were a student, and examine how the program handles errors or mistakes the student may make
    B. Try the computer program as if you were a student, read any online information about the program, have a student use the program and provide feedback
    C. Read the instructions and load it onto your computer, try out the program yourself as if you were a student, have a student use the program and provide feedback
    D. Read the instructions, have a student use the program, try it out yourself

Answer: A. Read the instructions to ensure it will work with the computer you have, try it out as if you were a student, and examine how the program handles errors or mistakes the students may make
You should not have students use the program until you have read all of the material related to the use, tried it out yourself as if you were a student and made many different types of mistakes when using it. You should try to make as many different types of errors as possible, so that you can see how the program responds and ensure it is how you want your student's errors handled.

65. **When a teacher wants to utilize an assessment that is subjective in nature, which of the following is the most effective method for scoring?**
    (Easy)

    A. Rubric
    B. Checklist
    C. Alternative assessment
    D. Subjective measures should not be utilized

Answer: A. Rubric
Rubrics are the most effective tool for assessing items that can be considered subjective. They provide the students with a clearer picture of teacher expectations and provide the teacher with a more consistent method of comparing this type of assignment.

66. **What is an example of formative feedback?**
    (Average)

    A. The results of an intelligence test
    B. Correcting the tests in small groups
    C. Verbal behavior that expresses approval of a student response to a test item
    D. Scheduling a discussion prior to the test

Answer: C. Verbal behavior that expresses approval of a student response to a test item
Standardized testing is currently under great scrutiny, but educators agree that any test that serves as a means of gathering and interpreting information about children's learning and that can provide accurate, helpful input for nurturing children's further growth is acceptable. All testing must be formative in nature. Formative evaluation is the basic, everyday kind of assessment that teachers continually do to understand students' growth and to help them learn further.

67. **Norm-referenced tests:**
    (Rigorous)

    A. Give information only about the local samples results
    B. Provide information about how the local test takers did compared to a representative sampling of national test takers
    C. Make no comparisons to national test takers
    D. None of the above

Answer: B. Provide information about how the local test takers did compared to a representative sampling of national test takers
This is the definition of a norm-referenced test.

68. **What is the best definition for an achievement test?**
    (Average)

    A. It measures mechanical and practical abilities
    B. It measures broad areas of knowledge that are the result of cumulative learning experiences
    C. It measures the ability to learn to perform a task
    D. It measures performance related to specific, recently acquired information

Answer: B. It measures broad areas of knowledge that are the result of cumulative learning experiences
The ways that a teacher uses test data is a meaningful aspect of instruction and may increase the motivation level of the students especially when this information is available in the form of feedback to the students. This feedback should indicate to the students what they need to do in order to improve their achievement. Frequent testing and feedback is most often an effective way to increase achievement.

69. **How are standardized tests useful in assessment?**
    (Average)

    A. For teacher evaluation
    B. For evaluation of the administration
    C. For comparison from school to school
    D. For comparison to the population on which the test was normed

Answer: D. For comparison to the population on which the test was normed
While the efficacy of the standardized tests that are being used nationally has come under attack recently, they are actually the only device for comparing where an individual student stands with a wide range of peers. They also provide a measure for a program or a school to evaluate how their own students are doing as compared to the populace at large.

70. **Mr. Brown wishes to improve his parent communication skills. Which of the following is a strategy he can utilize to accomplish this goal?**
    (Easy)

    A. Hold parent-teacher conferences
    B. Send home positive notes
    C. Have parent nights where the parents are invited into his classroom
    D. All of the above

Answer: D. All of the above
Increasing parent communication skills is important for teachers. All of the listed strategies are methods a teacher can utilize to increase his skills.

71. **When communicating with parents for whom English is not the primary language, you should:**
    (Easy)

    A. Provide materials whenever possible in their native language
    B. Use an interpreter
    C. Provide the same communication as you would to native English speaking parents
    D. All of the above

Answer: D. All of the above
When communicating with non-English speaking parents, it is important to treat them as you would any other parent and utilize any means necessary to ensure they have the ability to participate in their child's educational process.

72. **Which statement best reflects why family involvement is important to a student's educational success?**
    (Easy)

    A. Reading the class newsletter constitutes strong family involvement
    B. Family involvement means to attend graduation
    C. There are limited ways a parent can be active in their child's education
    D. The more family members are involved, the more success a student is likely to experience

Answer: D. The more family members are involved, the more success a student is likely to experience
Although reading the class newsletter and coming to graduation are obvious parts of parental involvement, it is not the sole involvement for which teachers hope. Unlike the statement in choice C, there are many unique ways parents can participate and share talents toward their child's education. Parents are invited in to assist with workshops, attend class trips, participate as room parents, organize special events, read to the class, speak of an occupation, help with classroom housekeeping, and more. Parents can also be involved by volunteering for the PTO/A, library help, office help, and other tasks. Some teachers plan a few events a year in the classroom for special parties, presentations and events.

73. **Which of the following is NOT an appropriate method for teachers to interact with families of diverse backgrounds?**
    (Easy)

    A. Show respect to parents
    B. Share personal stories concerning the student
    C. Display patience with parents
    D. Disregard culture of student

Answer: D. Disregard culture of student
The culture of the student must be taken into account when interacting with families of diverse backgrounds. Teachers must show respect to all parents and families, and they need to realize that various cultures have different views of how children should be educated—this must be taken into consideration when dealing with families.

74. **A parent has left an angry message on the teacher's voicemail. The message relates to a concern about a student and is directed at the teacher. The teacher should:**
(Average)

   A. Call back immediately and confront the parent
   B. Cool off, plan what to discuss with the parent, then call back
   C. Question the child to find out what set off the parent
   D. Ignore the message, since feelings of anger usually subside after a while

Answer: B. Cool off, plan what to discuss with the parent, then call back
It is professional for a teacher to keep her head in the face of emotion and respond to an angry parent in a calm and objective manner. The teacher should give herself time to cool off and plan the conversation with the parents with the purpose of understanding the concern and resolving it, rather than putting the parent in his or her place. Above all, the teacher should remember that parent-teacher interactions should aim to benefit the student.

75. **Which is NOT considered a good practice when conducting parent-teacher conferences?**
(Average)

   A. Ending the conference with an agreed plan of action
   B. Figure out questions for parents during the conference
   C. Prepare work samples, records of behavior, and assessment information
   D. Prepare a welcoming environment, set a good mood, and be an active listener

Answer: B. Figure out questions for parents during the conference
Choices A, C, and D all reflect effective practices for holding a successful parent teacher conference. Teachers should prepare questions and comments for parents prior to the conference so they are optimally prepared.

76. **Which of the following should NOT be a purpose of a parent-teacher conference?**
(Average)

   A. To involve the parent in their child's education
   B. To establish a friendship with the child's parents
   C. To resolve a concern about the child's performance
   D. To inform parents of positive behaviors by the child

Answer: B. To establish a friendship with the child's parents
The purpose of a parent-teacher conference is to involve parents in their child's education, address concerns about the child's performance, and share positive aspects

of the student's learning with the parents. It would be unprofessional to allow the conference to degenerate into a social visit to establish a friendship.

77. **Which of the following is a technological strategy that keeps students and teachers interactively communicating about issues in the classroom and beyond?**
    (Rigorous)

    A. Distance learning
    B. Mentoring support system
    C. Conceptual learning modalities
    D. Community resources

    Answer: A. Distance learning
    Distance learning is the process of creating educational experiences for students outside the classroom. This growing technological tool is becoming widely used in schools and institutions around the country. With the recent trend of technological advances, distance learning is becoming highly appreciated as an effective learning strategy.

78. **In the past, teaching has been viewed as _____ while in more current society it has been viewed as _____.**
    (Rigorous)

    A. isolating…collaborative
    B. collaborative…isolating
    C. supportive…isolating
    D. isolating…supportive

    Answer: A. isolating…collaborative
    In the past, teachers often walked into their own classrooms and closed the door. They were not involved in any form of collaboration and were responsible for only the students within their classrooms. However, in today's more modern schools, teachers work in collaborative teams and are responsible for all of the children in a school setting.

79. **Which of the following is a good reason to collaborate with a peer?**
    (Easy)

    A. To increase your knowledge in areas where you feel you are weak, but the peer is strong
    B. To increase your planning time and that of your peer by combining the classes and taking more breaks
    C. To have fewer lesson plans to write
    D. To teach fewer subjects

Answer: A. To increase your knowledge in areas where you feel you are weak, but the peer is strong
One of the best reasons to collaborate is to share and develop your knowledge base.

80. **Which of the following is responsible for working with the school in matters concerning the business of running a school?**
    (Rigorous)

    A. Curriculum coordinators
    B. Administrators
    C. Board of Education
    D. Parent-Teacher organizations

Answer: C. Board of Education
The Board of Education is elected by the district to offer direction for the students and their schools. Among its many responsibilities, the Board establishes a long-term vision for the district and designs their policies and goals. The administrator carries out the school district's policies and manages the day-to-day operations of the school.

81. **What would happen if a school utilized an integrated approach to professional development?**
    (Average)

    A. All stakeholders needs are addressed
    B. Teachers and administrators are on the same page
    C. High-quality programs for students are developed
    D. Parents drive the curriculum and instruction

Answer: C. High-quality programs for students are developed
The implementation of an integrated approach to professional development is a critical component to ensuring success of programs for students. It involves teachers, parents, and other community members working together to develop appropriate programs to ensure students are receiving the necessary instruction to be successful in the future workforce.

82. **Which is true of child protective services?**
    (Rigorous)

    A. They have been forced to become more punitive in their attempts to treat and prevent child abuse and neglect
    B. They have become more a means for identifying cases of abuse and less an agent for rehabilitation due to the large volume of cases
    C. They have become advocates for structured discipline within the school
    D. They have become a strong advocate in the court system

Answer: B. They have become more a means for identifying cases of abuse and less an agent for rehabilitation due to the large volume of cases
Child protective serves is the agency a teacher/school district would contact for suspected child abuse in a student.

83. **What is a benefit of frequent self-assessment?**
    (Average)

    A. Opens new venues for professional development
    B. Saves teachers the pressure of being observed by others
    C. Reduces time spent on areas not needing attention
    D. Offers a model for students to adopt in self-improvement

Answer: A. Opens new venues for professional development
When a teacher is involved in the process of self-reflection and self-assessment, one of the common outcomes is that the teacher comes to identify areas of skill or knowledge that require more research or improvement on her part. She may become interested in overcoming a particular weakness in her performance or may decide to attend a workshop or consult with a mentor to learn more about a particular area of concern.

84. **Mrs. Graham has taken the time to reflect, completed observations, and asked for feedback about the interactions between her and her students from her principal. It is obvious by seeking this information out that Mrs. Graham understands which of the following?**
    (Rigorous)

    A. The importance of clear communication with the principal
    B. She needs to analyze her effectiveness of classroom interactions
    C. She is clearly communicating with the principal
    D. She cares about her students

Answer: B. She needs to analyze her effectiveness of classroom interactions
By utilizing reflection, observations, and feedback from peers or supervisors, teachers can help to build their own understanding of how they interact with students. In this way, they can better analyze their effectiveness at building appropriate relationships with students.

85. **Which of the following are ways a professional can assess his/her teaching strengths and weaknesses?**
    (Rigorous)

    A. Examining how many students were unable to understand a concept
    B. Asking peers for suggestions or ideas
    C. Self-evaluation/reflection of lessons taught
    D. All of the above

Answer: D. All of the above
It is important for teachers to involve themselves in constant periods of reflection and self-reflection to ensure they are meeting the needs of the students.

86. **In successful inclusion of students with disabilities:**
    (Average)

    A. A variety of instructional arrangements are available
    B. School personnel shift the responsibility for learning outcomes to the student
    C. The physical facilities are used as they are
    D. Regular classroom teachers have sole responsibility for evaluating student progress

Answer: A. A variety if instructional arrangements are available
Here are some support systems and activities that are in evidence where successful inclusion has occurred:

Attitudes and beliefs
- The regular teacher believes the student can succeed
- School personnel are committed to accepting responsibility for the learning outcomes of students with disabilities
- School personnel and the students in the class have been prepared to receive a student with disabilities

87. **Teachers may duplicate copies of informational materials provided that they meet the following requirement/s:**
    (Rigorous)

    A. Brevity
    B. Spontaneity
    C. Cumulative effect
    D. All of the above

Answer: D. All of the above
Copyright is a type of protection provided by the United States to an author's literary works which also includes dramatic, musical, artistic, and other intellectual works. The

conscientious use of these requirements will protect teachers and students from accusations of educational copyright infringement.

88. **Which of the following is one of the greatest obstacles that new teachers face when first entering the profession?**
    (Rigorous)

    A. Dealing with behavioral issues in the classroom
    B. Monitoring daily student success
    C. Developing rapport with parents and caretakers
    D. Creating weekly lesson plans

Answer: A. Dealing with behavioral issues in the classroom
Dealing with behavioral problems is one of the major concerns that teachers in the classroom face today. Disruptive behavior results in lost curriculum time and creates a classroom environment that is not always conducive to learning. Teachers should be proactive in dealing with behavioral issues at the time of the occurrence.

89. **How can a teacher use a student's permanent record?**
    (Average)

    A. To develop a better understanding of the needs of the student
    B. To record all instances of student disruptive behavior
    C. To brainstorm ideas for discussing with parents at parent-teacher conferences
    D. To develop realistic expectations of the student's performance early in the year

Answer: A. To develop a better understanding of the needs of the student
The purpose of a student's permanent record is to give the teacher a better understanding of the student's educational history and provide her with relevant information to support the student's learning. Permanent records may not be used to arrive at preconceived judgments or to build a case against the student. Above all, the contents of a student's permanent record are confidential.

90. **To what does the validity of a test refer?**
    (Rigorous)

    A. Its consistency
    B. Its usefulness
    C. Its accuracy
    D. The degree of true scores it provide

Answer: B. Its usefulness
The *Joint Technical Standards for Educational and Psychological Testing* APA, AERA, NCME, 1985) states: "Validity is the most important consideration in test evaluation. The

concept refers to the appropriateness, meaningfulness and usefulness of *the specific inferences made from test scores*. Test validation is the process of accumulating evidence to support such inferences. A variety of inferences may be made from scores produced by a given test, and there are many ways of accumulating evidence to support any particular inference. Validity, however, is a unitary concept. Although evidence may be accumulated in many ways, validity always refers to the degree to which that evidence supports the inferences that are made from test scores."

TExES GENERALIST 4-8 111

LANGUAGE ARTS SAMPLE TEST

1. **If a student has a poor vocabulary the teacher should recommend that:**
   (Rigorous)

   A. The student read newspapers, magazines, and books on a regular basis
   B. The student enroll in a Latin class
   C. The student write the words repeatedly after looking them up in the dictionary
   D. The student use a thesaurus to locate synonyms and incorporate them into his/her vocabulary

2. **The arrangement and relationship of words in sentences or sentence structure best describes**
   (Rigorous)

   A. Style
   B. Discourse
   C. Thesis
   D. Syntax

3. **Which of the following is a formal reading assessment?**
   (Rigorous)

   A. A standardized reading test
   B. A teacher-made reading test
   C. An interview
   D. A reading diary

4. **The literary device of personification is used in which example below?**
   (Average)

   A. "Beg me no beggary by soul or parents, whining dog!"
   B. "Happiness sped through the halls cajoling as it went."
   C. "O wind thy horn, thou proud fellow."
   D. "And that one talent which is death to hide."

5. **Which teaching method would be the most effective for interesting underachievers in the required senior English class?**
   (Rigorous)

   A. Assign use of glossary work and extensively footnoted excerpts of great works
   B. Have students take turns reading aloud the anthology selection
   C. Let students choose which readings they'll study and write about
   D. Use a chronologically arranged, traditional text, but assigning group work, panel presentations, and portfolio management

6. **Which definition is the best for defining diction?**
   (Rigorous)

   A. The specific word choices of an author to create a particular mood or feeling in the reader
   B. Writing which explains something thoroughly
   C. The background, or exposition, for a short story or drama
   D. Word choices which help teach a truth or moral

7. **Which is not a true statement concerning an author's literary tone?**
   (Rigorous)

   A. Tone is partly revealed through the selection of details
   B. Tone is the expression of the author's attitude towards his/her subject
   C. Tone in literature is usually satiric or angry
   D. Tone in literature corresponds to the tone of voice a speaker uses

8. **What were two major characteristics of the first American literature?**
   (Rigorous)

   A. Vengefulness and arrogance
   B. Bellicosity and derision
   C. Oral delivery and reverence for the land
   D. Maudlin and self-pitying egocentricism

9. **An example of the subject of a tall tale is**
   (Rigorous)

   A. John Henry
   B. Paul Bunyan
   C. George Washington
   D. Rip Van Winkle

10. **Which term best describes the form of the following poetic excerpt?**
    (Rigorous)

    And more to lulle him in his slumber soft,
    A trickling streake from high rock
    tumbling downe,
    And ever-drizzling raine upon the loft.
    Mixt with a murmuring winde, much like a swowne
    No other noyse, nor peoples troubles cryes.
    As still we wont t'annoy the walle'd towne,
    Might there be heard: but careless Quiet lyes,
    Wrapt in eternall silence farre from enemyes.

    A. Ballad
    B. Elegy
    C. Spenserian stanza
    D. Octava rima

11. **Which sonnet form describes the following?**
    (Rigorous)

    My galley charg'd with forgetfulness,
    Through sharp seas, in winter night doth pass
    'Tween rock and rock; and eke mine enemy, alas,
    That is my lord steereth with cruelness.
    And every oar a thought with readiness,
    As though that death were light in such a case.
    An endless wind doth tear the sail apace
    Or forc'ed sighs and trusty fearfulness.
    A rain of tears, a cloud of dark disdain,
    Hath done the wearied cords great hinderance,
    Wreathed with error and eke with ignorance.
    The stars be hid that led me to this pain
    Drowned is reason that should me consort,
    And I remain despairing of the poet

    A. Petrarchan or Italian sonnet
    B. Shakespearian or Elizabethan sonnet
    C. Romantic sonnet
    D. Spenserian sonnet

12. **A figure of speech in which someone absent or something inhuman is addressed as though present and able to respond describes**
    (Average)

    A. Personification
    B. Synechdoche
    C. Metonymy
    D. Apostrophe

13. **The quality in a work of literature which evokes feelings of pity or compassion is called**
    (Easy)

    A. Colloquy
    B. Irony
    C. Pathos
    D. Paradox

14. **An extended metaphor which compares two very dissimilar things—one lofty, one lowly, is a definition of a/an**
    (Average)

    A. Antithesis
    B. Aphorism
    C. Apostrophe
    D. Conceit

15. **Which of the following is a complex sentence?**
    (Easy)

    A. Anna and Margaret read a total of fifty-four books during summer vacation.
    B. The youngest boy on the team had the best earned run average which mystifies the coaching staff.
    C. Earl decided to attend Princeton; his twin brother Roy, who aced the ASVAB test, will be going to Annapolis.
    D. "Easy come, easy go," Marcia moaned.

16. **Middle and high school students are more receptive to studying grammar and syntax**
    (Rigorous)

    A. Through worksheets and end of lessons practices in textbooks
    B. Through independent, homework assignment
    C. Through analytical examination of the writings of famous authors
    D. Through application to their own writing

17. **A punctuation mark indicating omission, interrupted thought, or an incomplete statement is a/an**
    (Easy)

    A. Ellipsis
    B. Anachronism
    C. Colloquy
    D. Idiom

18. **Which of the following contains an error in possessive inflection?**
    (Easy)

    A. Doris's shawl
    B. Mother's-in-law frown
    C. Children's lunches
    D. Ambassador's briefcase

19. **Wally groaned, "Why do I have to do an oral interpretation of "The Raven."**
    (Average)

    A. Groaned "Why… of 'The Raven'?"
    B. Groaned "Why… of "The Raven"?
    C. Groaned ", Why… of "The Raven?"
    D. Groaned, "Why… of "The Raven."

20. **Mr. Smith respectfully submitted his resignation and had a new job.**
    (Average)

    A. Respectfully submitted his resignation and has
    B. Respectfully submitted his resignation before accepting
    C. Respectfully submitted his resignation because of
    D. Respectfully submitted his resignation and had

21. **There were fewer pieces of evidence presented during the second trial**
    (Average)

    A. fewer peaces
    B. less peaces
    C. less pieces
    D. fewer pieces

22. **The teacher implied from our angry words that there was conflict between you and me.**
    (Easy)

    A. Implied… between you and I.
    B. Inferred… between you and I.
    C. Inferred… between you and me.
    D. Implied… between you and me.

23. **Which of the following is not one of the four forms of discourse?**
    (Average)

    A. Exposition
    B. Description
    C. Rhetoric
    D. Persuasion

24. **"Clean as a whistle or "Easy as falling off a log" are examples of**
    (Average)

    A. Semantics
    B. Parody
    C. Irony
    D. Clichés

25. **What is the figure of speech present in line one below in which the dead body of Caesar is addressed as though he were still a living being?**
    (Average)

    O, pardon me, though Bleeding piece of earth
    That I am meek and gentle with These butchers.

    Marc Antony from *Julius Caesar*

    A. Apostrophe
    B. Allusion
    C. Antithesis
    D. Anachronism

26. A sixth-grade science teacher has given her class a paper to read on the relationship between food and weight gain. The writing contains signal words such as "because," "consequently," "this is how," and "due to." This paper has which text structure?
 (Rigorous)

   A. Cause & effect
   B. Compare & contrast
   C. Description
   D. Sequencing

27. A form or discourse which explains or informs is
 (Average)

   A. Exposition
   B. Narration
   C. Persuasion
   D. Description

28. The following passage is written from which point of view?
 (Rigorous)

   As she mused the pitiful vision of her mother's life laid its spell on the very quick of her being –that life of commonplace sacrifices closing in final craziness. She trembled as she heard again her mother's voice saying constantly with foolish insistence: Dearevaun Seraun! Dearevaun Seraun!*
   * "The end of pleasure is pain!" (Gaelic)

   A. First person, narrator
   B. Second person, direct address
   C. Third person, omniscient
   D. First person, omniscient

29. Which of the following should not be included in the opening paragraph of an informative essay?
 (Average)

   A. Thesis sentence
   B. Details and examples supporting the main idea
   C. A broad general introduction to the topic
   D. A style and tone that grabs the reader's attention

30. Which of the following is not a technique of prewriting?
(Average)

    A. Clustering
    B. Listing
    C. Brainstorming
    D. Proofreading

31. Which of the following is not an approach to keep students ever conscious of the need to write for audience appeal?
(Rigorous)

    A. Pairing students during the writing process
    B. Reading all rough drafts before the students write the final copies
    C. Having students compose stories or articles for publication in school literary magazines or newspaper
    D. Writing letters to friends or relatives

Answer Key

1.	A
2.	D
3.	A
4.	C
5.	C
6.	A
7.	C
8.	D
9.	B
10.	D
11.	A
12.	D
13.	C
14.	D
15.	B
16.	D
17.	A
18.	B
19.	A
20.	C
21.	D
22.	C
23.	C
24.	D
25.	B
26.	A
27.	A
28.	C
29.	B
30.	D
31.	B

Rigor Table

Easy
13, 15, 17, 18, 22

Average
4, 12, 14, 19, 20, 21, 23, 24, 25, 27, 29, 30

Rigorous
1, 2, 3, 5, 6, 7, 8, 9, 10, 11, 16, 26, 28, 31

LANGUAGE ARTS SAMPLE TEST WITH RATIONALES

1. If a student has a poor vocabulary the teacher should recommend that:
   (Rigorous)

   A. The student read newspapers, magazines, and books on a regular basis
   B. The student enroll in a Latin class
   C. The student write the words repeatedly after looking them up in the dictionary
   D. The student use a thesaurus to locate synonyms and incorporate them into his/her vocabulary

   Answer: A. The student read newspapers, magazines, and books on a regular basis
   It is up to the teacher to help the student choose reading material, but the student must be able to choose where s/he will search for the reading pleasure indispensable for enriching vocabulary.

2. The arrangement and relationship of words in sentences or sentence structure best describes
   (Rigorous)

   A. Style
   B. Discourse
   C. Thesis
   D. Syntax

   Answer: D. Syntax
   Syntax is the grammatical structure of sentences.

3. Which of the following is a formal reading assessment?
   (Rigorous)

   A. A standardized reading test
   B. A teacher-made reading test
   C. An interview
   D. A reading diary

   Answer: A. A standardized reading text
   If assessment is standardized, it has to be objective, whereas B, C and D are all subjective assessments.

4. **The literary device of personification is used in which example below?**
   (Average)

   A. "Beg me no beggary by soul or parents, whining dog!"
   B. "Happiness sped through the halls cajoling as it went."
   C. "O wind thy horn, thou proud fellow."
   D. "And that one talent which is death to hide."

Answer: C. "O wind thy horn, thou proud fellow."
Personification gives human characteristics to an inanimate object, such as wind in the sentence above.

5. **Which teaching method would be the most effective for interesting underachievers in the required senior English class?**
   (Rigorous)

   A. Assign use of glossary work and extensively footnoted excerpts of great works
   B. Have students take turns reading aloud the anthology selection
   C. Let students choose which readings they'll study and write about
   D. Use a chronologically arranged, traditional text, but assigning group work, panel presentations, and portfolio management

Answer: C. Let students choose which readings they'll study and write about
It will encourage students to react honestly to literature. Students should take notes on what they're reading so they will be able to discuss the material. They should not only react to literature, but also experience it. Small-group work is a good way to encourage them. The other answers are not fit for junior-high or high school students. They should be encouraged, however, to read critics of works in order to understand criteria work.

6. **Which definition is the best for defining diction?**
   (Rigorous)

   A. The specific word choices of an author to create a particular mood or feeling in the reader
   B. Writing which explains something thoroughly
   C. The background, or exposition, for a short story or drama
   D. Word choices which help teach a truth or moral

Answer: A. The specific word choices of an author to create a particular mood or feeling in the reader
Diction refers to an author's choice of words, expressions, and style to convey his/her meaning.

7. **Which is not a true statement concerning an author's literary tone?**
   (Rigorous)

   A. Tone is partly revealed through the selection of details
   B. Tone is the expression of the author's attitude towards his/her subject
   C. Tone in literature is usually satiric or angry
   D. Tone in literature corresponds to the tone of voice a speaker uses

Answer: C. Tone in literature is usually satiric or angry
Tone in literature conveys a mood and can be as varied as the tone of voice of a speaker (see D), e.g., sad, nostalgic, whimsical, angry, formal, intimate, satirical, sentimental, etc.

8. **What were two major characteristics of the first American literature?**
   (Rigorous)

   A. Vengefulness and arrogance
   B. Bellicosity and derision
   C. Oral delivery and reverence for the land
   D. Maudlin and self-pitying egocentricism

Answer: D. Maudlin and self-pitying egocentricism
This characteristic can be seen in Captain John Smith's work as well as William Bradford's, and Michael Wigglesworth's works.

9. **An example of the subject of a tall tale is**
   (Rigorous)

   A. John Henry
   B. Paul Bunyan
   C. George Washington
   D. Rip Van Winkle

Answer: B. Paul Bunyan
A tall tale is a Folklore genre, originating on the American frontier, in which the physical attributes, capabilities, and exploits of characters are wildly exaggerated. This is the case of giant logger Paul Bunyan of the American Northwestern forests. James Stevens traced Paul Bunyan to a French Canadian logger named Paul Bunyon. He won a reputation as a great fighter in the Papineau Rebellion against England in 1837 and later became famous as the boss of a logging camp. Paul Bunyan's first appearance in print seems to be in an advertising pamphlet, *Paul Bunyan and His Big Blue Ox*, published by the Red River Company. It immediately became very popular and was reissued many times.

10. **Which term best describes the form of the following poetic excerpt?** *(Rigorous)*

And more to lulle him in his slumber soft,
A trickling streake from high rock tumbling downe,
And ever-drizzling raine upon the loft.
Mixt with a murmuring winde, much like a swowne
No other noyse, nor peoples troubles cryes.
As still we wont t'annoy the walle'd towne,
Might there be heard: but careless Quiet lyes,
Wrapt in eternall silence farre from enemyes.

A. Ballad
B. Elegy
C. Spenserian stanza
D. Octava rima

Answer: D. Octava rima
The Octava Rima is a specific eight-line stanza whose rhyme scheme is abababcc.

11. **Which sonnet form describes the following?**
    (Rigorous)

    My galley charg'd with forgetfulness,
    Through sharp seas, in winter night doth pass
    'Tween rock and rock; and eke mine enemy, alas,
    That is my lord steereth with cruelness.
    And every oar a thought with readiness,
    As though that death were light in such a case.
    An endless wind doth tear the sail apace
    Or forc'ed sighs and trusty fearfulness.
    A rain of tears, a cloud of dark disdain,
    Hath done the wearied cords great hinderance,
    Wreathed with error and eke with ignorance.
    The stars be hid that led me to this pain
    Drowned is reason that should me consort,
    And I remain despairing of the poet

    A. Petrarchan or Italian sonnet
    B. Shakespearian or Elizabethan sonnet
    C. Romantic sonnet
    D. Spenserian sonnet

Answer: A. Petrarchan or Italian sonnet
The Petrarchan sonnet, also known as the Italian sonnet, is named after the Italian poet Petrarch (1304-74). It is divided into an octave rhyming *abbaabba* and a sestet normally rhyming *cdecde*.

12. **A figure of speech in which someone absent or something inhuman is addressed as though present and able to respond describes**
    (Average)

    A. Personification
    B. Synechdoche
    C. Metonymy
    D. Apostrophe

Answer: D. Apostrophe
Apostrophe gives human reactions and thoughts to animals, things, and abstract ideas alike. This figure of speech is often present in allegory: for instance, the Giant Despair in John Bunyon's *Pilgrim's Progress*. Also, fables use personification to make animals able to speak.

13. **The quality in a work of literature which evokes feelings of pity or compassion is called**
    (Easy)

    A. Colloquy
    B. Irony
    C. Pathos
    D. Paradox

Answer: C. Pathos
A very well known example of pathos is Desdemona's death in Othello, but there are many other examples of pathos.

14. **An extended metaphor which compares two very dissimilar things—one lofty, one lowly, is a definition of a/an**
    (Average)

    A. Antithesis
    B. Aphorism
    C. Apostrophe
    D. Conceit

Answer: D. Conceit
A conceit is an unusually far-fetched metaphor in which an object, person, or situation is presented in a parallel and simpler analogue between two apparently very different things or feelings, one very sophisticated and one very ordinary, usually taken either from nature or a well known every day concept familiar to both reader and author alike. The conceit was first developed by Petrarch and spread to England in the sixteenth century.

15. **Which of the following is a complex sentence?**
    (Easy)

    A. Anna and Margaret read a total of fifty-four books during summer vacation.
    B. The youngest boy on the team had the best earned run average which mystifies the coaching staff.
    C. Earl decided to attend Princeton; his twin brother Roy, who aced the ASVAB test, will be going to Annapolis.
    D. "Easy come, easy go," Marcia moaned.

Answer: B. The youngest boy on the team had the best earned run average which mystifies the coaching staff.
Here, the use of the relative pronoun "which", whose antecedent is "the best run average", introduces a clause that is dependent on the independent clause "The youngest boy on the team had the best run average". The idea expressed in the subordinate clause is subordinate to the one expressed in the independent clause.

16. **Middle and high school students are more receptive to studying grammar and syntax**
    (Rigorous)

    A. Through worksheets and end of lessons practices in textbooks
    B. Through independent, homework assignment
    C. Through analytical examination of the writings of famous authors
    D. Through application to their own writing

Answer: D. Through application to their own writing
At this age, students learn grammatical concepts best through practical application in their own writing.

17. **A punctuation mark indicating omission, interrupted thought, or an incomplete statement is a/an**
    (Easy)

    A. Ellipsis
    B. Anachronism
    C. Colloquy
    D. Idiom

Answer: A. Ellipsis
In an ellipsis, a word or words that would clarify the sentence's message are missing, yet it is still possible to understand them from the context.

18. Which of the following contains an error in possessive inflection?
    (Easy)

    A. Doris's shawl
    B. Mother's-in-law frown
    C. Children's lunches
    D. Ambassador's briefcase

Answer: B. Mother's-in-law frown
Mother-in-Law is a compound common noun and the inflection should be at the end of the word, according to the rule.

19. Wally <u>groaned, "Why</u> do I have to do an oral interpretation of "The Raven."
    (Average)

    A. Groaned "Why… of 'The Raven'?"
    B. Groaned "Why… of "The Raven"?
    C. Groaned ", Why… of "The Raven?"
    D. Groaned, "Why… of "The Raven."

Answer: A. Groaned "Why… of 'The Raven'?"
The question mark in a quotation that is an interrogation should be within the quotation marks. Also, when quoting a work of literature within another quotation, one should use single quotation marks ('…') for the title of this work, and they should close before the final quotation mark.

20. Mr. Smith <u>respectfully submitted his resignation and</u> <u>had</u> a new job.
    (Average)

    A. Respectfully submitted his resignation and has
    B. Respectfully submitted his resignation before accepting
    C. Respectfully submitted his resignation because of
    D. Respectfully submitted his resignation and had

Answer: C. Respectfully submitted his resignation because of
Choice A eliminates any relationship of causality between submitting the resignation and having the new job. Choice B just changes the sentence and does not indicate the fact that Mr. Smith had a new job before submitting his resignation. Choice D means that Mr. Smith first submitted his resignation then got a new job.

21. There were <u>fewer pieces</u> of evidence presented during the second trial
(Average)

A. fewer peaces
B. less peaces
C. less pieces
D. fewer pieces

Answer: D. fewer pieces
"Less" is impossible in the plural, and "peace" is the opposite of war, not a "piece" of evidence.

22. The teacher <u>implied</u> from our angry words that there was conflict <u>between you and me.</u>
(Easy)

A. Implied... between you and I.
B. Inferred... between you and I.
C. Inferred... between you and me.
D. Implied... between you and me.

Answer: C. Inferred....between you and me.
The difference between the verb "to imply" and the verb "to infer" is that implying is directing an interpretation toward other people; to infer is to deduce an interpretation from someone else's discourse. Moreover, "between you and I" is grammatically incorrect: after a preposition here "and", a disjunctive pronoun (me, you, him, her, us, you, them) is needed.

23. Which of the following is not one of the four forms of discourse?
(Average)

A. Exposition
B. Description
C. Rhetoric
D. Persuasion

Answer: C. Rhetoric
Exposition, description, and persuasion are styles of writing and ways of influencing a reader or a listener. Rhetoric, on the other hand, is theoretical. It is the theory of expressive and effective speech. Rhetorical figures are ornaments of speech such as anaphora, antithesis, metaphor, etc.

24. "Clean as a whistle or "Easy as falling off a log" are examples of
    (Average)

    A. Semantics
    B. Parody
    C. Irony
    D. Clichés

Answer: D. Clichés
A cliché is a phrase or expression that has become dull due to overuse.

25. **What is the figure of speech present in line one below in which the dead body of Caesar is addressed as though he were still a living being?**
    (Average)

    O, pardon me, though Bleeding piece of earth
    That I am meek and gentle with
    These butchers.

    Marc Antony from *Julius Caesar*

    A. Apostrophe
    B. Allusion
    C. Antithesis
    D. Anachronism

Answer: B. Allusion
This rhetorical figure addresses personified things, absent people or gods. An antithesis is a contrast between two opposing viewpoints, ideas, or presentation of characters. An anachronism is the placing of an object or person out of its time with the time of the text. The best known example is the clock in Shakespeare's *Julius Caesar*.

26. A sixth-grade science teacher has given her class a paper to read on the relationship between food and weight gain. The writing contains signal words such as "because," "consequently," "this is how," and "due to." This paper has which text structure?
(Rigorous)

   A. Cause & effect
   B. Compare & contrast
   C. Description
   D. Sequencing

Answer: A. Cause & effect
Cause and effect is the relationship between two things when one thing makes something else happen. Writers use this text structure to show order, inform, speculate, and change behavior. This text structure uses the process of identifying potential causes of a problem or issue in an orderly way. It is often used to teach social studies and science concepts. It is characterized by signal words such as because, so, so that, if... then, consequently, thus, since, for, for this reason, as a result of, therefore, due to, this is how, nevertheless, and accordingly.

27. A form or discourse which explains or informs is
(Average)

   A. Exposition
   B. Narration
   C. Persuasion
   D. Description

Answer: A. Exposition
Exposition sets forth a systematic explanation of any subject. It can also introduce the characters of a literary work and their situations in the story.

28. **The following passage is written from which point of view?**
    (Rigorous)

    As she mused the pitiful vision of her mother's life laid its spell on the very quick of her being –that life of commonplace sacrifices closing in final craziness. She trembled as she heard again her mother's voice saying constantly with foolish insistence: Dearevaun Seraun! Dearevaun Seraun!* * "The end of pleasure is pain!" (Gaelic)

    A. First person, narrator
    B. Second person, direct address
    C. Third person, omniscient
    D. First person, omniscient

Answer: C. Third person, omniscient
The passage is clearly in the third person (the subject is "she"), and it is omniscient since it gives the characters' inner thoughts.

29. **Which of the following should not be included in the opening paragraph of an informative essay?**
    (Average)

    A. Thesis sentence
    B. Details and examples supporting the main idea
    C. A broad general introduction to the topic
    D. A style and tone that grabs the reader's attention

Answer: B. Details and examples supporting the main idea
The introductory paragraph should introduce the topic, capture the reader's interest, state the thesis and prepare the reader for the main points in the essay. Details and examples, however, should be given in the second part of the essay, so as to help develop the thesis presented at the end of the introductory paragraph, following the inverted triangle method consisting of a broad general statement followed by some information, and then the thesis at the end of the paragraph.

30. **Which of the following is not a technique of prewriting?**
    (Average)

    A. Clustering
    B. Listing
    C. Brainstorming
    D. Proofreading

Answer: D. Proofreading
Proofreading should be reserved for the final draft.

31. Which of the following is not an approach to keep students ever conscious of the need to write for audience appeal?
    (Rigorous)

    A. Pairing students during the writing process
    B. Reading all rough drafts before the students write the final copies
    C. Having students compose stories or articles for publication in school literary magazines or newspaper
    D. Writing letters to friends or relatives

Answer: B. Reading all rough drafts before the students write the final copies
Reading all rough drafts will not encourage the students to take control of their text and might even inhibit their creativity. On the contrary, pairing students will foster their sense of responsibility, and having them compose stories for literary magazines will boost their self esteem as well as their organization skills. As far as writing letters is concerned, the work of authors such as Madame de Sevigne in the seventeenth century is a good example of epistolary literary work.

MATHEMATICS SAMPLE TEST

1. $\dfrac{2^{10}}{2^5} =$
   (Average)

   A. 2^2
   B. 2^5
   C. 2^{50}
   D. $2^{\frac{1}{2}}$

2. $\left(\dfrac{-4}{9}\right) + \left(\dfrac{-7}{10}\right) =$
   (Average)

   A. $\dfrac{23}{90}$
   B. $\dfrac{-23}{90}$
   C. $\dfrac{103}{90}$
   D. $\dfrac{-103}{90}$

3. $0.74 =$
   (Easy)

   A. $\dfrac{74}{100}$
   B. 7.4%
   C. $\dfrac{33}{50}$
   D. $\dfrac{74}{10}$

4. $(5.6) \times (^-0.11) =$
   (Average)

   A. $^-0.616$
   B. 0.616
   C. $^-6.110$
   D. 6.110

5. An item that sells for $375 is put on sale at $120. What is the percent of decrease?
   (Easy)

   A. 25%
   B. 28%
   C. 68%
   D. 34%

6. Which denotes an irrational number?
   (Easy)

   A. 4.2500000
   B. $\sqrt{16}$
   C. 0.25252525
   D. π=3.141592

7. What is the greatest common factor of 16, 28, and 36?
   (Average)

   A. 2
   B. 4
   C. 8
   D. 16

8. Compute the surface area of the prism below.
   (Average)

   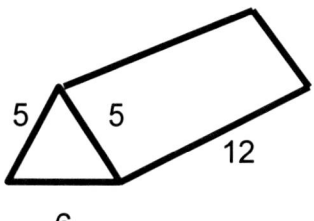

   A. 204
   B. 216
   C. 360
   D. 180

9. What is the area of a square whose side is 13 feet?
   (Easy)

   A. 169 feet
   B. 169 square feet
   C. 52 feet
   D. 52 square feet

10. The owner of a rectangular piece of land 40 yards in length and 30 yards in width wants to divide it into two parts. She plans to join two opposite corners with a fence as shown in the diagram below. The cost of the fence will be approximately $25 per linear foot. What is the estimated cost for the fence needed by the owner?
    (Rigorous)

    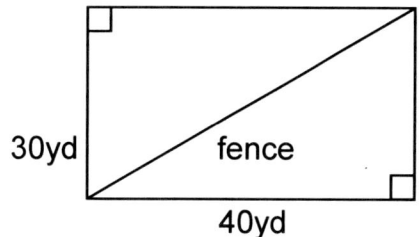

    A. $1,250
    B. $62,500
    C. $5,250
    D. $3,750

11. Find the surface area of a box which is 3 feet wide, 5 feet tall, and 4 feet deep.
    (Average)

    A. 47 sq. ft.
    B. 60 sq. ft.
    C. 94 sq. ft
    D. 188 sq. ft.

12. The trunk of a tree has a 2.1 meter radius. What is its circumference?
(Average)

    A. 2.1π square meters
    B. 4.2π meters
    C. 2.1π meters
    D. 4.2π square meters

13. Set A, B, C, and U are related as shown in the diagram. Which of the following is true, assuming not one of the six regions is empty?
(Average)

    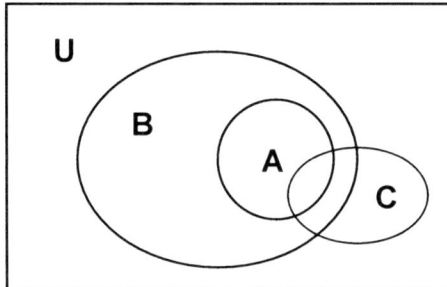

    A. Any element that is a member of set B is also a member of set A.
    B. No element is a member of all three sets A, B, and C.
    C. Any element that is a member of set U is also a member of set B.
    D. None of the above statements is true.

14. If $4x - (3-x) = 7(x-3) + 10$, then
(Rigorous)

    A. $x = 8$
    B. $x = -8$
    C. $x = 4$
    D. $x = -4$

15. It takes 5 equally skilled people 9 hours to shingle Mr. Joe's roof. Let t be the time required for only 3 of these men to do the same job. Select the correct statement of the given condition
(Rigorous)

    A. $\dfrac{3}{5} = \dfrac{9}{t}$

    B. $\dfrac{9}{5} = \dfrac{3}{t}$

    C. $\dfrac{5}{9} = \dfrac{3}{t}$

    D. $\dfrac{14}{9} = \dfrac{t}{5}$

16. Find the equation of a line through (5,6) and (-1,-2) in standard form.
(Rigorous)

    A. $3y = 4x - 2$

    B. $-2y = \dfrac{4}{3}x - 1$

    C. $6y + 5x - 1$

    D. $y = 4x - 6$

17. Find the real roots of the equation $3x^2 - 45 + 22x$.
    (Rigorous)

    A. $\dfrac{-5}{3}$ and 9

    B. $\dfrac{5}{3}$ and -9

    C. 5 and 9

    D. -5 and -9

18. {1,4,7,10, . . .} What is the 40th term in this sequence?
    (Rigorous)

    A. 43
    B. 121
    C. 118
    D. 120

19. Which term most accurately describes two coplanar lines without any common points?
    (Average)

    A. Perpendicular
    B. Parallel
    C. Intersecting
    D. Skew

20. Given similar polygons with corresponding sides 6 and 8, what is the area of the smaller polygon if the area of the larger polygon is 64?
    (Rigorous)

    A. 48
    B. 36
    C. 144
    D. 78

21. Study figures A, B, C, and D. Select the letter in which all triangles are similar.
    (Easy)

    A.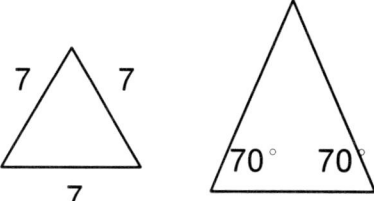

    B.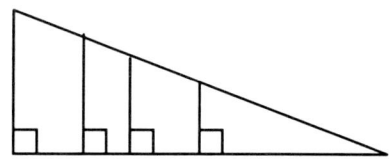

    C.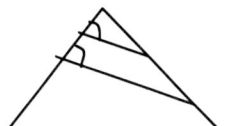

    D.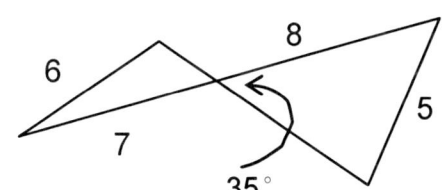

22. Find the midpoint of (2,5) and (7,-4).
    (Rigorous)

    A. (9,-1)
    B. (5, 9)
    C. (9/2, -1/2)
    D. (9/2, 1/2)

23. The following chart shows the yearly average number of international tourists visiting Palm Beach for 1990-1994. How many more international tourists visited Palm Beach in 1994 than in 1991?
(Average)

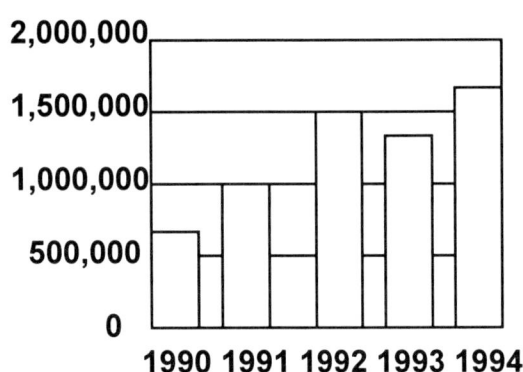

A. 100,000
B. 600,000
C. 1,600,000
D. 8,000,000

24. What conclusion can be drawn from the graph below?
(Rigorous)

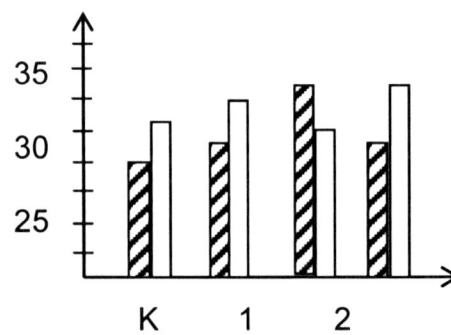

MLK Elementary Student Enrollment — Girls / Boys

A. The number of students in first grade exceeds the number in second grade
B. There are more boys than girls in the entire school
C. There are more girls than boys in the first grade
D. Third grade has the largest number of students

25. Mary did comparison shopping on her favorite brand of coffee. Over half of the stores priced the coffee at $1.70. Most of the remaining stores priced the coffee at $1.80, except for a few who charged $1.90. Which of the following statements is true about the distribution of prices?
    (Rigorous)

    A. The mean and the mode are the same
    B. The mean is greater than the mode
    C. The mean is less than the mode
    D. The mean is less than the median

26. What is the mode of the data in the following sample?
    (Easy)

    9, 10, 11, 9, 10, 11, 9, 13

    A. 9
    B. 9.5
    C. 10
    D. 11

27. A coin is tossed and a die is rolled. What is the probability of landing on the head side of the coin and rolling a 3 on the dice?
    (Rigorous)

    A. $\dfrac{1}{2}$

    B. $\dfrac{1}{6}$

    C. $\dfrac{1}{12}$

    D. $\dfrac{1}{15}$

28. What is the probability of drawing 2 consecutive aces from a standard deck of cards?
    (Rigorous)

    A. $\dfrac{3}{51}$

    B. $\dfrac{1}{221}$

    C. $\dfrac{2}{104}$

    D. $\dfrac{2}{52}$

Answer Key

1. B
2. D
3. A
4. A
5. C
6. D
7. B
8. B
9. B
10. D
11. C
12. B
13. D
14. C
15. A
16. A
17. B
18. C
19. B
20. B
21. B
22. D
23. B
24. B
25. B
26. A
27. C
28. B

Rigor Table

Easy
3, 5, 6, 9, 21, 26

Average
1, 2, 4, 7, 8, 11, 12, 13, 19, 23

Rigorous
10, 14, 15, 16, 17, 18, 20, 22, 24, 25, 27, 28

MATHEMATICS SAMPLE TEST WITH RATIONALES

1. $\dfrac{2^{10}}{2^5} =$

   (Average)

   A. 2^2
   B. 2^5
   C. 2^{50}
   D. $2^{\frac{1}{2}}$

Answer: B. 2^5

The quotient rule of exponents says $\dfrac{a^m}{a^n} = a^{(m-n)}$ so $\dfrac{2^{10}}{2^5} = 2^{(10-5)} = 2^5$

2. $\left(\dfrac{-4}{9}\right) + \left(\dfrac{-7}{10}\right) =$

   (Average)

   A. $\dfrac{23}{90}$

   B. $\dfrac{-23}{90}$

   C. $\dfrac{103}{90}$

   D. $\dfrac{-103}{90}$

Answer: D. $\dfrac{-103}{90}$

Find the LCD of $\dfrac{-4}{9}$ and $\dfrac{-7}{10}$. The LCD is 90, so you get $\dfrac{-40}{90} + \dfrac{-63}{90} = \dfrac{-103}{90}$

3. **0.74 =**
   (Easy)

   A. $\dfrac{74}{100}$

   B. 7.4%

   C. $\dfrac{33}{50}$

   D. $\dfrac{74}{10}$

Answer: A. $\dfrac{74}{100}$

0.74 ⑧ the 4 is in the hundredths place, so the answer is $\dfrac{74}{100}$

4. $(5.6) \times (^-0.11) =$
   (Average)

   A. $^-0.616$
   B. 0.616
   C. $^-6.110$
   D. 6.110

Answer: A. $^-0.616$
Simply multiply 5.6 by -0.11. The answer will be negative because a positive times a negative is a negative number.

5. **An item that sells for $375 is put on sale at $120. What is the percent of decrease?**
   (Easy)

   A. 25%
   B. 28%
   C. 68%
   D. 34%

Answer: C. 68%
Use $(1 - x)$ as the discount. $375x = 120$.
$375(1 - x) = 120 \rightarrow 375 - 375x = 120 \rightarrow 375x = 255 \rightarrow x = 0.68 = 68\%$

6. **Which denotes an irrational number?**
   (Easy)

   A. 4.2500000
   B. $\sqrt{16}$
   C. 0.25252525
   D. π=3.141592

Answer: D. π=3.141592
An irrational number is neither terminal nor repeating. Rational numbers are either terminal or repeating. Of the choices given, only the value of pi (π) is an irrational number.

7. **What is the greatest common factor of 16, 28, and 36?**
   (Average)

   A. 2
   B. 4
   C. 8
   D. 16

Answer: B. 4
The smallest number in this set is 16; its factors are 1, 2, 4, 8 and 16. 16 is the largest factor, but it does not divide into 28 or 36. Neither does 8. 4 does factor into both 28 and 36.

8. **Compute the surface area of the prism below.**
   (Average)

   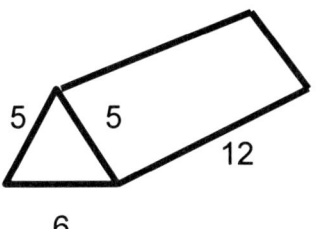

   A. 204
   B. 216
   C. 360
   D. 180

Answer: B. 216
There are five surfaces which make up the prism. The bottom rectangle has area 6 x 12 = 72. The sloping sides are two rectangles each with an area of 5 x 12 = 60. The height of the triangles is determined to be 4 using the Pythagorean Theorem. Therefore each triangle has area 1/2bh = 1/2(6)(4) =12. Thus, the surface area is 72 + 60 + 60 + 12 + 12 = 216.

9. **What is the area of a square whose side is 13 feet?**
   (Easy)

   A. 169 feet
   B. 169 square feet
   C. 52 feet
   D. 52 square feet

Answer: B. 169 square feet
Area = length times width (*lw*).
Length = 13 feet
Width = 13 feet (square, so length and width are the same).
Area = $13 \times 13 = 169$ square feet.
Area is measured in square feet.

10. The owner of a rectangular piece of land 40 yards in length and 30 yards in width wants to divide it into two parts. She plans to join two opposite corners with a fence as shown in the diagram below. The cost of the fence will be approximately $25 per linear foot. What is the estimated cost for the fence needed by the owner?
(Rigorous)

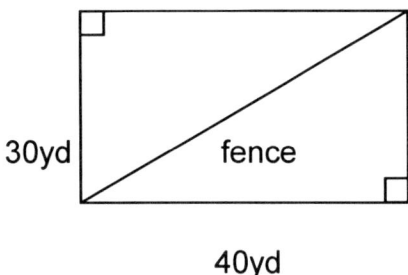

A. $1,250
B. $62,500
C. $5,250
D. $3,750

Answer: D. $3,750
Find the length of the diagonal by using the Pythagorean theorem. Let x be the length of the diagonal.

$$30^2 + 40^2 = x^2 \rightarrow 900 + 1600 = x^2$$
$$2500 = x^2 \rightarrow \sqrt{2500} = \sqrt{x^2}$$
$$x = 50 \text{ yards}$$

Convert to feet. $\dfrac{50 \text{ yards}}{x \text{ feet}} = \dfrac{1 \text{ yard}}{3 \text{ feet}} \rightarrow 150 \text{ feet}$

It cost $25.00 per linear foot, so the cost is (150 ft)($25) = $3750

11. **Find the surface area of a box which is 3 feet wide, 5 feet tall, and 4 feet deep.**
    (Average)

    A. 47 sq. ft.
    B. 60 sq. ft.
    C. 94 sq. ft
    D. 188 sq. ft.

Answer: C. 94 sq. ft.
Let's assume the base of the rectangular solid (box) is 3 by 4, and the height is 5. Then the surface area of the top and bottom together is 2(12) = 24. The sum of the areas of the front and back are 2(15) = 30, while the sum of the areas of the sides are 2(20)=40. The total surface area is therefore 94 square feet.

12. **The trunk of a tree has a 2.1 meter radius. What is its circumference?**
    (Average)

    A. 2.1π square meters
    B. 4.2π meters
    C. 2.1π meters
    D. 4.2π square meters

Answer: B. 4.2π meters
Circumference is $2\pi r$, where r is the radius. The circumference is $2\pi 2.1 = 4.2\pi$ meters (not square meters because not measuring area).

13. Set A, B, C, and U are related as shown in the diagram. Which of the following is true, assuming not one of the six regions is empty?
(Average)

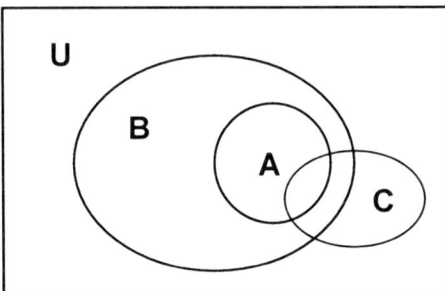

   A. Any element that is a member of set B is also a member of set A.
   B. No element is a member of all three sets A, B, and C.
   C. Any element that is a member of set U is also a member of set B.
   D. None of the above statements is true.

Answer: D. None of the above statements is true.
Answer A is incorrect because not all members of set B are also in set A. Answer B is incorrect because there are elements that are members of all three sets A, B, and C. Answer C is incorrect because not all members of set U is a member of set B. This leaves answer D, which states that none of the above choices are true.

14. If $4x-(3-x)=7(x-3)+10$, then
(Rigorous)

   A. $x = 8$
   B. $x = -8$
   C. $x = 4$
   D. $x = -4$

Answer: C. $x = 4$
The answer is **C.** Solve for x.
$4x-(3-x)=7(x-3)+10$
$4x-3+x=7x-21+10$
$5x-3=7x-11$
$5x=7x-11+3$
$5x-7x=8$
$^{-}2x=^{-}8$
$x=4$

15. It takes 5 equally skilled people 9 hours to shingle Mr. Joe's roof. Let t be the time required for only 3 of these men to do the same job. Select the correct statement of the given condition
(Rigorous)

A. $\dfrac{3}{5} = \dfrac{9}{t}$

B. $\dfrac{9}{5} = \dfrac{3}{t}$

C. $\dfrac{5}{9} = \dfrac{3}{t}$

D. $\dfrac{14}{9} = \dfrac{t}{5}$

Answer: A. $\dfrac{3}{5} = \dfrac{9}{t}$

$\dfrac{3 \text{ people}}{5 \text{ people}} = \dfrac{9 \text{ hours}}{t \text{ hours}}$

16. Find the equation of a line through (5,6) and (-1,-2) in standard form. *(Rigorous)*

   A. 3y=4x-2

   B. $-2y = \dfrac{4}{3}x - 1$

   C. 6y + 5x – 1

   D. y = 4x -6

Answer: A. 3y=4x-2

$$\text{slope} = \frac{y_2 - y_1}{x_2 - x_1} = \frac{-2-6}{-1-5} = \frac{-8}{-6} = \frac{4}{3}$$

$$Y - y_a = m(X - x_a) \to Y + 2 = \frac{4}{3}(X + 1) \to$$

$$Y + 2 = \frac{4}{3}X + \frac{4}{3}$$

$$Y = \frac{4}{3}X - \frac{2}{3} \qquad \text{This is the slope-intercept form.}$$

Multiply by 3 to eliminate fractions

$$3y = 4x - 2 \qquad \text{This is the standard form.}$$

17. Find the real roots of the equation $3x^2 - 45 + 22x$.
    (Rigorous)

    A. $\dfrac{^-5}{3}$ and 9

    B. $\dfrac{5}{3}$ and $^-9$

    C. 5 and 9

    D. -5 and -9

Answer: B. $\dfrac{5}{3}$ and $^-9$

Factor the equation $3x^2 - 45 + 22x$
(-   )(+   )
$(3x - 5)(x + 9)$ Set each part equal to 0 and solve for x.
$3x - 5 = 0$
$3x = 5$
$x = \dfrac{5}{3}$

$x + 9 = 0$
$x = ^-9$

18. $\{1, 4, 7, 10, \ldots\}$ What is the 40th term in this sequence?
    (Rigorous)

    A. 43
    B. 121
    C. 118
    D. 120

Answer: C. 118

To find a term in an arithmetic series in which each term is separated from the next by a fixed number, use the following formula: $a_n = a_1 + (n - 1)d$, where a_1 = the first term in the series, a_n = the nth term in the series, and d = the common difference between the terms.

$a_n = 1 + (40 - 1)3$
$a_n = 1 + (39)3$
$a_n = 118$

19. Which term most accurately describes two coplanar lines without any common points?
    (Average)

    A. Perpendicular
    B. Parallel
    C. Intersecting
    D. Skew

Answer: B. Parallel
By definition, parallel lines are coplanar lines without any common points.

20. Given similar polygons with corresponding sides 6 and 8, what is the area of the smaller polygon if the area of the larger polygon is 64?
    (Rigorous)

    A. 48
    B. 36
    C. 144
    D. 78

Answer: B. 36
In similar polygons, the areas are proportional to the squares of the sides. 36/64 = x/64.

21. Study figures A, B, C, and D. Select the letter in which all triangles are similar.
    (Easy)

A.

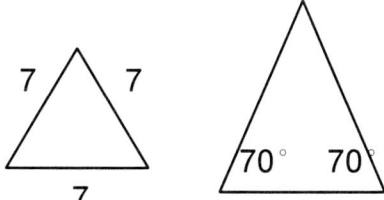

B.

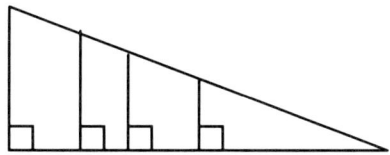

C.

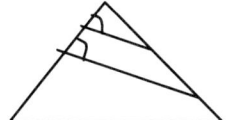

D.

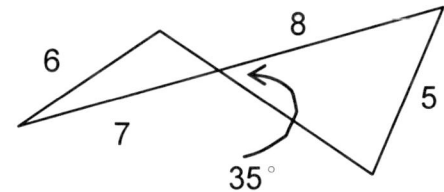

Answer: B.
Choice A is not correct because one triangle is equilateral and the other is isosceles. Choice C is not correct because the two smaller triangles are similar, but the large triangle is not. Choice D is not correct because the lengths and angles are not proportional to each other. Therefore, the correct answer is B because all the triangles have the same angles.

22. Find the midpoint of (2,5) and (7,-4).
    (Rigorous)

    A. (9,-1)
    B. (5, 9)
    C. (9/2, -1/2)
    D. (9/2, 1/2)

Answer: D. (9/2, 1/2)
Using the midpoint formula x = (2 + 7)/2   y = (5 + -4)/2

23. The following chart shows the yearly average number of international tourists visiting Palm Beach for 1990-1994. How many more international tourists visited Palm Beach in 1994 than in 1991? *(Average)*

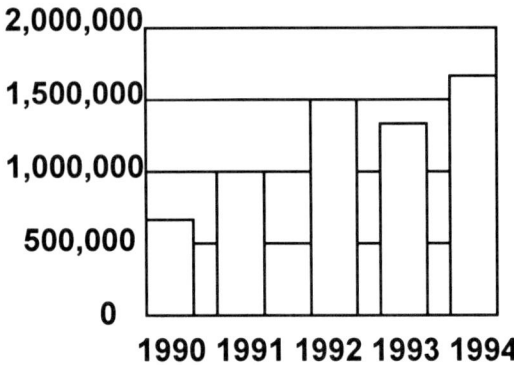

- A. 100,000
- B. 600,000
- C. 1,600,000
- D. 8,000,000

Answer: B. 600,000
The number of tourists in 1991 was 1,000,000 and the number in 1994 was 1,600,000. Subtract to get a difference of 600,000.

24. What conclusion can be drawn from the graph below?
    (Rigorous)

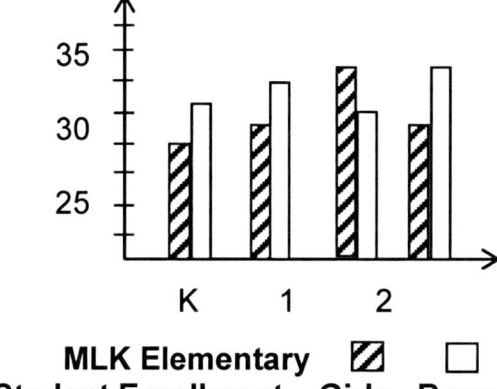

**MLK Elementary
Student Enrollment   Girls   Boys**

   A. The number of students in first grade exceeds the number in second grade
   B. There are more boys than girls in the entire school
   C. There are more girls than boys in the first grade
   D. Third grade has the largest number of students

Answer: B. There are more boys than girls in the entire school
In Kindergarten, first grade, and third grade, there are more boys than girls. The number of extra girls in grade two is more than made up for by the extra boys in all the other grades put together.

25. Mary did comparison shopping on her favorite brand of coffee. Over half of the stores priced the coffee at $1.70. Most of the remaining stores priced the coffee at $1.80, except for a few who charged $1.90. Which of the following statements is true about the distribution of prices?
    (Rigorous)

   A. The mean and the mode are the same
   B. The mean is greater than the mode
   C. The mean is less than the mode
   D. The mean is less than the median

Answer: B. The mean is greater than the mode
Over half the stores priced the coffee at $1.70, so this means that this is the mode. The mean would be slightly over $1.70 because other stores priced the coffee at over $1.70.

26. **What is the mode of the data in the following sample?**
    (Easy)

    9, 10, 11, 9, 10, 11, 9, 13

    A. 9
    B. 9.5
    C. 10
    D. 11

Answer: A. 9
The mode is the number that appears most frequently. Nine appears 3 times, which is more than the other numbers.

27. **A coin is tossed and a die is rolled. What is the probability of landing on the head side of the coin and rolling a 3 on the dice?**
    (Rigorous)

    A. $\dfrac{1}{2}$

    B. $\dfrac{1}{6}$

    C. $\dfrac{1}{12}$

    D. $\dfrac{1}{15}$

Answer: C. $\dfrac{1}{12}$

$P(\text{head}) = \dfrac{1}{2}. \quad P(3) = \dfrac{1}{6}$

$P(\text{head and 3}) = P(\text{head}) \times P(3)$
$\phantom{P(\text{head and 3})} = \dfrac{1}{2} \times \dfrac{1}{6} = \dfrac{1}{12}$

28. What is the probability of drawing 2 consecutive aces from a standard deck of cards?
    (Rigorous)

    A. $\dfrac{3}{51}$

    B. $\dfrac{1}{221}$

    C. $\dfrac{2}{104}$

    D. $\dfrac{2}{52}$

Answer: B. $\dfrac{1}{221}$

There are 4 aces in the 52 card deck. P(first ace) = $\dfrac{4}{52}$. P(second ace) = $\dfrac{3}{51}$.

P(first ace and second ace) = P(one ace)xP(second ace|first ace) = $\dfrac{4}{52} \times \dfrac{3}{51}$ = $\dfrac{1}{221}$.

SOCIAL SCIENCE SAMPLE TEST

1. The belief that the United States should control all of North America was called:
   (Easy)

   A. Westward expansion
   B. Pan Americanism
   C. Manifest Destiny
   D. Nationalism

2. The area of the United States was effectively doubled through purchase of the Louisiana Territory under which President?
   (Average)

   A. John Adams
   B. Thomas Jefferson
   C. James Madison
   D. James Monroe

3. A major quarrel between colonial Americans and the British concerned a series of British Acts of Parliament dealing with:
   (Easy)

   A. Taxes
   B. Slavery
   C. Native Americans
   D. Shipbuilding

4. The international organization established to work for world peace at the end of the Second World War is the:
   (Average)

   A. League of Nations
   B. United Federation of Nations
   C. United Nations
   D. United World League

5. Which famous battle fought on Texas soil resulted in Texas independence from Mexico?
   (Rigorous)

   A. The Battle of the Alamo
   B. The Battle of San Jacinto
   C. The Battle of the Rio Grande
   D. The Battle of Shiloh

6. **Why is the system of government in the United States referred to as a federal system?**
   (Rigorous)

   A. There are different levels of government
   B. There is one central authority in which all governmental power is vested
   C. The national government cannot operate except with the consent of the governed
   D. Elections are held at stated periodic times, rather than as called by the head of the government

7. **The U.S. Constitution, adopted in 1789, provided for:**
   (Rigorous)

   A. Direct election of the President by all citizens
   B. Direct election of the President by citizens meeting a standard of wealth
   C. Indirect election of the President by electors
   D. Indirect election of the President by the U.S. Senate

8. **From about 1870 to 1900 the settlement of America's "last frontier," the West, was completed. One attraction for settlers was free land, but it would have been to no avail without:**
   (Rigorous)

   A. Better farming methods and technology
   B. Surveying to set boundaries
   C. Immigrants and others to seek new land
   D. The railroad to get them there

9. **Slavery arose in the Southern Colonies partly as a perceived economical way to:**
   (Average)

   A. Increase the owner's wealth through human beings used as a source of exchange
   B. Cultivate large plantations of cotton, tobacco, rice, indigo, and other crops
   C. Provide Africans with humanitarian aid, such as health care, Christianity, and literacy
   D. Keep ships' holds full of cargo on two out of three legs of the "triangular trade" voyage.

10. **The post-Civil War years were a time of low public morality, a time of greed, graft, and dishonesty. Which one of the reasons listed below would not be accurate reasons for this?**
    (Rigorous)

    A. The war itself, because of the money and materials needed to conduct the War
    B. The very rapid growth of industry and big business after the War
    C. The personal example set by President Grant
    D. Unscrupulous heads of large impersonal corporations

11. **A number of women worked hard in the first half of the 19th century for women's rights, but decisive gains did not come until after 1850. The earliest accomplishments were in:**
    (Average)

    A. Medicine
    B. Education
    C. Writing
    D. Temperance

12. **Of all the major causes of both World Wars I and II, the most significant one is considered to be:**
    (Average)

    A. Extreme nationalism
    B. Military buildup and aggression
    C. Political unrest
    D. Agreements and alliances

13. **Meridians, or lines of longitude, not only help in pinpointing locations but are also used for:**
    (Rigorous)

    A. Measuring distance from the Poles
    B. Determining direction of ocean currents
    C. Determining the time around the world
    D. Measuring distance on the equator

14. **The study of the ways in which different societies around the world deal with the problems of limited resources and unlimited needs and wants is in the area of:**
    (Average)

    A. Economics
    B. Sociology
    C. Anthropology
    D. Political science

15. **Capitalism and communism are alike in that they are both:**
    (Easy)

    A. Organic systems
    B. Political systems
    C. Centrally planned systems
    D. Economic systems

16. **The purchase of goods or services on one market for immediate resale on another market is:**
    (Average)

    A. Output
    B. Enterprise
    C. Arbitrage
    D. Mercantile

17. **The economic system promoting individual ownership of land, capital, and businesses with minimal governmental regulations is called:**
    (Easy)

    A. Macro-economy
    B. Micro-economy
    C. Laissez-faire
    D. Free enterprise

18. **The American labor union movement started gaining new momentum:**
    (Rigorous)

    A. During the building of the railroads
    B. After 1865 with the growth of cities
    C. With the rise of industrial giants such as Carnegie and Vanderbilt
    D. During the war years of 1861-1865

19. **It can be reasonably stated that the change in the United States from primarily an agricultural country into an industrial power was due to all of the following except:**
    (Average)

    A. Tariffs on foreign imports
    B. Millions of hardworking immigrants
    C. An increase in technological developments
    D. The change from steam to electricity for powering industrial machinery

20. There is no doubt of the vast improvement of the U.S. Constitution over the weak Articles of Confederation. Which one of the four accurate statements below is a unique yet eloquent description of the document?
    (Rigorous)

    A. The establishment of a strong central government in no way lessened or weakened the individual states
    B. Individual rights were protected and secured
    C. The Constitution is the best representation of the results of the American genius for compromise
    D. Its flexibility and adaptation to change gives it a sense of timelessness

21. Marbury vs Madison (1803) was an important Supreme Court case which set the precedent for:
    (Rigorous)

    A. The elastic clause
    B. Judicial review
    C. The supreme law of the land
    D. Popular sovereignty in the Territories

22. Which one of the following is not a function or responsibility of U.S. political parties?
    (Rigorous)

    A. Conducting elections or the voting process
    B. Obtaining funds needed for election campaigns
    C. Choosing candidates to run for public office
    D. Making voters aware of issues and other public affairs information

23. Which of the following choices lists elements usually considered to be responsibilities of citizenship under the American system of government?
    (Easy)

    A. Serving in public office, voluntary government service, military duty
    B. Paying taxes, jury duty, upholding the Constitution
    C. Maintaining a job, giving to charity, turning in fugitives
    D. Quartering of soldiers, bearing arms, government service

24. In which of the following disciplines would the study of physical mapping, modern or ancient, and the plotting of points and boundaries be least useful?
 (Average)

    A. Sociology
    B. Geography
    C. Archaeology
    D. History

25. The study of the exercise of power and political behavior in human society today would be conducted by experts in:
 (Average)

    A. History
    B. Sociology
    C. Political science
    D. Anthropology

Answer Key

1. C
2. B
3. A
4. C
5. B
6. A
7. C
8. D
9. B
10. C
11. B
12. A
13. C
14. A
15. D
16. C
17. D
18. B
19. A
20. C
21. B
22. A
23. B
24. A
25. C

Rigor Table

Easy
1, 3, 15, 17, 23

Average
2, 4, 9, 11, 12, 14, 16, 19, 24, 25

Rigorous
5, 6, 7, 8, 10, 13, 18, 20, 21, 22

SOCIAL SCIENCE SAMPLE TEST WITH RATIONALES

1. **The belief that the United States should control all of North America was called:**
   (Easy)

   A. Westward expansion
   B. Pan Americanism
   C. Manifest Destiny
   D. Nationalism

   Answer: C. Manifest Destiny
   The belief that the United States should control all of North America was called Manifest Destiny. This idea fueled much of the violence and aggression towards those already occupying the lands such as the Native Americans. Manifest Destiny was certainly driven by sentiments of nationalism, and gave rise to westward expansion.

2. **The area of the United States was effectively doubled through purchase of the Louisiana Territory under which President?**
   (Average)

   A. John Adams
   B. Thomas Jefferson
   C. James Madison
   D. James Monroe

   Answer: B. Thomas Jefferson
   The Louisiana Purchase, an acquisition of territory from France in 1803, occurred during the presidency of Thomas Jefferson. John Adams (1735-1826) was president from 1797–1801, before the purchase. James Madison (1751-1836) was president after the purchase (1809-1817). James Monroe (1758-1831) was actually a signatory on the Purchase, but did not become President until 1817.

3. **A major quarrel between colonial Americans and the British concerned a series of British Acts of Parliament dealing with:**
   (Easy)

   A. Taxes
   B. Slavery
   C. Native Americans
   D. Shipbuilding

   Answer: A. Taxes
   Acts of Parliament imposing taxes on the colonists always provoked resentment. Because the colonies had no direct representation in Parliament, they felt it

unjust that that body should impose taxes on them, with so little knowledge of their very different situation in America and no real concern for the consequences of such taxes. While slavery (B) continued to exist in the colonies long after it had been completely abolished in Britain, it never was a source of serious debate between Britain and the colonies. By the time Britain outlawed slavery in its colonies in 1833, the American Revolution had already occurred and the United States was free of British control. There was no series of British Acts of Parliament passed concerning Native Americans (C). Colonial shipbuilding (D) was an industry which received little interference from the British.

4. **The international organization established to work for world peace at the end of the Second World War is the:**
   (Average)

   A. League of Nations
   B. United Federation of Nations
   C. United Nations
   D. United World League

Answer: C. United Nations
The international organization established to work for world peace at the end of the Second World War was the United Nations. From the ashes of the failed League of Nations, established following World War I, the United Nations continues to be a major player in world affairs today.

5. **Which famous battle fought on Texas soil resulted in Texas independence from Mexico?**
   (Rigorous)

   A. The Battle of the Alamo
   B. The Battle of San Jacinto
   C. The Battle of the Rio Grande
   D. The Battle of Shiloh

Answer: B. The Battle of San Jacinto
It was the Battle of San Jacinto in which Sam Houston and the Texicans roundly defeated the Mexican army and captured Mexican General and Commander Santa Anna. The result was the independence of the Republic of Texas from Mexican control. The Battle of the Alamo (A), despite the defeat of the Texans by Santa Anna's troops, was a critical event which enabled Houston to gather troops and prepare for the Battle of San Jacinto. The Battle of Shiloh (D) occurred during the Civil War, and it was not in Texas. There was no major battle called the Battle of the Rio Grande (C).

6. **Why is the system of government in the United States referred to as a federal system?**
   (Rigorous)

   A. There are different levels of government
   B. There is one central authority in which all governmental power is vested
   C. The national government cannot operate except with the consent of the governed
   D. Elections are held at stated periodic times, rather than as called by the head of the government

Answer: A. There are different levels of government
The United States is composed of fifty states, each responsible for its own affairs, but united under a federal government. A centralized system (B) is the opposite of a federal system. That national government cannot operate except with the consent of the governed (C) is a founding principle of American politics but is not a political system like federalism. A centralized democracy could still be consensual, but would not be federal. (D) is a description of electoral procedure, not a political system like federalism.

7. **The U.S. Constitution, adopted in 1789, provided for:**
   (Rigorous)

   A. Direct election of the President by all citizens
   B. Direct election of the President by citizens meeting a standard of wealth
   C. Indirect election of the President by electors
   D. Indirect election of the President by the U.S. Senate

Answer: C. Indirect election of the President by electors
The United States Constitution has always arranged for the indirect election of the President by electors. The question, by mentioning the original date of adoption, might mislead someone to choose B, but while standards of citizenship have been changed by amendment, the President has never been directly elected. Nor does the Senate have anything to do with presidential elections. The House of Representatives, not the Senate, settles cases where neither candidate wins in the Electoral College.

8. **From about 1870 to 1900 the settlement of America's "last frontier," the West, was completed. One attraction for settlers was free land, but it would have been to no avail without:**
   (Rigorous)

   A. Better farming methods and technology
   B. Surveying to set boundaries
   C. Immigrants and others to seek new land
   D. The railroad to get them there

Answer: D. The railroad to get them there
From about 1870 to 1900, the settlement of America's "last frontier" in the West was made possible by the building of the railroad. Without the railroad, the settlers never could have traveled such distances in an efficient manner.

9. **Slavery arose in the Southern Colonies partly as a perceived economical way to:**
   (Average)

   A. Increase the owner's wealth through human beings used as a source of exchange
   B. Cultivate large plantations of cotton, tobacco, rice, indigo, and other crops
   C. Provide Africans with humanitarian aid, such as health care, Christianity, and literacy
   D. Keep ships' holds full of cargo on two out of three legs of the "triangular trade" voyage.

Answer: B. Cultivate large plantations of cotton, tobacco, rice, indigo, and other crops
The Southern states, with their smaller populations, were heavily dependent on slave labor as a means of being able to fulfill their role and remain competitive in the greater U.S. economy. When slaves arrived in the South, the vast majority would become permanent fixtures on plantations, intended for work, not as a source of exchange. While some slave owners instructed their slaves in Christianity, provided health care or some level of education, such attention were not their primary reasons for owning slaves – a cheap and ready labor force was their reason. Whether or not ships' holds were full on two or three legs of the triangular journey was not the concern of Southerners as the final purchasers of slaves. Such details would have concerned the slave traders.

10. **The post-Civil War years were a time of low public morality, a time of greed, graft, and dishonesty. Which one of the reasons listed below would not be accurate reasons for this?**
    (Rigorous)

    A. The war itself, because of the money and materials needed to conduct the War
    B. The very rapid growth of industry and big business after the War
    C. The personal example set by President Grant
    D. Unscrupulous heads of large impersonal corporations

Answer: C. The personal example set by President Grant
The post-Civil War years were a particularly difficult time for the nation, and public morale was especially low. The war had plunged the country into debt, and ultimately into a recession by the 1890s. Racism was rampant throughout the South and the North, where freed Blacks were taking jobs for low wages. The rapid growth of industry and big business caused a polarization of rich and poor, workers and owners. Many people moved into the urban centers to find work in the new industrial sector. These jobs typically paid low wages, required long hours, and offered poor working conditions. The heads of large impersonal corporations treated their workers inhumanely, letting morale drop to a record low. The heads of corporations tried to prevent and disband labor unions.

11. **A number of women worked hard in the first half of the 19th century for women's rights, but decisive gains did not come until after 1850. The earliest accomplishments were in:**
    (Average)

    A. Medicine
    B. Education
    C. Writing
    D. Temperance

Answer: B. Education
Although women worked hard in the early nineteenth century to make gains in medicine, writing, and temperance movements, the most prestigious accomplishments of the early women's movement were in the field of education. Women such as May Wollstonecraft (1759-1797), Alice Palmer (1855-1902), and, of course, Elizabeth Blackwell (1821-1910) led the way for women, particularly in the area of higher education.

12. Of all the major causes of both World Wars I and II, the most significant one is considered to be:
    (Average)

    A. Extreme nationalism
    B. Military buildup and aggression
    C. Political unrest
    D. Agreements and alliances

Answer: A. Extreme nationalism
Although military buildup and aggression, political unrest, and agreements and alliances were all characteristic of the world climate before and during World War I and World War II, the most significant cause of both wars was extreme nationalism. Nationalism is the idea that the interests and needs of a particular nation are of the utmost and primary importance above all else. Some nationalist movements could be liberation movements while others were oppressive regimes, much depends on their degree of nationalism.

The nationalism that sparked WWI included a rejection of German, Austro-Hungarian, and Ottoman imperialism by Serbs, Slavs and others culminating in the assassination of Archduke Ferdinand by a Serb nationalist in 1914. Following WWI and the Treaty of Versailles, many Germans and others in the Central Alliance Nations, malcontent at the concessions and reparations of the treaty, started a new form of nationalism. Adolf Hitler and the Nazi regime led this extreme nationalism. Hitler's ideas were examples of extreme, oppressive nationalism combined with political, social, and economic scapegoating and were the primary cause of WWII.

13. Meridians, or lines of longitude, not only help in pinpointing locations but are also used for:
    (Rigorous)

    A. Measuring distance from the Poles
    B. Determining direction of ocean currents
    C. Determining the time around the world
    D. Measuring distance on the equator

Answer: C. Determining the time around the world
Meridians, or lines of longitude, are the determining factor in separating time zones and determining time around the world.

14. **The study of the ways in which different societies around the world deal with the problems of limited resources and unlimited needs and wants is in the area of:**
    (Average)

    A. Economics
    B. Sociology
    C. Anthropology
    D. Political science

Answer: A. Economics
The study of the ways in which different societies around the world deal with the problems of limited resources and unlimited needs and wants is a study of economics. Economists consider the law of supply and demand as fundamental to the study of the economy. However, sociology and political science also consider the study of economics and its importance in understanding social and political systems.

15. **Capitalism and communism are alike in that they are both:**
    (Easy)

    A. Organic systems
    B. Political systems
    C. Centrally planned systems
    D. Economic systems

Answer: D. Economic systems
While economic and political systems are often closely connected, capitalism and communism are primarily economic systems. Capitalism is a system of economics that allows the open market to determine the relative value of goods and services. Communism is an economic system where the market is planned by a central state. While communism is a centrally planned system, this is not true of capitalism. Organic systems (A) are studied in biology, a natural science.

16. **The purchase of goods or services on one market for immediate resale on another market is:**
    (Average)

    A. Output
    B. Enterprise
    C. Arbitrage
    D. Mercantile

Answer: C. Arbitrage
Output is an amount produced or manufactured by an industry. Enterprise is simply any business organization. Mercantile is one of the first systems of

economics in which goods were exchanged. Arbitrage is an item or service that an industry produces. The dictionary definition of arbitrage is the purchase of securities on one market for immediate resale on another market in order to profit from a price discrepancy.

17. **The economic system promoting individual ownership of land, capital, and businesses with minimal governmental regulations is called:**
(Easy)

   A. Macro-economy
   B. Micro-economy
   C. Laissez-faire
   D. Free enterprise

Answer: D. Free enterprise
Free enterprise or capitalism is the economic system that promotes private ownership of land, capital, and business with minimal government interference. Laissez-faire is the idea that an "invisible hand" will guide the free enterprise system to the maximum potential efficiency.

18. **The American labor union movement started gaining new momentum:**
(Rigorous)

   A. During the building of the railroads
   B. After 1865 with the growth of cities
   C. With the rise of industrial giants such as Carnegie and Vanderbilt
   D. During the war years of 1861-1865

Answer: B. After 1865 with the growth of cities
The American Labor Union movement had been around since the late 18th and early 19th centuries. The Labor movement began to first experience persecution by employers in the early 1800s. The American Labor Movement remained relatively ineffective until after the Civil War. In 1866, the National Labor Union was formed, pushing such issues as the eight-hour workday and new policies of immigration. This gave rise to the Knights of Labor and eventually the American Federation of Labor (AFL) in the 1890s and the Industrial Workers of the World (1905). Therefore, it was the period following the Civil War that empowered the labor movement in terms of numbers, militancy, and effectiveness.

19. It can be reasonably stated that the change in the United States from primarily an agricultural country into an industrial power was due to all of the following except:
    (Average)

    A. Tariffs on foreign imports
    B. Millions of hardworking immigrants
    C. An increase in technological developments
    D. The change from steam to electricity for powering industrial machinery

Answer: A. Tariffs on foreign imports
It can be reasonably stated that the change in the United States from primarily an agricultural country into an industrial power was due to a great degree to three of the reasons listed above. It was a combination of millions of hard-working immigrants, an increase in technological developments, and the change from steam to electricity for powering industrial machinery. The only reason given that really had little effect was the tariffs on foreign imports.

20. There is no doubt of the vast improvement of the U.S. Constitution over the weak Articles of Confederation. Which one of the four accurate statements below is a unique yet eloquent description of the document?
    (Rigorous)

    A. The establishment of a strong central government in no way lessened or weakened the individual states
    B. Individual rights were protected and secured
    C. The Constitution is the best representation of the results of the American genius for compromise
    D. Its flexibility and adaptation to change gives it a sense of timelessness

Answer: C. The Constitution is the best representation of the results of the American genius for compromise
The U.S. Constitution was indeed a vast improvement over the Articles of Confederation and the authors of the document took great care to assure longevity. It clearly stated that the establishment of a strong central government in no way lessened or weakened the individual states. In the Bill of Rights, citizens were assured that individual rights were protected and secured. Possibly the most important feature of the new Constitution was its flexibility and adaptation to change which assured longevity.

21. **Marbury vs Madison (1803) was an important Supreme Court case which set the precedent for:**
    (Rigorous)

    A. The elastic clause
    B. Judicial review
    C. The supreme law of the land
    D. Popular sovereignty in the Territories

Answer: B. Judicial review
Marbury vs. Madison (1803) was an important case for the Supreme Court as it established judicial review. In that case, the Supreme Court set precedence to declare laws passed by Congress as unconstitutional.

22. **Which one of the following is not a function or responsibility of U.S. political parties?**
    (Rigorous)

    A. Conducting elections or the voting process
    B. Obtaining funds needed for election campaigns
    C. Choosing candidates to run for public office
    D. Making voters aware of issues and other public affairs information

Answer: A. Conducting elections or the voting process
U.S. political parties have numerous functions and responsibilities. Among them are obtaining funds needed for election campaigns, choosing the candidates to run for office, and making voters aware of the issues. The political parties, however, do not conduct elections or the voting process, as that would be an obvious conflict of interest.

23. **Which of the following choices lists elements usually considered to be responsibilities of citizenship under the American system of government?**
    (Easy)

    A. Serving in public office, voluntary government service, military duty
    B. Paying taxes, jury duty, upholding the Constitution
    C. Maintaining a job, giving to charity, turning in fugitives
    D. Quartering of soldiers, bearing arms, government service

Answer: B. Paying taxes, jury duty, upholding the Constitution
Only paying taxes, jury duty and upholding the Constitution are responsibilities of citizens as a result of rights and commitments outlined in the Constitution. For example, the right of citizens to a jury trial in the Sixth and Seventh Amendments and the right of the federal government to collect taxes in Article 1, Section 8. Serving in public office, voluntary government service and military duty,

maintaining a job, giving to charity and turning in fugitives are all considered purely voluntary actions, even when officially recognized and compensated. The United States has none of the compulsory military or civil service requirements of many other countries. The quartering of soldiers is an act which, according to Amendment III of the Bill of Rights, requires a citizen's consent. Bearing arms is a right guaranteed under Amendment II of the Bill of Rights.

24. **In which of the following disciplines would the study of physical mapping, modern or ancient, and the plotting of points and boundaries be least useful?**
    (Average)

    A. Sociology
    B. Geography
    C. Archaeology
    D. History

Answer: A. Sociology
In geography, archaeology, and history, the study of maps and plotting of points and boundaries is very important as all three of these disciplines hold value in understanding the spatial relations and regional characteristics of people and places. Sociology, however, mostly focuses on the social interactions of people and while location is important, the physical location is not as important as the social location such as the differences between studying people in groups or as individuals.

25. **The study of the exercise of power and political behavior in human society today would be conducted by experts in:**
    (Average)

    A. History
    B. Sociology
    C. Political science
    D. Anthropology

Answer: C. Political science
Experts in the field of political science today would likely conduct the study of exercise of power and political behavior in human society. However, it is also reasonable to suggest that such studies would be important to historians (study of the past, often in an effort to understand the present), sociologists (often concerned with power structure in the social and political worlds), and even some anthropologists (study of culture and their behaviors).

SCIENCE SAMPLE TEST

1. **Chemicals should be stored**
   (Easy)

   A. In the principal's office
   B. In a dark room
   C. In an off-site research facility
   D. According to their reactivity with other substances

2. **When measuring the volume of water in a graduated cylinder, where does one read the measurement?**
   (Average)

   A. At the highest point of the liquid
   B. At the bottom of the meniscus curve
   C. At the closest mark to the top of the liquid
   D. At the top of the plastic safety ring

3. **When is a hypothesis formed?**
   (Easy)

   A. Before the data is taken
   B. After the data is taken
   C. After the data is analyzed
   D. Concurrent with graphing the data

4. **Which of the following is the most accurate definition of a non-renewable resource?**
   (Average)

   A. A nonrenewable resource is never replaced once used
   B. A nonrenewable resource is replaced on a timescale that is very long relative to human life-spans
   C. A nonrenewable resource is a resource that can only be manufactured by humans
   D. A nonrenewable resource is a species that has already become extinct

5. A scientist exposes mice to cigarette smoke, and notes that their lungs develop tumors. Mice that were not exposed to the smoke do not develop as many tumors. Which of the following conclusions may be drawn from these results?
(Rigorous)

   I. Cigarette smoke causes lung tumors
   II. Cigarette smoke exposure has a positive correlation with lung tumors in mice
   III. Some mice are predisposed to develop lung tumors
   IV. Cigarette smoke exposure has a positive correlation with lung tumors in humans

   A. I and II only
   B. II only
   C. I, II, III and IV
   D. II and IV only

6. Which of the following is a correct explanation for an astronaut's 'weightlessness'?
(Average)

   A. Astronauts continue to feel the pull of gravity in space, but they are so far from planets that the force is small
   B. Astronauts continue to feel the pull of gravity in space, but spacecraft have such powerful engines that those forces dominate, reducing effective weight
   C. Astronauts do not feel the pull of gravity in space, because space is a vacuum
   D. The cumulative gravitational forces, that the astronaut is experiencing, from all sources in the solar system equal out to a net gravitational force of zero

7. Physical properties are observable characteristics of a substance in its natural state. Which of the following are considered physical properties?
(Rigorous)

   I. Color
   II. Density
   III. Specific gravity
   IV. Melting point

   A. I only
   B. I and II only
   C. I, II, and III only
   D. III and IV only

8. The change in phase from liquid to gas is called:
   (Rigorous)

   A. Evaporation
   B. Condensation
   C. Vaporization
   D. Boiling

9. Which of the following statements is true of all transition elements?
   (Rigorous)

   A. They are all hard solids at room temperature
   B. They tend to form salts when reacted with Halogens
   C. They all have a silvery appearance in their pure state
   D. All of the above

10. A boulder sitting on the edge of a cliff has which type of energy?
    (Easy)

    A. Kinetic energy
    B. Latent energy
    C. No energy
    D. Potential energy

11. A converging lens produces a real image _____.
    (Rigorous)

    A. always
    B. never
    C. when the object is within one focal length of the lens
    D. when the object is further than one focal length from the lens

12. Which of the following is not a factor in how different materials will conduct seismic waves?
    (Average)

    A. Density
    B. Incompressiblity
    C. Rigidty
    D. Tensile strength

13. The Law of Conservation of Energy states that:
    (Average)

    A. There must be the same number of products and reactants in any chemical equation
    B. Mass and energy can be interchanged
    C. Energy is neither created nor destroyed, but may change form
    D. One form energy must remain intact (or conserved) in all reactions

14. When you step out of the shower, the floor feels colder on your feet than the bathmat. Which of the following is the correct explanation for this phenomenon?
 (Rigorous)

   A. The floor is colder than the bathmat
   B. The bathmat, being smaller than the floor, quickly reaches equilibrium with your body temperature
   C. Heat is conducted more easily into the floor
   D. Water is absorbed from your feet into the bathmat so it doesn't evaporate as quickly as it does off the floor, thus not cooling the bathmat as quickly

15. Identify the correct sequence of organization of living things from lower to higher order:
 (Average)

   A. Cell, organelle, organ, tissue, system, organism
   B. Cell, tissue, organ, organelle, system, organism
   C. Organelle, cell, tissue, organ, system, organism
   D. Organelle, tissue, cell, organ, system, organism

16. Catalysts assist reactions by _____.
 (Easy)

   A. lowering required activation energy
   B. maintaining precise pH levels
   C. keeping systems at equilibrium
   D. changing the starting amounts of reactants

17. Which process results in a haploid chromosome number?
 (Rigorous)

   A. Mitosis
   B. Meiosis I
   C. Meiosis II
   D. Neither mitosis nor meiosis

18. A carrier of a genetic disorder is heterozygous for a disorder that is recessive in nature. Hemophilia is a sex-linked disorder. This means that:
 (Easy)

   A. Only females can be carriers
   B. Only males can be carriers
   C. Both males and females can be carriers
   D. Neither females nor males can be carriers

19. **Which of the following is a correct explanation for scientific biological adaptation?**
    (Average)

    A. Giraffes need to reach higher for leaves to eat, so their necks stretch. The giraffe babies are then born with longer necks. Eventually, there are more long-necked giraffes in the population.
    B. Giraffes with longer necks are able to reach more leaves, so they eat more and have more babies than other giraffes. Eventually, there are more long-necked giraffes in the population.
    C. Giraffes want to reach higher for leaves to eat, so they release enzymes into their bloodstream, which in turn causes fetal development of longer-necked giraffes. Eventually, there are more long-necked giraffes in the population.
    D. Giraffes with long necks are more attractive to other giraffes, so they get the best mating partners and have more babies. Eventually, there are more long-necked giraffes in the population.

20. **An animal choosing its mate because of attractive plumage or a strong mating call is an example of:**
    (Average)

    A. Sexual selection
    B. Natural selection
    C. Mechanical isolation
    D. Linkage

21. **Many male birds sing long, complicated songs that describe thier identity and the area of land that they claim. Which of the answers below is the best decription of this behavior?**
    (Rigorous)

    A. Innate territorial behavior
    B. Learned competitve behavior
    C. Innate mating behavior
    D. Learned territorial behavior

22. **A wrasse (fish) cleans the teeth of other fish by eating away plaque. This is an example of _____ between the fish.**
    (Average)

    A. parasitism
    B. symbiosis (mutualism)
    C. competition
    D. predation

23. **Which of the following causes the aurora borealis?**
    (Rigorous)

    A. Gases escaping from earth
    B. Particles from the sun
    C. Particles from the moon
    D. Electromagnetic discharges from the North pole

24. **The transfer of heat from the earth's surface to the atmosphere is called:**
    (Average)

    A. Convection
    B. Radiation
    C. Conduction
    D. Advection

25. **What is the most accurate description of the Water Cycle?**
    (Rigorous)

    A. Rain comes from clouds, filling the ocean. The water then evaporates and becomes clouds again.
    B. Water circulates from rivers into groundwater and back, while water vapor circulates in the atmosphere.
    C. Water is conserved except for chemical or nuclear reactions, and any drop of water could circulate through clouds, rain, ground-water, and surface-water.
    D. Water flows toward the oceans, where it evaporates and forms clouds, which causes rain, which in turn flow back to the oceans after it falls.

26. **What makes up the largest abiotic portion of the Nitrogen Cycle?**
    (Average)

    A. Nitrogen fixing bacteria
    B. Nitrates
    C. Decomposers
    D. Atomsphere

27. **What are the most significant and prevalent elements in the biosphere?**
   (Easy)

   A. Carbon, Hydrogen, Oxygen, Nitrogen, Phosphorus
   B. Carbon, Hydrogen, Sodium, Iron, Calcium
   C. Carbon, Oxygen, Sulfur, Manganese, Iron
   D. Carbon, Hydrogen, Oxygen, Nickel, Sodium, Nitrogen

28. **Neap Tides are especially weak tides that occur when the Sun and Moon are in a perpendicular arrangment to the Earth, and Spring Tides are especially strong tides that occur when the Sun and Moon are in line. At which combination of lunar phases do these tides occur (respectively)?**
   (Rigorous)

   A. Half Moon and Full Moon
   B. Quarter Moon and New Moon
   C. Gibbous Moon and Quarter Moon
   D. Full Moon and New Moon

29. **The planet with true retrograde rotation is:**
   (Rigorous)

   A. Pluto
   B. Neptune
   C. Venus
   D. Saturn

30. **The phases of the Moon are the result of its _____ in relation to the Sun.**
   (Average)

   A. revolution
   B. rotation
   C. position
   D. inclination

31. **The end of a geologic era is most often characterized by:**
   (Average)

   A. A general uplifting of the crust
   B. The extinction of the dominant plants and animals
   C. The appearance of new life forms
   D. All of the above

32. **The best preserved animal remains have been discovered in:**
   (Rigorous)

   A. Resin
   B. Fossil mold
   C. Tar pits
   D. Glacial ice

33. Which type of student activity is most likely to expose a student's misconceptions about science?
(Average)

A. Multiple-choice and fill-in-the-blank worksheets
B. Laboratory activities, where the lab is laid out step-by-step with no active thought on the part of the student
C. Teacher- lead demonstrations
D. Laboratories in which the students are forced to critically consider the steps taken and the results obtained

34. In an experiment measuring the inhibition effect of different antibiotic discs of bacteria grown in Petri dishes, what are the independent and dependent variables respectively?
(Rigorous)

A. Number of bacterial colonies and the antibiotic type
B. Antibiotic type and the distance between antibiotic and the closest colony
C. Antibiotic type and the number of bacterial colonies
D. Presence of bacterial colonies and the antibiotic type

Answer Key

1.	D		18.	A
2.	B		19.	B
3.	A		20.	A
4.	B		21.	D
5.	B		22.	B
6.	A		23.	B
7.	C		24.	C
8.	A		25.	C
9.	B		26.	D
10.	D		27.	A
11.	D		28.	B
12.	D		29.	C
13.	C		30.	C
14.	C		31.	D
15.	C		32.	C
16.	A		33.	D
17.	C		34.	B

Rigor Table

Easy
1, 3, 10, 16, 18, 27

Average
2, 4, 6, 12, 13, 15, 19, 20, 22, 24, 26, 30, 31, 33

Rigorous
5, 7, 8, 9, 11, 14, 17, 21, 23, 25, 28, 29, 32, 34

SCIENCE SAMPLE TEST WITH RATIONALES

1. **Chemicals should be stored**
   (Easy)

   A. In the principal's office
   B. In a dark room
   C. In an off-site research facility
   D. According to their reactivity with other substances

   Answer: D. According to their reactivity with other substances
   Chemicals should be stored with other chemicals of similar properties (e.g., acids with other acids), to reduce the potential for either hazardous reactions in the store-room, or mistakes in reagent use. Certainly, chemicals should not be stored in anyone's office, and the light intensity of the room is not very important because light-sensitive chemicals are usually stored in dark containers. In fact, good lighting is desirable in a store-room, so that labels can be read easily. Chemicals may be stored off-site, but that makes their use inconvenient.

2. **When measuring the volume of water in a graduated cylinder, where does one read the measurement?**
   (Average)

   A. At the highest point of the liquid
   B. At the bottom of the meniscus curve
   C. At the closest mark to the top of the liquid
   D. At the top of the plastic safety ring

   Answer: B. At the bottom of the meniscus curve
   To measure water in glass, you must look at the top surface at eye-level, and ascertain the location of the bottom of the meniscus (the curved surface at the top of the water). The meniscus forms because water molecules adhere to the sides of the glass, which is a slightly stronger force than their cohesion to each other. This leads to a U-shaped top of the liquid column, the bottom of which gives the most accurate volume measurement. (Other liquids have different forces, e.g., mercury in glass, which has a convex meniscus.)

3. **When is a hypothesis formed?**
   (Easy)

   A. Before the data is taken
   B. After the data is taken
   C. After the data is analyzed
   D. Concurrent with graphing the data

Answer: A. Before the data is taken
A hypothesis is an educated guess, made before undertaking an experiment. The hypothesis is then evaluated based on the observed data. Therefore, the hypothesis must be formed before the data is taken, not during or after the experiment.

4. **Which of the following is the most accurate definition of a non-renewable resource?**
   (Average)

   A. A nonrenewable resource is never replaced once used
   B. A nonrenewable resource is replaced on a timescale that is very long relative to human life-spans
   C. A nonrenewable resource is a resource that can only be manufactured by humans
   D. A nonrenewable resource is a species that has already become extinct

Answer: B. A nonrenewable resource is replaced on a timescale that is very long relative to human life-spans
Renewable resources are those that are renewed, or replaced, in time for humans to use more of them. Examples include fast-growing plants, animals, or oxygen gas. (Note that while sunlight is often considered a renewable resource, it is actually a nonrenewable but extremely abundant resource.) Nonrenewable resources are those that renew themselves only on very long timescales, usually geologic timescales. Examples include minerals, metals, or fossil fuels.

5. A scientist exposes mice to cigarette smoke, and notes that their lungs develop tumors. Mice that were not exposed to the smoke do not develop as many tumors. Which of the following conclusions may be drawn from these results?
(Rigorous)

   I. Cigarette smoke causes lung tumors
   II. Cigarette smoke exposure has a positive correlation with lung tumors in mice
   III. Some mice are predisposed to develop lung tumors
   IV. Cigarette smoke exposure has a positive correlation with lung tumors in humans

   A. I and II only
   B. II only
   C. I, II, III and IV
   D. II and IV only

Answer: B. II only
Although cigarette smoke has been found to cause lung tumors (and many other problems), this particular experiment shows only that there is a positive correlation between smoke exposure and tumor development in these mice. It may be true that some mice are more likely to develop tumors than others, which is why a control group of identical mice should have been used for comparison. Mice are often used to model human reactions, but this is as much due to their low financial and emotional cost as it is due to their being a "good model" for humans, and thus this scientist cannot make the conclusion that cigarette smoke exposure has a positive correlation with lung tumors in humans based on this data alone.

6. **Which of the following is a correct explanation for an astronaut's 'weightlessness'?**
   (Average)

   A. Astronauts continue to feel the pull of gravity in space, but they are so far from planets that the force is small
   B. Astronauts continue to feel the pull of gravity in space, but spacecraft have such powerful engines that those forces dominate, reducing effective weight
   C. Astronauts do not feel the pull of gravity in space, because space is a vacuum
   D. The cumulative gravitational forces, that the astronaut is experiencing, from all sources in the solar system equal out to a net gravitational force of zero

Answer: A. Astronauts continue to feel the pull of gravity in space, but they are so far from planets that the force is small
Gravity acts over tremendous distances in space (theoretically, infinite distance, though certainly at least as far as any astronaut has traveled). However, gravitational force is inversely proportional to distance squared from a massive body. This means that when an astronaut is in space, s/he is far enough from the center of mass of any planet that the gravitational force is very small, and s/he feels 'weightless'. Space is mostly empty (i.e., a vacuum), and spacecraft do have powerful engines. However, none of these has the effect attributed to it in the incorrect answer choices (B) or (C). Although, theoretically there is a point in space where the cumulative gravitational forces of sources within the solar system would equal a net force of zero, that point would be in constant motion and difficult to find, making answer D unlikely at best.

7. Physical properties are observable characteristics of a substance in its natural state. Which of the following are considered physical properties?
(Rigorous)

I. Color
II. Density
III. Specific gravity
IV. Melting point

A. I only
B. I and II only
C. I, II, and III only
D. III and IV only

Answer: C. I, II, and III only
Of the possibilities only the melting point of a substance cannot be found without altering the substance itself. Color is readily observable. Density can be measured without changing a substances form or structure, and specific gravity is a ratio based on density, so once one is known the other can be calculated. Thus answer (C) is the only possible answer.

8. The change in phase from liquid to gas is called:
   (Rigorous)

   A. Evaporation
   B. Condensation
   C. Vaporization
   D. Boiling

Answer: A. Evaporation
Condensation is the change in phase from a gas to a liquid. Vaporization is the conversion of matter to vapor - not all gases are vapors. Boiling is one method of inducing the change from a liquid to a gas; the process is called evaporation.

9. Which of the following statements is true of all transition elements?
   (Rigorous)

   A. They are all hard solids at room temperature
   B. They tend to form salts when reacted with Halogens
   C. They all have a silvery appearance in their pure state
   D. All of the above

Answer: B. They tend to form salts when reacted with Halogens
Answer (A) is incorrect because of Mercury, which has a low melting point and is thus a liquid at room temperature. Answer (C) is incorrect because Copper and Gold do not have a silvery appearance in their natural states. Since answers (A) and (C) are not correct then answer (D) cannot be correct either. This leaves only answer (B).

10. A boulder sitting on the edge of a cliff has which type of energy?
    (Easy)

    A. Kinetic energy
    B. Latent energy
    C. No energy
    D. Potential energy

Answer: D. Potential energy
Answer (A) would be true if the boulder fell off the cliff and started falling. Answer (C) would be a difficult condition to find since it would mean that no outside forces where operating on an object, and gravity is difficult to avoid. Answer (B) might be a good description of answer (D) which is the correct energy. The boulder has potential energy is imparted from the force of gravity.

11. A converging lens produces a real image _____.
    (Rigorous)

    A. always
    B. never
    C. when the object is within one focal length of the lens
    D. when the object is further than one focal length from the lens

Answer: D. when the object is further than one focal length from the lens
A converging lens produces a real image whenever the object is far enough from the lens (outside one focal length) so that the rays of light from the object can hit the lens and be focused into a real image on the other side of the lens. When the object is closer than one focal length from the lens, rays of light do not converge on the other side; they diverge. This means that only a virtual image can be formed, i.e., the theoretical place where those diverging rays would have converged if they had originated behind the object.

12. Which of the following is not a factor in how different materials will conduct seismic waves?
    (Average)

    A. Density
    B. Incompressiblity
    C. Rigidty
    D. Tensile strength

Answer: D. Tensile strength
Density affects the speed at which seismic waves travel through the material. Incompressibilty has to do with how quickly a material compresses and rebounds as the waves hit it. The more compressable a material (and thus the slower the rebound) the slower the wave travels trhough the material. Seismic waves create a shearing force as they travel through a material, rigidity is the measure of the material's resistance to that shearing force. Tensile strength measures how far something can be stretched before breaking. Since seismic waves compress materials and are not stretching them that makes answer (D) the correct answer.

13. **The Law of Conservation of Energy states that:**
    (Average)

    A. There must be the same number of products and reactants in any chemical equation
    B. Mass and energy can be interchanged
    C. Energy is neither created nor destroyed, but may change form
    D. One form energy must remain intact (or conserved) in all reactions

    Answer: C. Energy is neither created nor destroyed, but may change form
    Answer (C) is a summary of the Law of Conservation of Energy (for non-nuclear reactions). In other words, energy can be transformed into various forms such as kinetic, potential, electric, or heat energy, but the total amount of energy remains constant. Answer (A) is untrue, as demonstrated by many synthesis and decomposition reactions. Answers (B) and (D) may be sensible, but they are not relevant in this case.

14. **When you step out of the shower, the floor feels colder on your feet than the bathmat. Which of the following is the correct explanation for this phenomenon?**
    (Rigorous)

    A. The floor is colder than the bathmat
    B. The bathmat, being smaller than the floor, quickly reaches equilibrium with your body temperature
    C. Heat is conducted more easily into the floor
    D. Water is absorbed from your feet into the bathmat so it doesn't evaporate as quickly as it does off the floor, thus not cooling the bathmat as quickly

    Answer: C. Heat is conducted more easily into the floor
    When you step out of the shower and onto a surface, the surface is most likely at room temperature, regardless of its composition (eliminating answer (A)). The bathmat is likely a good insulator and is unlikely to reach equilibrium with your body temperature after a short exposure so answer (B) is incorrect. Although evaporation does have a cooling effect, in the short time it takes you to step from the bathmat to the floor, it is unlikely to have a significant effect on the floor temperature (eliminating answer (D)).

    Your feet feel cold when heat is transferred from them to the surface, which happens more easily on a hard floor than a soft bathmat. This is because of differences in specific heat (the energy required to change temperature, which varies by material). Therefore, the answer must be (C), i.e., heat is conducted more easily into the floor from your feet.

15. **Identify the correct sequence of organization of living things from lower to higher order:**
(Average)

   A. Cell, organelle, organ, tissue, system, organism
   B. Cell, tissue, organ, organelle, system, organism
   C. Organelle, cell, tissue, organ, system, organism
   D. Organelle, tissue, cell, organ, system, organism

Answer: C. Organelle, cell, tissue, organ, system, organism
Organelles are parts of the cell; cells make up tissue, which makes up organs. Organs work together in systems (e.g., the respiratory system), and the organism is the living thing as a whole.

16. **Catalysts assist reactions by _____ .**
(Easy)

   A. lowering required activation energy
   B. maintaining precise pH levels
   C. keeping systems at equilibrium
   D. changing the starting amounts of reactants

Answer: A. Lowering required activation energy
Chemical reactions can be enhanced or accelerated by catalysts, which are present both with reactants and with products. They induce the formation of activated complexes, thereby lowering the required activation energy—so that less energy is necessary for the reaction to begin. Catalysts may require a well maintained pH to operate effectively, however they do not do this themselves. A catalyst, by lowering activation energy, may change a reaction's equilibrium point however, it does not maintain a system at equilibrium. The starting level of reactants is controlled separately from the addition of the catalyst, and has no direct correlation. Thus the correct answer is (A).

17. Which process results in a haploid chromosome number?
    (Rigorous)

    A. Mitosis
    B. Meiosis I
    C. Meiosis II
    D. Neither mitosis nor meiosis

Answer: C. Meiosis II
Meiosis is the division of sex cells. The resulting chromosome number is half the number of parent cells, i.e., a haploid chromosome number. Meiosis I mirrors Mitosis, resulting in diploid cells. It is only during Meiosis II that the number of chromosomes is halved. Mitosis, however, is the division of other cells, in which the chromosome number is the same as the parent cell chromosome number. Therefore, the answer is (B).

18. A carrier of a genetic disorder is heterozygous for a disorder that is recessive in nature. Hemophilia is a sex-linked disorder. This means that:
    (Easy)

    A. Only females can be carriers
    B. Only males can be carriers
    C. Both males and females can be carriers
    D. Neither females nor males can be carriers

Answer: A. Only females can be carriers
Sice Hemophilia is a sex-linked disorder, the gene only appears on the X chromosome, with no counterpart on the Y chromosome. Since males are XY, they cannot be heterozygous for the trait; whatever is on the single X chromosome will be expressed. Females being XX can be heterozygous.

Answer (C) would describe a genetic disorder that is recessive and expressed on one of the somatic chromosomes (not sex-linked). Answer (D) would describe a genetic disorder that is dominant and expressed on any of the chromosomes. An example of answer (C) is sickle cell anemia. An example of answer (D) is Achondroplasia (the most common type of short-limbed dwarfism), in fact for this condition people that are Homozygous dominant for the gene that creates the disorder usually have severe health problems if they live past infancy, so almost all individuals with this disorder are carriers.

19. **Which of the following is a correct explanation for scientific biological adaptation?**
    (Average)

    A. Giraffes need to reach higher for leaves to eat, so their necks stretch. The giraffe babies are then born with longer necks. Eventually, there are more long-necked giraffes in the population.
    B. Giraffes with longer necks are able to reach more leaves, so they eat more and have more babies than other giraffes. Eventually, there are more long-necked giraffes in the population.
    C. Giraffes want to reach higher for leaves to eat, so they release enzymes into their bloodstream, which in turn causes fetal development of longer-necked giraffes. Eventually, there are more long-necked giraffes in the population.
    D. Giraffes with long necks are more attractive to other giraffes, so they get the best mating partners and have more babies. Eventually, there are more long-necked giraffes in the population.

Answer: B. Giraffes with longer necks are able to reach more leaves, so they eat more and have more babies than other giraffes. Eventually, there are more long-necked giraffes in the population.
Although evolution is often misunderstood, it occurs via natural selection. Organisms with a life/reproductive advantage will produce more offspring. Over many generations, this changes the proportions of the population. In any case, it is impossible for a stretched neck (A) or a fervent desire (C) to result in a biologically mutated baby. Although there are traits that are naturally selected because of mate attractiveness and fitness (D), this is not the primary situation here, so answer (B) is the best choice.

20. **An animal choosing its mate because of attractive plumage or a strong mating call is an example of:**
    (Average)

    A. Sexual selection
    B. Natural selection
    C. Mechanical isolation
    D. Linkage

Answer: A. Sexual Selection
The coming together of genes determines the makeup of the gene pool. Sexual selection, the act of choosing a mate, allows animals to have some choice in the breeding of its offspring.

21. Many male birds sing long, complicated songs that describe thier identity and the area of land that they claim. Which of the answers below is the best decription of this behavior?
    (Rigorous)

    A. Innate territorial behavior
    B. Learned competitve behavior
    C. Innate mating behavior
    D. Learned territorial behavior

Answer: D. Learned territorial behavior
Birds often learn their songs, through a combination of trial and error, and listening to the songs of other members of their species (in some cases other species; this is called mimicry). Thus answers (A) and (C) are not correct. Typically a male bird will use a short song to impress a mate, the longer song is territorial because it is trying to convey to other males both identity and the territory that it claims.

22. A wrasse (fish) cleans the teeth of other fish by eating away plaque. This is an example of _____ between the fish.
    (Average)

    A. parasitism
    B. symbiosis (mutualism)
    C. competition
    D. predation

Answer: B. symbiosis (mutualism)
When both species benefit from their interaction in their habitat, this is called symbiosis, or mutualism. In this example, the wrasse benefits from having a source of food, and the other fish benefit by having healthier teeth. Note that parasitism is when one species benefits at the expense of the other; competition is when two species compete with one another for the same habitat or food, and predation is when one species feeds on another.

23. Which of the following causes the aurora borealis?
    (Rigorous)

    A. Gases escaping from earth
    B. Particles from the sun
    C. Particles from the moon
    D. Electromagnetic discharges from the North pole

Answer: B. Particles from the sun
Aurora Borealis is a phenomenon caused by particles escaping from the sun. The particles escaping from the sun include a mixture of gases, electrons and

protons, and are sent out at as force that scientists call solar wind. Together, we have the Earth's magnetosphere and the solar wind squeezing the magnetosphere and charged particles everywhere in the field. When conditions are right, the build-up of pressure from the solar wind creates an electric voltage that pushes electrons into the ionosphere. Here they collide with gas atoms, causing them to release both light and more electrons.

24. **The transfer of heat from the earth's surface to the atmosphere is called:**
    (Average)

    A. Convection
    B. Radiation
    C. Conduction
    D. Advection

Answer: C. Conduction
Radiation is the process of warming through rays or waves of energy, such as the Sun's rays warming the earth. The Earth returns heat to the atmosphere through conduction. Conduction is the transfer of heat through matter, such that areas of greater heat move to areas of lesser heat in an attempt to balance temperature.

25. **What is the most accurate description of the Water Cycle?**
    (Rigorous)

    A. Rain comes from clouds, filling the ocean. The water then evaporates and becomes clouds again.
    B. Water circulates from rivers into groundwater and back, while water vapor circulates in the atmosphere.
    C. Water is conserved except for chemical or nuclear reactions, and any drop of water could circulate through clouds, rain, ground-water, and surface-water.
    D. Water flows toward the oceans, where it evaporates and forms clouds, which causes rain, which in turn flow back to the oceans after it falls.

Answer: C. Water is conserved except for chemical or nuclear reactions, and any drop of water could circulate through clouds, rain, ground-water, and surface-water.
All natural chemical cycles, including the Water Cycle, depend on the principle of Conservation of Mass. Any drop of water may circulate through the hydrologic system, ending up in a cloud, as rain, or as surface or ground-water. Although answers (A), (B) and (D) describe parts of the water cycle, the most comprehensive and correct answer is (C).

26. **What makes up the largest abiotic portion of the Nitrogen Cycle?**
    (Average)

    A. Nitrogen fixing bacteria
    B. Nitrates
    C. Decomposers
    D. Atomsphere

Answer: D. Atomsphere
Since answers (A) and (C) are both examples of living organisms, they are biotic components of the nitrogen cycle. Nitrates are one type of nitrogen compound, (making it abiotic) that can be found in soil and in living organisms, however it makes up a small portion of the avaible nitrogen. The atmosphere being 78% Nitrogen gas (an abiotic component) makes up the largest source available to the Nitrogen Cycle.

27. **What are the most significant and prevalent elements in the biosphere?**
    (Easy)

    A. Carbon, Hydrogen, Oxygen, Nitrogen, Phosphorus
    B. Carbon, Hydrogen, Sodium, Iron, Calcium
    C. Carbon, Oxygen, Sulfur, Manganese, Iron
    D. Carbon, Hydrogen, Oxygen, Nickel, Sodium, Nitrogen

Answer: A. Carbon, Hydrogen, Oxygen, Nitrogen, Phosphorus
Organic matter (and life as we know it) is based on Carbon atoms, bonded to Hydrogen and Oxygen. Nitrogen and Phosphorus are the next most significant elements, followed by Sulfur and then trace nutrients such as Iron, Sodium, Calcium, and others. If you know that the formula for any carbohydrate contains Carbon, Hydrogen, and Oxygen, that will help you narrow the choices to (A) and (D) in any case.

28. **Neap Tides are especially weak tides that occur when the Sun and Moon are in a perpendicular arrangment to the Earth, and Spring Tides are especially strong tides that occur when the Sun and Moon are in line. At which combination of lunar phases do these tides occur (respectively)?**
    (Rigorous)

    A. Half Moon and Full Moon
    B. Quarter Moon and New Moon
    C. Gibbous Moon and Quarter Moon
    D. Full Moon and New Moon

Answer: B. Quarter Moon and New Moon
Spring tides are especially strong tides that occur when the Earth, Sun and Moon are in line, allowing both the Sun and the Moon to exert gravitational force on the Earth and increase tidal bulge height. These tides occur during the full moon and the new moon.

Neap tides occur during quarter moons, when the sun is illuminating half of the Moon's surface (the term quarter is used to refer to the fact that the Moon has traveled 1/2 of it's way through its cycle, not the amount of the surface illuminated by the Sun).

29. **The planet with true retrograde rotation is:**
    (Rigorous)

    A. Pluto
    B. Neptune
    C. Venus
    D. Saturn

Answer: C. Venus
Venus has an axial tilt of only 3 degrees and a very slow rotation. It spins in the direction opposite of its counterparts (who spin in the same direction as the Sun). Uranus is also tilted and orbits on its side. However, this is thought to be the consequence of an impact that left the previously prograde rotating planet tilted in such a manner.

30. The phases of the Moon are the result of its _____ in relation to the Sun.
    (Average)

    A. revolution
    B. rotation
    C. position
    D. inclination

Answer: C. position
The Moon is visible in varying amounts during its orbit around the earth. One half of the Moon's surface is always illuminated by the Sun (appears bright), but the amount observed can vary from full Moon to none.

31. The end of a geologic era is most often characterized by:
    (Average)

    A. A general uplifting of the crust
    B. The extinction of the dominant plants and animals
    C. The appearance of new life forms
    D. All of the above

Answer: D. All of the above
Any of these things can be used to characterize the end of a geologic era, and often a combination of factors are applied to determining the end of an era.

32. The best preserved animal remains have been discovered in:
    (Rigorous)

    A. Resin
    B. Fossil mold
    C. Tar pits
    D. Glacial ice

Answer: C. Tar pits
Tar pits provide a wealth of information when it comes to fossils. Tar pits are oozing areas of asphalt, which were so sticky as to trap animals. These animals, without a way out, would die of starvation or be preyed upon. Their bones would remain in the tar pits, and be covered by the continued oozing of asphalt. Because the asphalt deposits were continuously added to, the bones were not exposed to much weathering, and we have found some of the most complete and unchanged fossils from these areas, including mammoths and saber toothed cats.

33. **Which type of student activity is most likely to expose a student's misconceptions about science?**
    (Average)

    A. Multiple-choice and fill-in-the-blank worksheets
    B. Laboratory activities, where the lab is laid out step-by-step with no active thought on the part of the student
    C. Teacher- lead demonstrations
    D. Laboratories in which the students are forced to critically consider the steps taken and the results obtained

Answer: D. Laboratories in which the students are forced to critically consider the steps taken and the results obtained

Answer (A) is a typical retain and repeat exercise, where a student just needs to remember the answer and doesn't need to understand it. Answer (B) is often called a cookie cutter lab because everything fits into a specific plan. Students are often able to guess the right answer without understanding the process. Teacher-lead demonstrations can be interesting for the students, and may challenge a student's misconceptions but misconceptions are often firmly routed and will require critical thought and reflection to change. Answer (D) requires active mental participation on the part of the student and thus is most likely to alter their understanding. These types of labs are often refered to as guided discovery laboratories.

34. In an experiment measuring the inhibition effect of different antibiotic discs of bacteria grown in Petri dishes, what are the independent and dependent variables respectively?
(Rigorous)

   A. Number of bacterial colonies and the antibiotic type
   B. Antibiotic type and the distance between antibiotic and the closest colony
   C. Antibiotic type and the number of bacterial colonies
   D. Presence of bacterial colonies and the antibiotic type

Answer: B. Antibiotic type and the distance between antibiotic and the closest colony
To answer this question, recall that the independent variable in an experiment is the entity that is changed by the scientist, in order to observe the effects of the change on the dependent variable. In this experiment, the antibiotic used is purposely changed so it is the independent variable.

Answers (A) and (D) list antibiotic type as the dependent variable and thus cannot be the correct answer, leaving answers (B) and (C) as the only two viable choices. The best answer is (B), because it measures at what concentration of the antibiotic the bacteria are able to grow, (as you move from the source of the antibiotic, the concentration decreases).

SAMPLE ESSAYS: SCIENCE

1. Use your accumulated knowledge to discuss the components of biogeochemical cycles.

BEST

Essential elements are recycled through an ecosystem. At times, the element needs to be made available in a useable form. Cycles are dependent on plants, algae and bacteria to fix nutrients for use by animals. The four main cycles are: water, carbon, nitrogen, and phosphorous.

Two percent of all the water is fixed in ice or the bodies of organisms, rendering it unavailable. Available water includes surface water (lakes, ocean, and rivers) and ground water (aquifers, wells). The majority (96%) of all available water is from ground water. Water is recycled through the processes of evaporation and precipitation. The water present now is the water that has been here since our atmosphere was formed.

Ten percent of all available carbon in the air (in the form of carbon dioxide gas) is fixed by photosynthesis. Plants fix carbon in the form of glucose; animals eat the plants and are able to obtain the carbon necessary to sustain themselves. When animals release carbon dioxide through respiration, the cycle begins again as plants recycle the carbon through photosynthesis.

Eighty percent of the atmosphere is in the form of nitrogen gas. Nitrogen must be fixed and taken out of gaseous form to be incorporated into an organism. Only a few genera of bacteria have the correct enzymes to break the strong triple bond between nitrogen atoms. These special bacteria live within the roots of legumes (peas, beans, alfalfa) and add bacteria to the soil so it may be taken-up by the plant. Nitrogen is necessary in the building of amino acids and the nitrogenous bases of DNA.

Phosphorus exists as a mineral and is not found in the atmosphere. Fungi and plant roots have structures called mycorrhizae that are able to fix insoluble phosphates into useable phosphorus. Urine and decayed matter returns phosphorus to the earth where it can be fixed in the plant. Phosphorus is needed for the backbone of DNA and for the manufacture of ATP.

The four biogeochemical cycles are present concurrently. Water is continually recycled, and is utilized by organisms to sustain life. Carbon is also a necessary component for life. Both water and carbon can be found in the air and on the ground. Nitrogen and phosphorous are commonly found in the ground. Special organisms, called decomposers, help to make these elements available in the environment. Plants use the recycled materials for energy and when they are consumed, the cycle begins again.

BETTER
Essential elements are recycled through an ecosystem. Cycles are dependent on plants, algae and bacteria to make nutrients available for use by animals. The four main cycles are: water, carbon, nitrogen, and phosphorous. Water is typically available as surface water (large bodies of water) or ground water. Water is recycled through the states of gas, liquid (rain), and solid (ice or snow). Carbon is necessary for life as it is the basis for organic matter. It is a byproduct of photosynthesis and is found in the air as carbon dioxide gas. Nitrogen is the largest component of the atmosphere. It is also necessary for the creation of amino acids and the nitrogenous bases of DNA. Phosphorous is another elemental cycle. Phosphorous is found in the soil and is made available by decomposition. It is then converted for use in the manufacture of DNA and ATP.

BASIC
Elements are recycled through an ecosystem. This occurs through cycles. These important cycles are called biogeochemical cycles. The water cycle consists of water moving from bodies of water into the air and back again as precipitation. The carbon cycle includes all organisms, as mammals breathe out carbon dioxide and are made of carbon molecules. Nitrogen is an amino building block and is found in soil. As things are broken down phosphorous is added to the earth, enriching the soil.

2. Examine the components of a eukaryotic cell.

BEST

The cell is the basic unit of all living things. Eukaryotic cells are found in protists, fungi, plants, and animals. Eukaryotic cells are organized. They contain many organelles, which are membrane bound areas for specific functions. Their cytoplasm contains a cytoskeleton that provides a protein framework for the cell. The cytoplasm also supports the organelles and contains the ions and molecules necessary for cell function. The cytoplasm is contained by the plasma membrane. The plasma membrane allows molecules to pass in and out of the cell. The membrane can bud inward to engulf outside material in a process called endocytosis. Exocytosis is a secretory mechanism, the reverse of endocytosis.

Eukaryotes have a nucleus. The nucleus is the brain of the cell that contains all of the cell's genetic information. The genetic information is contained on chromosomes that consist of chromatin, which is a complex of DNA and proteins. The chromosomes are tightly coiled to conserve space while providing a large surface area. The nucleus is the site of transcription of the DNA into RNA. The nucleolus is where ribosomes are made. There is at least one of these dark-staining bodies inside the nucleus of most eukaryotes. The nuclear envelope is two membranes separated by a narrow space. The envelope contains many pores that let RNA out of the nucleus.

Ribosomes are the site for protein synthesis. They may be free floating in the cytoplasm or attached to the endoplasmic reticulum. There may be up to a half a million ribosomes in a cell, depending on how much protein is made by the cell.

The endoplasmic reticulum (ER) is folded and provides a large surface area. It is the "roadway" of the cell and allows for transport of materials through and out of the cell. There are two types of ER. Smooth endoplasmic reticulum contains no ribosomes on their surface. This is the site of lipid synthesis. Rough endoplasmic reticulum has ribosomes on its surfaces. They aid in the synthesis of proteins that are membrane bound or destined for secretion.

Many of the products made in the ER proceed on to the Golgi apparatus. The Golgi apparatus functions to sort, modify, and package molecules that are made in the other parts of the cell. These molecules are either sent out of the cell or to other organelles within the cell. The Golgi apparatus is a stacked structure to increase the surface area.

Lysosomes are found mainly in animal cells. These contain digestive enzymes that break down food, substances not needed, viruses, damaged cell components and eventually the cell itself. It is believed that lysomomes are responsible for the aging process.

Mitochondria are large organelles that are the site of cellular respiration, where ATP is made to supply energy to the cell. Muscle cells have many mitochondria because they use a great deal of energy. Mitochondria have their own DNA, RNA, and ribosomes and are capable of reproducing by binary fission if there is a greater demand for additional energy. Mitochondria have two membranes: a smooth outer membrane and a folded inner membrane. The folds inside the mitochondria are called cristae. They provide a large surface area for cellular respiration to occur.

Plastids are found only in photosynthetic organisms. They are similar to the mitochondria due to the double membrane structure. They also have their own DNA, RNA, and ribosomes and can reproduce if the need for the increased capture of sunlight becomes necessary. There are several types of plastids. Chloroplasts are the sight of photosynthesis. The stroma is the chloroplast's inner membrane space. The stoma encloses sacs called thylakoids that contain the photosynthetic pigment chlorophyll. The chlorophyll traps sunlight inside the thylakoid to generate ATP which is used in the stroma to produce carbohydrates and other products. The chromoplasts make and store yellow and orange pigments. They provide color to leaves, flowers, and fruits. The amyloplasts store starch and are used as a food reserve. They are abundant in roots like potatoes.

The Endosymbiotic Theory states that mitochondria and chloroplasts were once free living and possibly evolved from prokaryotic cells. At some point in our evolutionary history, they entered the eukaryotic cell and maintained a symbiotic relationship with the cell, with both the cell and organelle benefiting from the relationship. The fact that they both have their own DNA, RNA, ribosomes, and are capable of reproduction helps to confirm this theory.

Found in plant cells only, the cell wall is composed of cellulose and fibers. It is thick enough for support and protection, yet porous enough to allow water and dissolved substances to enter. Vacuoles are found mostly in plant cells. They hold stored food and pigments. Their large size allows them to fill with water in order to provide turgor pressure. Lack of turgor pressure causes a plant to wilt.

The cytoskeleton, found in both animal and plant cells, is composed of protein filaments attached to the plasma membrane and organelles. They provide a framework for the cell and aid in cell movement. They constantly change shape and move about. Three types of fibers make up the cytoskeleton:

1. Microtubules – the largest of the three, they make up cilia and flagella for locomotion. Some examples are sperm cells, cilia that line the fallopian tubes, and tracheal cilia. Centrioles are also composed of microtubules. They aid in cell division to form the spindle fibers that pull the cell apart into two new cells. Centrioles are not found in the cells of higher plants.

2. Intermediate filaments – intermediate in size, they are smaller than microtubules but larger than microfilaments. They help the cell to keep its shape.

3. Microfilaments – smallest of the three, they are made of actin and small amounts of myosin (like in muscle tissue). They function in cell movement like cytoplasmic streaming, endocytosis, and ameboid movement. This structure pinches the two cells apart after cell division, forming two new cells.

BETTER
The cell is the basic unit of all living things. Eukaryotic cells are found in protists, fungi, plants, and animals. Eukaryotic cells are organized. Their cytoplasm contains a cytoskeleton that provides a protein framework for the cell. The cytoplasm is contained by the plasma membrane. The plasma membrane allows molecules to pass in and out of the cell.

Eukaryotes have a nucleus. The nucleus is the brain of the cell that contains all of the cell's genetic information. The chromosomes house genetic information and are tightly coiled to conserve space while providing a large surface area. The nucleus is the site of transcription of the DNA into RNA. The nucleolus is where ribosomes are made.

Ribosomes are the site for protein synthesis. There may be up to a half a million ribosomes in a cell, depending on how much protein is made by the cell.

The endoplasmic reticulum (ER) is folded and provides a large surface area. It is the "roadway" of the cell and allows for transport of materials through and out of the cell. It may be smooth or rough.

Many of the products made in the ER proceed on to the Golgi apparatus. The Golgi apparatus functions to sort, modify, and package molecules that are made in the other parts of the cell.

Mitochondria are large organelles that are the site of cellular respiration, where ATP is made to supply energy to the cell. Mitochondria have their own DNA, RNA, and ribosomes and are capable of reproducing by binary fission if there is a greater demand for additional energy.

Plastids are found only in photosynthetic organisms. They are similar to the mitochondria. They also have their own DNA, RNA, and ribosomes and can reproduce if the need for the increased capture of sunlight becomes necessary.

Found in plant cells only, the cell wall is composed of cellulose and fibers. It is thick enough for support and protection, yet porous enough to allow water and dissolved substances to enter.

The cytoskeleton, found in both animal and plant cells, is composed of protein filaments attached to the plasma membrane and organelles. They provide a framework for the cell and aid in cell movement. They constantly change shape and move about. Three types of fibers make up the cytoskeleton (in order of size: largest-smallest): microtubules, intermediate filaments, microfilaments.

BASIC
The cell is the basic unit of all living things. Eukaryotic cells contain many organelles. Eukaryotes have a nucleus. The nucleus is the brain of the cell that contains all of the cell's genetic information. The nucleus is the site of DNA transcription. There is at least one nucleolus inside the nucleus of most eukaryotes. Ribosomes are the site for protein synthesis and can be found on the endoplasmic reticulum (ER). The Golgi apparatus functions to sort, modify, and package molecules that are made in the other parts of the cell. Mitochondria are large organelles that are the site of cellular respiration, where ATP is made to supply energy to the cell.

In plant cells, the cell wall is composed of cellulose and fibers. The cytoskeleton, found in both animal and plant cells, is composed of protein filaments. The three types of fibers differ in size and help the cell to keep its shape and aid in movement.

3. Discuss the scientific process.

BEST

Science may be defined as a body of knowledge that is systematically derived from study, observations, and experimentation. Its goal is to identify and establish principles and theories that may be applied to solve problems. Pseudoscience, on the other hand, is a belief that is not warranted. There is no scientific methodology or application. Some of the more classic examples of pseudoscience include witchcraft, alien encounters or any topic that is explained by hearsay.

Scientific theory and experimentation must be repeatable. It is also possible to be disproved and is capable of change. Science depends on communication, agreement, and disagreement among scientists. It is composed of theories, laws, and hypotheses.

> Theory - the formation of principles or relationships which have been verified and accepted.

> Law - an explanation of events that occur with uniformity under the same conditions (laws of nature, law of gravitation).

> Hypothesis - an unproved theory or educated guess followed by research to best explain a phenomena. A theory is a proven hypothesis.

Science is limited by the available technology. An example of this would be the relationship of the discovery of the cell and the invention of the microscope. As our technology improves, more hypotheses will become theories and possibly laws. Science is also limited by the data that is able to be collected. Data may be interpreted differently on different occasions. Science limitations cause explanations to be changeable as new technologies emerge.

The first step in scientific inquiry is posing a question to be answered. Next, a hypothesis is formed to provide a plausible explanation. An experiment is then proposed and performed to test this hypothesis. A comparison between the predicted and observed results is the next step. Conclusions are then formed and it is determined whether the hypothesis is correct or incorrect. If incorrect, the next step is to form a new hypothesis and the process is repeated.

BETTER
Science is derived from study, observations, and experimentation. Its goal is to identify and establish principles and theories that may be applied to solve problems. Scientific theory and experimentation must be repeatable. It is also possible to disprove or change a theory. Science depends on communication, agreement, and disagreement among scientists. It is composed of theories, laws, and hypotheses. A theory is a principle or relationship that has been verified and accepted through experiments. A law is an explanation of events that occur with uniformity under the same conditions. A hypothesis is an educated guess followed by research. A theory is a proven hypothesis.

Science is limited by the available technology. An example of this would be the relationship of the discovery of the cell and the invention of the microscope. The first step in scientific inquiry is posing a question to be answered. Next, a hypothesis is formed to provide a plausible explanation. An experiment is then proposed and performed to test this hypothesis. A comparison between the predicted and observed results is the next step. Conclusions are then formed and it is determined whether the hypothesis is correct or incorrect. If incorrect, the next step is to form a new hypothesis and the process is repeated.

BASIC
Science is composed of theories, laws, and hypotheses. The first step in scientific inquiry is posing a question to be answered. Next, a hypothesis is formed to provide a plausible explanation. An experiment is then proposed and performed to test this hypothesis. A comparison between the predicted and observed results is the next step. Conclusions are then formed and it is determined whether the hypothesis is correct or incorrect. If incorrect, the next step is to form a new hypothesis and the process is repeated. Science is always limited by the available technology.

CPSIA information can be obtained at www.ICGtesting.com
Printed in the USA
BVOW05s0449101213

338679BV00001B/5/P